H.J.S. GUNTRIP

Harry in the Highlands of Scotland

H.J.S. GUNTRIP

A Psychoanalytical Biography

JEREMY HAZELL

Free Association Books / London / New York

Published in 1996 by
FREE ASSOCIATION BOOKS LTD
57 Warren Street, London W1P 5PA
and 70 Washington Square South,
New York, NY 10012–1091

A CIP record for this book is available from
the British Library

ISBN 1 85343 332 2 hbk

Impression 01 00 99 98 97 96   5 4 3 2 1

Produced for Free Association Books Ltd by
Chase Production Services, Chipping Norton OX7 5QR
Printed in the EC by The Cromwell Press, Broughton Gifford

A problem created in childhood is 'never too late to mend', and if we know how to let our unconscious speak to us, a lifelong tension can be relieved even in the seventies. Age does not necessarily bring loss of capacity for emotional change and relief of longstanding tension.

H.J.S. Guntrip 1973

To V.J.H. *with love and gratitude.*

Contents

Preface ix

1   Early Influences 1
2   Growing Away and the Salvation Army Years (1908–21) 11
3   The University Years and the Ipswich Pastorate (1921–34) ...18
4   The Salem Pastorate (1934–47) and the Beginning of
    Dream Analysis 26
5   The Emergent Psychotherapist 45
6   The Professional Psychotherapist 63

THE FAIRBAIRN ANALYSIS

7   1949 73
8   1950 95
9   1951 113
10   1952 131
11   1953 140
12   1954 152

TRANSITION

13   1955–62 165

THE WINNICOTT ANALYSIS

14   1962 207
15   1963 213
16   1964 223
17   1965 236
18   1966 255
19   1967 272
20   1968 286
21   1969 298

RESOLUTION

22   1969–75 307

Bibliography   345

Index   348

Preface

After Guntrip died in 1975, the newly established International Review of Psychoanalysis published a paper (Guntrip 1975, in Hazell 1994, p. 351) which cast an intriguing light upon his personal background, and upon his experience of analysis with Fairbairn and Winnicott. Guntrip had submitted the paper some six months earlier, because he felt that 'time was running out' for the more ambitious task of using his records of the analyses to 're-examine Fairbairn in historical perspective', and to show how his own development of Fairbairn's theory had found expression in his analysis with Winnicott. Not that he submitted the paper to the Review with much optimism, for he believed that its contents might prove 'too disturbing for the orthodox'!

At the time of the analyses, Guntrip had kept the records 'simply to work over each session afterwards and get the most out of it'. He then locked them away, with a vague feeling that sometime he might be interested to look over them again. A need to do so arose in the New Year of 1971 when he received the news that Winnicott had died. That same night he began a vividly compelling dream sequence which broke through an amnesia for his baby brother's death, that had occurred when Guntrip was three and a half, and when, according to his parents, he had himself nearly died. Guntrip unearthed the records in an attempt to find out why two analyses had failed to disperse the amnesia. At the same time he re-discovered some earlier records of 'self-analysed' dreams during a ten-year period (1936–46) before he entered analysis with Fairbairn in 1949. He then realised that taken together the records formed a virtually continuous account of his dream-experience over thirty-five years from 1936–71, and he began to think in terms of 'a possible study of a detailed kind – an "autobiographical psychoanalytic" study of the continuous dreaming process', which he believed would provide 'factual data about psychodynamic processes of a kind that critics of psychoanalysis have no access to' (personal communication to J.D. Sutherland, 24 April 1973). Guntrip was himself extremely surprised at the power and clarity of many of the dreams. Moreover, he was especially glad to discover that the 'mostly Oedipal' interpretations of the early period had had no influence on the contents of the dreams, since his 'unconscious knew its own business and went its own way' despite the fact that his 'self-analysis' had been influenced by some sessions with a Freudian psychoanalyst.

Guntrip's compelling dream-sequence in 1971 had gone 'right back to the actual events' surrounding his brother's death, and the correlation between the dream contents and the external circumstances caused Guntrip to explore the 'historic background' of the entire span of his recorded dreams, without which, he believed, they would be 'uninterpretable' (personal communication, *op. cit.*), Accordingly, in the last two years of his life, he embarked upon a 'total project', consisting of personal history, his records of the two analyses, and the final dream sequence, with the dream record providing an underlying theme throughout. It was a greatly condensed version of this project that eventually appeared in the *International Review*, and in addition Guntrip conceived the further project of re-examining Fairbairn in historical perspective, and of evaluating Winnicott's work as the first 'post-Fairbairnian development' of object-relations theory.

With the agreement of Guntrip's family, the bulk of the notes and records that he left behind were stored by J.D. Sutherland in the Menninger library in Kansas, where they remain available for detailed research. Sutherland's own intention to work on the material was sadly prevented by his sudden demise in 1991, and it was at this point that the present writer took on the task, with the generous agreement of Molly Sutherland, and Bertha Guntrip, whose constant interest and support, together with that of Guntrip's daughter and son-in-law, Gwen and Denis Greenald, has been invaluable. It was a matter of starting from scratch, for although Sutherland had collected a great deal of material (including copies of the papers in the Menninger library) he had not committed anything to paper.

Guntrip himself was aware that the volume of the material was prohibitive and that much of it was repetitive. The purpose of this present volume is to present for wider readership the essential elements of it, whilst also drawing on memorabilia, and correspondence between Guntrip and his family, his analysts and Sutherland, in order to give as rounded a picture as possible of Guntrip. I also have my own recollection of him from a training analysis (1964–69), about which I have written elsewhere (Hazell 1991).

The records of the analyses with Fairbairn and Winnicott have been subject to a process of selection. I have endeavoured to retain the main elements, while keeping the reader in touch both with the passage of time, and also with the characteristically 'uneven' nature of the psychotherapeutic process. Psychotherapist and patient are tried repeatedly by disappointments resulting from the latter's fearful inability to consolidate and develop therapeutic gains, and by his compulsion to return to the familiarity of 'sickness patterns'. Whilst it is a tribute to Guntrip's honesty and intellectual vigour that these oscillations are so assiduously mapped (he points out that he had a 'photographic memory' for such matters), it was also an over-dependence upon, and exaggerated use of, cerebral capacities which constituted his main form of 'resistance' to the psychotherapeutic process. But equally it was his determination to remain intellectually true to what he genuinely experienced which was the source of his ability to convert emotional experience into thought for the development of a 'psychodynamic science'. Winnicott, in particular, valued Guntrip's ability to express intuitive perceptions in clear, internally consistent concepts, and we owe it to that same clarity of thought that Guntrip was able to develop Fairbairn's theory of endo-psychic structure, in terms which earned the latter's full approval.

In fact his disturbed experience left him little choice about examining what David Scharff has referred to as 'a painful and bleak frontier that was simultaneously within himself and in the realm of the science of psychoanalysis' (in Hazell 1994, p. xi). As Guntrip himself put it: 'The long quest for a solution to that problem has been too introverted an interest to be wholly welcomed, but I had no option, could not ignore it, and so turned it into a vocation through which I might help others. (Guntrip 1975, in Hazell 1994, pp. 351–2). It is as well that he did. His extension of Fairbairn's theory has proved significant beyond all proportion to its position in the total theoretical model, forming an effective link between Fairbairn's scheme and the 'True Self' concept of Winnicott, and anticipating, by its emphasis upon personal relations as the essential matrix of the self, the Self-Psychology of Kohut and his colleagues (see Bacal and Newman 1990, p. 162). As Scharff (op. cit.) has further pointed out, Guntrip's work 'has been absorbed into the sensibility of the field with far less attribution and direct appreciation than is warranted'. To a degree, this was probably due to Guntrip's stated dislike of 'schools', dogma and techniques of treatment. Once theory became static, he believed it to be schizoid, conceptualising the ego-defences of its proponents. In 1972, he told the American psychoanalyst, Bernard Landis,

The fact is, I've become much less interested in theory. Theory is only a schizoid defence. It doesn't lead to change. This only occurs in an enduring personal relationship. The problem with Object Relations theory is that it's piecemeal; what one sees at any one time is an aspect of the whole person, and we shouldn't think of that aspect apart from the whole. We also can't use the old static concepts. We need new concepts that imply process and change. (Landis 1981, p. 114)

Thus, just as he felt the ego ('the evolution of the intrinsic nature of the self') to be a function of growth in personal relations, so he believed that psychoanalytic therapy was a

process of interaction, a function of two variables, the personalities of two people working together towards free spontaneous growth [in which] the analyst grows as well as the analysand. (Guntrip 1975, in Hazell 1994, p. 366).

It was, of course, only as Guntrip himself became aware of such experiences, particularly as the analysis with Winnicott progressed, that he was moved to conceptualise them. Thus the difference is marked between the Guntrip who, in 1962, described the Regressed Ego as 'the headquarters of the most serious fears', bringing a sense of utter and hopeless alone-ness, (Guntrip 1962, in Hazell 1994, pp. 231–2), and the person who called for the starting-point of structural theory to be 'our latent natural health', and not 'the forms of illness so soon imposed by an unfacilitating environment' (Guntrip 1968, p. 425). The first statement represented Guntrip stranded between analyses, contemplating having to settle for a schizoid compromise in a therapeutic stalemate, whereas the second represented a person who could 'hardly convey the powerful impression it made' to find Winnicott entering into the emptiness left by his non-relating mother, so that he could experience the security of being himself (Guntrip 1975, in Hazell 1994, p. 366).

Both aspects of this remarkable person are amply illustrated in this book. Notwithstanding the subjective nature of the records, there is an unmistakable note of integrity running through them. At times it may be difficult for readers to reconcile so abject and troubled a person with the clear and compelling style of his public lecturing and writing. But it is salutary to bear in mind that the latter invariably arose from, and refined the experience of the former to the greater benefit of psychodynamic knowledge.

It remains for me to record my deep appreciation of the courteous efficiency with which Gill Davies and her team at Free Association Books have facilitated this venture, and to express my very great gratitude to the Guntrip family, Mrs Bertha Guntrip, and Gwen and Denis Greenald, for their friendship and generous interest and backing for this venture, and to my wife for her consistent support and active co-operation throughout the four years of this book's production.

Jeremy Hazell
July 1995

CHAPTER 1

Early Influences

Harry Guntrip was born on 29 May 1901 at Herne Hill in South
East London. His mother and father came from widely varying
backgrounds. Henry Guntrip was a favoured youngest son in a
family of seven children, whose father, 'a saintly man of great
gentleness, unselfconscious charm and attractiveness' died early,
leaving Henry in the care of his authoritarian mother, with whom
he lived until he became engaged at the age of thirty-three to
Harriet Jessop. In his twenties Henry 'rebelled' politically by forsak-
ing the Tories for the Liberals, and religiously by leaving High
Anglicanism for Wesleyan Methodism. There he once again insti-
gated a breakaway movement of Evangelical Fundamentalist
Preachers, known as 'The Ranters', whom he led with considerable
success for seventeen years, before establishing an active Church
on a permanent site in East Dulwich.

Henry was a good looking man, over six feet tall with close cut
beard and side whiskers. He was a keen cricketer, a slow left-arm
bowler of good club standard, and an impressive public speaker,
with a love of poetry and music. However, he appears to have been
the odd-one-out in his large family, for he made little effort to keep
in touch with them after his mother died, and it is noticeable that
he remained closely attached to the maternal figure against whose
values he rebelled. Indeed, it seems probable that his mother's
death at the time of his impending marriage to Harriet, caused
him to draw back from a vocation in the Wesleyan ministry, and
to pursue a safe but dull clerical position in a City firm, a position
beyond which he never moved.

Harriet Jessop, Guntrip's future mother, met Henry when she and
her mother went to hear 'The Ranters'. Before long Harriet and her
brother Sam became active workers at Herne Hill Mission Hall, the
'tin tabernacle' that was the forerunner of the East Dulwich church.
Harriet impressed everyone by her capacity for hard work. She had
learned in a hard school for she was the third of twelve children, four
of whom died in infancy, and by the time her father died when she

was in her twenties, she was worn out with the care of her younger siblings. Her father, whose favourite she was, bequeathed to her his business, a Dyers and Cleaners, and charged her with the care of her feather-brained and irresponsible mother, with the ominous words, 'Look after your mother. She's only a child.' Her father, though a powerful figure in the business world, and a respected Grand Master of Good Templars, a Temperance Friendly Society, nevertheless revealed a basically depressed personality in a bullying attitude to his sons whom he regularly thrashed. On one occasion, when Harriet, whom he never beat, intervened, she sustained a badly bruised arm, and her father was so aghast that he never beat his children again. At twelve Harriet tried to run away, but was found and brought back to resume her responsibilities, and when a teacher drew her mother's attention to her academic potential, the latter replied, 'If she can read and write and do arithmetic that's all she needs. I need her at home to help me.' Accordingly, when her father died Harriet was left to support her mother, two younger sisters and a brother. To make matters worse still, her elder brother, with whom she had worked in her father's business, contested her right to it, and eventually virtually took it over by force. Thus Harriet was obliged to start another business of her own to support her four dependants, and a lifelong feud developed between Harriet and her elder brother.

By the time she met Henry, Harriet was already of an extremely embittered and domineering personality, struggling with notable determination to maintain a dutiful serviceableness and responsibility to her charges. It is not difficult to see how Henry, faced with the probable death of his mother, was drawn towards this strong-willed energetic figure when she came to his 'tin tabernacle'; nor is it hard to suppose that Harriet, her father's favourite, saw in this fine looking, eloquent and sensitive leader, the warmer and more impressive side of her recently deceased father. Neither of them could have realised that too many years as an 'overburdened little mother' had rendered Harriet emotionally unable either to want or to cope with a child of her own.

When they married in 1898, she gave up her business and used the proceeds to settle her mother in a small flat, while she and Henry accepted Mary, Minnie and Sam into their home. Minnie and Sam soon married and moved away, but Mary, a chronic invalid with a heart valve defect, remained with the Guntrips for the rest of her life. She idolised Harriet, and despite her frailty always helped with the housework. For her part, Harriet relied more than she knew on her sister's affection, and she reacted drastically many years later when Mary died.

By the time Harry was born in 1901, his parents relationship had begun to deteriorate. Harriet had miscarried in 1900, and although she breast-fed Harry for eleven months, she maintained that she did so because she thought it would prevent a further pregnancy. Moreover, it is likely that her breast milk was inadequate for Harry developed rickets, and was a 'crying baby' in general. Beneath an unwavering admiration for Henry as her 'ideally Christian man' she was unremittingly hostile to his interests, especially insofar as they represented independence of herself. Within a very short time he had stopped playing cricket, and he ceased reading poetry for Harriet declared, on hearing him read 'Paradise Lost', that Milton's description of Eve was disgusting. Perhaps the most devastating change in Henry was the deterioration in his public speaking, of which one listener now remarked that one could draw a horse and cart between each sentence and the next. Eventually, he gave up preaching, and with it went his active personality. All that was left to him was a capacity for 'passive resistance', exemplified typically by his refusal to sign a petition in support of the Boer War. Although this defiance almost cost him his job in the City, Henry, with great dignity, remained true to his principles. Doubtless, he had not foreseen the effect that the threat of his unemployment might have on Harriet. By far the more practical of the two, she took advantage of the crisis to set herself up in a new draper's business and trading as 'Guntrip and Jessop', secured premises in East Dulwich, too far from Herne Hill for Henry to continue his superintendency of the Mission Hall. Thence forward the family was established on an entirely new basis, with Harriet running the shop with occasional assistance from Mary, who was deputed to clean the living quarters and to look after the one-year-old Harry. When Henry returned from the City, he would spend his evenings at the shop desk, recording the takings and doing the clerical work for each day – a practice he was to continue for many years: an idealised passive father-figure, 'superintending' not his beloved Mission Hall, but a business in which he played no real part. He did not 'rebel' as he had with his mother, but he retained a 'quiet integrity', which Harry later came to regard as a true and enduring quality of his father's personality. This integrity was also something of an antedote to Harriet's increasingly violent rages, for she never lost her temper in Henry's presence. However, neither parent ever called Harry by name, always 'son' or 'the boy', and he could not recall physical intimacy with either parent ever. In later life Harriet would openly declare that she could never get on with children.

The new business did not do well, partly because Harriet had chosen a poor site in an area known as Goose Green, half-way between two shopping centres at Peckham Rye and Upper Lordship Lane. Apart from the general disruptions, and Harriet's lack of maternal feeling, three events in particular must have impinged upon Harry in the first two years. The first was the presence, certainly at Herne Hill, and quite probably for a time at East Dulwich, of a domestic help, Mrs Prentice, who had worked for Harriet in the shop she ran before she was married. In a letter to Harry in 1944 Harriet alleged that Mrs Prentice's three babies all died under one year old because 'she broke their spirits', so that they 'fretted and pined away', a view which she claimed had been confirmed by the family doctor. In the letter Harriet maintained that she had found Harry looking unhappy and crying, 'Prentice says I'm sickenin'' whereupon she took him into the shop with her and consoled him; for although Mrs Prentice always wanted Harry with her – 'in his high chair or in the evenings on her lap' – Harriet could see that he was 'so lonely and unhappy' that she intervened.

The second influence suggests that being in the shop with Harriet offered only qualified 'consolation', for in order to boost her takings, she dressed Harry entirely in girls' clothes, as an advertisement for her dressmaking skills, a practice that she continued until her customers protested that it was inappropriate. After that she dressed him in effeminate boys' clothes: silk blouses and velvet suits with lace collars.

The third influence was the birth, on 6 July 1903 of a brother, Percy. As well as the usual ambivalent feelings that any elder brother has for a younger, Harry was said by Harriet to have displayed a marked devotion to Percy, letting him get the better of him 'in every way', though it would also appear that Harry never actually allowed his baby brother to dispossess him of food, but 'just held on calling, "Auntie, this little mannie is taking my cake"'. This 'devotion' is all the more remarkable for the fact that Harriet often compared Harry unfavourably with his brother, especially insofar as he did not actively oppose him. She did not like what she called his 'Peace at any price' attitude, and curiously described it as 'one of the evilest things' about Harry – an example of a curiously dual attitude she took to 'goodness' both in Harry and in his father, admiring it in principle and scorning it in practice, especially when it appeared to be 'unmanly'. Thus she would describe Percy as 'a little mannie', who would have 'made two of Harry', and concerning the departure of Mrs Prentice, who became disenchanted with both Harry and his mother, declaring that she wanted nothing to do with a second baby, Harriet wrote, 'I wish she had. He would have been a match for her.' Harriet seemed set to oppose that which she most admired, perhaps because of a misguided policy of 'character toughening'. In all likelihood, Harriet would have preferred a daughter whose role could have been, like Mary's, to supply the undeveloped feminine side of herself. As for Harry, he came to believe that he adopted Percy as his major interest in an emotionally bleak existence, and as a kind of buffer state between himself and his mother; and moreover that he identified him with the unmothered aspect of himself so that, in his devotion to Percy he was better able to to repress his own unmet need.

The only abiding memory that he had of this period during Percy's first year was of standing in the garden of a Herne Bay boarding house, waiting for Mary to get Percy ready for the beach and looking at a rabbit in a small wooden hutch. He felt sorry for the rabbit and on an impulse he unlatched the wire front and let the rabbit out. All the other information came from Harriet's later written or verbal responses, which, despite their frequent inconsistencies, that were usually in pursuit of self-justification, nevertheless create a scenario of unmistakable bleakness when considered from a child's point of experience. For instance, she told Harry in his teens, that she refused to breast-feed Percy and refused further intimacy to Henry. That Harry's only clear memory of that time should be of securing the release and escape of a timid creature may serve to emphasise the effect upon him of the oppressive atmosphere of his home.

On 10 November 1904, a major catastrophe occurred which was to influence the whole of Harry's future life. His brother Percy died at the age of sixteen months, and Harry came face to face with him, lying naked and dead on Harriet's lap. In one of her 1944 letters she gave her account as follows: 'When I was performing the last sad duty, somehow you got away from Mary and came into the room. I said "Go to Aunty" but for once you would not obey me, but came right up to me, catching hold of the baby. You said firmly "What's the matter with Babs?" Not knowing what to say, I said, "He's gone to sleep." You caught hold of him and said: "Wake him up. I don't want him to sleep." I then said, "Well darling, he's gone to live with Jesus." You then gave a loud cry, "Don't let him go, Mummie. You'll never get him back." I put my free arm around you and we cried together. After a time you went away with Mary quietly and it was a long time before you spoke of our darling again.'

In fact ten days later Harry was so ill that the doctor was

called. According to Harriet, he said, 'Mrs Guntrip, if your mother-wit will not help you, nothing can. This child is fretting for the baby.' Here Harriet's 1944 account became inconsistent with her verbal account when Harry was in his early twenties. In the former she reported that she lay awake for two nights with Harry in her arms until Sunday when the shop was closed, whereupon she made an early morning journey by horse-bus, with Harry wrapped in a blanket in her arms to Uncle George at Edmonton. Her purpose was to bring back cousin Annie as company for Harry. According to Harriet in 1944 this was a remarkable success for Harry calmly accepted the loss of Percy thereafter as 'being with Jesus', especially when assured by his mother that Percy would not remain a baby but would 'go on growing', like himself. In the latter, more immediate account, however, Harriet told Harry that he went into a decline and was thought to be dying soon after Percy's death; whereupon, on an impulse, she took him to Aunt Dolly and Uncle George, hoping that their family of small children would take his mind off Percy. Harry accepted the latter account as the true one. Both Fairbairn and Winnicott were of the opinion that he would have died, had Harriet not sent him away from herself in that situation. As for Harry, with the exception of the 'rabbit memory', the whole period, and indeed the whole of Percy's life was hidden by an amnesia.

Harriet's account of the causes of Percy's death are similarly inconsistent, possibly as a consequence of guilty feelings. She angrily denied Henry's claim that Percy would have lived if she had breast-fed him. But her own explanations were sometimes quite wild, as for example, her claim that a maid tipped him out of his push-chair, so that he fell on his head and incurred an abscess on the brain! Others were simply bland: 'I expect you know that he died in full health, fell dead in my arms.'

The most probable explanation, supported by those parts of her explanations which are common to letters and verbal accounts, both in the 1920s and the 1940s, is that Percy died during a febrile convulsion which coincided with teething to bring about what she described as 'a teething fit'. But, whatever the physical cause of Percy's demise, the sheer lack of maternal feeling for him as an unintended and unwanted second baby must surely have been a strong contributory factor. Whenever Harriet spoke about Percy during Harry's late teens and early twenties, she always emphasised what a 'sturdy bouncing baby' he was, by comparison with his weaker older brother; and although these references always made Harry feel that she would have preferred him to die instead of Percy, his ultimate conclusion, supported by his experience of analysis, was that his mother wanted neither child, and that apart from a brief period of early maternal feeling for him as her first born, she failed to relate personally to them.

In the eighteen-month period that followed Harry's return to Goose Green the family endured a bad time. Harriet's business lost money steadily because of its poor site, and had to be subsidised by Henry's dwindling capital. Harriet's typically determined reaction was to work harder, often continuing dressmaking into the early hours, while the shop stayed open until eight or even ten o'clock at night, and until midnight on Saturdays, as was customary in pre-First World War London. The combination of work pressure and anxiety caused her temper to deteriorate, and although Henry's very presence seemed to have a calming effect upon her, his inflexible routine and comparative inertia must have provided a somewhat unhelpful contrast to Harriet's own workrate. Henry would come home from the City, lie on his black horse-hair sofa and read the *News Chronicle* for half an hour, have his evening meal, (prepared by Mary) and spend the rest of the evening at the shop desk making up the books and giving change. Sexual relations were non-existent since Harriet was determined to avoid further conception, and she frequently and openly expressed her dislike of being touched. All that remained of Henry's former activity was his chairmanship of the 'Men's Brotherhood Meeting' at the local Congregational Church, which he attended every Sunday evening.

In this atmosphere, for the next eighteen months until his fifth birthday Harry developed a series of fevers, stomach aches, heat spots, constipation and loss of appetite. Worried by his repeated high temperatures Harriet called the doctor who could find no physical cause. Indeed the only measure that availed was for Harriet herself to leave the shop to Mary, and make Harry a 'tent-bed' on the kitchen sofa so as to shield his eyes against the light, to which he had become over-sensitive. She would then feed him bread and milk and next day he would be quite recovered. Indeed Harriet did all that could reasonably be expected in the provision of physical care, especially in view of her lack of maternal feeling and the pressures of the business. She left sweets and chocolate around the house, hoping to tempt Harry to eat, but whenever he found one, he would simply look at them 'with a wan smile', leaving them uneaten. Her treatment for constipation was more summary. She would lay him across her lap and insert glycerine suppositories into his rectum – a process intended to be helpful, but whose sole effect was to leave Harry feeling humiliated, presumably because of an absence of sensitivity on Harriet's part superimposed on an already highly disturbed little boy. The 'psychosomatic' nature of his illnesses was to become the focus of many psychoanalytic hours in years to come.

It is noticeable that even at this early age Harry's symptoms seem to have been specific to being at home with his mother, for he had no problems during this same period at the small private 'Dame School', just opposite the shop, which was kept by a large, slow, kindly elderly lady called Miss Turner. Thus, when, at the age of five he began to experience irritation under his foreskin, Harriet's meagre patience would appear to have become exhausted. After several attempts at cleaning his penis by standing him in the kitchen sink, she suddenly had him circumcised, without explanation, on the table in the very parlour where he had seen Percy lying dead on her lap. When the doctor removed his stitches a few days later, he found Harry most unnaturally passive and submissive, and from that time on all the physical disturbances of the previous eighteen months disappeared. Doubtless further traumatised by this drastic and insensitive treatment, Harry withdrew from Harriet and began a slow process of 'growing away from her' – a process aided by his move to a larger private school run by Mrs East, an efficient bustling woman, where he played vigorous 'Red Indian' games 'scalping enemies by the score', thus unconsciously turning the tables in some sense upon those who had 'scalped' him. However, despite a greater measure of freedom at Mrs East's school Harry, who was naturally left-handed, was made to wear a glove on that hand so that he would learn to use his right. A particular friend at this time was Alfie Blows, whose father came to manage a grocery shop in Lordship Lane. Their bond was so close that when their Sunday School teacher decreed that, because of an age difference, Alfie and Harry should be in different classes, Harry refused point blank to attend; for Alfie was the first of many 'brother figures' from whom Harry was to find separation unsupportable after the death of Percy. A further echo of that grim event occurred in Harry's sixth year, when Aunt Mary almost died with rheumatic fever. At the nadir of her illness Harriet, fearing that her sister would die, made Harry enter Mary's dimly-lit room, and lay his 'cool hand' on her forehead. The experience of seeing the invalid, lying still, white and silent, unable to make any response or to show the slightest sign of recognition, was to spark off one of Harry's most terrifying dreams years later.

Under the double impact of a failing business and her sister's illness Harriet's temper began to deteriorate further and perhaps further provoked by Harry's unresponsiveness to her, she beat him cruelly on several occasions. Like many parents of her generation, she always kept a cane on the mantelshelf, and when an old cane broke she sent Harry to buy a new one from the 'Oil shop'. Once he stayed out all day with the new cane only to pay the inevitable penalty when he returned home.

The worst beating, which occurred when Harry was six, came as a result of a customer's malicious gossip regarding a head injury which Harry had sustained a week or so earlier while romping about the house playing 'tig' with a little girl from a neighbouring shop. Thus, he was taken completely by surprise when Harriet rushed in from the shop in a towering rage, shouting, 'A customer has just told me you have been telling lies at school about how you cut your head', and with that, began to beat him repeatedly and uncontrollably, until he was reduced to sobbing helpless terror, clinging to her skirt to support himself. When the shop bell rang he was dragged, still clinging to his mother into the shop, sobbing helplessly, and when the customer expressed concern, Harriet said, 'He's a bad boy. He's been telling lies.' In a letter to Fairbairn dated 15 June 1955, Guntrip refers to 'the penis game with Gillie Stiles or Roland Audoire' as an example of a thrashing offence, because it bore witness to his existence as 'an ordinary boy . . . of flesh and blood', whom his mother could not tolerate; though she also despised the other-worldly self she demanded of him. It is possible that a sexual element was present in his game with the girl at this time, which Harriet may have suspected, but which Harry would certainly have denied, thus becoming 'a bad boy, telling lies'. The mystery was never solved, but Harry's terrified realisation of the extent of his mother's loss of control was mixed with a deep resentment at the injustice for which he never forgave her. Although Harriet later denied the beatings, it is significant, that when after Henry and Mary died, she tried keeping a dog, she had to give it up because she could not stop herself beating it.

There is also the probability that in this, as in much of her general personality, she was unconsciously identified with her beating father. Thus, even on more peaceful occasions, as for example, on Sunday evenings when Henry and Mary were in church, and Harriet would sit with Harry on the sofa, reading to him from 'The Bible in Fortnightly Parts', the theme of violence preoccupied him. For he was fascinated, above all, by an illustration of Nimrod, the mighty hunter, standing at the back of his speeding chariot with spear poised above the open roaring mouth of a great lion as it clung with its front paws to the chariot. Later he was to wonder: was he Nimrod defying his roaring, attacking mother, or was he the hungry lion clinging on to his mother with her cane raised and about to strike? – a question which was to be taken up in both his analyses. At any rate, Harry insisted that, whatever else she read to him, Harriet should always finish by reading that story, while he gazed at the illustration. Another memory from this period, 1906–1909, remained similarly lodged in Harry's mind years later and again it concerned sudden unprovoked attack, this time upon the vulnerable by the ruthless strong: the family cat's kittens were attacked and killed by a tomcat after what appeared to have been a terrible fight with fur strewn everywhere. Harry was terribly distressed.

CHAPTER 2

Growing Away and the Salvatian Army Years (1908–21)

When Harry was seven two events supported his 'growing away' from his family. The first was a move to Grove Lane School on Denmark Hill, about a mile from the shop, and for a time he walked there every morning with Henry, who walked to Camberwell to get his tram to the City. Despite a certain reputation for roughness, the larger school suited Harry, and he greatly valued his walks with his impressive looking father. In June 1951, in analysis with Fairbairn, Guntrip recalled that it was after this period walking up Dog Kennel Hill to school that he began to develop 'obsessional characteristics' in an attempt to 'organise himself inwardly' and thus grow away from Harriet. He would walk in the squares, avoiding the lines, touching every other railing, and striving to reach the next lamp post 'before a tram came up, but not by running, only by taking long strides', like his father.

The second event concerned the arrival of the East Dulwich Salvation Army to hold their Sunday Evening Open Air Meeting outside the shop. Eventually Harriet allowed Harry to join the gathering, where he was warmly received, and provided with a warm, cheerful family throughout the remainder of his childhood and adolescence. Harriet, for her part was freed to join Henry and Mary at church, and years later she recalled how Harry would often say, 'That'll cheer you up.' Presumably he sensed that he was largely a burden to her.

The following year, by great good fortune, Mr Blows told Harriet that the shop next door to his, further up Lordship Lane, was to let. The shop was in the centre of a regular shopping area, and she did not hesitate – so much so that, by her own account she arranged the entire lease herself, only informing Henry on the day of the move, believing him to be too nervous to commit himself to a decision. In practice, of course, Henry's signature would have been essential to secure the lease, but however that may be, the new business thrived, and Harriet's temper improved. Doubtless delighted to be able to give financially what she was unable to give emotionally, she supported

Harry in his developing hobbies of wood and metal work, sport and scouting and eventually music, making over to him the larger top-floor bedroom where he and Alf Blows later built a carpenter's bench with a vice, and even added a fretwork machine and a turning lathe! Meantime Harry was always playing next door with Alf and his sister, and his last 'parting shot', so to speak, in his mother's direction was to soil his trousers in blithe disregard, having rushed out to play. For his pains he received one final beating – which he felt he asked for. In 1951 in the Fairbairn analysis Harry recalled that at nine or ten years of age, he had 'revelled in helping in the shop, setting toys out at Christmas', and that despite his underlying problems with Harriet, this was a time when he felt they 'understood each other' superficially.

Adolescent interests flourished apace. Alongside carpentry Harry and Alf became keen cricketers. They joined the Salvation Army Scout troop, where Harry became solo drummer and learned bugle and violin. Noise-tolerance must have been among Harriet's strengths! Even Mary played a part by giving him piano lessons. At twelve Harry passed the entrance examination to Alleyn's School, a minor public school of the Dulwich College Foundation. There, his interests were sporting rather than intellectual. He batted at number one for his house cricket eleven, played at outside left for the soccer team, and tried his hand at gymnastics, athletics, and even boxing. Practically speaking he was happy, and the only clear evidence of the repressed anxieties of the Goose Green period was a memory around the age of thirteen of standing in the back garden and saying to himself, 'I wish I was old enough to get away from home and do as I like.' Presumably the feeling with which this was said was not one of 'healthy' adolescent initiative and purpose. Perhaps a more ominous sign of underground anxiety was betokened by his thinking at the age of fourteen, 'I don't believe in Hell. A good God couldn't possibly create that torment'; only suddenly to be panicked by the thought, 'But what if it's true?' What is remarkable by its absence is any mention at all in Guntrip's biographical notes of his father's response to or participation in Harry's sporting achievements or indeed in any of his hobbies, although he later mentioned to Fairbairn that his father came to watch him play cricket on a number of occasions. Neither is there any record of parental reaction when, at fifteen, Harry left Alleyns against the explicit advice of the staff, to follow Alf Blows in training for the Civil Service. In addition to his determination to stick close to his 'brother figure', a precipitating factor may have been a separation from his first girl-friend, Madeleine Webber, daughter of the Commanding Officer of the Dulwich Salvation Army Corps. According to Harry's account Madeleine was a sweet-natured girl and he was sad when her family moved away. This was one 'adolescent interest' which Harry took care not to reveal to his mother.

Harry's period with the Civil Service, where he worked in the Treasury, was shortlived. The new adjutant of his Salvation Army Corps was an extreme religious zealot, and Harry, who never did anything by halves, threw himself into 'witnessing and evangelism', even to the extent of forcing himself to wear his Salvation Army jersey under his jacket for his first three days at the Treasury, despite the mild titterings around him. It was a period of some falsification of experience, for he carried on a highly conventional 'religious friendship' with a girl in the Corps, and even prolonged it in defiance of Harriet, who had posted a Salvationist to 'spy' on their activities. By 1918, after the threat of military call-up receded, and, after nine months in the Civil Service, Harry's zealousness was recognised, and he accepted a temporary appointment as Sub-Lieutenant of Corps in a slum area of the Old Kent Road. Harry was thrilled, and, as on former occasions, the protestations of his head of department in the Treasury only made him more deter-mined to go his own way. It is also to be noted that, at the same time, Harriet had discussed with him the possibility of his joining her in the business. Not surprisingly, he declined. In a realistic appraisal during his analysis with Fairbairn Harry acknowledged that he had 'inherited' his mother's determination to survive. He also saw that if he had 'inherited' too much of his father's gentler nature he might have grown up to be 'a wholly undeveloped sub-ordinate, dependent on mother in her business' – in the event of which he believed he would have predeceased her.

Despite Harry's religious zeal, his critical faculty remained sharp. Thus from August 1918 to February 1921 he kept a private Devo-tional Diary in which he recorded his impressions – among them the perception that many people managed to convince themselves that they had experienced 'conversion' and 'the Second Blessing of Entire Sanctification'. Another means of 'reality testing' was his first-hand experience of the appalling poverty and housing conditions of the people to whom he ministered. A third influence was a series of books called 'The Home University Library' which included books on a wide variety of subjects by leading experts and among which he found *Social Psychology* (1908) by Professor William McDougal. It was almost certainly this book which first awakened him intellectu-ally to the significance of psychological understanding for himself and others. But however far afield his divergent interests may have lead him, he never allowed them to sour his friendships, of which he regarded his association with Theo Holbrook as among the richest. Holbrook, who rose to the highest rank of Commissioner, became a lifelong friend, and their wide differences of opinion were always mutually respected.

Amid the general relief brought about by the Armistice of 1918 the Salvation Army Training Course was reopened and Harry began a belated training. At a gathering of the parents of cadets, he was astonished to find that his father had been asked to speak for the parents. To Harry's delighted surprise, Henry held the attention of the large audience for ten minutes of purely extempore speech. As a child he had once asked his mother, 'Was father alive in Moses' time?', and here on this moving occasion, he saw an inner dynamism augment his father's impressive appearance. It was the one time when Harriet told Harry that she was proud of his father. The training officers were also impressed, and at the end of the course, Harry was one of eight cadets chosen to remain as sergeants at the college, whence he was later posted to Canning Town, as sergeant in charge of the Cycle Brigade.

A feature of Harry's years in the Salvation Army was his assiduous keeping of the Devotional Diary. Apart from a period in 1945 when Harry unearthed the diary during a period of self-analysis, it was to remain buried among his papers, forgotten until 1972, when he began to compile his autobiographical record. In 1945 he was struck by the realisation that it revealed an intense desire to develop a completely 'other-wordly religious experience', which, by then he had come to recognise as schizoid in nature. It became clear to him in 1972 that the diary was also a record of the lifelong conflict within him between flagging energies and compulsive overwork, unconsciously expressed in religious terms. Texts such as Colossians 3:2–3, 'Set your affections on things above, not on things on the earth. For ye are dead and your life is hid with Christ in God', carried an unconscious reference to his dead brother whom Harriet had assured him was continuing to live and grow in Jesus. Moreover, the interpretation of religious experience in terms of evangelical fundamentalism and biblical literalism cultivated by the Salvation Army had introduced him to the possibility of following Percy. On the other hand, he noted in his retrospective view that the more actively involved in external events he was the less intensive his diary-keeping became as his Christian service vied with his desire to be apart. With St Paul in his Epistle to the Phillipians 1:23–4, he could say, 'I am in a strait betwixt two, having a desire to depart and be with Christ, which is far better. Nevertheless to abide in the flesh is more needful for you.' Throughout the diary, entries describing a strong yearning for 'unbroken communion' and to be 'entirely wrapped up in the Spirit of God', all reflecting his lifelong experience of feeling apart, and 'out of touch', are countered by injunctions to himself, that he 'must overcome sloth and fainting', and the setting down of twenty-four 'Rules for Life and Work' under three headings: (1) Pray without ceasing; (2) Practise self-denial; and (3) Redeem the time. In 1945 he was to make the partially intellectual assessment: 'My need of communion suggests that I had missed the basis of that experience in the kind of mother-love that is warm, understanding, yet helps the child to freedom. I must have grown to feel that love could only be bought with the price of suubmission, and I turned all that into the religious channel. I was seeking in religion something that I had missed in human experience'. Meanwhile, his attempt to force himself into a 'passion for the salvation of the unsaved' dictated that the minimum of time should be spent in sleeping and eating, with periodical 'half-nights' spent in prayer, the denial of all luxuries and any practice that was 'self-pleasing', and maximum full-time commitment to 'labour, prayer, study and meditation'. That this regime was foreign to his nature, and quite unlike his earlier and more healthy normal adolescent period was evidenced by the fact that, after 1920, Harry began gradually to 'grow away' from the Salvation Army, just as he had from his dominating mother – and for not dissimilar reasons.

At the end of the second year of his training he was commissioned as Captain of the Corps at Bideford in Devon. With Jack Hunt, another lifelong friend, as Lieutenant, Harry built up a dwindling group to indoor gatherings of three hundred, drawn partly by Jack's superb musicianship on the solo cornet, which Harry would accompany enthusiastically on the concertina. In this freer atmosphere Harry's developing intellectual interest grew to include modern scholarship which questioned the verbal authority of the Bible. His experience in the London slums imparted an essentially practical rather than a purely theological tone to his preaching, and one of the arguments which most caught his attention was that of Huxley, who in his essays on Evolution posed the question: By what right did Jesus send devils into the Gadarene swine, thus robbing the poor swineherd of his living? Such liberality was not to last. In 1921, probably due to overwork, Harry developed chest pains, which caused him to wonder if he had tuberculosis. But rather than consult a doctor, he decided, in an attitude of religiously dedicated fatalism, to work himself to death in the cause of Christ. Immediately the text, 'Having a desire to depart and be with Christ which is far better' came obsessively into his mind, and its sudden and unexpected emergence at a time of anxiety and stress was the first unambiguous sign of many, that the early shock of his brother's death was still active within him.

The chest pains and mood soon eased, however, and Harry and Jack Hunt were granted permission to remain at Bideford for another year, only to have the permission peremptorily rescinded by a telegram from headquarters: 'Arrange Farewell. Proceed to Training College. Junior Staff Appointment.' The authoritarian tone of the telegram reflected the general atmosphere in the Salvation Army 'high command' at that time, where the founder, William Booth, was becoming too old to bear the responsibilities of leadership, while remaining unwilling to retire and intolerant of any policy disagreements. A spirit of restlessness began to be felt 'in the ranks' and Harry was appalled to find, when asked to give a lecture series on 'doctrine', that he was expected to read from duplicated copies of stock lectures.

Dissatisfaction continued to grow under the leadership of General Bramwell Booth, son of the founder, and a small but decisive incident occurred when Harry used his discretion to excuse a cadet from a weekend posting which involved Sunday travel, to which the latter had a conscientious objection. Although he did not share this narrow conscience, Harry was prepared to respect it, and he arranged an alternative posting. However, on mentioning this casually to his superior, Captain Wycliffe Booth, the son of Bramwell, he was amazed to hear him reply curtly, 'Go at once and tell him he must go where the Salvation Army sends him.' Harry replied angrily, 'I'll do nothing of the sort. If you want to tell him that, go and tell him yourself.' Captain Booth's reaction was to by-pass his immediate superior, and report the incident to his father, who accused Harry of insubordination. No further action was taken, but Harry had seen enough to realise that he could not reconcile his personal values with the authoritarian structure of the Salvation Army at that time. He did not refer to the incident in his letter of resignation, but he did write a personal letter to Captain Wycliffe Booth, regretting the manner of their parting. He received a brief note by way of reply in which the Captain said that he was very hurt by Harry's letter, and when the time of parting came, he refused to shake Harry by the hand. Many of his fellow officers wrote supporting his decision, but characteristically the more people tried to dissuade him, the more determined he became to stick to his decision. Not surprisingly, his father completely supported him, for it was exactly the kind of 'matter of principle' on which he too would have made a stand. However, there must surely have been considerable ambivalence on both sides as Harry did not finally part from his surrogate family until his second year at University.

CHAPTER 3

The University Years and
The Ipswich Pastorate (1921–34)

With the support of both his parents Harry prepared to enter New College and University College, both constituent colleges of London University, to read respectively Divinity, and joint honours Philosophy and Psychology. New College was Congregationalism's London Theological College, where the principal, Dr Garvie, was a noted progressive theologian, and it was with the ambition of training for the Congregational Ministry that Harry began his preparation for the entrance examination. For the first year of preparation Harry lived at home. But although he took up cricket again and joined a lively Literary and Debating Society, the effect of living at home with his mother again forced him, for the first time, to look consciously and objectively at her character and personality. It was in her reaction to his relationship with his future wife, to whom she herself had casually introduced him at the annual church bazaar, that Harriet's instability became most obvious. Fortunately for Harry, however, he had seen and fallen in love with Bertha in advance of Harriet's introduction. Bertha had been one of Harriet's favourite lieutenants in the church Girl Guide troop for some years, and although Harriet had resigned as Captain following a disagreement with the Guide Commissioner, she nevertheless assumed rights over her former subordinate. Moreover, she had herself marked out another girl as Harry's future wife, whom she personally invited to his twenty-first birthday party. Unwittingly, for she knew nothing of the true position – she also invited Bertha, to be one of her own guests. During the summer months, as his relationship with Bertha developed, Harry learned that her father had been killed in the war in the slaughter of Paschendale, leaving her mother with four children, of whom Bertha was the eldest. She had just left school when her father was killed, and had taken a job as a messenger girl for a large City firm, taking the opportunity of getting to the office early in the mornings to teach herself to type on the office machines. She improved her skill at evening classes for shorthand and typing, and by the time that she met

Harry, she had become a shorthand typist with a City firm of stockbrokers. In order to supplement the family income, her mother and her mother's younger sister Charlotte trained for Midwifery in turn, and thus were enabled to take cases in the neighbourhood of their home. Even so, Bertha was expected to look after the younger children for much of her free time. It was a hard life, and in some ways not dissimilar from Harriet's situation when she met Henry. Both were hard-working eldest daughters, forced by circumstances into premature responsibility for younger siblings. They were both attracted to young preachers. But there was a world of difference in the capacity of the two women to love and relate to their partners.

Harriet knew nothing of these developments and when, two months later, Harry informed her that he and Bertha intended to marry her reaction was characteristically odd. She was silent for some minutes and then said sharply, 'If you're going to marry Bertha Kind you must treat her well and not hurt her.' Disconcerted by this proprietorial attitude to his fiancée, Harry replied tersely, 'What do you expect me to do?' Gradually he became aware that his mother was becoming increasingly critical of Bertha, in contrast to her former regard for her, and he concluded that she was trying to keep a hold on him because she had become resentful over her exclusion from his life. It was in this atmosphere that Harry succumbed to a state which was to occur repeatedly later in his life. He suffered a drastic loss of energy, with a tight sensation in the head and eye-strain, so that he had no choice but to lie down with his eyes covered from the light for a week. It reminded him of the tent-bed illnesses of his childhood, but without the temperatures, for, as on those occasions, the state suddenly disappeared and he was well again. At the time he put it down to overwork in his studies. Only later did he come to recognise the state as a reaction to 'living at home with mother again'. It seems probable that his state may also have represented a 'schizoid withdrawal' from the emotional demands of the developing relationship with Bertha, for he was to describe a similar state in the case of a patient's reaction to engagement many years later in 1962 in his paper 'The Manic Depressive State in the Light of the Schizoid Process'.[1] He and Bertha were engaged as he ended his first year at New College. In his third year Bertha embarked upon a nursing training in Exeter and Harriet objected violently to Harry's purchase of a motorbike and sidecar in order to visit his fiancée, arguing that he was incurring too much expense. But she was not normally mean where finance was concerned, and in the ensuing

row it became clear that she was angry at Harry having the freedom to travel to Exeter to be with Bertha.

The academic side of University life was a disappointment to
Harry, though he found the lectures of Professor J.G. Flugel on
Psychoanalysis stimulating, and affirming of his own feeling of
dissatisfaction, both with Freud's 'hybrid mixture' of biology and
psychology, and also with the tendency in General Psychology to
confuse physiology and psychology. He was also greatly encouraged
by the Personal Relations Philosophy of Professor John MacMurray.
However, most of the lecturers used the same verbal dictation
method, which he himself found tiresome in the Salvation Army,
and it was in sport that he found his greatest fulfilment; playing
soccer, and captaining the cricket team as opening batsman for five
years. During his time at New College, Harry formed a particularly
close friendship with a student in the year above his, Leslie
Tizard,[2] who later became one of Congregationalism's most outstanding preachers. A sense of the tone of their friendship is conveyed in Harry's introduction to the book *Facing Life and Death*,
which Leslie wrote during his final illness in 1957 and which
Harry himself completed. He describes (p. 14) how he met Tizard
on his first day at New College and was immediately struck by his
appearance, in contrast to another student with whom he was
playing billiards:

> One was definitely shorter than average and . . . plump and
> rotund. By contrast his opponent [Tizard] was at least twice the
> other's height and as thin as a lath. When he stood up I thought
> at once of a lamp post. I did not then know what close contact
> with this man lay in the hidden future.

They came closer through cricket and shared interest in sport,

> for Leslie was most humanly interested in sport, even though
> his physique did not lend itself to marked personal success . . .
> I have two college photos on my study walls of New College
> cricket and football teams of that era, in both of which we both
> appear. In the football team his role is indicated by the towel
> draped over his shoulder. In cricket he was a playing member of
> the team, and at one time he nearly achieved a reputation as a
> fast bowler, assisted by his great height and length of arm. But
> alas, the only distinct memory is of an occasion on a very wet
> wicket when he slipped in the act of delivering a 'snorter', and
> fell full length along the pitch. He seemed to us to stretch from

wicket to wicket. Many a time I have heard him chuckle with glee over a reference to this incident. I mention it now because it was characteristic of him that humour played a quiet and most important part in his life, and among friends made him a most pleasant companion. He was never voluble or talkative, and was always a good listener, but he was sociable and his apt and quizzical turns of phrase and humorous comment of an invariably kind sort were one of the most appreciated of his personal characteristics . . .

Tizard's value to Harry as a clear-sighted ally was demonstrated on a memorable occasion during an acrimonious debate at a 'House Business Meeting' of their college. Tizard sat near to Harry, listening and saying nothing as the House grew more and more divided.

Then, just as most of us were feeling that there was little hope of an agreed policy, Leslie rose and made a short and perfectly clear speech . . . I have retained a very strong impression of this man, without fuss or emotion, with a clear mind sorting out the relevant and irrelevant in what had been said, and simplifying the whole issue. I remember the powerful impression he made on the meeting, and on me: one of sound sense.

In Harry's third year the two men occupied neighbouring studies, where they would meet for 'Saturday mid-morning toast', and with their respective future wives they travelled by Harry's motor bike and sidecar for holidays on Dartmoor. However, at the end of Harry's penultimate year Leslie left for Mansfield College, Oxford, with consequences that were becoming ominously familiar. With his 'brother-figure' gone Harry was quite unable to devote his summer vacation to the reading for his final year, as he had planned. As soon as he returned home, he felt his energy oozing away. He became so exhausted, 'tight-headed' and photophobic that he could do nothing but lie and rest for the whole sixteen-week vacation, while the pressure of the final year's demands accumulated. Thus emerged a further 'trigger' for Harry's 'exhaustion illness', in addition to 'being at home with mother', namely the loss of a brother-figure. Fortunately for him his symptoms cleared up when he returned for the Michaelmas term and he was able to resume normal working. Not for many years was he able to assimilate the coincidence of separation from men friends of his own age with the loss of Percy – or the return home to mother afterwards with his collapse into apparent dying that had followed Percy's death. Back at college, with his other 'brothers', he was perfectly fit again and completed his final year with an Honours degree in Philosophy and Psychology from University College, taking the 'Class Psychology Prize', and a Bachelor of Divinity degree at New College.

Midway through Harry's University years, Harriet's own energies began to fail and her health became uncertain. However, she had made sufficient money to buy a plot of land at Benfleet in the Thames Estuary, where she and Henry had a bungalow built and on its completion they moved there in readiness for Henry's retirement in three years' time. Thus it was to Benfleet that Harry returned after obtaining his degrees, with the encouraging news that he had accepted the pastorate of St John's church, Ipswich, and that he and Bertha intended to be married that summer at the little Congregational church in Thundersley where his parents worshipped. But as he walked into the garden at Benfleet he was surprised to see his father lying back in a deck-chair, his face a strange yellowish colour. Henry later explained that 'a touch of indigestion' had kept him from going to work in the City, but Harriet told Harry that the doctor feared his father had cancer of the liver, and when a specialist examined Henry two days later he called Harry, his mother and Aunt Mary together and confirmed that diagnosis. He told them that there was nothing to be done and that he expected Henry to live for about a week. At that moment Harriet lost control and began to cry, and Harry moved to comfort her. Before he could do so, however, the specialist said, 'Sit down. Your mother will control herself.' Overawed by the gravity of the situation, Harry obeyed. But he was later greatly to regret having lost this opportunity of crossing the emotional barrier between himself and his mother – the one occasion when a deeper personal relationship might have grown between them. Harriet never revealed her need again, even on the day Henry died, exactly a week later. Harry was often to reflect upon the manner of his father's passing. Henry got up and dressed every day of that last week, until the Saturday when he was unable to rise. When the end was approaching he threw off the effects of morphia and sat upright in bed. Addressing Harriet, Mary, Bertha and Harry in turn, he said, 'Goodbye', his face lighting up with a serene smile. Thus Henry died in his son's arms, maintaining his gentle, patient nature to the last.

The extent to which Harry identified emotionally with his father may be gauged from the fact that during that last week he had begun to experience pains in the area of the liver. Indeed, so disturbed was he that he consulted his father's specialist who assured him that there was nothing wrong. In retrospect he believed that this degree of identification with his dying father, linking, as it surely did, with the memory of the deathly invalid Mary, and his unconscious identification with the dead Percy, would almost certainly have broken him down, had it not been for his imminent marriage. It was decided that the wedding should go ahead as arranged and afterwards Harry and Bertha spent a happy and successful honeymoon at Dovedale in the Peak District. Harriet's opposition to their relationship remained implacable. She was quite incapable of sharing their happiness, and called them 'disgusting' for walking with their arms around each other. During the period after Henry's death Harriet was looked after by the expedient intervention of Mrs Kind, who stayed with her, as she later revealed, in order to make certain the wedding went ahead, for she had heard from church friends in Dulwich that Harriet had been telling them that the engagement was breaking down because Harry had seen that Bertha was merely infatuated with him. However, in one respect Harry was grateful to Harriet: even though an arrangement for herself and Mary to stay at a small seaside hotel after the wedding broke down because she couldn't stand it, she did not disrupt the honeymoon.

Harry's pastorate in East Anglia was productive. He responded to the needs of the unemployed men and their families during the slump following the 1926 General Strike by making the school hall available to them as a social centre. Then he gathered a committee of local businessmen to raise funds for the purchase of a disused school in which a sewing room, a boot repairing room, and a carpentry room were installed, along with necessary materials for the men and their wives to make their own things. The venture was so successful that several centres were formed in the town. It was also in Ipswich that Harry first practised 'pastoral psychotherapy'. His interest in re-interpreting the 'psychobiology' of Freud in terms of the personal relations philosophy of MacMurray, led him to register for an MA degree at London University under the latter's supervision. Whilst he lacked at this stage the practical experience of helping emotionally disturbed people that was needed to supplement this work, he set about applying the knowledge he derived from his reading in his pastoral ministry. This worked to good effect in the case of a severely depressed, recently bereaved widower whose wife had been a prominent churchgoer. The man became convinced that he had committed 'the unforgivable sin', and Harry, realising that the man's wife had longed patiently, but in vain, for him to join her in church, suggested to him that the cause of his depression was not that God could not forgive him, but that he could not forgive himself for denying his wife companionship in that important aspect of her life. The man recovered from his depression, and from that time, 'personal-relations psychotherapy' became a major influence in Harry's work, both in his pastorate and in a lecture series on psychology which he gave to the Workers' Educational Association. Indeed, so fulfilling did the lecturing become, that in his third year at Ipswich, Harry seriously considered giving up the Ministry for teaching. Ultimately he was to choose neither, but he always maintained that his close involvement with 'persons' at every level of their interest and activity, greatly enhanced his psychotherapy practice.

Harriet, in her bereavement, was a continual source of unrest. On her first visit to Ipswich after delivering a spate of petty criticism on such matters as colour scheme and decor, she walked into Harry and Bertha's bedroom one morning before they were up, and stood looking down at them with an 'arch smirk' on her face. Harry furiously ordered her out and forbade her ever to enter their bedroom again. This was the first occasion on which Harry had actively opposed her and the effect was immediate: for the next two years Harriet travelled abroad, cruising in the Mediterranean, and visiting her brother Sam in Canada. The respite was short-lived. In December 1929 her sister Mary died and the effect of Harriet's, largely unacknowledged, dependence upon her younger sister, became manifest. Even the birth in April the following year of Harry and Bertha's daughter Gwen did not assuage her bitterness, for at the christening, she at once began gossiping malevolently about them to members of their congregation. She was packed off back to Benfleet, but with Mary gone and her funds exhausted by travel, Harriet was to return to Ipswich on several occasions between 1930 and 1933. On every occasion she worked up an open quarrel and flung out of the house, back to Benfleet. When this happened the impact upon Harry, though considerable, did not result in overt exhaustion illnesses, no doubt because of his marriage, and the fact that he was now on his own home ground, so to speak. But he suffered from repeated bouts of what was termed 'gastric flu', and when the position became intolerable he forbade Harriet to visit again, promising instead to visit her every three months, and to write every week, which he did.

During their last, relatively undisturbed year at Ipswich, Harry was invited to become a partner in a joint pastorate at Salem Church in Leeds, originally the creation of Smith and Wrigley, two of Congregationalism's most distinguished ministers. Harry accepted the appointment eagerly, looking forward to working closely with the present incumbent, Mr Turner, who was by reputation 'a very human, kindly, sympathetic man and a first rate pastor'. Only after his installation was it reported to Harry that his predecessor, Mr Briggs, an excellent speaker and organiser, had felt compelled to resign as a result of rumours, set going by Mrs Turner, that he had tried to put Turner in the shade. As a result the church was said to be split between a 'Turnerite' camp and a 'Briggsite' camp, and attendances, though enormous by modern standards, had been dropping steadily since the last few years of Smith and Wrigley's regime. It was of course a quite arbitrary and unwarrantable assumption on the deacons' part that the installation of two strangers could replace such an established and renowned partnership. Smith and Wrigley had been close friends since college days, and both remained bachelors until, late in life, Wrigley married. Their ministry became the subject of Harry's first book, *Smith and Wrigley of Leeds: The Story of a Great Pastorate*, published by the Independent Press Limited in 1944.

Notes

1. *International Journal of Psycho-Analysis* 1962, Vol. 43, pp. 98–112; in Hazell (ed.) 1994, p. 187.
2. The Reverend Leslie Tizard B.A. B.D. B.Litt. (Oxon.) 1902–1957. Chairman of the Congregational Union of England and Wales, and minister of the highly renowned Carr's Lane Church, Birmingham.

CHAPTER 4

The Salem Pastorate (1934–47)
and the Beginning of Dream Analysis

Despite the rumblings at Salem, Harry was delighted with his new position. It was agreed that he should conduct all the business and committee meetings, while Turner remained responsible for the Communion services. The church was very alive intellectually, and after the Sunday evening service, Harry would open discussions with a group of some hundred, mainly young people, on such varied topics as 'The History of Greek Philosophy', and 'The Rise of Mussolini and Italian Fascism'. During the week a 'Men's Meeting' of many hundreds attended lectures and debates, one of which was between a Conservative City Councillor and a Communist University Lecturer on 'Could a Popular Front work in Britain?'.

The course of these proceedings was about to be abruptly interrupted by the coincidence, in January 1936, of a visit by Harriet and a severe bout of flu which laid the whole family low. Whilst Harry appeared to be the first to recover, he soon began to show signs of increasing exhaustion, and his condition worsened to include sleeplessness, despite a period of rest on his doctor's advice at the home of a fellow clergyman, Arnold Mee, in the Yorkshire Dales. Greatly alarmed by his insomnia, which was hitherto unknown to him, Harry visited a local doctor who discovered a badly infected left sinus and referred him to a Harrogate surgeon. Antibiotics were not generally available in 1936, and the surgeon operated on the sinus. For the severe exhaustion and anxiety, the surgeon recommended that Harry should consult a London psychoanalyst, Dr Crichton-Miller, from whom he himself had received some treatment. Thus after a brief period of convalescence, during which the insomnia did not abate, Harry's increasing desperation led him to billet his family with Harriet at Benfleet, while he himself travelled up to London by train to consult Dr Crichton-Miller. After three exploratory sessions Crichton-Miller referred him to his pupil, Dr Clifford Allen, with whom Harry undertook a short period of daily analytical treatment, for the duration of which the family took rooms in London. Although Harry was later to deplore Crichton-Miller's 'spot-diagnosis, in terms of character-trait psychology', on the grounds that 'it took no account of the complex and insecure family situation of the most important early years', it was an accurate enough description based on what was known at the time. Crichton-Miller identified Harry's hyperactivity, together with the tension that prevented sleep and relaxation, as a reaction-formation against a fear of succumbing to his father's passivity, by means of identifying with his dominating mother whom he had taken as his ideal. He was thus diagnosed as 'a mother-fixated Narcissan, living in defence of an Ego-Ideal' – a diagnosis which he felt to be 'moralistic' and whose effect, he later believed, was to sidetrack him for many years into a 'self-analysis' based upon severe self-criticism for any sign of self-assertiveness, rivalry, jealousy of others' success and so on. In effect it operated as a latter-day 'psychological' version of his '24 rules for Life and Work', and so deeply ingrained did this self-criticism become that Harry was later astounded by the way he accepted classical Oedipal interpretations, in the psychotherapeutic situation, with which he was already in fundamental intellectual disagreement.

What disturbed him even more in retrospect was the realisation that during the whole period of his self-analysis, interspersed by periodic visits to both Crichton-Miller and Allen, between 1936 and 1942, he had been influenced against the clear evidence of his own unconscious experience, revealed to him through his dream and phantasy life. The full irony of this situation was to be brought home in 1971, when, after his two major analyses were over, it was Harry's dreaming that finally broke through the amnesia which shrouded Percy's death and revealed the true root of his psychopathology.

Those momentous dreams were culminative however, for he began recording his dreams on 7 May 1936 and kept a continuous record of them for the remainder of his life. It was this record, which when he re-discovered it in 1972, he believed to betoken, in deeply symbolic form, the true nature of his struggle to grow 'a viable self' in the harsh and remote atmosphere of his early life. For reasons of space only a selection can be reproduced here, the more complete record having been stored, after Harry's death, in the Menninger Library in Kansas. It is hoped that the selection will serve to acquaint the reader with the 'direction' of Harry's unconscious experience.

In his posthumously published paper (1975, in Hazell 1994) he was to define dreaming, 'so far as psychopathological material is concerned' as 'a way of experiencing, on the fringes of consciousness, our internalised conflicts, our memories of struggles originally in our outer world and then as memories and fantasies of conflicts

that have become our inner reality'. Their purpose was to 'to keep
"object-relations" alive, even if only 'bad object relations' because
we need them to keep possession of our ego'.

At this time, in 1936, however, such a view was not generally
held, and certainly not by Crichton-Miller and Clifford Allen who
were of a Freudian orientation. An example of the 'Oedipal' nature
of Dr Allen's analysis was his interpretation of Guntrip's first
recorded dream which was as follows:

> There was a procession in the street. I was not supposed to be
> in it. We halted and I turned 'right about face' and back again. I
> discovered father immediately behind me. He recognised me,
> but we signed that we should not appear to know each other.
> Father looked tall, passive, but dignified and erect.

Allen interpreted the dream in terms of Oedipal 'father rivalry': of
Harry wanting to be the one in front. Harry later felt that this had
been a misleading model for his future analysis, since, apart from a
few dreams which clearly showed a desire for his father to be more
vigorous, by far the majority showed his father, and father-figures
in general, in a supportive rôle, as indeed Harry felt him to be in
this dream – silently affirming his right to be there and to move
forward. A second dream which depicted a movement in the opposite direction, away from life, was interpreted, and accepted by
Harry at the time, as arrogant intellectual ambition in breaking
with religion. No connection was made with a need to escape from
'mother church', nor yet with the strong yearning to 'be apart' and
the exhaustion illnesses. In a third dream his uncontrolled grief at
his father's death was interpreted as disguised uncontrolled joy at
the removal of his rival.

However misleading these interventions may have been, they
took hold to such an extent that Harry did not return to Leeds
until 21 June – some five months after his departure, and even
then only at the prompting of a letter from the Church Secretary
who enquired whether there was any chance of Harry's returning to
work, as his colleague, Turner was badly in need of a holiday.
During the next two years a situation was to arise at Salem which
greatly exacerbated Harry's unconscious dread of loss. During his
long absence the deacons had concluded that unless extra money
was found, the church could not afford to pay two stipends. Turner
felt that it would be wrong to press the congregation for more
money, and suggested that he should be the one to move on.
Harry agreed about the financial exigency, but offered the option

that, if one of the pastors had to leave it should be he as the junior minister (he was ten years younger than Turner), and he told the deacons that he was prepared to resign his pastorate. Turner, however, insisted that he could no longer stand to be left in sole charge. He pointed out that he had already undergone nine months of sole responsibility before Harry arrived, and that he could not bear the thought of it as a permanency. Turner's feeling was reported to the Moderator who agreed to find another position for him. However, the situation was allowed to drag on, in steadily deteriorating circumstances, for almost two years. After eighteen months of inaction, rumours began to circulate that Harry was seeking to drive Turner out and that a repetition of the Briggs situation was about to occur. Harry tackled his colleague at once, repeating his own willingness to leave, but again Turner begged him not to, and finally set about actively seeking another pastorate for himself. But the combination of these underground parochial rumblings, so reminiscent of his mother's church gossip, and the protracted sense of his colleague's imminent departure inevitably stirred deep anxieties in Harry – anxieties disproportionate to the external situation. Outwardly he entered energetically into the life of the great church, playing his full part in preaching, chairing meetings and committees, arranging speakers, giving lectures, and visiting his congregation. He revelled in the young people's outdoor activities that summer, rambling, cricket, and organising the August camp in the Lake District, for the slowly growing anxiety about Salem's future as a joint pastorate in no way diminished it's 'activity programme'; and it was not until the winter of 1937–38 that it became a serious conscious influence. Yet the contrast between Harry's energetic participation in the ongoing programme of church events and the mental undercurrents of his dream life is striking. Throughout 1936 and the early half of 1937 the dreams reveal a persistent level of anxiety, which, though not basically due to Salem, nonetheless exploited his forebodings about the church to find disguised expression of his long repressed rivalrous feelings towards his infant brother and of his 'flight into illness' after losing him. Thus, in the following dream his conscious fear that people in the church might force a rift between himself and Turner stirred up one of the few buried experiences of 'sibling rivalry' with Percy.

I was working with a woman and Mussolini and I said to him 'She's never on holiday'. I wanted Mussolini to myself, but disapproved of him.

Whereas he had little difficulty in seeing that Mussolini was 'a little fat mannie, like Percy', with whom Turner had become associated in his deeper feelings, it was only later that he came to realise that although he was devoted to Percy/Turner as a 'buffer state' between himself and mother/church, he could also feel jealous of Percy ('disapprove' of him) where the attentive Mary was concerned. Again his need for a more vigorous version of his father to support him in these situations was expressed in a dream that mother was married again 'to someone's father, but with squarer jaws and ginger whiskers' who lay on the sofa with a newspaper chatting animatedly and interestingly. The figure was clearly Henry himself, but 'gingered up' so to speak. Conversely, his own tendency to become over-influenced by and unconsciously identified with his punitive mother was expressed when he dreamed:

> My daughter wouldn't obey me. I knocked her head on the table till I hurt her, but I couldn't hit her with my hand, which was held up by an invisible check six inches from her body every time I tried.

The dream was provoked by some parent–child clash at the time, but Harry felt that its deeper significance lay in the conflict in his unconscious where the girl-child represented his weak inner self and his own mother-influenced ambivalent attitude to it. He was later to relate this dream to his daughter Gwen in the context of her adolescent struggle with him. The extent to which he felt trapped and beset both at Salem and in his inner world was revealed when he dreamed:

> I was at the zoo. The entrance was guarded by a lion, a black jaguar and a snake. I skipped between them, but when I made to go out I just escaped the jaguar's paw as I rushed back in. Then the jaguar's face seemed human as it seized the snake which now had human shoulders. I got away but returned to see a cage where some tragedy had occurred.

He associated the lion with his non-interventionist father, and the black jaguar with his mother with her heavy 'paw' preventing his escape. He felt that the snake represented Percy, and the tragedy to be Percy's death, killed by the jaguar/mother: the first disguised remembering of the event for which he had a conscious amnesia. In terms of the contemporary scene, one might suppose that the zoo represented many-layered Salem with its wholesome exterior and lurking dangers. He had got in and could not get out. Nor was his position much helped by his communications with Crichton-Miller, whom he consulted when the death occurred of the Church Secretary, Joe Armstrong. Armstrong had been a very good father-figure to Harry, and his death triggered Harry's repressed grief for his father. He dreamed of being with his wife and a woman family-friend after his father's death. They came to stand on either side of him as he wept uncontrollably, while they went up and down in a warehouse lift. One would suppose this to be a simple expression of grief for his dead father while being supported through the ups and downs of emotion. But so influenced was he by the Oedipal interpretations of Crichton-Miller, that he recorded his view as follows:

A simple Oedipal dream. All associations about lifts and ware-houses are of going there as a boy with mother. At one of them, Rylands I think, there was a primitive lift. Father is dead, my rival is out of the way, and Mrs Storrer (a mother figure) and I go up in the lift, a piece of sex-symbolism. My tears over father are only a disguise at the joy over the removal of my rival, and I am now the centre of all this ministry.

The same night he dreamed simply:

Mr H.B. was taken very ill. I grieved for Salem's sake because Joe Armstrong was gone and now H.B. was nearly gone.

In both dreams he was surely feeling genuine grief for his father, which in turn masked repressed grief for his brother. But in October 1936 after another visit to Crichton-Miller, Harry recorded the following summary:

The analysis of May to October 1936 showed that a strong Oedipus Complex was the basis of my psychology. A strong unconscious determination to monopolise mother, gave rise to secondary motives such as father-rivalry and hostility, guilt and self-punishment. Bound up with this 'mother-monopoly' wish are Narcissism, Exhibitionism and Ambition. The trouble was a repressed complex. Now it is the hard core of Narcissism that grew out of it in conflict with my world. Then my unconscious was busily wanting mother. Now it is busily wanting a free field. Both situations are Narcissistic and the second gives rise to hostilities likewise.

He was overriding his intellectual disagreement with Freud's theories because they were the only ones available to him, even though they bore little or no relation to the actual dream contents. At that time Harry could do no better than assent to Crichton-Miller's own character-trait and Oedipal interpretations, which the latter promptly wrote back and confirmed. And since this was the only potentially therapeutic relationship to which he had access, Harry continued his self-analysis, interspersed with periodic visits to both Crichton-Miller and Allen for the next eight years. However, an experience of a hallucinatory type which Harry had at this time would seem to have eluded the 'Oedipal net', suggesting instead that his relation to his mother was based on an objectively justified fear of her loss of temper. Lying between waking and sleep Harry distinctly 'saw' a small boy dart across the room from door to fireplace and disappear up the chimney. Although he realised that he was hallucinating, he recalled having been told of an occasion when his mother had discovered him walking in his sleep. He had silently opened the kitchen door, darted across the room and was just disappearing through the scullery to the back door when she caught him, and led him back to bed. It had happened when he was five or six years old after the circumcision when he gave up his 'hysterical illnesses', and his mother had begun to beat him. It will be noted that the hallucinatory experience strongly resembles the dream in which the black jaguar prevents his escape from the zoo. The deepest feeling his mother evoked in him was fear, and it is not surprising that at this time he fantasied escaping from Salem also, to take refuge in a peaceful country church. The overall real-life situation was further complicated by the fact that Harriet was becoming increasingly disturbed. Numerous compromise arrangements for her, such as staying with friends, and renting rooms, had repeatedly failed, and it was becoming clear that she would soon become incapable of living alone, due to her equal inability either to live by herself or with anyone else.

As the situation worsened Harry's dreams became increasingly disturbed. Church activities such as anniversary services, choir concerts, bazaars, men's lectures, anything for which he had responsibility all served as triggers for his anxieties, and in February 1937 he noted,

> I am feeling uncertain about myself and the future, not feeling fit, and again having vague thoughts about taking a small church and getting away from Salem.

In early March he noted,

> I must have an inferiority complex, as I fear that reality will
> prove that I am not up to my Ego-Ideal standard.

Two more dreams in which his undermined ego was revealed provoked another visit to Crichton-Miller. Both referred in some way
to the external situation. On 16 March 1937 he dreamed:

> There were two armies at war. Mine was in great danger of
> defeat unless it could get into a strategic position. In a previous
> action my army had been defeated and was in full retreat. We
> got into a safe position but I was not well and could not have
> managed the manoeuvre without taking tablets. It was now on
> the Salem Bazaar Hall stage.

Four nights later on 20 March 1937 he dreamed:

> My wife and I wandered on to the seafront with our arms
> around each other [as they had on the last evening of their
> honeymoon]. We suddenly became afraid of Mrs X (a somewhat
> forbidding Salem mother-figure). We should have been at the
> Salem Choir Concert, but then Clifford Allen and I were dis-
> cussing the Jews who suffered from suppressed hate. One of his
> patients had a murder wish and made sucking or chewing
> noises as if eating his victim.

At this time Harry was unable to see the clear indications of
sadistic oral hate aroused by the intrusion of the forbidding
mother-figure in the second dream or that the earlier dream
involved a repressed memory of a previous defeat – his collapse
after Percy's death, subsequent illness and circumcision. Nor could
he fully see that he was unwittingly experiencing a reactivation of
all that by the growing suspicion that Salem, mother church,
would prove divided and fail to support him as he had hoped.
Moreover, in the background his mother's fixed paranoid jealousy
of Bertha was troubling him greatly. Crichton-Miller appears to
have drawn his attention to none of these factors, but simply to
have re-affirmed the old Oedipal formula, saying that Harry was on
the right lines and should go ahead. Thus he was led to visit upon
himself a full-scale, supposedly psychological version of the old
religious self-castigation of 1918–21. He wrote:

> I have lived in the service of an Ego-Ideal which I could not bear
> to have challenged, driven on to prove that I was the man who
> worked harder than anyone else, the most zealous Christian, the
> most studious student, most active leader. My devotion had to
> outstrip all others. I could give myself no rest . . . Behind all this
> was not pure love of the work, but a very sensitive self-reference
> . . . I have an unconscious need to go absurdly out of my way to
> help people . . . so as to realise my Ego-Ideal. I must face and
> break my self-love, and weed out my Ego-Ideal compulsions.

Completely absent was the realisation which came to him years
later that his compulsion to care so assiduously for others was
rooted in a fear that they might die like Percy, if he did not keep
them (and himself) alive.

Ten months had passed since his colleague had agreed to look
for another church and nothing had happened. In his dream-life his
colleague's prospective departure became increasingly associated
with his brother's death. At the end of May 1937 he wrote again
to Crichton-Miller, feeling that he was getting nowhere with his
self-analysis. Again Crichton-Miller replied that Harry was on the
right track and that he did not need to see him again. The deeper
reality was abruptly revealed in two dreams, in the first of which
he seemed to be trying to re-enter the earliest period of his life at
Goose Green, while in the second he re-experienced the grim
atmosphere of that period. On 29 May 1937 he dreamed:

> I went back to the Goose Green shop and waited about, won-
> dering if I should go in. I went on, went back, then waited at
> the door while the man inside served a customer. Then I went
> inside and told him I used to live there and that my parents'
> name was 'Guntrip', and we had moved further up Lordship
> Lane at a later date.

Five nights later on 3 June he dreamed:

> I was in a bare room in an air-raid that went on and on
> without stopping day after day. Everything outside was blazing
> and I saw smoke and flames through a window high up. I
> seemed helpless and thought that presumably I would have to
> hide under the ruins. I had a huge bomb . . . with a time fuse.
> I set it to explode and at first the time hand on the clock face
> was going around quickly and then more and more slowly, and
> then it was not to explode until later on. My room was not

actually destroyed. I did not know whether I had really let it explode.

The mood of the second dream was one of fatalistic desperation arousing a nearly uncontrollable destructive hate of the whole world, such as to induce in a child an indifference to his own survival. In the contemporary atmosphere of 1937 his mother was herself a 'time-bomb', as it were, ticking away, liable to explode at any time, and Harry could only deal with her by 'exploding back'. The dream of trying to penetrate the Goose Green of his infancy suggested that this situation together with the growing unrest in the church were stirring up repressed feelings belonging to that time. Thus he felt that the air-raid that went on day after day was his mother's ill temper, generating in him a growing pent-up hatred which he felt to be like a time-bomb itself, but which he nonetheless had to repress, indefinitely postponing the explosion. The repressed rage was surely a contributor to his heat-spots and high fevers, and indeed all through his life he had occasional thoughts of breaking out into some violent action, although he never did: not even in this dream. He was always slow to defend himself when under attack, but he could, and when necessary did show plenty of aggression in the defence of anyone else whom he felt to be wronged. However, the dream sparked off a further series of dreams in which he tried to elevate himself to the position of 'a psychologist' who could deal with high blood pressure, and other possible manifestations of smothered rage, only to feel ultimately that his 'self-analysis' was futile. In one dream someone told him that St Augustine cured himself of a bad memory by auto-suggestion, but Harry woke with the impression that he himself had tried 'that sort of thing' and failed. In a further dream he warned someone against something with authority but could not say why. He seemed to be a 'disguised psychologist'. Again, he dreamed of being in the GP surgery with Dr Danks and his partners as 'the psychologist among them', but his sense of disillusionment with 'self-analysis' was mounting and his last recorded dream of that period suggests that he had come to feel unable to help himself. On 23 June 1937, he dreamed:

I was on a wooden pier in the centre of a harbour surrounded by water all night and trying with an electric torch to attract attention and get rescued.

At this point he recorded no further dreams for six months. By the time he recommenced his self-analysis in January 1938 his colleague had begun actively to seek a new post, and the frequency of Harry's dreams lessened as he faced the practical problems of Turner's departure. Significantly, only three of the dreams were specifically about Salem, and a sign that deeper problems were lurking in the unconscious appeared in a powerful and frightening dream of 11 February 1938:

> I saw a big fish in a river and a rowing boat on a rope far out. I pulled it in, disturbed the fish and a monster rushed out from under the water, on to land, very dangerous. I tried to attract it and keep it busy until it could be dealt with.

Turner finally left in May 1938, after an acrimonious church meeting at which clear insinuations were made that Harry had forced him out. It was characteristic of Harry at that time that he made no attempt to defend himself publicly, arguing that to do so would only divide the church still further. However, he wrote a strong letter of protest to Turner after he left.

The ravages of the last two years had brought repeated attacks of sinusitis, and with his brother-colleague's departure Harry succumbed to a recurrence of the exhaustion illnesses. Dr Danks warned the deacons that unless Harry was given two months' complete rest there was risk of serious breakdown, and the Guntrips went north to Bertha's mother in Scotland. Those months in Scotland were to provide Harry with one of the most crucial purely psychological events of his life. He was reduced to near-total helplessness for two weeks, unable to sleep in bed at night, and able only to lie out on the grass during the day, feeling more deprived of energy than ever before. When the two weeks had elapsed, and he had all but decided that he had no option but to resign from Salem and leave them free to get a fit man, he had one of the most vivid dreams of his life. It occurred on the tenth anniversary of his father's death, 15 July 1938, and it presaged a considerable though temporary recovery. He dreamed:

> I was researching and went down some steps into an underground room. Inside a dead man lay clothed on top of a coffin. He seemed to have been there a very long time, with a weight of books on his legs. It was as if I was entering an ancient tomb. I was going to copy an inscription I found on him. His name seemed to be Aemilia. I took the weight of books off and he stirred and raised his hand. I laid him down but he sat up again, and said he would have got up a long time ago but for

the weight. I got him down again and replaced the weight of books and watched him as I went out to see that he did not move. He watched me, and the moment I reached the door, he got up. He had a pointed face and beard and seemed Spanish. I went back angrily and tried to push him down again but he would not go, till I said I would fetch the doctor and nurse, (that is, threaten him with illness) if he didn't. He said, 'Oh! Don't', and lay down at once. I rushed out and locked the door.

The dream has many aspects. At the time Harry did not attempt much analysis, but simply rejoiced in his returning energy and health. It was only when he came to review his dream-record that he saw its many-layered significance. That the 'tomb-man' resembled his father was clear from the start. He had exactly Henry's close cut beard and shape of face, and was recognisably the same height as he lay in much the same way as Harry had seen his father on the sofa: a passive figure with whom he felt emotionally close, but who gave no active support. He was reminded of the Salem deacons, who, in their fear of making matters worse, had left him unsupported. Crichton-Miller had drawn his attention to a possible fear of being drawn down into his father's passivity and he saw in the dream a buried part of himself identified with his dead father, 'taking it lying down' in the face of 'mother-church', as he had with Harriet also until he had grown away from her. He recalled how only his marriage had saved him from an exhaustion illness when his father died, and how, ever since, he had been afraid that he might die, like father, at sixty-three. But another aspect of the dream pointed to a hidden vitality in his father. The bearded Aemilia wanted to get up and come out, and showed considerable determination to do so. His appearance reminded Harry at the time of an illustration of the Spanish Ambassador who had plotted to assassinate Queen Elizabeth I. Harry must have felt that something in his father never accepted that passive rôle, and that his 'repressed vitality' consumed him in the end, destroying him in the form of pent-up anger against Harriet. He realised that there must have been times when Henry had felt murderous rage, as he had himself, both with his mother and with the largely female church faction, but had remained quiet for the sake of peace. The dream revealed the extent to which he was now buried alive in the tomb of his unconscious and determinedly wanting to get out. But he could not express either the recent or the ancient anger, feeling that his only alternatives were either to keep the angry self buried by repression, or incapacitated by illness, whilst his intellectual faculty (the weight of books) functioned as a defence. He was later to see that the dream had a 'three tier structure', referring at bottom to his reaction to mother after Percy's death, in which he became identified with both his dead father and his dead brother. He must also have identified with the apparently dying Aunt Mary, and the three identifications, coalescing, exerted such a powerful 'pull' that it was capable of undermining his normally active personality, whenever any roughly parallel event in real life reactivated it. The removal of his brother–colleague in circumstances provoked by the female faction in 'mother-church' was such an event, and it evoked both frightened and angry reactions. The latter surely played a part in enabling him to recover, as indeed it may have when his mother's lack of genuine maternalism culminated, as he thought, in her 'letting Percy go', despite his agitated appeal. However this may be, the dream also reflected his 'long-standing strategy of survival', by means of keeping an active self in real life, at the expense of a deeply repressed infantile trauma, which was nevertheless always a potential threat. Although he was to refer often to this dream in the future, he never made reference to possible interpretations in terms of 'sexual libido' in the dream, believing the sexual drive to reflect the state of the ego, and not vice versa, and thus to be 'secondary'.

Harry returned to work on 1 September, with his energies much restored. However, the demands of the divided church, for which he was now solely responsible, were extremely heavy, for Salem had a high standard to maintain. In addition to his pastoral work, it was his duty to supply the men's meeting with regular guest speakers of a high standard. Among those who spoke from the Salem platform were Ramsey Macdonald, Attlee, Cripps, Gaitskill, Greenwood, Alexander, a number of Conservative and Liberal MPs, Archbishop Temple, successive bishops of Ripon, and successive vice-chancellors and professors of the University. Not surprisingly Harry's dreams at this period reflected both the 'highs' of such major events and also the 'lows' of the exhausted inner self, whilst the strain of maintaining the former in defiance of the latter was registered once again in sinusitis and insomnia. By November he was writing to Crichton-Miller that 'insomnia has returned in acute form and I feel a rather dangerous degree of overstrain'. He did not mention the tomb-man dream, doubtless anticipating an unhelpful interpretation, but merely reported that although he had benefited from his rest, he had 'not succeeded in regaining natural sleep' and had 'constant headaches and lack of energy'.

A dream of 8 November seems to show his desperate struggle to maintain his 'mechanised' personality with inadequate resources.

> I was driving my car and became aware that petrol was flooding out on to the road behind me. I found a hole in the cap of the tank, and then it seemed as if the car was on two small legs at the back and one had come off. I had to screw it on again.

He felt that his energy would run out, secretly used up in maintaining a powerful repression on the angry man in the tomb, forced to lie there passively. In his retrospective survey in 1973 he felt that his dream of the following night reflected the fact that he was forced back on to dependence upon the 'phallic mother' in his unconscious search for nourishment:

> An elderly woman presented me with two cakes with cream on top, shaped like penises. I angrily rejected them.

However, at that time, Harry wrote to Clifford Allen, and using the only formulation at his disposal, suggested that the dream reflected an oral attachment to his mother in defence of his Ego Ideal. He records Allen's reply in the affirmative, as follows: 'You are quite right about ceasing analysis too soon, since we never dug out the oral material which is undoubtedly there, but now you have found it, no doubt it will soon become conscious. It is probable that that is attaching you to the mother (after all the breast is a great point of attachment of the child to the mother) and when you break away there, you will have no further difficulty and will sleep like a top. In any case you seem to have passed through the worst.' Despite this inaccurate prognosis, Harry would appear to have been reassured, for during the next month he had no less than eighteen dreams in which he felt supported by a variety of father-figures – doubtless a function of an idealising positive transference, for in his deepest experience, despite a succession of supportive father-figures throughout his life, he showed a strong tendency to place his trust, somewhat uncritically in 'medical men'.

A period of snowy weather in January brought poor congregations, causing Harry to become rather discouraged and withdrawn. In these bleak circumstances, he returned in his dreaming to the fruitless search to find Percy in an 'Arctic atmosphere'.

> Queen Victoria (mother's Queen), but then it was my wife and I were carrying a dead baby, wrapped up so no-one would know it was dead. A desolate Arctic place, nowhere to bury it. Then it put

its hands out and stirred in the shawl and seemed to have revived
and come back to life.

The same night, he dreamed of 'taking part in a funeral', as if coming
to terms with Percy's death, only to dream again three nights later of
returning to the Goose Green shop where his mother examined a
'numb swelling' on the left side of his jaw. She leaned over the
counter, and felt his top teeth, finding them to be suppurating as
well, so that he had to have an operation. He had returned to the
post-Percy period of compelling his mother's attention by physical
ill-health. At that time in 1939 war clouds were gathering and Harry
first had dreams depicting sexually-toned aggressive counter-attack
with penis-shaped guns, insufficiently supported by father-figures.
These later then gave place to a dream of a 'return to the womb' as
the fight motive gave way to one of flight, prefiguring his later observation that the schizoid position involved a 'two-stage withdrawal'
first from a harsh or remote external reality into an inner world
where the same struggles were fought out, and finally into the deepest unconscious as a substitute womb hoping for 'a mental conva-
lesce' (Guntrip 1968). He dreamed:

> I left a party of people and went in a small boat to a little
> island, through a little dark entrance into a house hollowed out
> inside the rock, for food. An old lady was there, and a young
> man but I did not see him.

In his notes at that time Harry laid emphasis upon 'reversing the
birth process' rather than on a positive search for primary security
in the womb. Neither did it then occur to him to connect his
dream with the recurrence in his mind of the Pauline text, 'Having
a desire to depart etc.', nor yet that the unseen young man might,
in his deepest unconscious represent a fantasy that Percy lay hidden in the womb. On the very next night however, his dreams
returned to the more familiar ground of the post-natal phallic
mother of the 'penis cakes':

> At a circus. A female jester named Wamba had flesh on each
> side of the chin growing out into red horns.

– a theme continued in a dream three weeks later in which he was

> sitting on the floor in Mother's bedroom in Lordship Lane,
> kissing her and thinking it was pleasant, and then suddenly
> found pus coming out of her breasts.

Harry was later to observe that for the schizoid individual 'having someone to hate', and thereby feeling a 'somebody', was far preferable to an emotional vacuum in which one could only feel 'nobody'. It was this latter state which so often accompanied the 'retreat to the womb', impelling a return to sado-masochistic relations in an active internal world where one had 'someone to hate' and be hated by. Crichton-Miller made no comment on the dreams, leaving Harry with no option but to continue to 'conduct a witch-hunt' for any symptoms in himself or his dreams, that betokened his identification with mother's dominating personality. He therefore could only continue with an attitude of moralistic self-criticism in his dream interpretations, which Crichton-Miller confirmed, and which thus served only to perpetuate the very state they were meant to alleviate, whilst offering no help with, or insight into the perpetual threat of being undermined from within by the regressive compulsion.

War was declared on 23 September 1939, and its gradual progression brought about great changes in Salem, and in the nature of Harry's pastorate, which became increasingly centred upon social work, care of refugees, and psychotherapy. Ultimately, well over three hundred from Salem joined the Forces, and with the aid of voluntary secretarial help, Harry was able to send a monthly letter to them all throughout the war. Air-raids were not as intense in Leeds as had been feared at first, and the remaining congregation, who began by operating a refugee centre for bombed-out citizens, later formed a Reception Centre for refugees from overseas. These came first from the Channel Islands and France, then from the Mediterranean countries, and then from further East, until finally the church received a multi-racial group of some two dozen who had come from Hong Kong through Manchuria, Siberia, Russia, Finland, Sweden and Norway, until they arrived by ship at Glasgow. From there they travelled by train to Leeds, where they were housed and fed until the Public Assistance Committee could find permanent housing for them. Harry's organisation was characteristically efficient: the women of the church formed three eight-hour shifts, so that whenever the Public Assistance Committee telephoned Harry, day or night he would drive round to the relevant shift, and within half an hour arrange meals and beds for the newcomers. The former meeting-hall became the dining room, and the former dance-hall a dormitory, equipped with camp-beds. Harry recalled no undue difficulties until, with the first onslaught of 'flying-bombs' on London a rush of his own 'Eastenders' caused overcrowding, and showed a tendency to return drunk in the evenings and start fights in the corridors!

However one may gather a sense of a 'two tier' existence, consisting of Harry's clearly valuable social and pastoral work on one level, and his seemingly autonomous dream life on another, it should be remembered that the linking factor was the ever-present influence of Harriet. It is probable, for example, that the 'phallic mother' dreams of the horns and the poisonous breasts was sparked off by her presence in Harry and Bertha's home for three months in 1938, when Bertha nursed her through a long illness. Indeed, in spite of Harry's resolve not to have her in his home after the Ipswich conflict, she had continued to make periodic visits to their small house at 147 Cross Flatts Grove, and had made trouble virtually every time.

At the time of her long visit in 1938 she seemed grateful to Bertha, but as on former occasions she gradually deteriorated into her former jealousy and hostility. A period of extreme estrangement occurred in 1939 when Harriet was invited by Bertha's mother to spend a three-month holiday at the home of the latter's father in Newton Don near Kelso. There Harriet seemed to lose all sense of reality, pouring out a spate of odd and invented criticisms of Bertha, while apparently unaware that she was talking to Mrs Kind. When he heard of this, Harry resolved once again to put a stop to further visits. However, on one of his own now regular monthly visits to Thundersley the terrifying sight of a squadron of German planes attacking gun emplacements in the Thames Estuary caused him to fear for Harriet's safety. The war was at its height at the time of the Battle of Britain, and Harry and Bertha brought Harriet back to Leeds in September 1940. She stayed for ten months, during which time she had worked up such a degree of hostility to Bertha that she finally stormed out of the house in a temper and returned to Thundersley. From midsummer 1939, when relations with his mother were at their worst, Harry's insomnia worsened progressively into the new year of 1940, one of the longest spells of sleeplessness that he had had, and his dreaming was infused with anxieties of a hypochondriacal nature. Later he saw that if he could have been helped to understand that his basic persistent fear was of an eruption of that traumatic collapse at age three and a half, he could have made decisive progress out of that nagging poor health and insomnia. At that time, however, no such understanding was available, and although he felt he had exhausted the usefulness of Crichton-Miller and Clifford Allen's line of interpretation, he knew of no other alternative. He had tried to apply the theories of Jung and Adler with minimal help, and once again his dreams revealed a disillusionment with psychological help. By February 1940 he was having dreams of pure anxiety, escalating towards breakdown; an example of which occurred when he dreamed:

> I am going in a train down a steep hill and halfway down I realised it was rushing down at tremendous speed and must rush off the rails and crash, but it did not. It rushed around a sweeping bend at the bottom and was under control.

Five days later, as if to head off this headlong rush towards breakdown, he dreamed that he went across the road to Dr Martin at Goose Green for treatment of a badly crushed left forefinger. Dr Martin was the doctor who had carried out his circumcision at the age of five, putting a sudden and total stop to his attempts to coerce his mother's attention by recurring psychosomatic illness. Now it appeared that he was returning in his unconscious to that desperate measure to avert what he felt to be imminent breakdown.

In this atmosphere he was considerably relieved to come across Dr Henry Dicks' book, *Clinical Studies in Psychopathology* (1939), which contained a more enlightened theoretical approach than he had so far encountered. Fairbairn's journal articles had not yet been published, and it was not until later that Harry discovered Ian Suttie's earlier seminal book, *Origins of Love and Hate* (1935) with its strong affirmation of the basically social nature of persons. Although Dicks was still operating on the basis of Freudian 'instinct theory' he adopted a broader approach, and had Harry read and mastered the whole book at that time he might well have saved himself much wasted theoretical misinterpretation. However, he referred only to Chapter 4 on 'Obsessional States' in order to help his understanding of a patient, and thus missed the vital, simple and direct statement on page 234, that 'Every patient with mental illness was more afraid than he could tolerate as a baby, and the faults in his psychic structure represent the gallant attempts to allay this intolerable feeling by the inadequate means at his disposal.' In the light of what his future analyses were to reveal, it would be difficult to find a more accurate and compassionate account of Harry's own state. It would have thrown a flood of light on his recent dreams and fears of breakdown, and of reversion to the poisonous, castrating phallic breast-mother, saving him from further moralistic self-criticism. As it was he applied what he had read about Obsessional Neurosis to his overwork, attributing it's cause not to anxiety over breakdown, but instead to a need to find an outlet for his repressed aggression, yielding 'the diagnosis of father-rivalry and brother-rivalry as the root of jealousy and ambition', overlaid by an obsessional super ego with

'Christian Ideals'. Apparently unaware of any identification with his aggressive mother, he wrote in his 'dream-book', 'My aggression finds an outlet in self-assertiveness in argument, fantasies of "telling people off", impatient pushing at overwork. I "go at it" as if I were attacking Life and the World.' He was of course, also unaware that these attitudes might also represent Dicks' 'gallant attempts' to allay fear and weakness, although he did note that his sleeplessness, 'lying awake thinking', had its origins in 'some basic anxiety, causing a lack of joy and happiness and a dullness of mind, even in what I enjoy'. As further instances he recalled how afraid he had been of dogs as a boy, how he had been assailed by a sudden panic when out alone on his motorbike in his twenties lest he should get stranded, and how his anxiety had assumed a religious form in his boyhood fear that 'Hell might be true', and that the ceiling might fall on him if he failed to say his prayers – fears that belonged to the age of nine or ten, when he first moved into the front bedroom at Lordship Lane.

CHAPTER 5

The Emergent Psychotherapist

It was in the disrupted atmosphere of wartime Leeds that Harry's psychotherapy practice began to form, at first through his relationship with Dr Danks, his GP, with whom he shared an interest in the psychogenic element in illness. Danks first invited Harry to take a patient for 'pastoral psychotherapy' in 1938, but Harry declined, on the grounds that he had only theoretical knowledge and no training in psychotherapeutic practice. He suggested instead that the patient should see Crichton-Miller at the Tavistock Clinic. This she did for two weeks, and on her return to Leeds Danks approached Harry again. This time he assented, with the proviso that Crichton-Miller should supervise him. Somewhat to his surprise, Miller agreed. The patient's condition, a lifelong chronic anxiety, presented a formidable 'first case', and Harry felt that he learned more from her and the supervision, than he was able to give. Danks thought otherwise, however, and referred three more patients to Harry, all of whom presented with family problems. By the time war was declared other GPs had begun to send patients to Harry specifically for psychotherapy. The fall in congregations and a consequently reduced Salem programme, meant that Harry had more time for this work, but as it developed apace, he saw that his new interest was taking precedence over his pastoral ministry. He therefore made a practice of explaining his position to his patients, inviting them to place a contribution to the church in a collecting box on the study desk. That the pervasive influence of 'instinct theory' was still very much rooted in his approach is shown by his interpretation of one of his own dreams in February 1940:

> I was trying to collect together all my belongings but seemed to be crippled in my legs, which were defective so that I was low on the ground.

His written comment was, 'I am crippled in the primitive ground-work of my nature, my instincts have been denied proper growth and recognition.' Had he been able to jettison instinct theory and recall long-forgotten events which damaged his then immature ego, he could have drawn nearer to understanding his basic psychic reality in that simple dream, so redolent of what he later termed 'ego weakness'.

It is doubtless significant that throughout this period when Harriet was causing such disturbance, and especially during her ten months' stay in Leeds during the blitz, Harry neither recorded nor analysed his dreams. Later, he was inclined to the view that her very presence had an inhibiting effect at the deeper dream level, even though her behaviour towards Bertha often drove him to frank and open anger with her; for in his unconscious inner world he still felt he was a small boy at her mercy, in terror of provoking her violent rages. The first dream he recorded in August 1941 clearly supported this view:

> I and a youngish middle-aged couple were in a castle which we were holding to keep someone out, probably someone who had been ousted from power. Suddenly, an elderly woman, probably the ousted Queen, burst into the room, though all doors were locked, and we fled in terror.

Although he now had ten patients in psychotherapy he had not as yet had any experience of very disturbed personalities, and his mother's long stay had had a profound effect. He had long recognised that she could be intermittently extremely difficult and in between 'quite nice', but this was the first time since childhood that he had been exposed to ten months' unavoidable experience of her tempers. It shook him deeply to see how she was 'going to pieces' in her old age. A vivid dream in October 1941 revealed her various disturbing manifestations in his inner world, and the way in which he sought refuge in his relationship with Bertha, and as he had earlier, to a limited extent with Aunt Mary.

> There was an old lady, a widow in black, and she put on a black cape made of feathers. We had to guess what she represented and I said 'Raven'. She said 'Right' and then made the cape stand up like a big cup-shaped frill round her neck and I said 'A hooded falcon or hawk'. Then she represented a third bird, a dangerous attacking bird, and I was hesitant to say what it was for fear of provoking an attack. She had now turned into this bird and was pecking at me. I thought I could pin it down but did not seem able to, for fear it should seriously and dangerously attack me, and I

might not be able to cope with it. I turned to a younger woman for help.

Meanwhile the tension between Harry's pastoral duties and his psychotherapy was attracting the attention of Bertram Smith. Salem was his creation, and he advised Harry to devote his entire time and energy to it, its organisations and its people, and to use his psychological knowledge 'to understand average human nature'. Moreover, Smith as father-figure came together with Harry's actual father in one of very few recorded dreams in which the role of father and mother were reversed. He dreamed that his views were criticised in an edition of the Congregational Quarterly, and that he met father who criticised him further for 'having nothing better to do', whereupon his mother sided with Harry. Perhaps the dream indicates the likely truth that Henry, as well as being largely passive could at times be obstructive to the more adventurous nature that Harry shared with his mother. In addition Harry must have felt that his father, like Bertram Smith, would be suspicious of his new interest, which was diverting his energies from pastoral work. But it was equally the case that Harriet distrusted psychotherapy, as she distrusted anything over which she had no control, for, as she once said, 'I don't like this psychotherapy. I don't know what it is.' Thus, whilst his mother's disturbed personality formed a strong motive in his search for psychological understanding, it also impelled her to oppose any venture of his which marked his independence of herself. The fact that, according to the prevailing culture, Harriet was more 'male' by comparison with Henry's gentler 'female' personality already gave rise to confusion in Harry's unconscious mind where the 'male' thinking principle and the 'female' feeling principle became associated with psychotherapy and religion respectively. In view of this, the experience of the earlier dream in which his parents had reversed their familiar rôles had compounded his confusion. He dreamed:

> I was in a small church with my wife. A neatly dressed girl who looked to be a good type was sharing the Bible reading, alternate verses, with a man. Her confident voice rather surprised me. At first he was on the right, then they changed places and she seemed to become the leading figure of the two.

That same night he had a second dream of a 'neatly dressed girl' to whom he had to become a friend. To him the dreams seemed to indicate a need for the feeling and thinking functions of his personality, which had become artificially opposed as unconscious disturbed feeling and conscious compulsive thinking, to be integrated in one whole self. He had long been aware that Bertha represented for him undeveloped aspects of his own nature, and that it was to her that he owed the fact that he did not grow to be a more one-sided personality than he was. Whereas he was happy if he could 'do things' for people practically or intellectually, he was always aware that his wife made a more genuinely personal relation to people, for she showed a quality of interest in them, in all the 'trivia' of their lives, that he was unable to feel. He knew that people sensed 'a certain impersonality or intro-version' about him and that he found much pastoral visitation 'bor-ing', because it called for a live emotional response which he felt unable to give. It was this kind of developing perception that led him to interpret his next simple dream from a quite different overall theoretical standpoint, not based on 'instinct theory': 'I was examin-ing a bombed property with a view to its reconstruction.'

In his notes at the time, June 1942, he wrote, 'Bombed property is disintegrated into its elements, like my Ego under the impact of psychic reality. Hence insomnia which is the physical reflection of a perpetual unsolved problem. But Reconstruction involves accepting and integrating my "feeling function", which arouses fears of being swept away by irrational forces.' Unknown to him, in using the concept of 'ego-disintegration' he was moving towards the 'object-relations theory' that had already begun to develop in Fairbairn's thinking at this time, and which would come to replace 'physicalistic psychobiology and instinct theory', for Harry, as a means of under-standing the roots of his problem. Meanwhile he saw with greater clarity how he was more able more to 'relate' to individuals with a 'specific need' concerning a definite 'personal problem', than he could in friendly generalities in a crowd of people. His self-analysis was beginning to identify the 'schizoid' element in his make-up, as he began to see that his deep emotion was too disturbed and fragile to be allowed more natural outward expression. Thus he dreamed, ten days later, of a small defenceless animal which was to become a familiar symbol for his fragile inner self.

> I was walking in a forest and came across a closed hutch in which was a small animal, possibly a dog or a kitten, trying to get out between the bars and it couldn't. I felt it might be in danger if it got out and was alone. Then I stood by the hutch holding our kitten 'Pinky' tight in my hands.

A few weeks later the divorce of his emotion from conscious think-ing was demonstrated by a dream in which a rationalised attempt on Harry's part to interpret to his mother her unconscious hostility to sexual intimacy was interrupted by a horrendous train crash in which 'another man was helping the injured' while Harry himself remained uninvolved. The impact of this dream was heightened by a fantasy that preceded it of 'a great circular waterspout, boiling up out of the depths of the sea and exploding into small clouds', which together with the frightful crash surely represented his rage at Harriet's hostile rejection of all affectionate intimacy.

By August 1942 Harry's spirits were at a low ebb. His dreaming was in abeyance for the time being, and he recorded his conscious thinking in a diary which he called a 'Psychological Autobiography'. The following extract describes his state at the time:

> August 3rd. 10.45 p.m. I am firewatching alone at Salem, tired after a heavy Sunday; three addresses plus three hospital visits, and am ready for our holiday at Wilsil (a village near Pateley Bridge, from which I can get back to Leeds quickly in the event of an air raid). I feel somewhat depressed and need to release my m
>
> troubles, ministerial disappointment in the Salem internal crisis and the low level of organised church life owing to the war, and I have just turned the corner of middle age at forty-one, youth has gone and I have not fulfilled my hopes. I know I have had plenty of successes and helped a lot of people. But I have not yet achieved a philosophy or theology and religious faith that grips me, and I have not settled the problem of my own mental make-up, and the tendency to feel depressed, as for a time at home when I left the Salvation Army, in my second year of the Philosophy Course at U.C.L., the third year at Ipswich, and now in this third year of war I have lost the thrill of wartime church leadership. I am aware of a profound change in my attitude to life in general. I used to be idealistic, with naively simple assumptions about people respond-ing to example and reason. I heard the Bishop of Bradford (Dr Blunt) say recently that as you get older you can easily lose faith in human nature. I see that much less can be done to better the world than I had always believed and hoped. Is this a mood or a recognition of hard facts? Here perhaps is the spiritual crisis of middle age, to see the world with disillusioned eyes, and go on and win for oneself, all over again, a faith.

He was not to know then that the last sentence was prophetic, and yet even as he wrote, circumstances were developing in a way which held promise for his future.

At the beginning of 1943 Harry was invited to dine with Professor William McAdam of Leeds University Medical School. Having been somewhat surprised by the invitation Harry was uncertain, after an evening of hard discussion, as to whether the professor approved or disapproved of his views. However, next morning McAdam telephoned him, asking if he would see a patient for psychotherapy, and from that time the professor referred to him a steady flow of patients. Further recognition was swift to follow. McAdam and his colleague Professor Stuart, Professor of Pathology and Dean of the Faculty of Medicine, were hoping to develop a department of Psychiatry when the war was over, for which money had already been promised by Lord Nuffield. Meanwhile, they were looking for knowledgeable personnel to prepare the ground, and Harry was keen to accept their offer of a temporary lectureship in 'Psychology in Relation to Medicine', involving sixteen lectures per annum, until the new department should be inaugurated. In 1943 no-one could say when, or even if, that would be! But for Harry the way was opening towards a new career. He discussed this matter with his deacons, drawing their attention to the number of patients referred to him, which had vastly exceeded anything he had expected, and he pointed out that the influx was largely due to the confidence in his work shown by the Leeds medical community. The deacons readily accepted Harry's proposal that his lecture fees, together with the income from his patients, should be used to provide Salem with a part-time Assistant Minister to help with the preaching, pastoral visiting and organisation. Vernon Sproxton, at that time part-time Secretary of the Student Christian Movement, was appointed with effect from 29 March 1944 for two years. Meanwhile Harry began his Lectureship in anticipation of Sproxton's arrival, in the Michaelmas term of 1943. In fact he had accepted the post in May, following his meeting with the deacons, and he at once began searching for further training for himself. Finding a suitable training analyst was not easy, partly because so many, such as J.D. Sutherland, were in the Army Psychiatric Services. Moreover, Harry's experience of the limitations of instinct theory had made him extremely cautious, and he realised his good fortune when Dr Alan Maberley, the Acting Wartime Director of the Tavistock Clinic, London, agreed to accept him for some private training sessions. Maberley was not a Freudian, and in fact he inclined heavily towards the theories of Jung, with which Harry had already made himself familiar. Indeed, Maberley did not commit himself in a doctrinaire way to any theory, but retained an independence of mind which Harry found liberating. Furthermore, he recognised how difficult it was for Harry to get any professional support for his new commitment, and usually gave him sessions lasting a good hour and a half. Due to the travel involved, the sessions were arranged on a somewhat piecemeal basis. There were six that May, twenty-six in August (two per day for two weeks while Harry was in London writing *The Life of Smith and Wrigley*) two a month in September, October and December, three in January, two in March, three in October 1944, and some sporadic sessions in January and April 1945.

During the period of intensive sessions in August, Harry dreamed that he was simultaneously offering to stand down from his pastorate in order, 'not to stand in the church's way of growing', whilst also working at a Psychology degree in a university building which was connected in some way with what he might do if he left Salem. The dream, which he reported to Maberley, summed up the inner significance of the events of 1943 as a critical turning point in his life, even though a final decision lay three years in the future. He had long felt temperamentally unsuited to a ministerial pastorate, and that he was by nature equipped for individual work and concentrated research, yet his fear of the unknown made itself known in 'a dream flash of being on a precipice and in danger of falling over'. Maberley offered a useful 'semi-Jungian' interpretation: 'You feel that in giving up the church you may be retreating from the challenge of fuller emotional development. To deal with an individual you can use the conscious level, to deal with a crowd one must be able to release the unconscious. Hitler is all unconscious, he has no conscious thinking self. You need to overcome your fear of the unconscious. The distinction between good and evil is not horizontal but vertical. We have ultimately to get beyond "good and evil" and the tension of opposites of thinking and feeling, to real integration.'

One might suppose that this interpretation, carrying the implication that Harry's unconscious had value, came as something of a revelation after the moralistic self-criticism inspired by the Freudians. Nor is it surprising that it encountered Harry's 'super-ego opposition' in a subsequent dream, in which the unconscious inner contents were associated with faeces which at first 'looked pretty' to the dreamer, and then had to be 'cleaned out' by him. The influence of Maberley's experience in child-guidance was clear, when he said, 'to a child faeces are a gift of precious material, an infant's treasure, something it has itself made. I make a gift of tenderness to mother but have a sense of guilt about it: she won't like it, and I stifle it, get rid of it.' This at once encouraged

Guntrip to explore not the postulated desire to monopolise mother and eliminate father, but the actual quality of his relationship to his mother. He recalled her shrinking from physical expressions of affection, sitting like a statue when he climbed on her knee at eight years, and her rejection of any expression of sympathetic tenderness as 'sentimental and sloppy'. In two subsequent dreams he was first 'having a desperate struggle with a Medieval Roman Catholic' (under the domination of 'mother-church'), and then being criticised for trying to show sympathy to 'a bundly dressed woman in trouble' – a reference to the fact that his mother, although a skilled dressmaker, could never make herself look smart. He had often remarked that she looked like 'a bundle of clothes', and presumably expressed some sympathy for her, only to encounter her hostile criticism. Harry was quick to associate this 'guilt inhibition' on natural expressions of feeling with his feeling of being emotionally restricted in his public work. Certainly his sessions with Maberley were directed towards the freeing of his emotional self for personal relating in a way he had previously not experienced; a way more relevant to the 'crippled primitive ground-work' of his nature – crippled because not his 'instincts' but his 'very self' had been denied proper recognition and growth. However, the analysis was too sporadic, and too merely explanatory to deal with the very deep material which was to emerge. For the present it centred upon the need for Harry to integrate the 'male' and 'female', thinking and feeling elements of his personality, with con-sequent resistance on his part. Maberley also shed a different light upon the way that women were always intruding into Harry's private affairs in his dreams when he suggested that they might represent both 'the excluded feeling self' which he did not want to lose, and also the instinctive side, which, when aroused, interfered with his intellectuality. The last dream of the intensive period of sessions in August 1943 drew from the the first eight years when mother's inhibiting influence on Harry's self-assertive and, when provoked, aggressive impulses was at its height.

> I was examining a very small model house, a kind of doll's house, the hut of a primitive head-hunter. In one corner was a collection of tiny heads or skulls. I arranged them in a row with a vague idea that the hunter was going to make another attack on them a second time. Then a group of tiny models of a family were to be massacred, a taller female was to be raped as well.

The dream had a contemporary external trigger in newspaper accounts of German atrocities on the Russian front, but for Harry its inner meaning was evoked by a memory of his mother showing him the bottom of a cupboard where mice had shredded up a lot of paper; tiny but destructive creatures: the aggression of a tiny infantile world. It seems probable that genuine progress could have been made along these lines had Harry been able to continue his twice-daily sessions, especially as he was visiting Harriet during that period, and reading the above mentioned correspondence, concerning Percy. The letters showed that Harriet's state of mind was already unstable, and as Harry returned to Leeds, the need for Harriet to live with him and Bertha began to weigh more heavily upon him.

The combined effect of ending the intensive period of analysis and the growing weight of responsibility for Harriet made Harry acutely sensitive to the destructive elements of her personality. The following dream, which he had on his return to Leeds, vividly caricatures his impression of what his mother did to his father, and of what she really wanted to do to him, hence her jealousy and resentment of Bertha.

A lady was driven around in a carriage drawn by a bird-man. He had a human face and body, but small wings for arms, pinned under his coat, and thin bird legs. Drawing the carriage he looked like an ostrich. She went into a draper's shop and tied him to a lamp-post and he just stood still there. There seemed to be no carriage then.

Although Harry was able to take advantage of a London Ministerial Committee meeting to snatch a session with Maberley, such sporadic visits only served to underline his need for a proper training analysis, for they understandably failed to hold the upsurge of disturbed experience sparked off by his current difficulties with his mother. In one dream he re-experienced an early fear that his mother and the doctor had severely damaged or cut off his penis during the circumcision. In another, he dreamed of 'A cage in a park with a tiny catlike animal two inches long, perfectly made and very agile and fierce', thus 'staging a comeback' so to speak. In yet another dream he lost courage, seeming to re-experience a child's confusion over whether he ought to want to retain his organ or to sacrifice it. Finally, after a hurried visit to London to see Maberley, he dreamed simply 'I was playing with our new kitten.' The kitten had been a symbol for his genitals in previous dreams,

and now he felt securely in possession of it. On his return from
London, Bertha, who had been more ready than he to associate his
depression with the irregularity of sessions, was relieved to find
that he was his old self again. Greatly to his misfortune however,
he could only manage five sessions over the next four months, and
had to do the best he could to follow up the developments alone.
Partly as a result of the ensuing strain, he suffered another acute
sinus attack, for which Maberley referred him to a Harley Street
physician. For the next two and half years he was treated with
ephedrine and vaccines, but with only short-term success, until
finally surgery seemed the only course. Regretably, at that time,
medical men were obsessed with the idea of 'focal infections' and a
Harley Street surgeon diagnosed a focal infection in the soft alveolar tissue of Harry's upper jaw. A 'radical alveolectomy' was carried
out in a London nursing home, at great expense, which he and
Bertha could ill afford. The operation involved the removal of all
Harry's top teeth and the soft alveolar bone beneath, and the sewing back of the skin over the hard bone. It was a total disaster, for
the dentures he had to wear continually cut through the skin
covering the hard bone so that his mouth became full of sores. It
was, in the social sense, a 'castration' since Harry was never able
to eat in company with other people. Moreover, the operation completely failed to relieve the sinus attacks which continued to occur
each winter as before.

It is hardly surprising that towards the end of 1943, Harry
experienced once again the powerful 'pull to get out of life' which
was the core of his psychopathology, and the underlying cause of
his relentless over-driving of his energies. It appeared first in a
simple dream in which he had 'decided to commit suicide' with no
clear reason, but was 'postponing it' for the sake of his wife and
Salem. About a month later part of the reason appeared in the
form of a clear regression dream:

> I was standing in an open arch, holding the top and drawing
> myself up into the position of a baby in the womb.

It will be noticed however, that even this depended upon his own
efforts to draw himself up, and furthermore it was impinged upon
by sexual excitement, for the dream ended:

> I was suspended in the air and had an erect penis. It was as if
> mother was holding me like that.

Two nights later he dreamed,

> I was waiting for some news about someone, a baby, perhaps a
> brother. It was very vague and uncertain. Meanwhile I was in bed
> (i.e. ill) held at a woman's breast which seemed wrinkled and not
> comforting. I felt some vague dislike or repugnance for her.

The atmosphere of these dreams constituted the unconscious context
over against which Harry continued to carry on his consciously
directed work. By the time Vernon Sproxton arrived to take up his
duties as part-time Assistant Minister, Harry was severely overworked. In addition to twenty-seven hours a week with his patients
and all the usual Salem work, he was carrying on his Medical School
lecturing, and lecturing on Wednesday evenings on psychology at
Swarthmore Psychiatric Hospital. Altogether he was working twelve
hours a day, about eighty hours a week. Indeed it seems as though in
the absence of consistent psychotherapeutic support, he could only
keep the inner turmoil unconscious by making the external pressure
equally taxing. An imbalance occurred however, when the external
pressure grew to include Harriet. When Harry and Bertha returned
from a week's recuperation at Pateley Bridge, they received a telegram
from Harriet peremptorily informing them that she was selling her
bungalow and coming to live with them. At the same time a further
telegram arrived from a neighbour of hers, 'Come at once or your
mother will have given away her home.' Harry caught the first available train, and found that she had already sold her bungalow to a
neighbour's son for less than it was worth. He was just in time to
stop her giving away her household effects at random, and to salvage
enough furniture for her to be able to furnish the main bedroom at
Cross Flatts Road with her own possessions. That night, sleeping in
the bungalow at Thundersley he had a dream which needs no interpretation:

> I had to conduct the funeral of a female. The corpse was
> wrapped in a paper parcel and brought into what seemed like an
> Anglican church.

On 29 April 1944 Harriet came to live permanently and finally
with Harry and Bertha. She was to remain there for the next nine
years, becoming increasingly helpless and difficult, until ultimately
she had to be nursed by Bertha. On 1 May, Harry dreamed:

> I was watching a tame tiger but was half afraid of it and felt it
> might turn savage.

Indeed Harriet was relatively 'tame' at this time due to her low
state of health. Nevertheless, for the first two months of her resi-
dence Harry found himself seriously sexually impotent for the only
time in his life. On 14 June he dreamed:

> I was in some building and there was a great tiger there, then it
> seemed to be a bear that would hug one to death. I was high up
> somewhere trying to escape from it. Details vague, but fear
> intense.

He noted 'This tiger or bear is mother . . . Now mother is with us
we can't get away from her. She won't go to bed at night and
we've got to take her on holiday with us.' In a further dream it
would appear that Bertha was the only antidote to his mother's
emasculation of him:

> I got into a rowing boat with a not very impressive looking man
> who had come to find a girl to take out. I was approaching the
> girl. But then I went out of the house and met my wife who
> was waiting outside for me.

It was in this atmosphere that Harry had one of the most memorable
of his 'big dreams', and one which aroused more intense fear in him
than any other.

> I was sitting at a table in a downstairs living room, working
> with books and papers, writing. Suddenly I became aware that
> in a bedroom upstairs, there was a pale, passive invalid, white,
> lying motionless in bed: but an invisible substance, a kind of
> ectoplasm emerged from the body and was stretching all the
> way downstairs and into the room where I was, and at this end
> it was somehow fused into my body and was drawing me
> relentlessly out of the room. I knew that it would draw me into
> the invalid's room and I would become absorbed into her. I was
> terrified and fought against the pull. I held on to the table and
> it drew me and the table along towards the door. I let go of the
> table and clutched the mantelpiece fixed to the wall. Suddenly
> the spell broke and I knew that I was free from the danger and
> was able to go back to my work.

Both at the time and ever thereafter, Harry felt certain that the
dream expressed his terror of being drawn into that collapse illness
after Percy's death, though it was not until later that he saw that it

also contained hidden identifications with Percy and Father. The dream exploited the memory (doubtless stirred up by Harriet's presence in the home) of going up into Aunt Mary's bedroom when she was believed to be dying, and it surely also expresses a need to merge with the affectionate aunt so as not to lose her as the one source of tenderness in his family. Deeper still, no doubt, lay the powerful urge to regress to the womb which formed a permanent threat to his hyperactive self, until many years later he came at last to experience the therapeutic possibilities of regression. Meanwhile he was consciously committed to compulsive overwork, general overactivity and inability to relax and enjoy leisure. He even made holidays strenuous, marking off the stages of car journeys in terms of time and distance, unable to risk relaxing and falling asleep at night lest he should allow the unconscious menace to erupt as it had done in a big way when his colleague left. It was indeed fortunate for Harry that Vernon Sproxton's arrival had preceded that of Harriet by a month. He was an excellent colleague and Harry was undoubtedly spared a great deal of strain, for he wrote, 'Sproxton is a grand lad, and in some ways temperamentally better suited to the ministry than I am. He is a natural preacher. I am more suited to lecturing and research. Moreover, I begin to see a way ahead and am right off sleeping tablets.' In fact, Sproxton was newly married, and he and his wife lived with the Guntrip's for six months while they were house-hunting, thus somewhat diluting the impact of Harriet's influence.

One aspect of this influence was the striking similarity in 'constitutional type' between Harriet, Harry, and his daughter Gwen. Harry did not make much of his similarity to his mother in this way, understandably in view of her destructive influence upon him. But one of his cousins had remarked on it at their first meeting, saying, 'You're a proper Jessop, Harry. We're all like it, active all the time, on the go', and when Harriet's arrival coincided with the start of Gwen's early adolescence, Harry sensed a degree of resemblance which at times he found disconserting. He noted that Gwen was becoming a 'challenging adolescent . . . at times aggressively independent. She is a very good companion when all is going to her liking, but she fires up at the least difference of opinion, or if asked to do what she doesn't want to, and I believe I am afraid of her having no use for me, of her giving me no chance to help her, and am anxious that she should not become hard.' This problem, which is so typical of many an adolescent development, was to reach a climax when Gwen left home to go to the London School of Economics where she met her future husband, Denis Greenald.

For the time being Harry's dreaming reflected his ambivalence to his daughter's need for freedom, while consciously he supported her right to act out her growing independence. Although he had scarcely been actively encouraged to be free at the same age by his mother, who never approved 'of young people growing up', it is surely as well that by the time of his own early adolescence, he had at least 'grown away' from Harriet, with the aid of her financial support for his hobbies. Of more serious import was the effect upon Bertha of the disturbed emotions that Harriet was stirring up in Harry. Bertha was by nature a sympathetic person, and she was genuinely sorry to see Harriet in an ill and run-down condition. She had nursed Harriet already through a three-month illness, and was well aware that the old woman's gratitude was short-lived, and rapidly gave way to jealousy and paranoia. She also realised that it was impossible to place Harriet in an old people's home, partly because of the war, but also because no home would have kept her for any length of time, once she began telling people what to do and lodging complaints. Thus Bertha devoted herself to the utmost to making Harriet comfortable, looking after her and arranging little treats for her, while Harriet herself became increasingly demanding. The burden became almost intolerable when Harry, returning from his day's work, complained that Bertha, by allowing Harriet to monopolise her, was neglecting Gwen and himself. Uncharacteristically Bertha fought back, pointing out to Harry that he was unjustly displacing his anger towards his mother on to herself and thereby increasing her already very great burden. This wholly justified riposte shocked Harry into a greater awareness of his dependence upon Bertha, especially as far as his mother was concerned, while Bertha, for her part, found it easier than hitherto to share with Harry the day's troubles. Somehow they weathered the storm as Harriet's returning strength continued to sour her relations with Bertha, until she began to complain openly to Harry about how badly Bertha treated her, and finally started to quarrel with Bertha in front of him. At last, Harry exploded at her, and she flung out of the room and up to her bedroom, where she could be heard stamping up and down, talking at the top of her voice. Each time this happened she would emerge an hour later all smiles and for a week or so the house would be peaceful, until the situation recurred. Harry realised that, inadvertently, he had found a means of dealing with his mother, which enabled him to vent his lifelong resentment against her openly, and without guilt, since he saw that it also satisfied a need in her. The knowledge that he was prepared to be frankly angry with her, in a way that Henry had never been, made her feel safer, since she saw that her own violence could be contained. Harry was helped in this matter of realistically dealing with his mother on an occasion when he happened to glance at her as he was having a late tea after working late. She had moved from the table and was sitting in an armchair staring into space with a fierce thunderous scowl on her face. To his shocked surprise Harry felt an immediate and involuntary sharp stab of real fear. When he recovered himself, he was struck by the incongruity of a man in his late forties feeling physically afraid of an old lady in her seventies. He realised that, taken by surprise and off guard, he had re-experienced a state which had often overwhelmed him as a small defenceless child, a state to which his dream-life so amply testified. The realisation helped him consciously to feel justified in protecting himself and his family against his mother's moods.

However successfully he and Bertha came to manage Harriet at home, Harriet in church was another matter. She was too old to play an active part in church life, but she would attend the services with Bertha and sit throughout the proceedings with a black scowl on her face. She deeply resented having to wait after the service while members of the congregation discussed affairs with Harry and Bertha, and although those members who understood the situation would talk to Harriet while she waited, there was no telling what she might say. On one occasion, when Harry found her standing at the front of an aisle with the usual hard scowl on her face, she said to him, 'I've just heard someone saying, "I don't know how Mrs Guntrip puts up with it."' Harry answered, somewhat tartly, 'They meant Bertha. She is Mrs Guntrip to the people here.' On other occasions Harriet told people that she had bought Harry and Bertha's house for her retirement, and that their car was a hired car. Harry and Bertha had cause to be relieved that, of the nine years that Harriet lived with them, only the first two were during his Salem ministry. Even so, her extreme jealousy of their family relationships continued to make home life very difficult. On one memorable occasion in 1945 Harry and Bertha arranged for Harriet to be looked after by Mrs Kind and her sister Charlotte, while they took Gwen for her first visit to London to see the 'VJ Day'[1] celebrations, and then on to Bournemouth for their annual summer holiday. Immediately on their return, Harriet called Harry to her room and poured out a bizarre story of the ill-treatment she had received at the hands of the two sisters. Adopting his 'direct approach', Harry told her he did not believe a word of it, to which she replied 'Then you are accusing me of telling lies.' Harry said, 'If you want to put it that way, Yes I am.' and left her in

her room. Within a week it became clear that her quite paranoid
reaction was all of a piece with her acute jealousy over his taking
Bertha and Gwen on holiday and leaving her at home. She then
demanded that he arrange a holiday for her. Harry relented and
arranged a holiday for her at Pateley Bridge with a middle-aged
woman and her mother who let rooms. Harriet liked the woman and
the rooms and agreed to stay a fortnight. Within three days she wrote
saying Harry must collect her immediately as they were beating her
cruelly. Harry did so, only to take her back a few days later, com-
plaining that she had not had her holiday. Within three days the
same thing happened again. This time he took her for a walk, gave
her an extremely frank dressing down and took her back home,
making it quite clear that there must be an end to the nonsense.
When reviewing this period almost thirty years later, Harry wrote, 'It
is impossible to do justice to my wife's forbearance and patience over
the nine years that my mother finally lived with us.' Harry's record
casts his mother firmly in the rôle of 'bad object', and there is objective validation for this from others who knew her. But, however
silently benevolent his father may have been, he was certainly inadequate both as a protection from Harriet's hostility and as any kind of
companion for his son. Indeed one wonders whether Harry realised
the full implication of his famous dictum that 'a bad relationship is
better than none', which he used to explain the adhesiveness of the
bad object. Did he realise the likely inference that the 'bad object'
relationship with Harriet was effectively his only one? At any rate a
dream which he had after the holiday debacle on 1 September 1944,
would seem to suggest that he was at least semi-consciously aware of
Henry as 'pottering and ineffective', and a drag on him:

> I was conducting a religious service and I seemed to be not
> properly prepared for it. Father was pottering around ineffec-
> tively wanting to help but I wouldn't let him. He complained of
> the gulf between us and said we didn't really share interests.
> Then I seemed to be engaged in a struggle with him and finally
> subdued him till he collapsed.

The dream was a prelude to a series in which he registered his
desire to leave Salem and engage fully in psychoanalysis. In a
particularly striking dream in mid-December he discovered 'a new
block of buildings at the back of Salem', which unknown to him
'had always been there', and in which Andrew Lang and F.W.H.
Myers had regularly been chairing a 'Men's Meeting' without his
knowledge. Andrew Lang, the anthropologist, and Myers, the poet

who studied psychic research, both stood for scholarly investiga-
tions into human nature, and Harry's discovery that they had been
working in an 'undiscovered block of rooms at the back' would
seem to suggest an unconscious awareness that the facet of him
that they represented 'always' had been 'working in the background', in his busy organisational activities at Salem. He had
often found that the discovery of a hitherto unknown room in a
dream, that had 'always been there', represented the unconscious
capacities of the dreamer waiting to be brought to light. Lang and
Myers did not stand for the 'preacher' but for the 'researcher and
writer', and probably the 'lecturer': all facets of his personality
which were to play a far larger part in his life than at that time he
could ever have imagined.

With the growing perception that his developing interest would
involve a radical change in his whole life set-up, came the realisation that he needed a steady radical analysis in place of the present
ad hoc arrangement. He had four dreams of seeing both Maberley
and Clifford Allen in which they seemed friendly but vague and
ineffective, while further dreams betokened feelings of lack of parental support in the face of growing anxiety. He saw Maberley for
the last time in April, and from that point he stopped dream
recording and self-analysis for two years and nine months.

As the war ended in 1945 Salem began to return to its normal
pattern of busy activity, and Harry realised that he must either
phase out his psychotherapy or else himself from Salem while
easing someone else in. By great good fortune the Rev. Norman
Beard came to preach at Salem one Sunday and made a great
impression on everyone. From this moment events acquired their
own momentum. Vernon Sproxton was due to leave at the end of
July to take over the full-time Secretaryship of the Student Christian Movement, and at around the same time Dr Henry V. Dicks
of the Tavistock Clinic was appointed the first Nuffield Professor of
Psychiatry at Leeds. Somewhat to Harry's consternation, Dicks
attended one of his lectures to the senior year medical students
and shortly afterwards invited him to join the new department on
'any terms [he] might propose'. Beard was approached with a view
to taking on the pastorate at Salem, which he was keen to do, and
he was duly installed. For his part, Harry, while not wanting to
take on a full-time lectureship, which he felt might be too restrictive, quickly realised that with a combination of a part-time
lectureship in the Department of Psychiatry, and his fast-growing
psychotherapy practice, he could be financially viable. The title
'Long-Term Research Worker in Psychotherapy' was decided upon,

and it was agreed that he should devote two half-day sessions to seeing patients in the Department (Monday morning and Friday afternoon), attend staff meetings, and do any lecturing which might be required. His decision having been made, he was further assisted by the provision of a small consulting-room which his GP, Dr Danks, was vacating.

Note

1. Victory in Japan Day – effectively the end of the Second World War.

CHAPTER 6

The Professional Psychotherapist

The new 'Department of Psychiatry' was located in an empty house next door to the School of Dentistry. When Harry arrived, he found the new Nuffield Professor in one room with nothing but a chair and a table. His young secretary occupied another room with nothing but a chair, table and typewriter. It was the depth of winter, and bitterly cold. The secretary had a severe cold and both she and Dicks were wearing outdoor clothes. In the course of a week or two some furniture arrived, and so did another member of staff, a German refugee psychiatrist, Dr Rosenbusch. Over the next two years that nucleus grew steadily into a well-equipped and staffed department. In the weekly case-conferences Harry found that he was able to learn a great deal from his colleagues as well as contributing much from his eight years' experience of psychotherapy whilst at Salem. Dicks, whose book had earlier so impressed Harry, had a deep respect for the cure of souls. He once expressed the view that the people in Harry's profession (that is, the pastorate) knew more about emotional disturbance than those in his own, while often remarking of himself, 'I can't diagnose now, I can only describe psychopathology.' The psychopathology to which Harry was exposed at the Department clinic was of a severe kind, and during 1948 he became very discouraged by the lack of therapeutic results in the cases of patients whom he later realised were 'schizoid', presenting not problems of 'conflicting impulses' or 'super-ego guilt' but of sheer fundamental 'ego weakness'. He knew nothing of that at that time, though he must surely have been aware of a similarity to his own feeling of being apart from others. Dicks advised him to read Fairbairn's writings, but these had not as yet been published in book form and in his discouraged state Harry lacked the initiative, or perhaps the know-how, to contact Fairbairn directly. Indeed he hovered on the brink of feeling that he would have to give up psychotherapy and return to the Congregational ministry. Clearly his schizoid patients were presenting him with the very psychopathology for which he himself was unable to find understanding. Furthermore, as the department grew in size it began to lose the intimate 'family atmosphere' which was so valuable to Harry in the first two years, and when Professor Dicks announced his resignation, it seemed like a final blow. Dicks had forged a working department from scratch, commuting from London where he spent every weekend with his wife and children. It was a schedule that no-one could be expected to continue for long, and after two years he had wisely decided to hand over to a successor and return home. Harry had invested more than he realised in the warmth and stability of Dicks, who had become a new 'father-figure' to him. He dreamed of dining with Dicks and his wife in 'a large roomy scholarly [house] with a big library'. They both looked reliable and stable. Again, he dreamed of staying with Dicks and 'playing with his two children, freely sitting on the floor'. Without doubt the new department, with Dicks in charge, had become his new 'professional family'. When he knew of the former's plans to resign, Harry returned in his dreaming to that other good surrogate family, the Salvation Army, where 'a woman with a cheerful face framed in her bonnet smiled at me'. However, the imminent loss of Dicks inevitably took its toll in his inner world, where he felt once more exposed to the threat of his internalised bad mother. This was manifested in another of his 'big' dreams in February 1948.

> Two bedrooms opened into each other by two doors on opposite sides of two double beds, both of which had their heads to the dividing wall. I was holding my wife in my arms on one side, kissing her, but mother came through the door on the opposite side, from the left hand room, intruding. I picked my wife up and carried her through the door on our side into the other room, but mother followed through the door on her side. I kept carrying my wife from one room to the other to get away from mother. She was quite passive as if she had lost her personality.

Harry felt that the most serious aspect of the dream was its implication that his mother was destroying Bertha's personality just as she had destroyed Percy's and father's. He felt that she could not help interfering between himself and anyone who mattered to him by her insidious influence. In practice, Bertha never did succumb to her pressure through all the years of nursing, even though she could never be certain whether Harriet was really unwell or 'just playing up'. The dream was a measure not so much of 'objective reality', but of the extent to which his mother dominated Harry's inner world.

By the time Dicks finally left in July 1948, Harry had had five dreams of the bad mother and eight of Dicks as a supportive 'father-figure'. In one of the latter, Dicks' face was 'exactly like father's, including the same silver-grey hair', and in another final dream Harry was delighted to find the Dicks family installed in the Blows' house, in Lordship Lane, to which he had the side-door key. It would seem that Dicks had by then assumed the significance of a brother-figure, and characteristically after his departure, Harry fell prey to symptoms of exhaustion. Though the illness was similar in kind to the one following the departure of Turner, the symptoms were less severe. He wrote in his dream book on 28 July 1948,

> Felt ill all day, as I did in Scotland when my colleague left. It must go back to the illness after Percy's death. Lost interest in books and patients.

In fact he had been fighting against an urge to withdraw ever since he had first known that Dicks was to leave. In February he had written in his diary of how he had sought sanctuary from the turmoil of the emotions in intellectual life, a sanctuary now under renewed threat from his mother's presence:

> My feeling self does not live in this world, and I suspect many people have felt that I was the 'intellectual' whose heart does not go out to them. I know I could catch myself 'looking through' or 'looking over' people. A really sociable personality was something I desired rather than possessed, and in practice was more forced than felt. My friendliness was more my need for friendly relations than spontaneous friendliness towards others. My emotions did not flow spontaneously. I could organise, lecture, analyse, but something in me was inhibited. My religion was more thought than felt. Because of the conflict between angry assertiveness and defensive compliance, which mother forced on me very early, I must have withdrawn from the emotional into the intellectual life. Faced with mother, I did not want to become passive like father and Mary, so threw all my active assertive energies into religious zeal, and drew off my anger into intellectual revolt (where it did me a good turn). I would fight others battles but not my own. But now, the tensions of the emotional conflict I have tried to escape from in myself, are continually stirred up by mother once more, in direct confrontation. When I would like to show affection she drives me to anger, and so it has always been.

This accurate 'character analysis' shows the remarkable insight which is often characteristic of the 'schizoid intellectual'. In the course of time the discovery that intellectual insight does not in itself free one from internal conflict led Harry to emphasise the fundamental importance of the 'real relationship' between analyst and patient in psychoanalytic psychotherapy.

At this time in 1948, however, he had no analyst. Dicks had gone and he felt a pervading sense of insecurity centred on the thought that anyone he allowed himself to depend on for support in the face of the threat of mother, whether male or female, whether Percy, father, Mary, friend, colleague, or even his wife, would become lost to him. Thus he wrote of Bertha,

> I am afraid to need her emotional support too much in case I get dependent on her, and then feel forced into a state of anxious self-defence.

Indeed he showed that tendency to regard relationship and freedom as mutually exclusive which he was later to describe as a schizoid characteristic:

> I am afraid to depend on her love too much, a conflict between dependence and freedom.

He did, however, attempt to analyse the problem:

> I am very dependent on my wife's love. Probably this goes right down to my childhood need to find protection and comfort in Aunt Mary. This is the polar opposite to my drive and energy and activity, which is also natural but I have to use it to over-compensate the other [sic], for I believe I deeply fear the dependent side of me, and repress it. That dream of the invalid woman upstairs drawing me! I think this is stirred up whenever mother gets too much for my wife for a time, and I feel she becomes emotionally withdrawn and is not strong enough for me to depend on.

He was to find that his fear of weakness and dependence did not decrease when a strong person was present. Quite the reverse: it became greater. Meanwhile the loss of the supportive Dicks, with the attendant exhaustion and his fear of becoming over-dependent upon Bertha, caused him to redouble his efforts to remain active, and his insomnia, of which he had been free since leaving Salem, recurred.

On 16 October 1948 he wrote:

> It is worth considering all my problems of personality in terms of greed. I can't be content with what I have, and quietly enjoy it, but must be rushing on to get more or something different. I have to stop myself wanting the best of the food, do not like parting with money, and tend to think of a holiday in terms of loss of income: I say to myself that this is because we have had to scrape by on a small income for years but it is not wholly that. I am like it in other things. I try to read too many books at one time, and tend to rush on to others without finishing and digesting any properly. I feel to be wanting more friendly contacts with people, and at times become conscious of an unrelaxing drive to crowd more and more into life, to get more knowledge, more love, more money, more everything. I feel not sleeping is probably part of this pattern. I do not knock off and relax and do nothing and go to sleep. I go on being mentally active, go on living and getting things I want in imagination; even new ideas crowding in. I must feel I haven't got enough resources of value inside myself, and that life is slipping away in my late 40s, and I haven't yet done anything worthwhile. But this is dissipation of energy, starting and dropping things, and taking up others and doing nothing really well.

As he recognised in 1973, this pattern represented a somewhat hypermanic defence against an overwhelmingly strong underlying feeling of depletion due to early deprivation. Four years of mother living in their home had stirred up in Harry a small boy's longing in vain for 'mother love'.

Into this desolate situation came Dick's successor, formerly the professor of Psychiatry at the University of Aberdeen, Dr D.R. MacCalman. He was a son of a Scottish Manse, and he and Harry soon found that they had much in common. At his first address to the staff meeting at Leeds he gave a full exposition of the innovations in psychoanalytic theory made by Dr W.R.D. Fairbairn of Edinburgh, whom he knew personally. Harry listened, fascinated, for he saw that here was the very element that he had been searching for, a revision of Freudian theory in terms of 'personal human relationships', not 'instincts'. Here at last was the psychoanalytic counterpart to the 'Personal Relations' Philosophy of John MacMurray. Furthermore, the formidable 'schizoid problem' appeared to be the key concept in Fairbairn's work. After the lecture, Harry asked MacCalman if he could borrow Fairbairn's papers, to which the professor replied, 'Write and ask him for reprints.' He did so, and Fairbairn sent him copies of all the papers he had written. The effect was immediate, and Harry addressed himself with new heart to psychotherapy. He also began to sense the prospect of entering analysis with Fairbairn, in an attempt at last to make sense of his 'ego-experience' in terms of his struggle to come by a sense of personal meaning and reality in his family.

At that time, in November 1948, his feelings in relationship to his mother had hardened into 'a fixed unyielding hostility' to her as a 'hard, egotistical, unpleasant, selfish woman, whose superficial Christianity had evaporated'. He wrote:

> She takes everything and gives nothing. Her talk is scandalous, always about herself and embarrassing with visitors, as for example that she had the first wireless set in Benfleet, that father was useless, that she took good care that she had no more children etc. I dread leaving her alone with anyone. Her behaviour to us since we married has been appalling, vindictive to my wife, tempers, lying, criticism and neurotic tantrums during the first year here. She's hard and I've never had any real love from her. She did in her prime do and say the decent and right thing, but her behaviour since she lost father and Mary has shown her inner state of mind. I go into my shell with her. But in fact she is now only a lonely, pathetic, mentally-decayed old woman, though she can still play on my highly disturbed emotions of my long-distant childhood.

There could scarcely have been a more fertile ground or a greater need for an analysis based upon the 'object-relations theory' of the personality. For the preceding twelve years, since 1936, when the Salem crisis forced him to consult Crichton-Miller, Harry's self-analysis had served as 'an exhaust valve for inner emotional tension', by providing him with at least an intellectual understanding of his problem. Moreover, as he surveyed his assiduously kept record of dreams over that same period, he became convinced that they afforded 'indisputably clear' symbolic evidence that the highly disturbed family atmosphere of his first eight years was still very much alive in him, revealing both his intense early fear of his mother, and also his need of greater support from his father, 'though at least he was reliably present in his quiet way'. With these considerations in mind, he determined to visit Fairbairn in Edinburgh, and, as a means of introduction, he sent the latter a copy of his recently published book, *Psychology for Ministers and*

Social Workers,[1] in which he had already set out his credo regarding the essence of psychotherapy: 'psychotherapy is a co-operative effort of two people in the dynamic personal relationship of the analytical situation, to solve the problems of one of them' (p. 11).

Note

1   Independent Press, London, 1949.

The Fairbairn Analysis

CHAPTER 7

1949

Harry's first approach to Fairbairn was exploratory. Having read his papers, he wished to discuss and clarify their contents, but he also needed to assess Fairbairn's personality with a view to entering analysis with him. He took with him a case history of one of his own patients for Fairbairn to assess, and was greatly encouraged by the latter's suggestion that he should offer the paper to Dr Willi Hoffer for publication in the *International Journal of Psychoanalysis*. The fate of the paper appears to be obscure, but Hoffer was sufficiently impressed to suggest that Guntrip should consider going to London to do the Institute Training. Fairbairn's dry comment was: 'They regard you as a promising man gone to the wrong analyst!'

Harry had little difficulty in choosing Fairbairn. For one thing, his experience of Crichton-Miller and Clifford Allen had made him afraid that genuine intellectual difficulties might be interpreted as negative transference by an Institute analyst, rather than seriously considered and discussed. Given the general suspicion with which Fairbairn's theoretical papers were regarded by the Institute analysts it seems probable that Guntrip was justified in this view. When Fairbairn's book *Psychoanalytic Studies of the Personality* (1952) appeared, even relatively independent analysts such as Winnicott and Masud Khan (1953)[1] were more concerned about Fairbairn's challenge to Freud than with his pioneering clinical discoveries and theoretical advance. The point at issue for Harry was not, however, only about the fate of 'genuine intellectual differences' but about the whole approach of a psychoanalyst to his patient; and whether the latter was related to as a 'person' who mattered 'for his own sake in his own right', (Fairbairn 1952) or merely 'analysed' in terms of Freud's instinct theory. Not surprisingly, Guntrip preferred the former, though he was later to find that Fairbairn was more revolutionary in theory than he was able to be in practice.

Three months after his original approach Fairbairn agreed to take him on for four sessions a week – one on Tuesday evening, two on Wednesday, and one early on Thursday morning. Some

time earlier Harry and Bertha had agreed to save as much money
as possible towards a training analysis for Harry, but even so the
expense of travel and accommodation added considerably to the
financial burden. Fairbairn kindly agreed to take Harry on at the
very moderate rate of one guinea per session until his resources
increased. Accommodation was arranged with two elderly ladies,
and the arrangement continued unchanged for the next five years,
at which point the death of Fairbairn's first wife and his own
declining health necessitated the dropping of the early Thursday
session. The impact of these arrangements upon the Guntrips'
domestic life was very great. Since Harry's work at the Department
of Psychiatry occupied Thursday and Friday afternoons and Monday
mornings, he was obliged to see his private patients at weekends
and half-days on Mondays and Fridays. Bertha's unqualified support
was remarkable indeed, and Harry recorded his gratitude: 'I owe it
entirely to my wife that I was able to have this invaluable training
analysis, since she not only accepted the financial stringency and
my absence for some years two nights a week, but did all that at a
time when my difficult mother was still alive, nursing her as she
became increasingly demanding until her death in 1953.'[2]

The analysis began in Fairbairn's consulting rooms at 18 Grosvenor Crescent on 7 June 1949, and from then until its eventual
termination in 1960, Guntrip filled eleven exercise books of 200
pages each with his 'photographic' memories of his dreams, his own
'free associations', and Fairbairn's comments and interpretations.
The record would be written immediately after each session, 'to
strengthen the impression of each session on my mind', but he did
not study them at the time – or indeed at all until events precipitated
a need to do so in 1970[3] – for fear of 'intellectualising and disguising
my 'resistance'. Guntrip was aware that his own 'self-analytical'
thinking out of the meaning of his dreams had resulted in 'a good
deal of artificial meaning', and it was this tendency interpreted by
Fairbairn as 'a quest for mastery', and a substitute for immediate
feeling, which was the subject of the early sessions. In fact, it appears
that Harry's 'pursuit of power' was the result of a fear that Fairbairn
would see through his resistance and invade his innermost core.
Thus on his return to his rooms he experienced some 'anal tension',
and placed a table against the door because the lock was faulty. It is
also noticeable that, although Guntrip mentioned his sleeplessness,
sinusitis and constipation at the outset of his analysis, he made no
mention of his schizoid longing to be apart, or of the feeling of being
out of touch with others, which was so relevant to his basic problem
of 'ego weakness'. From the very start, his fear of invasion made him

strongly resistant, and he took it for granted, on the basis of the 'one up and the other down' pattern of relations in his family, that Fairbairn would dominate and invade him with intrusive interpretations (a negative transference from his mother), and consequently he unconsciously assumed that his role was to be one of stubborn resistance, 'automatically choosing' the couch rather than the chair, and then feeling 'dwarfed'. However, he recalled that, even at this early stage, what really frightened him was not so much the *invasiveness* of Fairbairn's intellectually precise interpretations, as the *bleakness* of the process. Thus it was principally the 'empty end of the large room' that made him feel dwarfed. And when, much later in the analysis, he mentioned this to Fairbairn, and the latter invited him to sit beside him on a chair near his desk, Guntrip related 'My stomach turned over in fear and I did not move.' Like so many of his schizoid patients, he feared the very relatedness he needed. Whilst it is not clear what Fairbairn made of this, the general tone of his interpretations remained broadly 'Oedipal', for he went on to link Guntrip's fear of the couch to the 'tent-bed illnesses', and a further feeling that if he acceded to his need to relax he would lose his 'masculinity' – whereas, as he later discovered, what he most deeply feared was 'the loss of definite selfhood' (see Guntrip 1961, in Hazell 1994, p. 163 ff.).

Guntrip began to realise that although part of his problem was one of 'fight' at the Oedipal level – though with *mother* rather than father – his basic problem consisted of the failure of either parent to foster and encourage a basic sense of selfhood in him, and it was the need to redress this failure he felt acutely with Fairbairn. He was conscious of wanting 'to build up Dr Fairbairn as a good object' before he could 'let [his] bad mother out' and it is noticeable that he assumed it was up to him to do this, as in the dream of 'gingering up' his father. The clearer this realisation grew, however, the more dissatisfied Guntrip became with Fairbairn's insistence that the heart of his problem lay in his mother's suppression of a basically strong libidinal nature. Whereas he could see the 'good Dr Fairbairn' as the ally he needed, Guntrip was to discover that he himself lacked the basic ego-strength to enter a therapeutic alliance at the level at which Fairbairn assumed he could. He felt he *could not reach Fairbairn*, since he lacked any solid basis in experience for a belief that such an outreach was open to him.

Meanwhile his dreaming continued to attest to his mother's potency as an internalised bad object – as for example when he dreamed early in his analysis of a female lion-keeper at a zoo, with whom he entered the male lions' cage. She shouted 'Back down' as they grew restive, and Guntrip grew afraid that his mother would disempower Fairbairn, just as she had everyone, and especially males, who had supported him. How pervasive and unaltered this fear remained, and how strongly he denied it, was demonstrated more than thirty years later when Guntrip was transcribing a memorable dream, in which Fairbairn, with 'mother's hard face', was analysing a patient in a setting which resembled both his consulting room and 'father's mission hall'. When he had finished transcribing the dream, Guntrip realised that he had unconsciously omitted the dream's ending in which 'a joke was being told, and Mrs Fairbairn, the mother, was going to whip her son for telling it wrong'. Thus, in one way or another, Fairbairn became in the transference either Guntrip's hard dominating mother, attacking him with interpretations, or his compliant, victimised father, who lost eventually even his gift for public speaking. Indeed Guntrip came to feel later that the very act of depending on Fairbairn exposed the latter to mother's destructiveness, though neither of them could see that at the time. Meanwhile his need for Fairbairn as a supportive father in the transference was somewhat frustrated when the latter consistently interpreted in a way which implied that he was 'expecting to find a broadly Oedipal pattern in [the] analysis' – that is to say a pattern in which Guntrip's problem was one of 'guilt over rivalry with father for mother's attention'.

In the face of Fairbairn's approach Guntrip began to waver, just as he had earlier in his period of analysis with Clifford Allen. He reminded himself of the comparison between Allen's interpretation of the 'Procession Dream' and that of Maberley. Whereas the former had said he was trying to get ahead of father in the procession, the latter had believed he was wanting father's support behind him. Now he believed, not only that 'all my twelve years of dreams had supported Maberley's view' but also that 'mother was the bad object in reality and father stood for the ideal', for even after his father had died he used to long to share experiences with him. Thus to Fairbairn he could only say 'Jealousy of father doesn't feel real to me', and point out that he had never found any evidence of it in his dreams.

Not surprisingly, he felt confused, and told Fairbairn that he felt stifled by his critical and judgemental style which reminded him of how his mother made him feel 'guilty over every bit of independence' – and thereby forcing him into rebellion, and into organising *a "thinking" self designed to prevent any spontaneous feeling. A compulsive intellectualising self.'* It was indeed this 'compulsive intellectualising self' rather than a 'bad Oedipal self' which, for Guntrip, constituted the greatest obstacle to accepting therapy: if there was any material for intellectual debate, he felt compelled to rise to the challenge, as if his battles with his mother had indeed become his whole means of self-definition. Yet he was also aware of of the great extent to which it precluded 'spontaneous feeling' and out of these deliberations there emerged a 'strikingly relevant dream':

> I had a small ginger-coloured kitten. It struggled fiercely to get free of my pocket. It belonged to someone else and I liked it so much that I borrowed it, but had to hold it so tight that its shoulder got broken. I was very upset and took it back to its owner with many expressions of regret. Then I was in a tram with Mr M. (a non-masculine type) and was naked and rushed to put his overcoat on. What would people think of me?

In the negative transference what Guntrip was later to describe (1975) as Fairbairn's 'very intellectually precise interpretations' had the force of his mother's hard emasculating attitude, and the dream shows the extent to which he had become identified with her in stifling himself and becoming, like Mr M., a non-masculine type, since, as he saw, he could not, as a small 'child-kitten', do without the mother who wanted him to be a girl. Submission was his only option, the handing back of his borrowed masculinity to an inadequately supportive father. He recalled the recent dream of the woman cowing the lions, and the earlier 'tomb-room dream', representing the repression of his anger against 'mother-church'; and also a dream from 1936 of 'stripping a piece of metal off the end of a poker with pliers', which Fairbairn accurately identified as representing circumcision – the operation which had put an end to his psychosomatic battle to get his mother to attend to him. He noted that he was re-experiencing in the analysis his 'repressed experience of helpless and frightened submission to mother and "demasculinization", and he was also enabled to see why 'the Salem Crisis' had loomed so large – for it represented 'the church as mother, my colleague as mother's little Mannie, Percy, and myself ill in Scotland as lying dying after Percy's death'. One effect of these events was registered the following week when Guntrip missed his sessions to attend a 'ministers' Summer School' under the direction of Professor MacCalman. While there he awoke to find his neck muscles taut and erect into the head, and as he realised how he had 'intellectualised life too much as a defence against deep unconscious fears' he became aware of an erection developing, and noted that his libido was 'flowing back where it belonged'. It was however, his *whole personal self* and not merely its sexual aspect of functioning to which his mother was opposed, and as can often happen in analysis, the recent disclosures gave rise to a fear, which he felt 'strongly deep down', that 'being analysed seems to mean giving up the active, striving assertive self that masters life, and lying on the couch with the analyst exalted'. In fact, there was much about Fairbairn's consulting room which supported this view. Guntrip later described (1975, in Hazell 1994, p. 355) how 'Fairbairn sat behind a large flat-topped desk, I used to think "in state" in a high-backed, plush-covered armchair', while 'the patient's couch had its head to the front of the desk. At times I thought he could reach over the desk and hit me on the head. It struck me as odd for an analyst who did not believe in the "mirror analyst". However, as Guntrip himself had 'chosen' the couch, it was clearly 'the fundamental pattern of relationship, one up and one down, forced on [him] and on everyone in the family by mother' which was primarily responsible for his basic reaction to starting analysis. As the first major break in the analysis approached, the five-week August holiday, Guntrip experienced some insomnia which Fairbairn attributed to anxiety over the coming separation. But it may also have represented the kind of inhibition imposed by his analyst/ mother's lack of interest in what he had to express, for Guntrip dreamed:

> I had a large bowl of golden urine, a nice bowl with white fluted sides. Every time I went to empty it down the lavatory, a woman was there with her back to me, blocking the way and I had to go away.

The imminent holiday was experienced by him as a blockage in the flow of sessional-communication with Fairbairn, whose needs came first, so to speak, in the same way that his mother blocked all his normal flow of feeling. By the last session before the holiday, however, he had reinstated Fairbairn as protector and ally in his inner world, dreaming of his analyst watching over him as he lay on the couch in his rooms where he had had an operation, and then fading into indistinctness as he lay alongside (like father) on another bed. Fairbairn, characteristically interpreted that Guntrip wanted him reliably there – but without any disturbing analysis – just 'a rock to cling to . . . a great source of resistance'. In fact it would appear that this 'resistance' was all too justified, so to speak, since, near the end of the session, Guntrip experienced 'the first emergence of [his] major trauma', for the facing of which his analyst's steady non-intrusive presence would surely have been vital. He recorded:

> I shut my eyes for a bit and began to see a dark blue-black background, then a yellowish-red spot which seemed to form vaguely into a fantasy of Percy in a pram, and then a vague stiff black woman with a stiff black baby across her knee, which seemed to be both me ill and Percy dead.

He was startled to hear Fairbairn say, 'These vague visions may be low-grade memories.' In fact, many years later, they were to form the substance of the most compelling dream-sequence of Guntrip's life, long after the analysis was over, and Fairbairn had died. It is note-worthy that these 'vague visions', in which the amnesia for Percy's death began to shift, and which appeared after only twenty-eight sessions of formal analysis, contained the nexus of Guntrip's deepest trauma: with the non-relating mother of his early life. Far from being 'cast out of the Garden of Eden' as Fairbairn once interpreted, he felt he had never been in it. Although he was consciously helped by the way Fairbairn enabled him to see how the pattern of his fight with his mother, in which someone was always 'one-up' on the other, was repeated in the negative transference, what was not considered was the situation that this fight concealed – namely the threatened disin-tegration of the ego in a vacuum of genuine relationship.

In the holiday period Guntrip dreamed and fantasised variously of Fairbairn dying of TB and valiantly exercising in a vain attempt to keep fit, or conversely of himself jumping up from the analytic couch in horror when confronted by a witch's face. He commented: 'If Fairbairn was not to be a witch, then he would have to be father – her victim.' A further dream appeared to refer again to Guntrip's three to five period, just after Percy's death:

> A woman brought a young child of about 3 to 5 years to my wife and said 'Why doesn't he smile with his mother?' My wife said 'Bring her. We can't say till we see how she handles him.' The mother came, a depressing figure, and at once the child went serious and lost all trace of a happy look. The mother was in black and looked as if she wanted to interfere and pull the child about.

He readily saw that mother, who was usually 'black' in his dreams, would have been wearing mourning clothes after Percy's death. Once again, there seemed a strong possibility of his mother's deadly influence overwhelming both Guntrip and his analyst, and his ambivalence was so extreme that when sessions resumed in September, he asked at the railway ticket office for Birmingham and then for Glasgow – not Edinburgh. He realised how he had striven to cultivate a 'tough self and reject a timid one – the sobbing little boy clinging terrified to mother, or lying ill on the "couch tent-bed" . . . who didn't fight but was afraid of dogs and bullies, who later didn't defend himself against Salem's insinuations, and who now lay on the analyst's "tent-bed" couch dependent', so that he was prone to see analysis as 'humiliation' at the hands of an analyst, who at times wore his mother's 'hard face' in his dreams. In his analysis with Maberley he had discovered the extent to which a 'vertical split' had become his means of building up an 'intellectualised conscious self' to repress the disturbed emotional self of childhood. This intellectualised conscious self had enabled him to achieve much and whilst it 'did not totally exclude his expression of tenderness in marriage, and of compassion in pastoral work', it nevertheless 'suppressed the emotionally castrated terrified small boy, traumatised by Percy's death', and the unconscious inner world where he was dominated by a destructive mother who for over twelve years, had appeared regularly and strikingly in his dreams.' However, Guntrip began to sense how disruptive the release of this repressed material would be to the effective working of his conscious self, when he noted, 'my defence in ordinary life now became my resistance to analysis, which seemed to be exposing me to what I most feared'. As the analytic sessions moved into autumn he came to identify Fairbairn and the analysis with the grey wintery weather and his mother's cold, aloof expression. Recalling his dream of the child who couldn't smile with his depressed black mother, he added 'I can't get back to the mother of early childhood. I can see the active, successful business-woman of my school years, but I can't see mother's face in my early childhood.' Fairbairn replied, 'There's something sealed off there', and added the cryptic comment: 'Something forecloses on the active process in the course of its development.'[4] Guntrip was reminded of his dream of crushing the ginger kitten as it tried to get free, and on leaving the session he was first to the door. Seeing his haste, Fairbairn said with a friendly smile, 'Are you wanting to get out?'

By the next session Guntrip was aware of thinking, 'It's not safe to show your feelings, it may provoke reprisals. Don't give yourself to anyone. It's not safe' – a feeling which in turn rapidly gave place to the opposite feeling of longing to see Fairbairn sooner than the following week.

Despite such oscillations, however, Guntrip made a firm decision to continue. He did, however, wish to clarify his financial position and wrote to Fairbairn in terms which at times suggest a certain confusion between financial and emotional resources:

Dear Dr Fairbairn,

As I am more keen than ever, after last week's sessions to go right through with this analysis, I think this is the point at which I would like to explain to you my financial position. A letter will save valuable time in sessions. I think I can see my way to carrying on as long as is necessary, if every three months, say at Xmas, Easter and the summer holiday, I could have a break of three or four weeks as last month, in which we could stabilise our finances; provided that would not be an inconvenient dislocation of your clinical programme. There must be heavy demands on your services and I would not want to lose my place on your list of patients under regular treatment, but I must find some way of preventing my resources running out before the job is done. One hesitation I had about suggesting this earlier was that I wondered whether my mind would settle down too much in the interval, but that is removed by finding last week that I resumed analysis at just as high a level of tension as when we left off in August.

Our position is as follows: while in the ministry, my wife and I managed over the years to put by £300 towards Gwen's University education and that sum represents our sole capital. Fortunately Gwen won a State Scholarship of £200 p.a. plus college fees, to which we add another £100 p.a. out of income. Thus that £300 plus my earning capacity represents the possibility of analysis for me.

If I lived in or near Edinburgh there would be no problem at all, but travelling and lodging expenses come to £4 a week, and I can't hope to meet an expense of £8 a week out of income. I am very grateful to you for charging only one guinea per session which, I take it, as with Dr Maberley, is half fee; and also for the frequency with which you arrange four sessions a week which I find of very great value.

At the end of July I had to overdraw £50 on our savings and did feel that our £300 looked like disappearing at an alarming rate. But in August I was able to pay off the overdraft and build up a reserve that will see us through to Xmas without much difficulty. By then I think we shall be feeling the pinch again, and if a short break would not be inconvenient to you, it would

enable me to carry on without strain. Naturally I would prefer
not to have to do this, but the only alternative that I see is to
run through our capital and at some time have to borrow
money from mother, which I do not want to do.

Fortunately my practice seems to be stable. The last financial
year, my third as a therapist, I earned £1200, of which £300
went in expenses (rooms etc.) another £300 in income tax,
Gwen and mother whose capital does not suffice to keep her.
That leaves us £600 to live on, and having had plenty of practice in living on £400 in the ministry, we shall manage very
well. I aim to preserve our capital so that later Gwen, and if
possible my wife, can have the benefit of analysis.

In the event neither Bertha nor Gwen entered analysis, although
the latter discussed the possibility very thoroughly with Fairbairn
by correspondence.

Guntrip's fear of being invaded by his analyst had now given
place to a fear of losing him, as he had lost his brother and father,
and his ministerial colleague, with consequent illness. It was, of
course, these equal and opposite fears which formed the core of his
ambivalent resistance, but gradually the conviction grew that Fairbairn was the only person who could help him avoid losing his
basic self under the threat of his destructive mother. Fairbairn had
observed the strength of Guntrip's fears of invasion or loss, and he
remarked, 'You are sealing off the repetition of a disaster you've
been menaced with before', and Guntrip recorded that Fairbairn
was 'now steadily becoming the one person with whose help I
could face this danger of inner breakdown'. In session Guntrip
reported two recent dreams in which he was attacked by aggressive
dogs owned by masculine women and a family who were 'not in
his class', a phrase often used by his mother. He held the dogs off
and stood up for himself, but one of them got his bare elbow in its
teeth before he could prevent it. The bare elbow reminded him of
his circumcised penis, and how his mother had dressed him as a
girl when he was two-plus, and how she would not tolerate any
assertiveness in him. It was after the circumcision that his psychosomatic illnesses stopped – effectively a castration of his active self.
Fairbairn was swift to associate this with the sealed-off catastrophe.
He said, 'That is the catastrophe you seal off, the loss of the penis,
the loss of masculinity that you nearly succumbed to once.' When
Guntrip came to survey his sessional record in the 1970s he saw
that although this was part of the catastrophe, by far the greater
part of his anxiety was that mother 'would not just seek to castrate

my penis, but crush "ME" as a little person in my own right, [for] the "person" or "Ego" is more than just the penis [and] I had the deep fear, created by the sight of my dead brother, of losing myself, my life, as I apparently nearly did . . . I was clearly feeling that my entire existence was at stake, truly . . . "a catastrophe I nearly succumbed to once"'. It is probable that he had some sense of this deeper level of trauma at the time, for he told Fairbairn – for the first time-about the 'older big dream' of the pale passive invalid threatening to absorb him into herself. Consciously, he felt tired and dull, and moved away from the inner trauma and back into intellectual discussion, a sign he knew, of dangerous anxiety within. He had a sense of 'something lurking to break out', and told Fairbairn that he had felt 'queer' on three occasions, as if he was 'going to have a breakdown'.

Reaction came in the shape of wanting to hit out at Fairbairn and his psychoanalysis, in a way which Guntrip had found impossible with his father, whom he had felt to be 'too inactive to be angry with'. Fairbairn commented 'Is that what you resented? He didn't give you anything to be angry at', and it occurred to Guntrip that indeed his father had given him nothing to stimulate his own competitive self-assertion with him, and had done nothing to offset his feeling that mother had robbed him of the chance to be any kind of positive person. His resentment over this would seem to have shown itself in the form of a 'vice versa' dream in which he was psychoanalysing his father – a process which proved to be easier than he had expected. The dream reached a point where father and son agreed that it was 'not so easy' to be spontaneous and vital with the 'Big Wigs' – that is, mother. Fairbairn himself, who was often silent in sessions partly because of Guntrip's 'hard talking', quietly suggested that Guntrip may have had something to do with his father's non-activity. Guntrip, however, sensing an 'Oedipal' inference, insisted that he sorely needed, not to cast out father in order to possess mother, but the vital stimulus of a vigorous competitive challenge from father to support his own emergent masculinity. He recalled a glorious day's cricket he had watched at Kennington Oval, seeing Fender and Hobbs score centuries. Henry had declined to come with him on the grounds that 'it might rain', and Harry had pulled his father's leg unmercifully when he got home. He now dreamed of Fairbairn as a better cricketer than himself – a left-arm bowler, like his father, who shared a 'Bovril tablet' with him (a reference to an advertisement for a tonic: 'Bovril puts a man on his feet' – with a picture of a bull making a weak little man jump on his feet!). He therefore felt

that his own challenging talking was an attempt to evoke, or provoke, a challenging potency in his father/analyst, a real relationship
at last. If such a relationship had seemed likely to develop with his
father, his mother had always been quick to squash it, and he
recalled an occasion when he had beaten his father at croquet with
a highly improbable shot at the last moment. It was one of the
rare and therefore memorable occasions when his father 'let himself go', bursting out with an exasperated expression of disbelief –
whereupon Harriet at once pulled him up, in front of a guest, 'for
showing that bit of emotion'. Fairbairn commented 'You and
mother can't stand your father asserting himself. You were together
against him' – which Guntrip regarded as an arbitrary interpretation based on an assumption of the inevitability of sexual rivalry,
regardless of the personalities involved. In fact Guntrip recalled
being 'a little embarrassed, but more surprised' at his father's
rather tame show of emotion.

It seems most likely that Guntrip sensed a potentiality for potency in his father: 'as a child I felt him as bearded, big, strong
and calm, and felt safe with him. He was never hurried. All my
dream father-figures have been supportive.' But the potential
potency remained tantalisingly elusive, and the mother, instead of
the father, received the son's resentment, since she *actively* interfered with any expression of potency in their relationship, whereas
the father merely failed to support it – a serious but less obvious
deficiency. Guntrip concluded that although he never had a father
to 'stimulate the masculine glow', he and his father had much in
common in their genetic personality type that neither of them
shared with mother. He based this view upon their shared interest
in religion and in seeking to help individual people – as distinct
from mother's money-making. While this may be so, it is difficult
not to conclude that Guntrip's hard-driven personality and general
restless contentiousness had more in common with his mother
than he wanted to believe – and indeed in his correspondence with
his daughter Gwen, many years later, he was to address the problem of the extent to which his mother's personality type had influenced them both, and how they might work together to dilute its
effects on the succeeding generation. Moreover, what he does not
seem to have considered is how he might have unconsciously
harmed his father by identification with his mother's driving personality – an eventuality for which Fairbairn allowed in his theory
of endopsychic structure in terms of an alliance between the anti-
libidinal ego and the rejecting object who together attack the libidinal ego, together with anyone – father or analyst – who supports it.

Meanwhile the new feeling of needing father/Fairbairn to give him a stimulating challenge to help his active development made the transference relationship very confusing. In the transference, Fairbairn could equally assume the significance of either the supportive father or the mother-menaced victim, or he could be experienced as mother herself, mentally castrating Guntrip, or yet again as a stimulating competitive father helping him to develop his active powers in friendly rivalry. And yet this more encouraging possibility only raised the fear that a jealous mother would interfere to squash father/Fairbairn – as she had in the croquet match, when he showed what Guntrip perceived as 'real emotion in friendly rivalry'. In addition to this, there was the effect upon mother herself, which Guntrip, despite his fear of her, could not ignore. Thus he dreamed that while Professor McCalman was helping him, a woman with whom he had 'some connection . . . had a deep crack in her flesh, laying bare the bone, as if her flesh were breaking apart', causing him to feel 'alarmed'. He was reminded of an earlier comment by Fairbairn about the woman as a victim of male aggression in response to his description of his mother's early family life with a child-thrashing father, and a quarrelsome brother. In this dream the tables were turned upon her, and he thought again of his insistence that she read him the ambiguous 'Nimrod story' about the hunter spearing the lion. Winnicott was later to pose the question: was Guntrip the lion or the hunter?

In a sense, his thinking about these complexities was itself a form of defence against re-experiencing the 'ultimate catastrophe'. Thus when Guntrip sought to 'explain' a dream of two ministers, one of whom was out to kill him in a 'battle of wits', while the other was 'friendly', by suggesting that they represented two aspects of Fairbairn, the latter made a wise intervention: 'Don't assign rôles to people in your dreams. Leave that to me and you go on experiencing. And dreams don't work in that neat way. Any figure in a dream might mean 10 or 20 people, economy, maximum meaning packed into minimum space. You are afraid of experiencing yourself. Why the blockage? You feel I'm that minister doing you down, trying to find out all sorts of bad things about you. That's not it. You need to experience yourself. What's the experience behind the barriers you put up?'

Guntrip at once replied, 'The disaster you said I nearly suffered once and sealed off.' We note, however, that the 'disaster' is referred to as an event reported by Fairbairn rather than Guntrip's own experience, and at the next session, Guntrip related a dream which perfectly illustrates both the nature of the catastrophe and of his 'unconscious resistance' to it. As in a number of his most significant dreams, two versions of himself appeared, one intellectually absorbed and the other in a state of collapse, with minimal connection between the two:

> I was writing and a young man in a chair beside me became ill, fell unconscious to the floor, hit his head with a whack and lay still. I left him to go for help, but forgot about him. Later in a vague way a similar thing happened, another man collapsed.

Once again, the sensing of the catastrophe of collapse caused Guntrip to 'forget about' his own near-death experience after finding his brother dead. And, although in discussing the dream he mentioned to Fairbairn 'for the first time fully' the 'tomb-man' dream of July 1938 after his 'brother-minister' departed, it did not occur to him at that time that the barrier that Fairbairn was trying to help him see beyond was 'in fact a deep fear of lifting my repression, my amnesia, on my collapse illness when Percy died, and literally feeling myself dying'. Both the experience and the memory were repressed and Guntrip himself sought refuge in the very 'sexual interpretations' he disagreed with, seeing the 'tomb-man dream' only in terms of castration, loss of potency and masculinity, which was less difficult to face than his fear of actual loss of life, of his total self. It was the last session of the week and he had 'escaped', so to speak. But it must surely have given him pause for thought that his own sharp intellectual critical faculty had once again been forced by fear to become an instrument of avoidance, for the 'sexual area' was a comparatively safe area into which to retreat from a fear of death, and, moreover, his mother's hostility to sexual expression, and the arbitrariness of the circumcision constituted fertile ground for Fairbairn's 'sexual interpretations'. But in fact, Guntrip's mother was hostile to *all* forms of self-expression in his most vulnerable years and not merely the sexual, and it was Guntrip and not Fairbairn, on this occasion who winced away from the ultimate consequences of her attitude: a profound fear 'of a living death, of being reduced to the state I saw Percy in, of actually collapsing into that state to everyone's alarm'. In fact, despite his conscious determination to uncover the cause of his primary trauma, Guntrip's unconscious fear-dictated resistance was so strong at this time that he could later find no mention in his records of his having told Fairbairn, at all, of the extremely traumatic details of how he had discovered Percy dead on his mother's lap. In his 1975 paper in which he later described his experience of analysis, he wrote:

There is a natural order peculiar to each individual and determined by his history, in which (1) problems can become conscious and (2) interpretations can be relevant and mutative. We cannot decide that, but only watch the course of the individual's development. (p.156, in Hazell 1994, p. 367)

In the first fifty sessions of his analysis with Fairbairn, all the material had come to light which could have led to the heart of the problem, but the therapeutic relationship had not matured to the point where he could allow himself to re-experience it. Thus he observed in his later survey of his sessional notes:

I could not go straight to the basic catastrophe, and had to work with the problems of the struggle with mother, the castrating mother, of the post-Percy period first, even though that functioned as a defence for the time being against going deeper.

Neither the patient nor his analyst could hasten the process. The 'tomb-man' could not surface without a breakdown into a real-life illness which neither felt able to risk. When he came to review the analysis, Guntrip interposed a section at this point in which he drew attention to Fairbairn's tendency early in the analysis to interpret his need for a security-giving relationship as resistance to the analysis, arising from a need to avoid the negative transference. He pointed out that 'even real negative transferences can be interpreted as signs of the patient feeling safe with the analyst, secure [sic] of being understood and therefore able to go on becoming conscious of who it was that he really felt that about as a child'. By the time he wrote that, Guntrip had found this security with Winnicott. But clearly in 1949 neither Fairbairn nor Guntrip could have developed it. Guntrip felt to be in 'an emotional chaos' where he did not 'feel any certainty of being loved and understood'. He had clearly been very frightened by the near emergence of the unconscious catastrophe, and for a time the transference analysis reverted emotionally to the 'safer' ground of his struggles either to force his mother to relate to him, or his father to support him, struggles in which good relations could only be had at the price of impotence, and potency could only be retained at the price of bad relations, whilst sexuality had to be either masochistic or sadistic. His dreams accordingly produced both sexual and aggressive symbolism. In one of these he was discussing with his flying instructor/father using 'a particularly destructive plane to attack the enemy'. The plane was in the form of an 'H' which stood for Henry and Harry in his mind – himself

and his father together against the enemy/mother – 'potency' of a
kind, but only as a sadistic attack. In another dream he became
aware of his penis 'hanging limp' as he abandoned sitting up at his
table and lay down on the couch, while Professor Dicks conducted
his analysis. He felt that he was 'oscillating between disowning and
then retrieving', his aggression, his 'capacity to stand up to mother'. Although he felt his 'flying instructor/father' was 'behind him'
in this battle with mother, he was surprised by one dream in
which he and his mother were under attack from 'male aggression'.
It was all the more surprising since it occurred at a time when
Fairbairn had become associated in his mind with a long line of
previous father-figures, all of whom were supportive, right back to
the 'impressive father' of his early years who 'must have been alive
in Moses' time'. He believed the trouble to lie in his basic assumption that immediately any 'parent-figure' became strong, he had no
option but to feel under threat, weak and inhibited by contrast, in
conformity with the basic one up/one down pattern in his family.
In the dream the attacker 'clearly symbolised a destructive father',
menacing both mother and himself who were under the threat of
attack by Russian guns as they huddled in a valley, while a gunner
(Guntrip?) slid a penis-shaped shell forward and back in the gun to
test its readiness. Whilst it is clear that, for Guntrip, if someone
was strong, someone else must be weak, two further causes for this
sense of his father's menace could surely be, first, father's suppressed hostility which he never expressed towards his wife or son,
and, second, a fantasised threat of reprisal against Harry and his
mother inasmuch as they were unconsciously identified in their
active challenging aspect. It seems that they were both 'too much'
for father, who, as Fairbairn had often pointed out 'wasn't much
use in helping [Guntrip] to be a man – who didn't go to football or
cricket' with him or share his manhood with his son in a natural
way. These issues were not discussed here, however, and Guntrip
experienced 'a flash of discouraged, embittered feeling: 30 years of
effort, religious and psychological, and not an inch forward. Life is
futile, effort wasted, still stuck in the old problems.' Fairbairn,
doubtless recalling that the dream of the menacing father had
arisen directly after, and as a possible response to, Guntrip's acceptance of himself as supportive, made the important observation
that Guntrip felt compelled to put up 'a barrier against all active
tendencies, against love as well as destructiveness'. The observation
brought forth from Guntrip a reaffirmation of faith in the therapeutic relationship, and he told Fairbairn, 'It's a good job I've got
you. Without you I'd never work through' – and as before, when he

had felt a deepening of the sense of Fairbairn's support, he began
to experience 'the spontaneous if vague image' of his mother – 'as
a blank grey shape' with no face, fixed and unchanging, with a
dead baby across her lap – the second occasion on which a deepening of the therapeutic relationship had presaged the surfacing of a
more profound trauma. It may also have been significant that this
second 'vague image' of the deeper trauma occurred just before a
two-week break in sessions while Fairbairn visited his eldest son –
a situation not dissimilar from that in which Guntrip experienced
the previous 'vague vision': a deepening of confidence in the therapeutic relationship followed by an absence, a separation in which
repression was likely to be reinstated.

It was during this separation that Guntrip clearly experienced,
for the first time in his analysis, the de-emotionalised schizoid
state which he was later to come to understand as so fundamental.
He noted at the time that he experienced 'a rather "estranged"
mood as if I were looking at myself living . . . doing things . . .
rather than really being IN [sic] the doing of them . . . a feeling of
separateness, an enclosed shut-in entity over against the world I
have no part in . . . two selves and two worlds, a world of my own
mood inside, a world of activities outside, and they don't meet'.
Fairbairn analysed the state as a reaction to feeling deserted during
the separation, and Guntrip confirmed that he felt more real at
work when he could feel some identification with Fairbairn. There
was also a sense in which Guntrip had always been compelled to
rely upon identifications with either mother or father, or their
various representatives, in order to sustain any feeling of personal
effectiveness, since he had received so little recognition to sponsor
the growth of his own proper nature. Significantly, it was at this
time that he began to gather material for a study of Fairbairn's
schizoid reactions,[5] for inclusion in his first professional paper – a
paper in which Fairbairn was to draw attention to some overlap-
ping with his own views.

At this point Guntrip had a brief but pertinent dream, 'A mixed
male and female gang were stealing my car', which he felt expressed
the truth that without Fairbairn he was left at the mercy of inadequate parents who robbed him of his personality, leaving him with
no alternative but to align himself with one or other of their's. In
reviewing his notes he was amazed to find that he had mentioned to
Fairbairn a remark of his mother's to Mrs Kind that 'he had poor
health because she had tried to get rid of him', and though the
reference to his poor health was spurious at the time that she made it
(in an attempt to sabotage his engagement!) it was certainly relevant

to the three and a half to five year period – the only time when he
was ill apart from odd bouts of tonsillitis or flu. He also recalled his
mother telling him that he was always crying as a baby and 'delicate'
as a small child; that breast-feeding was a 'device' to avoid a second
pregnancy, and that his father had been afraid to hold him as a baby.
He concluded that the family environment of his first few years was
seriously inadequate to his primary emotional needs, leaving him in
an 'emotional vacuum' where he was 'unable to grow the beginnings
of an active secure self'. It was this early emptiness to which he had
felt exposed by Fairbairn's 'desertion', bringing on a more marked
recurrence of the depersonalised, estranged state which he had experienced at moments throughout his life, and which had been expressed
both in his longing 'to be apart' and in his feeling of being 'out of
touch with people'.

During what he termed his 'schizoid week' of Fairbairn's absence,
Guntrip temporarily lost 'all sexual interest', and Fairbairn made the
illuminating comment that Guntrip was unable to enjoy an *equal
relationship* with an adult woman, even one as affectionate as Bertha.
He said, 'You always feel a child vis-a-vis parent figures, a child over
against a big dominating authoritative mother in both discipline and
sex. Then you have to reverse that and be the big dominating man
making the woman the child. But it is always a parent-child relationship, not two people "on a level". Being a man came to mean for you
"dominating", turning the tables, not "being grown up in the sense of
being equal", but of being "bigger".' This brought home to Guntrip
the painful realisation that he was unable to respond to his wife's
love because of the domination of his inner world by his mother as
an 'internalised bad object'. He said to Fairbairn, 'Mother has never
had the slightest understanding of what could be meant by an equal
relationship. It was always only "obedience".' Fairbairn replied 'No, I
don't think she has.' Fairbairn's interpretation had floated a new
concept in Guntrip's mind – of an 'on the level' relationship between
emotional equals – which was to have a profound influence upon his
thoughts and his emotional development. Of course, the whole
'schizoid incident' must also have brought home to him the extent of
his dependence upon the therapeutic relationship, since it was
Fairbairn's absence that provoked it, and it was surely extremely
felicitous to hear of Fairbairn's belief in an 'on-the-level relationship'
at that point. Thus Guntrip dreamed at that time of parents who
could facilitate spontaneous adolescent development:

> I was in love with a girl and her mother arranged for me to see
> her in her bedroom.

His conscious mind was far from convinced, however, and he left a briefcase, containing both his food and drink, and his notes for a lecture on the psychology of sex, on the train on his way to Manchester where he was due to deliver it! In fact he had dreamed that morning that he was giving the lecture to an audience containing a patient of his who was impotent and a schizoid intellectual. Fairbairn observed, 'Mother never gave you any physical intimacy of comfort, no sexuality. Your attaché case is perhaps not merely comfort, food, the breast, but the flesh, the sensuous element in intimate relationship. Mother gave you nothing of that, and you can only dream of libidinised intellectuality.' This interpretation, which reflects Fairbairn's view that Freud would have been better advised to call the satisfaction a child derived from sucking, 'sensuous' (of the senses) rather than 'sexual'[6] revived Guntrip's memory of climbing on to his mother's lap as a small boy: 'she sat like a statue and I slid off unwanted'. Moreover, his feeling of the value of Fairbairn's support and understanding of the 'sensuous element in intimate relationships' aroused in Guntrip the intense curiosity of his adolescent years, and his sudden realisation at that time that his parents slept together. He remembered a dream of dangerous females in the lionesses' pit, but this time with the inclusion of a part of the dream he had overlooked previously: 'that I had gone down into the pit into a little hut where a great lion and a lioness were sleeping together'.

Although he does not mention 'primal scene envy' and the painful feeling of exclusion from intimacy that such stirrings might have evoked, Guntrip saw the significance of his failure for so long to recognise that last aspect of the dream – and of its relevance to his next dream about Fairbairn:

> I understood my appointment with Dr F. was for 6 p.m., but he said it was 5 p.m. and I was an hour late. I said, 'We'll have to cancel the session then.' He said 'Yes, but stay and have a meal with us. What's your name?' Surprised I said 'Guntrip.' He replied 'No. What do they call you?' I said, 'Oh! Harry.' Then I was with him and the family and he spoke to someone about me and called me 'Harry'.

Here Guntrip was dreaming of the quality of relationship he knew he needed with Fairbairn. His parents had never called him 'Harry', only 'son' or 'the boy'. In sessions at this time he became 'highly sensitised' to little noises Fairbairn was making behind him as he lay on the couch. Rather surprisingly he appears to have accepted the interpretation that this sensitivity represented repressed sexual curiosity about father's relation to mother. Undoubtedly that was involved, but his dream about being accepted into Fairbairn's family contains no sexual aspect whatever – only the deeper need for acceptance as a 'person' in the family. Twenty years later Winnicott was to give a profound and mutative interpretation of that same sensitivity to slight movements of the analyst. Perhaps that need was so deep and the ache of its unfulfilment so painful, that Guntrip was relieved to remain at the less profound but important level of 'repressed sexual curiosity'.

A marked all-round improvement would seem to have resulted from these events, for Guntrip reported that he was 'feeling alert, well and interested, and normally sexually active again'. He had put on weight, topping eleven stones for the first time, and his wife and others had remarked on how well he looked. He was gaining greatly from the insights concerning his continual unconscious struggles, both against the suppressive force of his dominating mother, and also against the pull of the 'pale passive invalid'. In particular he realised, with Fairbairn's help, that he always regarded affection as feminine, ipso facto, which involved that he needed it in the woman but feared it in himself, since 'in mother's regime affection seemed to involve weakness'. Moreover, a strong degree of identification with mother's opposite, the semi-invalid Mary, for whom his mother was solicitous, meant that he had a strong tendency to regard his body negatively as 'suffering' and 'needing attention', like Mary's, a state imposed by mother, but also held in contempt by her – and also by the part of himself that was identified with her, as the sole example of active functioning in the family. He concluded that all his values were falsified, so that he 'automatically sorted things out into two groups of mutually exclusive opposites, feminine and masculine, soft and hard, weak and strong, passive and active, child and adult, love and power, masochism and sadism'. Thus he had denied his own nature to become either the disarming little girl-child with 'a halo straw, large-brimmed hat and silk blouse and a . . . saintly smile', or the suffering child coercing mother's attention by little recurrent illnesses. But he was never able to accept his physical being positively. He had gradually escaped into adolescent pursuits away from mother, and then away from the body into other-worldly religion and eventually to Bertha. But deep within him he felt the ominous presence of 'a menacing maternal superego' enforcing 'a clampdown on all spontaneous emotion and bodily activity or need, except as illness, a passive child-self masking frustration rage'. A frightening dream clearly depicted this terror of mother as an 'internalised bad-object':

> A flash of light in front of me and a bang, as if I had been shot at point-blank range by a pistol. The flash was a central point with rays shooting out all round.

He 'freely associated' the dream with a Titian painting of milk spurting out like rays from a woman's breast, and with an account by Ernest Jones of a boy pointing at a nipple and saying, 'That's what you shot me with.' The latter association was to prove prophetic.

As the three-week Christmas break approached, Guntrip feared that he might lose the insights he had derived since the summer, when his initial resistance had passed and the analysis had gained momentum. Doubtless he was also afraid of a return of the 'schizoid incident' in Fairbairn's absence. He dreamed that one of his male patients, who had a psychotic father, and with whom he had worked through a violent negative transference, laid his head on his shoulder while he talked. Guntrip's fear of his need for tenderness led him to describe this as a 'passive girlish homosexual act', but he was nonetheless able to surmise that, in anticipation of the break, he was 'feeling about Fairbairn like that'. Fairbairn replied, 'The analyst you lean on is the same as the analyst you resisted, and tried to keep out by putting that table against the hotel door. Now I'm not barred out, but turned into a sexual object, laying your head on my shoulder.' In view of Fairbairn's views on 'sensuous satisfaction' and Guntrip's on the secondary importance of sex in human relations, the comments of both men on this simple expression of the need for loving support might properly be understood as a product of the cultural atmosphere of the late 1940s. As Guntrip later pointed out, Fairbairn himself, in his 1954 paper, 'Observations on the Nature of Hysterical States', [7] demonstrated that all disturbed sexual phenomena can be understood psychoanalytically as 'hysterical conversion symptoms' used by the 'psychic self' to express its problems in personal relations, and especially those between parent and child. In fact, Guntrip's hysterical problems were not sexual in nature. His mother's rejective attitude towards his body resulted instead first in psychosomatic illnesses and later in passivity, so far as his relations with her were concerned, whilst he secretly kept possession of his body for active pleasure in sport, swimming, climbing, enjoyment of food (after he left home), and a normal sex-life in marriage. He did not care to probe for reasons, but was simply grateful for this relatively healthy aspect of his personality, salvaged from his mother's oppressive influence.

Notes

1   Review of Fairbairn's book by D.W. Winnicott and M. Khan, 'Review
    of Psychoanalytic Studies of the Personality by W.R.D. Fairbairn',
    International Journal of Psychoanalysis 1953, pp. 329–33.
2   Guntrip's manuscript is unclear as to the last phrase: 'nursing her . . .'
    which I have paraphrased according to the sense.
3   See Guntrip 1975, in Hazell 1994, p. 364 – 'an urge to write up my
    whole life history, as if I had to find out all that had happened to me'.
4   This phrase was cited by Guntrip (1975 in Hazell 1994 p. 356) as an
    example of Fairbairn's 'very intellectually precise interpretations'
    which, he felt, fostered the negative transference.
5   'A Study of Fairbairn's Schizoid Reactions', *British Journal of Medical
    Psychology* 1952, Vol. 25, pp. 86–103, in Hazell 1994 p. 39).
6   Fairbairn's earliest paper: *Edinburgh Medical Journal* 1929, 'Fundamen-
    tal Principles of Psychoanalysis'.
7   *British Journal of Medical Psychology*, Vol. 27.

CHAPTER 8

1950

As the analysis recommenced in 1950, Guntrip again dreamed of being in Fairbairn's home, where he was having a meal with Fairbairn and his wife. He and Fairbairn then began a session, sitting in chairs, but after a time Guntrip felt he should use the couch. He pulled it around by the desk – presumably into a less formal position, but it seemed that 'wasn't right', and the dream ended vaguely. Although Guntrip wrote, 'I felt I would have preferred a supportive friendship' instead of analysis, one senses a resistance, not to re-entering analysis as such, which he and Fairbairn supposed to be the case – but rather a fear of accepting the degree of emotional dependence expressed in the dream. It would appear that Guntrip had managed during the Christmas break to preserve the needed sense of belonging with Fairbairn, which the pre-holiday dream had also expressed, only for it to be interpreted as 'resistance' to analysis of his inner disturbance, rather than as he came later to feel, the only atmosphere in which he could stand re-experiencing his deepest trauma.

However, there is no doubt that he benefited on the 'professional level' from Fairbairn's steady encouragement. Whilst he was aware of 'feeling guilty about being an analyst at all' when in Fairbairn's consulting room, he felt progressively free outside, for Fairbairn gave 'exactly what mother never gave' in the way of practical straightforward recognition of his status as a professional – with the right to charge 'adequate fees'. Whilst he accepted that his professional self-doubts had been due to unconscious guilt over rivalry with father/Fairbairn, he sensed a deeper deference due to fear of 'expressing wishes' at all lest ego-destruction should result for him. His mother had instilled 'fear of reprisals rather than moral guilt'. Despite her rigid moral ideas, she didn't stop to preach (thereby provoking 'moral guilt') but simply lost her temper at any show of independence on Guntrip's part. The big beating over his alleged lying had left him ever after feeling, not 'guilty' but a cruel sense of injustice and he hated her for it, for 'she simply hit out at any defiance of her authority and aroused sheer fear, an ego-disintegrating experience'. Thus, he later felt that his accept-ance of Fairbairn's suggestion of 'guilt' was itself due to a fear of questioning it lest it provoke mother's reaction in Fairbairn. It was this kind of insight which led him to write in his Introduction to *Schizoid Phenomena, Object Relations and the Self* (1968, p. 12) '*pathological guilt*, is a struggle to maintain object-relations, a defence against ego-disintegration, a state of mind that is preferred to being undermined by irresistible fears'. He felt that it was much safer to have someone to accuse you, a relationship with a bad object, than to take flight into a vacuum and have no relationship at all, and whilst he had not developed these views with such clarity in 1950, he was not fully convinced by Fairbairn's interpre-tations in terms of 'guilty wishes'. He noted that he suspected 'the real issue with mother was not so much sex qua sex, but sex as subordination to a man (as for example in her mother's relation-ship to her father) and having to have babies'. In the face of her unremitting hostility he now felt 'in a weary lonely mood, T.S. Eliot's "Waste Land"': he felt trapped between semi-invalidism, caught in mother's 'octopus grip', and over-compensation by mak-ing 'a terrific sortie' to assert himself, and beneath these two states a profound sense of futility experienced as 'introverted moods, a loss of interest in the outer world, feeling shut up in myself'. He was once again experiencing the schizoid state, deeper than 'classi-cal depression', and as he was driving to see a regressed patient at Scalebor Park Hospital, he felt 'a severe sense of apartness and derealisation of the external world, which looked flat and uninter-esting'. Although he was intellectually alert and quite safe to drive, his feeling self was 'just not there'. This was similar to the mood which had enveloped him during Fairbairn's 'desertion', and it seems likely that he now felt 'deserted' in his inner world by Fairbairn's concentration on 'guilt and guilty wishes' rather than on his fear of ego-disintegration, so that he felt emotionally alone.

The state of profound emotional loneliness only served to empha-sise how Guntrip had had no choice as an infant but to identify with his mother in order to possess her. A powerful dream – his 'first clear oral-sadistic dream' – showed the degree to which he remained 'iden-tified with the breast mother who starved him', whilst also experienc-ing the gnawing hunger which had grown 'sadistic' as a result:

A young man had murdered a woman. A leg was cut off at the thigh. My wife was in bed and I sat on the edge. We were discussing it. I had the severed leg on my lap with my arms around it. I put two pieces of loose flesh in my mouth, but they were hard to chew and I threw them in the fire. My wife said, 'Don't eat that horrid flesh.' We were sorry for the youth. He'd done it because he was hungry and had no food.

Guntrip believed that the woman was mother, the leg was a breast and the two pieces of hard flesh were nipples. The two selves represented in the dream are the young man, the child of long ago with the ungiving breast-mother, hungry and without food, non-related to an impersonal world, and the other, a grown-up self with an understanding sympathetic wife – with whom he is nevertheless unable to have a complete relationship because of his plight. Due to her influence, however, the prevailing mood of the dream was not guilt over the young man's sadism, but sympathy for him in his plight. Fairbairn cogently pointed out that, whilst recounting the dream, Guntrip had clasped his own leg – thus demonstrating his identification with the mother, whom he must possess or die. The clear realisation of how his infant needs bound him to mother appalled Guntrip. He wrote 'The situation I had uncovered was an emotional deadlock.' Fairbairn suggested that his difficulty over sleeping might be a fear of 'sinking into the maw that will swallow you up'. In the transference, lying on the couch suggested the loss of his active self and 'being swallowed up in the passive self'. The therapist/mother, so urgently needed, was felt to be the horror that must be escaped from. He dreamed that he dozed off in the busy departmental clinic and awoke to find himself alone there 'disap-pointed, deserted'. Fairbairn pointed out that when he fell asleep, he sank into the 'unconscious where mother is' and consequently lost people outside and his 'striving working life'. Just then it occurred to Guntrip that perhaps he felt guilty about masturbation, because he was glad 'it never got a hold' over him. Fairbairn made an important interpretation: 'Masturbation is using the penis as something to be a baby with, to be comforted by, not to be a man with. Terrific conflict between lying back passive and nursed in the tent-bed, being a baby with bread and milk, and on the other hand the terrific programme of doing things, sport, study, organisation, preaching, analysis, work.' Although he found this illuminating, Guntrip failed at the time to see how this 'terrific conflict' was underlaid by his deep fear of 'collapsing with the dead Percy' – a fear which greatly magnified his mother's power over him.

In early March the flow of sessions was cut short by Fairbairn's absence for a fortnight with influenza. However, since Guntrip contrived to be in Edinburgh to deliver some lectures at the

Congregational College, Fairbairn put himself out to see him at earlier times for three of the four sessions of the first week. Nonetheless, sessions had to be cancelled for the second, and Guntrip again dreamed of staying with Fairbairn and his wife and children as one of the family – the kind of family he would have liked to grow up in, in which he could have an 'on-the-level' relationship. The dream served to make him feel lively and potent in Fairbairn's absence, only to feel passive and dispirited when Fairbairn wrote to say he was better. One is reminded of Guntrip's observation in *Schizoid Phenomena, Object Relations and the Self* (1968) that for the schizoid absence makes the heart grow fonder, while presence makes the heart less fond! Although he saw his inertia at the time as due to an automatic reinstatement of 'one-up-and-the-other-down' as he re-engaged in analysis, it seems probable that Guntrip's dream of the needed family (in which a little boy, wanting to help, 'clumsily broke an egg, but it didn't matter') was related to his intense hunger for love, which felt so prohibitively dangerous when the 'needed object' was present.

The same oscillations characterised his relations with his mother. His original childhood impetuosity represented in a further dream by a 'huge shaggy dog' which almost unbalanced a somersaulting girl, was held back by 'exceptionally strong anxieties'. He felt that the somersaulting girl was his mother in a whirlwind of anger with him, and that the anxieties which this aroused were redoubled by what happened to his fine bouncing baby brother. He dreamed again of 'an idiot boy who was paralysed and unconscious', and felt that he had been like the dog before he was paralysed and put out of action: 'That's what happens to bouncing babies or rushing dogs, especially if they rush at a female.' He recalled how his mother had tried to keep a dog, but had to give it up because she could not stop beating it. Another source of impetuosity at this time was Guntrip's daughter, Gwen, who suddenly decided that she wanted to get married, and would do so at Christmas. Negotiations had already been entered into regarding the possibility of Gwen beginning an analysis with Fairbairn in September or October 1951. However, in view of her desire for an early marriage, Fairbairn wisely advised against analysis until the marriage had had time to consolidate, since he felt it to be inadvisable to expose her to the emotional risk of analysis at this stage. Gwen had not realised this and was disappointed. But she may have given an impression of a somersaulting girl almost unbalanced by her own impetuosity! Guntrip makes no mention of his own reaction, merely saying that it was a preoccupation which drew his concentration on his own analysis into a real-life issue. But his reaction was probably fairly strong, given the general pattern of their relationship, and Gwen's similarity in some respects to Harriet. However he felt inwardly, he merely discussed it with her and let her decide. In his unconscious Guntrip felt he was forever caught between identification with the attacking woman, or assault on her, but Fairbairn pointed out that these were not equal alternatives, for identification could function as a safeguard against assaulting the woman, a way of immobilising the woman, since 'one anxiety that bars development of the active process is the fear of killing'. Guntrip saw that not only did the 'one-up-one-down' pattern spread through all his relationships with external persons, but that it dominated his relation to himself. Thus he saw the identification with his mother as the origin of his masochism in accepting the sinus operations by turning the tables on himself 'to save the woman in my inner sadomasochistic fantasy'. A more everyday example of inner conflict occurred when Guntrip bought a new car, and sought to justify the expenditure to Fairbairn. The latter responded: 'You feel you have to justify getting a new car, as if wanting a car is not a good enough reason. You feel guilty about doing or having anything.' Guntrip recalled his mother's opposition to his buying furniture on the hire-purchase system, and how 'she grudged everything she didn't choose'. While pondering this he suddenly had a mental picture of a baby on a mother's lap, screaming and red with anger, a state which he could not recall, though Fairbairn insisted that he had indeed felt like that before Percy was born. Guntrip's immediate reaction was to dream of a situation in which he was a victim. He dreamed:

A young man was condemned to death. he had to execute himself and a woman was there to supervise it. He couldn't bring himself to do it, so he was killed by an electric shock.

He said, 'Guilt about buying a car extends to guilt about doing anything at all; that leads to giving up living itself. I must feel I ought to be dead.' Fairbairn said emphatically 'Yes'. However, at that stage, instead of associating the deadly electric shock with his discovery of the brother who had died 'under mother's supervision', so to speak, and to the fear of a similar fate befalling himself, Guntrip concluded that he 'must have identified with father' and the 'tomb-man'. As he saw later, he could not allow 'the basic terrifying infantile situation' fully into consciousness at this time. Indeed, even the prospect of identification with father forced him to react away from that in turn to less frightening fantasies of rivalry with father, about which he experienced, for the first time, the theme of 'guilt' in his dreams – guilt over being successful and rivalling father as a minister, or Fairbairn as a therapist. However, even this attempt at a defence by experiencing his problem in terms of guilt rather than fear led eventually back to his conviction, implanted early in childhood, that mother would stop at nothing to subdue him. When she could not actively terrify him, she made him feel 'a subtler "guilt" about allowing her to sacrifice herself' for his benefit. Thus fear and guilt operated together to render him unable to 'go through with the active process of fulfilment', as Fairbairn put it. The latter continued, 'Something happened to make you too anxious to go ahead. Ever since you've stood at the door, wanting to go in, but too anxious to go. Sometimes it appears as guilt. What is it? What are the anxieties that make you afraid to go on?' Guntrip noted that this was 'a penetrating insight'. For the first time clearly, Fairbairn had suggested that guilt could be a cover for deeper fears, over ego-disintegration. The latter also suggested that this fear applied to success in the analysis. He said, "It's wrong to get better" turns into "It's not safe to get better", an insight which immediately provoked in Guntrip 'an acid tummy' by way of reaction. Indeed, on the everyday level, fear over succeeding as a writer caused Guntrip to feel overwhelmed by dizziness when banking the cheque after a rapid sale of half the first edition of his book *Psychology for Ministers and Social Workers* (1949).

He began to associate this blockage of the active process of fulfilment more directly with the very great fear that his 'frustrated murderous rage, wanting to squeeze viciously the unloving breast, bite the sour apple', would result in the destruction of the so-needed mother, a situation which became reproduced in the transference as he fantasied 'bullying Fairbairn to publish his papers . . . wanting to get something out of him'. At the same time he had 'a distinct impression of a phantom breast . . . a hollow shell with nothing in it' and of having to suck in his lips.

The sado-masochistic relationship with the breast-mother now came strongly into focus, in which Guntrip was both attacker and victim, feeling at the same time very forcibly the impact of finding his brother dead at such an early age, for he felt that his brother was a 'victim' who was 'finished off' by the sadistic mother: a formerly 'bouncy' child who 'went too far'. Thus it felt to him imperative that he should continue the conflict – never letting up, lest he meet the same fate, but also never 'succeeding' lest he destroy the mother and lose her. The deadlock of this situation was, as Fairbairn pointed out[1] symbolised by infected mucus trapped in his blocked sinuses, and by the faeces blocked in his constipated anus, both representative of his libidinal nature blocked and denied both relaxation and active self-expression by a frustrating, dominating and possessive mother. The extent of Guntrip's fear was exemplifed in a small but significant event. In moving to draw the curtain from the door at the end of a session, he felt that Fairbairn had 'cut him off' by saying 'I'll do that'. He had risked a little 'self-gesture', and such was his intense sensitivity in the transference, that Fairbairn's intervention 'stirred reactions that had roots in the deepest first year infancy experience': reactions which 'oscillated between the mouth and the penis, castration'. He dreamed:

> A woman in the Dental School was giving me an injection for having a bottom tooth out. But she gave it in my penis. There was no pain or feeling. I made no fuss.

The dream reflected a recent external event in which a female anaesthetist had handed him over to a male dentist, just as mother had removed the uncomfortable feeling from his penis before 'handing him over' to the doctor. On that occasion also, he had 'made no fuss', fearing to do so lest it become worse. So in the session the thought occurred: 'I put my hand out and Dr F. chopped me off: a castration threat if I put myself forward or become active.' The inner significance of this dream would seem to be that whilst the circumcision had brought about a displacement on to the penis, of the earliest deprivations associated with the mouth, the later sinus congestion had refocused the disturbed feeling on the nose and mouth – the organs involved in the highly disturbing relationship with the breast-mother. The full horror of this was disclosed in a fantasy, and a dream of terrifying violence. The fantasy, which developed in the session, was as follows:

> I am seeing that empty shell of a breast threatening to suffocate me . . . I hit it with a hammer and break it to bits. Now I see a human breast hanging from a body, flabby, the skin empty and drawn. Now it looks like my penis and scrotum in the dream into which the . . . needle was stuck, but it's me biting into mother's breast at the same spot. Penis and breast are then chopped in pieces. Now it's mother, with arms, legs and head chopped off.

Guntrip found himself thinking of the dream of the young man who murdered a woman because he was hungry and how he had nursed her severed leg and in session illustrated it by holding his own leg. He believed that he had identified himself with the mother whom in fantasy he had bitten to pieces, driven by hunger and that she had retaliated later by having his penis chopped off, (circumcised).

The fantasy was followed by a grossly disturbed and disturbing dream:

> War, invasion, a desperate struggle to throw back the enemy. People crouching low in a close mass, working away with knives and forks, cutting and thrusting, especially at penises. Then . . . vast halls, vague, as if savage Anglo-Saxons or Danes were invading. One group had bloodily slaughtered some people. Then I seemed to unhook from somewhere a saw and garments dripping with blood that these Danes had used, and was going to confront them with these. The halls were gloomy and empty and they were away on the left, and now they were hidden in jet blackness, terrified by the gory evidence of what they had done, and I woke trying to make that weird noise.

He was referring to 'a wavering noise' which had woken him in a previous dream and which seemed to express his own terrified attempt to scare off a hostile intruder in an empty building. In the light of his later emphasis upon 'ego-weakness' it would seem likely that this 'weird noise' represented the terrified reaction of the infantile 'psychic subject' at the mercy of such horrifying emotions and of the object or part object that evoked them. At any rate, Guntrip's adult consciousness repudiated the dream as 'ghastly nonsense . . . interfering with my living at my age', and he could find no record of Fairbairn having made any comment. On the other hand, he could not dismiss it, and he wrote in his review in 1970 'I have never, I think, had any dream to equal this one, as an expression of the chaos of rage and terror left behind in the unconscious by the experiences of my earliest childhood.' He was also quick to refute any suggestion by critics of psychoanalysis that 'patients' dreams are made up out of 'suggestions' from their analysts, recording his conviction that 'whatever symbolism we make use of in our dreaming', whether in or out of analysis, 'what we are expressing is the actual nature of the storms of emotion pent up in us from childhood. No analyst's "suggestion" could have made me produce this dream or have accounted for my acidity on waking.'

The emotions of the dream felt at least as frightening to him as his mother's later temper outbursts, which seemed 'utterly ungovernable', and his need for containment was expressed – oddly and comically – in a further dream of 'a big square-built Edinburgh Police Officer' whom he had seen on his way to Grosvenor Crescent.

He also needed to re-establish his faith in Fairbairn as a reliable and authoritative figure by asking 'a straight question . . . "What do *you* mean by libido?"' Fairbairn gave a 'good full answer' – surely an unconscious reference to an analytic 'good full breast'! He said,

> Libido is the active object-seeking processes [sic] in contrast to the anti-libidinal factor of aggression which negatives libido [and] is against all objects. Jung made libido stand for all active processes including aggression. Freud's fundamental discovery was the duality of libido and the anti-libidinal factor. Sublimation has no meaning. Also instincts floating about in an id have no meaning. Impulses are the activities of organised Egos reacting libidinally or anti-libidinally.

Guntrip records that he found this straight intellectual statement extremely valuable. Years later he told J.D. Sutherland that he felt closer to Fairbairn in theoretical discussions than in actual sessions, and there is certainly a sense that Fairbairn was more directly personal in this declaration of his views. In fact, the 'straightness' of the intellectual statement also expressed 'libido' in a way Guntrip would have valued in his own father, and it constituted a welcome structure amid the turbulence of his emotions. Thus supported, Guntrip was able to tolerate seeing again and with increased clarity how he swung 'between being the victim and the aggressor, masochist and sadist, the whole complex relation to mother, going on inside me'. Fairbairn pointed out that by his identification with the aggressor, the 'antilibidinal factor', he enabled himself to feel more powerful. He said,

> You changed yourself from your natural desires into something else to meet with approval from the puritanical crushing-down self. You changed into mother imposing restrictions on the child, on yourself. When you were a child mother imposed restrictions on you, you were helpless. When you identified with mother and imposed the restrictions you were powerful, you exercised mastery. You changed from the child subject to the parent, into the parent subduing the child . . . Mother's was the position of power. As a child you couldn't control the situation or mother. If you became mother, identified with her, you could control yourself as the child.

Pondering on this Guntrip came to feel that even his bodily pains were a product of this identification, imposed upon himself by his 'anti-libidinal Ego' identified with mother as the 'rejecting object' and expressed in his negative self-mastery. The realisation came to him afresh how strongly he was tied to the mother he consciously regarded a failure, and who 'always rejected tenderness, sex and love relationships'. A further indication of the extent of his identification with his mother in her power over his natural self came when he experienced an alarming dizziness after a happy love-making with Bertha. It was so severe as to make him clutch the side of the bed in fear of falling, and he felt that 'something else' in him that was tied to mother had interfered violently with his good conscious relation to Bertha, which was one of 'respect, appreciation and tender regard for her happiness and well-being, and a happy, spontaneous sexual relation'. Fairbairn pointed out that dizziness is the commonest anxiety symptom, and added, 'It occurred in the setting of your unconsciously feeling your wife is libidinally taboo, and then you defied it and had a successful relation with her. But you felt you risked death, all the more because you were successful.' The power of the internalised bad object seemed awesome to him driving him to participation in the suppression of any spontaneous self-expression, since even the hate she had inspired in him was turned against his libidinal self. He was both Nimrod attacking the lion and the lion attacking Nimrod in a kaleidoscopic welter of emotional tensions, over against which his adult workaday self felt to him to be merely 'a system, a playing of parts' into which feeling intruded randomly, from time to time from the volcanic depths. The splitting of self and object under this internal pressure gave rise to dreams of opposites, warm and cold, lively and inferior. In one dream a ginger kitten 'like a little tiger cub', which 'had to be watched to stop it bcoming a "lust-wanderer"' reminded him of the lion's golden mane in the Nimrod picture, of his bowl of golden urine, and also of his own golden curls as a child, which he felt for the very first time to be masculine. Fairbairn remarked that he would have been proud of his hair until it became associated with mother's attack on his masculinity.

As the seven-week summer break drew near, Guntrip experienced a great anxiety about being left with the child whom mother had damaged so badly and who was now being steadily drawn into the open. He described a patient of his who acted out upon herself the beatings originally administered by mother, and he was surprised when Fairbairn pointed out to him that he had demonstrated the process by hitting himself as he spoke. During the summer recess Guntrip and Bertha toured right round the north coast of Scotland. He had fewer dreams than during the previous break and those he had were not very urgent or significant. His last dream before the break was of telling Fairbairn that he had never had any serious illnesses other than the sinus and flu infection – doubtless in an attempt to demonstrate his ability to survive the separation. But he dreamed later that he and Bertha were in Edinburgh and saw Fairbairn crossing a road: the child mother had damaged was not entirely alone in the internal world.

When sessions resumed in September the paradoxical feeling of needing Fairbairn 'not to be there' while at the same time urgently needing his presence was reflected by four schizoid patients whom Guntrip saw at the weekend. They all felt 'greedy for food, starving, needy for help, not analysis, but something personal', and yet they were also 'breaking away' for fear of being smothered by people – only to feel 'emptied and collapsing when alone'. Confronted by this simultaneous urgent need and inability to accept the object of need, Guntrip felt a powerful sense of the hopelessness of his own quest. He said 'I felt a chasm was opening under me, hopeless, but couldn't see how I or they could work through.' Like his patients, he had found himself once again becoming detached from such extreme and painful feelings:

> a waning of interest, a lack of drive . . . carried along by my programme without any real interest . . . pictured in an earlier dream of a penis potent except at the top, the glans. My conscious self at times suddenly loses interest, becomes impotent, divorced from an urgent libido, a need to live that is active deeper down but hopeless. In that deepest part of me I've no-one to relate to.

Guntrip felt he had really come on something of enormous importance to him, a feeling which Fairbairn duly confirmed. After listening intently without comment, he said quietly, 'We have to stop now, but you will feel that you are being done out of something, and next session, when you want to switch on this feeling, you can't easily get going again.' However, the frankness and humanity of this response aroused the dormant hunger in Guntrip. At the next session (189), he spoke with a rare directness: 'My hungry, greedy self wants you, not analytically, but extra-analytically. I want love not analysis, mother not her lectures.'

Guntrip records that Fairbairn then made an important statement. However, it was not really a response to Guntrip's 'cri de coeur', but an oblique interpretation of how Guntrip found it im-

possible to accept analysis as a form of love: how in fact, he felt it
was the opposite of being loved since it was, like his mother's
'lectures', concerned only with his weaknesses and not with his
essential nature as a person. Guntrip concurred with this observation, but his deeper self evidently registered Fairbairn's qualified
response, for he said, 'I feel I've gone into my shell and lost
contact with you', and he drew back from his direct request for
maternal love and identified Fairbairn instead, once again, with his
father 'supportively behind' him, intuitively understanding their
'mutual problem with mother'.

Valuable though this undoubtedly was,[2] Guntrip knew that he
needed Fairbairn's love, not analysis, to counteract his mother's
depreciation of his father and himself, and told Fairbairn, 'I want a
father who is on my side in place of mother.' Fairbairn saw that,
much as Guntrip had wanted to turn to his father – emulating his
long strides up Dog Kennel Hill as a boy, and subsequently becoming a cricketer and preacher like Henry – he was nevertheless deep
down, unconsciously not in a position to get away from mother.
He told Guntrip 'You are needing to experience a relation to father,
but mother in you maintains the gap between you and him, you
and being a man . . . There were to be no men in mother's house.'
Reflecting on this Guntrip saw that his basic problem was the lack
of a 'positive dependence on mother in the first stage', so that he
remained tied to her, and unable to get away from her to father in
the second stage, but could only identify with what he knew of his
father's early active self, and seek similar father-figures in the
Salvation Army. When he fantasised a happy thriving family group,
he saw himself as a withdrawn onlooker and had a sudden attack
of 'acidity'. Fairbairn remarked: 'A happy picture and then acidity.
You can't digest it. You're not in it, but envious. You can't let
yourself enter into it, but you could spoil it. You've spoiled it for
yourself.' Guntrip's recalled his mother's dictum that 'only common boys' played out in the street.

Guntrip had now completed 200 sessions of analysis and his
defensive intellectual control had eased somewhat, freeing his
capacity for fantasy and imagination. In this respect he was greatly
encouraged by reading *On Not Being Able to Paint* by Joanna Field
(Marion Milner) and he now began to allow his unconscious experience to emerge more freely through his dreaming. Thus began:

> a two month spate of drawing that took me into the deepest
> depths of sado-masochistic emotional tensions of the first year,
> at the breast

which he described in his notebooks, but did not reproduce. The
first drawing was of

> an angular flying head . . . thin, sharp-featured, stretching and
> striving forward, no human feeling; not cruel but devoid of any
> tenderness. Urgent, perhaps flying from itself.

It seemed to him to denote 'flight' as an end in itself: flight from an
emptiness – the catastrophe he had almost succumbed to – but with
no-one to fly to, simply driving onward 'like a metal figure-head on a
car bonnet' – perhaps symbolising collapse hidden by amnesia and
overwork. The head had no environment; it was simply 'in the empty
air'. The drawing provoked a dream in which Guntrip was simply
being passively operated on, and as Fairbairn remarked, this passivity
characterised Guntrip's attitude to the analysis. Indeed, Fairbairn at
this early stage noted what was to become increasingly the main
problem in the analysis. He said, 'What doesn't appear is you and I
co-operating. You don't let the you inside you speak and communicate. You won't be yourself. Big obstacles of anxiety bar the way to
that.' The problem of the lack of a 'true meeting' was to surface again
in a big way in the Winnicott analysis, when the 'big obstacles of
anxiety' were worked through. At this stage it is noticeable that
although Fairbairn makes reference to anxiety, his use of the phrase
'You won't be yourself' carries the implication that Guntrip could, if
he would, surmount the anxiety and 'co-operate' with his analyst.
The ability to do that, however, was dependent upon how debilitating
the anxiety felt, and the full extent of Guntrip's 'ego-weakness' had
not been properly recognised at this stage. Two more drawings
appeared, both suggestive of an active ego straining to burst out of an
oppressive force: first, a closed pyramidal triangle containing the buried dead, but yet 'turning into into an erupting volcano with a vague
face, a spirit, in the smoke'; second, 'a vital dog straining at the ends
of reins held by invisible hands' – a vitalised vision of the first
drawing. The backward pull was stronger, however, for the dog's front
paws were in the empty air, with nothing to grip; and although
Guntrip could associate the volcanic drawing with the raging temperatures of the 'tent-bed' period, he nonetheless felt that the deadly
weight of the buried self was overwhelming – an even greater source
of anxiety than the volcanic reactions above. Further drawings
demonstrated the theme of bursting forward and being held back, but
always with a sense of dereliction, which could be interpreted either
as the feared result of an aggressive burst, or as the bleak experience
of having 'no environment' to promote growth. Thus in one drawing

a plane flying over a bombed landscape seemed to be disintegrating in the air whilst beneath just one wild tuft of grass remained as 'the only living thing'. Fairbairn's interpretations consistently emphasised the active 'bursting forward' aspect of Guntrip's battles with his mother, but the underlying motif of a struggle to grow in a bleak or barren environment persistently appeared. Thus another drawing depicted a daffodil bulb with one flower, but what looked like mouths in the soil under it, eating at the roots, and, as he let the picture develop in his imagination, the leaves disappeared and the whole top of the bulb became a mouth which closed upon his finger and held it fast. Another drawing showed smoke and flames bursting from a central chimney behind which a road forked. On the left (Guntrip's natural side) three planes or shrouded figures flew off at speed, whilst on the right was a sad face drawn on the sun held down by rays, tied to the earth. The daffodil theme appeared again in a later drawing in which a small daffodil bulb was growing out from the side of a big one, suggesting once again Guntrip's need to identify with father and Fairbairn in order to grow as an individual. But with this hungry need came an equally intense fear of passivity, falling into someone's power, and losing identity, a fear expressed in a dream that Fairbairn was hypnotising him during a session until with a great effort, Guntrip broke the spell and threw it off, thus disrupting the very security he longed for, as indeed he was often compelled to do at night when his insomnia prevailed. He felt polarised into forced activity and debilitating passivity, a situation represented in a drawing of a powerful striking shell-like structure, cone shaped, with great spiky teeth or spines sticking out all the way up to the top. At the base, inside, as if in a vault or tomb, totally inert, lay a passive figure, sexless, neither male nor female, as if in a shroud, buried alive. Guntrip made the important observation that this shell-like structure was 'static, no emotional rapport with people', like the hard head of the first drawing, and like the pyramidal triangle but without its volcanic element, whilst he saw that the passive person, buried alive, was 'perhaps more hopeful, could come alive, is libidinal, if passively so'. Perhaps this was an early sensing of his concept of the 'passive regressed libidinal ego' (Guntrip 1960, in Hazell 1994, p.155).

At another level, this drawing became linked with his dream of the analyst hypnotising him. It occurred to him that the phallic shell-like structure could represent not only his 'character armour' but Fairbairn's powerfully penetrative interpretations, which invaded his passive mind. In this respect he felt identified with his mother, 'suffering' the sexual relationship with his father. He wondered whether he had indeed witnessed his parents' sexual intercourse when he slept in their room during Mary's illness. But whether the scene was witnessed or imagined, he realised that he was once again split in two, always identified with one parent or the other, never free to be himself, and, moreover, that he had 'frozen' the primal scene in the drawing, since the spiky penis was a 'thing' and the passive figure a 'corpse'.

After a series of undisguised 'primal scene' dreams, which, maybe significantly, he did not record, Guntrip's drawings over a three-week period took on the significance of sado-masochistic infant and breast-mother relations in which his early pent-up rage fused with oral need in vivid symbolism. In the first of these drawings an obsequious toad was emerging out of half an eggshell, just born and 'looking pathetic', while a fierce eagle flies overhead. Guntrip saw the toad as representing his self of early childhood 'praying to be allowed to be born', feeling that the broken edges of shell might snap shut on him, whilst the eagle represented his need to get free. It seems surprising that he did not associate the fierce bird of prey either with his hostile mother or with his own in-turned rage. However, in the next drawing, his rage and fear were clearly depicted. He drew a woman's head with a baby held firmly between the teeth, but with a flying arrow making straight for her eye. A few days later, another horrifying fantasy manifested in a drawing of a large crab reaching out its pincers to grab the upper jaw of a crocodile which in turn was snapping its jaw on the lower half of one pincer. Guntrip commented: 'a small thing attacking a large creature, and it could only [escape] by tearing itself away and leaving part of itself behind. Only a mutilated freedom is permitted.'

The sheer terrifying violence of these drawings, which Guntrip was certain reflected the grossly disturbed relations between his infant self and his mother in the early feeding situation, was too frightening to contain. He found he could not carry on drawing for a time, and even his regular writing up of session notes was threatened in a dream of enemy planes flying over him as he wrote, forcing him to consider taking cover in the cellar.

After a space, he produced more drawings in which the horrifying sado-masochistic plight of the badly-mothered infant was again and even more vividly depicted, whilst beneath it and giving rise to the conflict, appeared the dragging exhaustion which had always been Guntrip's most pronounced and troublesome symptom. By this time the number of his drawings had increased to thirty-four, with a sketch of a back view of a man trapped in a bog, his feet buried in it, being sucked down. Although he was reaching out, the man had no hands, nor was there anything or anyone to reach. In the prevailing gloom and mist he was haunted by evil things, a stinging giant mosquito, a bloodsucking insect; and a grabbing pincer claw. Not until Fairbairn pointed out to him that the back view implied a renunciation of mouth and sex organs as well as hands – in short a sacrifice of all active organs – did Guntrip remember a thirty-fifth drawing which he had left in his pocket. He had drawn a beheading, so that even the head that had a mouth was gone, and the organism was entirely at the mercy of 'sucking, grabbing, biting things', whilst unable to take in anything for itself. The earlier battle between crab and crocodile, in which both baby and angry breast-mother were biting, had changed. Now the baby was too terrified to bite. Guntrip was reminded of Coleridge's 'Christabel' clasped at midnight by the evil witch to her dried and withered breast, so that she is rendered dumb, for him a clear example of Melanie Klein's view of the projection of the hungry baby's aggression into the bad, ungiving maternal breast. He recalled that in the thirty-fourth drawing he had sketched a ghostly reflection of the man's face in the misty air, and he said, 'All my environment reflects what I'm feeling. My world has become my rejected other half of me, so that . . . I can only be passive and suffer my own rages . . . I must be disowning my own hungry greedy incorporating mouth and then feel haunted by the terror of mother being like that to me.'

Guntrip recalled an earlier 'primal scene' drawing in which a vagina with teeth had become a fruity food, a breast that could bite back if bitten, and he noted how the Oedipal 'primal scene' drawings had gradually given place to 'oral sado-masochistic' drawings, while the same underlying theme appeared in both. In his next drawing, the thirty-sixth, the still deeper theme appeared, of a regression to the womb, represented by a sealed glass jar with an unborn embryo child in it of a kind he had once seen in the Medical School. This undoubtedly expressed the inner core of his withdrawn schizoid reactions: a flight deep into the unconscious as a symbolic womb, away from an unnourishing environment and the horrors of his own hungry cravings. It was the reaction of collapse and apparent dying which beset him alone with mother after Percy's death – alone with the black immobile statue-like female figure of his fantasy. But as on previous occasions when he touched on this level of experience, he now winced away from its profound implications, telling Fairbairn that he felt an urge to 'hustle the analysis and get it over – to rush from the couch'.

In fact, he only rushed as far as the sado-masochistic battle, and the oscillation between hungry active self and punished passive one, the biter bitten, expressed in further drawings. However, the urge to withdraw returned, and in one notable drawing, produced on the train journey back to Leeds, the sado-masochistic atmosphere appeared to have invaded the womb-security itself, causing Guntrip to wonder whether indeed his mother had hated him as an embryo, and to recall that she had told Bertha's mother that she tried to abort. He drew an embryo in the womb, not safely enclosed as in the glass bottle, but in a closed oval, like the vagina, with sharp teeth all around the inside. The same embryo lay in the centre, more developed and with hands. But there was a sharp spike coming up from the bottom of the oval and penetrating the embryo in the centre so that it looked speared.

From these terrifying depths Guntrip retreated to the level of what may well have been an objectively accurate picture of his mother's early feeding technique: a mechanical process. He had earlier recalled one of his own patients whose mother had been unable to recognise when her baby was hungry, and he now dreamed of watching a mother feeding a baby from a bottle without affection, 'just doing the job efficiently', Fairbairn made an apt interpretation: 'You feel mother was a professional parent, making a good job as she saw it of bringing you up, a finished job she could feel proud of. But she didn't value you as a person. You felt strong rebellion but you couldn't show it. Patients tend to see analysis like that, as if its purpose is to achieve a good result as the analyst sees it. And you set up a regime like that in yourself, your "superego" to crush down your individuality.' It was this theme of both mother – and also his mother-influenced self (his antilibidinal or super-ego), crushing both pleasurable spontaneity, and rage-reaction, which appeared in further drawings. Guntrip believed that the very intense emotion, of very early origin, depicted in the previous drawings could not have become available to his conscious mind in any other way.

Guntrip recalled, through another drawing, an experience of mutual masturbation with the son of a lodger at the Goose Green house.[3] He recalled the contrast between his own excitement and the perfunctory way the older boy manipulated his 'tiny organ'. In the same drawing, Guntrip drew himself as a little boy receiving the anaesthetic mask for his circumcision operation, clearly linking genital excitement with severe consequences. The same pattern was repeated in the transference when Fairbairn invited him to sit at the desk to discuss his paper on the latter's theory of schizoid reactions. Guntrip felt uneasy when Fairbairn's hand came near to his own and he 'shrank away imperceptibly'. Fairbairn interpreted: 'You felt I was that lodger's son enticing you. Then I might suddenly become your mother attacking you as in that previous dream.' Fairbairn further introduced the idea that Guntrip could have felt sadistic towards the lodger's son's penis from the start, since it might represent a tantalising object of desire, as Fairbairn's hand and originally his father's penis may also have done, since he was so deprived of libidinal satisfaction at his mother's breast. It would follow from this that Guntrip's identification with his father made them joint objects of his mother's attack, an attack in which he became involved also by his identification with her: a seemingly intractable internal closed system which was dramatised in his sinusitis and constipation. It was this theme which permeated the last week of sessions before the four-week Christmas break. In the transference, Guntrip felt that Fairbairn was the controlling mother as well as the tantalising father. Although he knew consciously that Fairbairn would not inhibit him, he wondered why he should trail up every week to lie on the couch to fit into Fairbairn's system. He felt that his analyst would be irritated if he got up and walked about. In his last dream before the break he was conducting a service at Salem, but from a bed: 'Just hopping up to speak and lying down again' – a situation which Fairbairn believed to be reflective both of Harriet's oppressive influence and also of Harry's perverse reaction to her at the time of the tent-bed illnesses, as if he were saying to her, 'If you won't let me do anything then I damn well won't do anything and you can look after me.' It was also markedly reflective of Guntrip's attitude to Fairbairn in the transference.

Notes

1   See Fairbairn 1954: 'Observations on the Nature of Hysterical States'. Guntrip is described under the pseudonym 'Jack'.
2   'Fairbairn built as a person on what my father did for me' (Guntrip 1975, in Hazell 1994, p. 367).
3   There is no account of this incident in the biographical section of Guntrip's notes.

CHAPTER 9

1951

During the Christmas break the Guntrips' daughter, Gwen, was married. Whatever the earlier misgivings, the occasion was very successful and both Guntrip and Bertha felt happy and well. But as the first session of the New Year approached, Guntrip felt sick as if flu symptoms were developing. It occurred to him to phone Fairbairn to ask whether he could visit him in his lodgings – an agreed provision in the event of illness in Edinburgh. But he decided that the symptoms arose from a need to avoid returning to the horrifying sado-masochistic dreams and drawings of the previous autumn, and a need to get back, either to a postulated good mother of the very earliest period, or at least to a good aspect of her – the nursing aspect of the tent-bed period. He realised that in thinking of phoning Fairbairn he was wanting not only to be nursed by father, not by mother, so to speak, but also as Fairbairn pointed out, to rival mother and take her place with father. In the end he attended his session and reported a dream in which Fairbairn and father became indistinguishable while he and a student friend (another version of himself) in nurse's uniform battled over whether analysis or nursing care should prevail. Fairbairn said, 'You want me as a nurse', and Guntrip realised that he was turning from the biting and devouring rages and terrors with mother to father/Fairbairn. He recalled how as a child he used to stand on the armchair watching for father coming home from church. He was searching for images and memories of the strong and active father of the Goose Green period with whom he might identify, and whose quiet and scholarly interests reminded him of Fairbairn. He dreamed,

> I was lying on the couch that mother bought for father when they moved to Benfleet. I was lying there with a man who was taller than me and handsome. I was smaller and lying at his side. I thought he might have been Fairbairn.

Here was a measure of co-operative side-by-side relation, and he recalled the dream he had had immediately before the first holiday break in analysis, of lying on Fairbairn's couch with Fairbairn beside him looking after him. But as soon as he realised that he must have supplanted mother to lie with father and so could feel 'one-up' on her, he immediately suffered a bout of urinary retentiveness, which lasted for several days. It was relieved only when he was able to leave home and return to Fairbairn, thereby escaping from his mother, with whom any active self-expression was inhibited, even though she was now in her eighty-first year. Although this was far from the case with Bertha, the event illustrates how all-pervading the blocking effect of his mother had become in Guntrip's inner world, especially insofar as he sought an alliance with his father/analyst. Gradually, however, Guntrip began to release more feeling in the transference. He dreamed of the King/father/Fairbairn visiting Salem without the Queen, and while one part of him wanted to show the King around, another part, a little boy, kept getting in the way. Fairbairn made the acute observation that some patients are more intent upon defeating the analyst than getting better: 'They pay the price of not being cured in order to get the better of him, and remaining ill relieves their guilt . . . You feel if you let go and show your feelings, you will lose what is precious . . . so you keep everything to yourself . . . You got your revenge by not giving out at all.' As he was leaving the session Guntrip surprised himself by colliding with Fairbairn's screen and kicking it. Fairbairn commented with a smile: 'You're letting some of it out now.' But, although this event was followed by a dream in which Guntrip felt free to urinate and defecate, 'and not mind much that he was seen going to the lavatory', before speaking at a conference, the feeling that such self-expression was dangerous was very strong, and he became preoccupied with a glass marble he had played with as a boy which had an internal pattern of well-organised wavy brown lines. He felt that the marble represented his closed internal system with all the mess safely controlled inside, and, as if to confirm that this was so, Bertha remarked that he was in his shell throughout the weekend. He told Fairbairn, 'I feel myself to be an abstraction poised between two dangers: you breaking in from outside and my inner world breaking out from inside, and I cannot let the conscious me break into my inner world.'

In the next session he was emotionally withdrawn, and felt that he was shut in mentally standing by the bookcase, watching the analysis, quite detached. Nevertheless, he recorded his feeling that of the twenty-one months of the analysis, the recent sessions had been the most important, and that Fairbairn had enabled him to

'get very deep indeed' into his unconscious. He realised that the
drawings which he had so unexpectedly produced went 'right down
to the baby biting the breast, and then the mother biting back', all
going on inside him, internalised at a time when he could not
easily distinguish between the mother and himself. Small wonder
that he needed to withdraw from such disturbed experience.

However, he only withdrew as far as the 'primal scene', for on
the way home on the train he drew a picture of parents having
intercourse and a baby lying on its back in a cot with its arms and
legs in the air. He had a powerful feeling that no-one must see the
drawing, and indeed he forgot about it until his next session,
which he began by knocking over Fairbairn's 'phallic' ashtray-stand.
He showed Fairbairn the drawing, with a strong feeling that the
latter would find it 'immoral', and also that he himself was parting
with something precious – all he had, so to speak, of a feeling of
relationship with his parents together. Fairbairn said, 'It's stretch-
ing out arms and legs as a baby does when it wants its mother.
You're sucking them in, drawing them into yourself. Somewhere
deep down you feel sexual intercourse is eating, the woman swal-
lowing the penis.' Guntrip immediately made a connection with
the baby biting the nipple. He had suffered nasal congestion at the
weekend and Fairbairn commented, 'The region is important. Your
eating organ gets excited and displaced into nasal catarrh. It's all
broadly the same area. You also said that you found it hard to
tolerate your dentures – Mouth, teeth, sinuses all got too closely
related emotionally for you through the sinus infection and the
operations on both areas.' Guntrip saw how he had unconsciously
exploited all these organs to express his repressed earliest conflicts,
keeping them all shut in himself. He said, 'I must have felt as if I
saw mother eating father and father eating mother, and me swal-
lowing both of them into myself, the tense feeling of a frightened
baby starved of genuine relationships with both parents, yet seeing
them there and can't get at them and they don't come to him.'
Thus the significance of the 'primal scene' was suffused with the
ravenous hunger of the deprived baby. That night he could not
allow himself to sleep, lest he either slip back into his bad internal
world, or release it into consciousness and so be robbed of its
'precious badness'. In a brief period of dozing, he had a vivid dream
in which he was carried down like a little child by a nurse to have
another nose operation. He gave himself the anaesthetic and the
surgeon stood on one side and did nothing. He associated the
surgeon with Fairbairn whom he feared would 'open him up' and
get something out of him and he said, 'It's all my early childhood

left me with. It's bad but I've nothing else.' It is also likely that
the nurse who carried him like a little child was created out of his
deep underlying need for emotional nurturance – for him the only
context in which he could afford to release the repressed material.
Meanwhile he kept it inside, in the internal closed system, and he
recalled how he, at the age of eight, had kept his faeces in his
trousers throughout the day until bedtime, the equivalent of his
constipation from three and a half to five years. As he left the
session he dropped the contents of his briefcase, his session notes
and study materials, at Fairbairn's front door: all he could 'let slip'
was his thinking, recording self, a necessary intellectual and professional activity. It is of interest at this time that Fairbairn encouraged Guntrip to convert his twice-abandoned MA thesis into a
PhD, for he did not view Guntrip's intellectual activity as 'only a
defence'. University College, London, accepted a thesis for a PhD
on 'The bearing of Recent Developments in Psychoanalytic Theory
on Sociology'. The inclusion of 'Sociology' enabled the thesis to be
accepted under the Faculty of Arts, since the Psychology Department felt unable to deal with a thesis on Psychoanalysis! The
thesis was to form the basis, ten years later, of Guntrip's first
major psychoanalytic book *Personality Structure and Human Interaction* (1961). Gradually, however, the defensive aspect of Guntrip's intellectual drive was beginning to yield for he dreamed that
he was in a race with an older man, whom he later associated with
Fairbairn, and keeping ahead of him, he could not keep up the
pace and lay down, exhausted. The following night he dreamed of
a possible sequel:

> Halfway through a session, I slipped out of my ordinary waking
> consciousness and went on talking in oblivion, and at the end I
> said, 'I forgot everything, almost even you, and have talked from
> deep down, living inside what I have been saying. But I feel
> more at ease, more en rapport with you because I had let go.

The sense of this greater emotional freedom gave rise to a less-
ening of concentrated intellectual energy, and Guntrip even felt
stripped of his professional identity, dreaming that his consulting
rooms were stripped bare for re-decoration', so that he had to
cancel a patient's sessions. He reacted with indignation to Fairbairn's suggestion of a modest increase in the analytic fee, and
sought to avoid the anxiety aroused by his dream of emotional
surrender, by reintroducing the theme of rivalry. If he was 'one-
down' it could only mean that Fairbairn was 'one-up' on him,

the dominating mother of his childhood. He felt he could only become a 'real person' by fighting to turn the tables. The underlying exhaustion suggested by the dream of the race with the older man, and its possible resolution in a therapeutic 'letting go' was denied in favour of another 'race'. It is also significant that the 'letting go' dream occurred in the week before the Easter break, as if Guntrip had felt 'able to risk it' knowing that anxiety over his separation would again force him to remuster his defences, in time to avoid too radical a regression. Furthermore Guntrip's professional viable 'self' was further reinforced by the publication of *You and Your Nerves* (1951), 'a simple account of the nature, causes and treatment of nervous illness'. The book was expanded from a series of the broadcast talks given by Guntrip on the BBC 'Silver Lining Programmes' in 1950. Dedicated to the broadcaster Stuart Hibbard, and with an extremely appreciative Foreword by Professor MacCalman, the book was to retain its relevance into the 1970s, when it was re-published with two additional chapters ('On Being a Real "Self", and 'Is there a "Cure"?') under the new title *Your Mind and Your Health* (1970).

When Guntrip returned after his two weeks' holiday his attention was once again 'safely' focused upon his septic sinus trouble, which had flared up just before Easter, and which he now regarded as 'undoubtedly psychosomatic and related to unconscious fantasies of having as a baby bitten off mother's breast, and then in the absence of any real relation to mother, turned to father, and fantasising biting off his penis, and then being attacked by it inside'. He recalled again how surprising he had found it when these kinds of phenomena had appeared in his drawings six months earlier, and realised that they had now reappeared in a variety of transient physical symptoms and finally as a septic sinus needing the use of the spray to clear it up. Fairbairn interpreted that in spraying his own septic sinuses he was identifying with both mother and father separately and in their intercourse together, both suffering it as the attacked vagina, (his septic sinus) and also impersonating the attacking father using the spray to push into the cavity, whilst in the transference he felt persecuted by father/Fairbairn's penetrative insights, 'opening him up'. He could only be excited in a suffering way since he could not satisfactorily experience his parents as persons but only hunger for them, and he could not dispose of them, since he was identified with them, and would therefore suffer 'self-castration'.

In the 1970s Guntrip was aware of the possibility that 'object-relations' thinkers might criticise him for being influenced by Fairbairn's more Freudian interpretations, especially as he had eschewed such an approach in his self-analysis. But, as he pointed out, he had not, at the time of his self-analysis, been experiencing a personal transference situation in which infantile bodily-cum-emotional experiences later repressed could be reactivated. Moreover, in his criticism of classical Freudian and Kleinian theory, he never denied the existence of 'impulse phenomena', but simply claimed that they were not primary. In a handwritten interpolation in his typewritten record, he makes it clear that his acceptance of Fairbairn's interpretations at this stage in the analysis should not be taken to imply that infants in the first year are capable of having such elaborate fantasies, since a baby in the first year would not, in his view, be mentally developed enough to fantasy literally in as sophisticated way as he drew and dreamed at fifty. But he maintained that the baby *experiences, and feels*, identified with the parents so that 'later acquired knowledge makes possible the explicit representations of early diffused experiences of frightening involvement'.

However that may be, Guntrip's deepest problem was once again avoided: namely that of being 'simply *unrelated* in an empty world with not even "bad objects" to relate to, [where he] felt threatened by *death*, not castration'. It was not father's penis that he wanted but father himself, and again he told Fairbairn, 'I need more than analysis, a personal fatherly interest and love.' He even thought of ending analysis, and dreamed of discontinuing a course of sinus syringing 'in another city' (that is, Edinburgh) and returning to Leeds for 'more thorough treatment', telling Fairbairn that 'treatment in Leeds would be in-patient. You only give out-patient treatment, sessions' – presumably by treating symptoms rather than causes. On the one hand he was aware of feeling that he could manage alone, but on the other, he felt a fear that he might prolong analysis in order not to lose Fairbairn. He said, 'Maybe as a small boy I felt I could never grow as big as father. He's a being of a different order.' Fairbairn replied, 'You felt forbidden to have a penis of your own. It's not for little boys to have a penis and be sexual.' The reply simply irritated Guntrip. It was, he felt 'a survival of Freudian sexology' which Fairbairn's own theory had already moved beyond, whereas an interpretation in terms of the penis ultimately representing the 'whole personality' which mother did her best to restrict and dominate would have felt much more realistic. In effect the analysis was becoming 'a penis analysis', not an 'ego-analysis', and, whereas Guntrip felt it was necessary to identify the penis and primal scene fantasies and transient symptoms, he felt it to be of the greatest importance to interpret them as defences against what Fairbairn himself had sensed early on:

namely the disaster he had nearly succumbed to once and had sealed off. This, he deeply sensed to be not castration but the loss of the sense of personal reality in a vacuum, the problem of basic ego-weakness and ego-breakdown in an early traumatised child, lying behind, and defended against, by these Oedipal phenomena. But whenever he thought of ending the analysis, he felt that old dread of the collapse which had followed Percy's death. He felt he had to hold on to mother and to Fairbairn, while secretly breaking away in another part of himself, and he saw that he, as much as Fairbairn, was once more effecting a 'schizoid compromise' by appearing to conform, whilst 'growing away' intellectually, being neither fully in, nor fully out of relationship, just as he had with mother. Accordingly, whilst he avoided re-experiencing the catastrophe he had almost succumbed to, by colluding with Fairbairn in the analysis of Oedipal defences as if they were causal, Guntrip 'secretly' began to 'reinterpret' Fairbairn's Oedipal sexual interpretations in terms of ego-psychology. For instance, when he dreamed that he showed Fairbairn the gold watch which his father and mother gave him as a twenty-first birthday present, and Fairbairn gave the by now predictable interpretation, 'You show me this watch, want my permission, father's permission, to be a man, come of age, be allowed to have a penis'. Guntrip made no reply.

On reading his notes twenty years later he was clear that 'Recognition' (in Balint's sense), not 'permission' had been the real issue. It was an 'ego question' not a 'sex question', and he had needed Fairbairn to confirm his status as an equal, a person in his own right, to build on the foundation laid by his father. At that time in 1951, however, Guntrip had not been able to achieve such clarity, and his secret 'growing away' began with a feeling of confusion over his relationship to Fairbairn: was the latter helping him to grow, or fitting him into his system? The gold watch dream was followed by another in which Guntrip was living in a house that was part of Salem. The old structure of Salem was rotten and crumbled and Guntrip informed the Women's Meeting that he would have to rebuild the house around his and Bertha's bedroom suite. Although the church had always been a symbol for 'the family situation' with certain women as 'bad-mother figures', Fairbairn interpreted the dream as the same old pattern of Guntrip destroying what he clung to in the act of leaving it: 'As soon as you become attached you destroy what you are attached to.' The interpretation does seem somewhat arbitrary, for not only were the mother-figures not destroyed as Fairbairn assumed, but the positive rebuilding theme was not mentioned in his interpretation.

Guntrip's confusion resulted in a growing antipathy to lying on the couch, which he mentioned to Fairbairn, apparently without response. He did not leave the couch, however, but dreamed that Fairbairn's car had a dent in the back, and that he assented to Fairbairn's request that he should take it to the garage for repairs while Fairbairn himself saw another patient. Fairbairn appears to have immediately interpreted the meaning of the dream as 'a penance intercourse, an attachment through guilt, making ties as a result of damaging my car'. On his way out Guntrip bumped a table in the hall with his bag, whereupon Fairbairn said 'You're destructive, hitting at me', which indeed he was – out of simple frustration with his analyst, whom he felt to be replicating his mother's restrictive influence, not merely in the transference but as a matter of objective fact. Nevertheless he could see how the analysis had valuably revealed how he had internalised the relationship between his mother and father, identifying with each of them, and carrying the whole conflict inside him, reflected in his blocked sinuses and constipation. He had also been enabled to see how the identifications with his parents as internal objects had both sealed him off from whole-hearted and spontaneous relations with actual external persons, and had also served as a defence against the experiencing his terrifying infantile sado-masochistic relations with the ungiving breast-mother. This was no mean achievement, and he later recorded his view that, in 1951, no other analyst could have got 'closer to the heart of the matter than Fairbairn', since it was not until 1960 that Winnicott wrote of a 'True and False Self' as a split in the personality, describing how, when the infant cannot find a real relationship in which to grow, his potential true self is put away in cold storage awaiting rebirth into a better environment. In 1951 Guntrip had no such terms in which to convey to Fairbairn that he felt 'out of touch' and unable either to reach out to him, or to co-operate with the therapeutic task in an 'on-the-level' relationship. It is hardly surprising, therefore, that he became frustrated when Fairbairn continually interpreted this inability as Guntrip 'keeping a penis to himself and hiding this from mother'. He told Fairbairn, 'I feel you won't let me talk my way and express myself. You restrict me and I won't have that', and although this shows a greater freedom to 'speak his mind' to Fairbairn, the underlying emotion was only one of reaction in the form of 'rebellion', and not a naturally spontaneous response. Even so, this increased frankness gave him a greater sense of being 'en rapport' with Fairbairn, so that he and Bertha were able to enjoy a good six weeks' summer holiday.

Ever since September 1950, when four of Guntrip's schizoid patients had declared 'starving needs for something more personal than analysis', Guntrip had been drawing together his impressions of their states, together with his own, in the light of Fairbairn's formulations. He had jotted down his observations during the long train journeys between Edinburgh and Leeds, and by June 1951, Bertha had typed a manuscript for 'A Study of Fairbairn's Theory of Schizoid Reactions' (Guntrip 1952, in Hazell 1994, p. 39), which Guntrip delivered to the Clinical Discussion Group at the Department of Psychiatry. The paper, which was clearly influenced by the spate of phantasy material that Guntrip produced from the autumn of 1950, points out the contrast between the energyless exterior of the schizoid and the ravenous hunger within ('love made hungry'), ceaselessly provoked by an internalised bad object who excites but never satisfies (Fairbairn's 'exciting object'). The therapeutic aim was described in terms of rescuing the patient's 'libidinal ego' from the allure of the exciting object (with whom it is identified) by means of a steadily developing personal relationship with the analyst.

Before he and Bertha left for their holiday, Guntrip sent his manuscript to Fairbairn for his consideration and the latter responded enthusiastically, though he was aware of a degree of overlap with an unpublished paper of his own which he intended to form the first chapter of a projected book (Fairbairn 1952: see Hazell 1994, pp. 5 and 6). Coincidentally the paper, which was published in the *British Journal of Medical Psychology*, was later to become the basis of the first chapter of Guntrip's second major psychoanalytical book (Guntrip 1968). On receipt of Fairbairn's favourable response Guntrip felt depressed, 'as if it was dangerous to enjoy success', but he was reassured by a pleasant dream on holiday, feeling that Fairbairn was with him in his inner world. Indeed it appears that in and through his frustration with Fairbairn some genuine sense of relationship and thus of 'true self' had begun to form, for on his return from holiday Guntrip dreamed that he was pregnant, though he wondered how the baby could be born since he had 'no natural outlet'. He felt sure that this must represent a sense of his natural self growing in relation to Fairbairn. The latter, however, made no comment and only later made an interpretation in terms of 'womb and vagina envy' in men, which, for Guntrip, again obscured the dream's deeper meaning, namely that a potential personal self remained shut up inside an inflexible closed system, and so was unable to develop further.

After further expressions of frustration, mostly 'unconscious', such as 'swaying away from Fairbairn at the door and knocking a grandfather clock on the other side', and more 'reversals', as for example a fantasy of 'falling on the spiked top of a railing' and thinking of himself as being impaled upon Fairbairn, Guntrip settled down to using Fairbairn's 'sexual terminology' to express ego-states, since it was the only language available. Thus, when Fairbairn said, 'In the inner scene you are preoccupied with father's penis in various guises, the doctor's capsule, the spray, the spike; and so far as the inner scene is reflected in the outer one, you're preoccupied with my penis ... but there is also a revulsion against someone of the opposite sex, your mother, that drives you to my penis and father's', Guntrip 'translated' it to mean that, since he could not live in a vacuum, as a little boy, revulsion against mother had made him long for a closer relationship with father, however this may have been symbolised, or felt by himself as a small child, whose experiences would so commonly have been registered in the body. Whilst he could well believe that after the circumcision, his 'fear of what mother might do' had made him switch his feeling and fantasy life to father, Guntrip believed that it was originally mother and not father who excited needs which she then frustrated. He recalled a time when, at nine or ten, he had achieved a superficial understanding with Harriet and had revelled in helping in the shop selling toys at Christmas, only to discover that she had betrayed a confidence about a friend which shattered his trust. He felt that she had also enticed him to share his burdens with her, as she martyrishly slaved for him and others, only to betray that trust when he needed to develop as a person. He was reminded of her 'letting Percy go' when he had cried out 'Don't let him go. You'll never get him back.' And when Fairbairn observed, 'But she held on to you by emotional blackmail. Look what I've done for you, slaved and given you a Public School education by my suffering. You can't leave me now. You've got to join me in it', Guntrip felt that they had 'really got close to the problem with mother' – that 'underneath her slaving for others, she was hard and grasping . . . and paranoid at heart', denying him any real sense of his significance as a person. Such frank criticism of mother, with Fairbairn's support, had the effect of bringing back the heat-spots, sore patches and stomach discomfort which he had suffered from three and a half to five years. But in his dream-life he reached an even earlier stage:

> I was standing in uniform in a Salvation Army ring. A naked little boy of 2½–3 years stumbled on the kerbstone and fell. I picked him up and set him on his feet.

He felt that the boy was himself, 'the lonely stumbling small child of under 3', six months before Percy's death, who appeared to have broken away from mother but came to disaster, and had to be helped by his older, compliant self who was 'part of a system'. He felt that he was unconsciously trying to reopen the battle with mother for a free self and, this time, to decide it in his favour. Moreover, Fairbairn's understanding of his struggle encouraged him again to feel that Fairbairn, like his father, was not hostile or critical but understanding and supportively behind him like the father of his very early dream, and he began to see that merely 'turning the tables' on mother could turn out to be not emancipation but only another method of holding on to her, when what he needed was 'genuine freedom for spontaneous relationships, equal ones'. A simple dream expressed a hope of genuine parental care:

A large wise old mother cat cleaning a new-born kitten.

The dream recalled how impressed he had been by the mother cat's care for her kittens at Goose Green, and he associated it with his latest feeling that Fairbairn might be introducing him 'to a new birth, a new start, independent of mother'. Fairbairn appears to have made no comment on this expression of faith in his care of Guntrip, but he listened intently and Guntrip felt he was 'very much with him'. This was not without its risks, however, and this time Guntrip dreamed of dethroning a father-figure and being waited on in bed, while in a second dream Fairbairn hinted at 'secret enjoyment of a safe dependent situation'. Guntrip was resisting, once again, the dependence he needed, and he said, 'Analysis stops me doing other things. It's like mother giving me something in the tent-bed, but I have to give up . . . freedom and activity to get it. I feel a stubborn resistance to her now.' Fairbairn commented, 'Repression is banishing mother, but you banish a bit of yourself along with her. Your resistance to her is "losing her", and in transference your resisting is losing me. But you feel that if you don't you'll lose yourself.' This interpretation bore deeply upon Guntrip's problem. Whereas he knew he needed 'a new birth', the risk of the loss of his known and familiar ('resistant') self seemed too great to be contemplated. The session 'dislodged something very deep', which manifested in two horrific dreams. In the first a criminal who had murdered and robbed his mother was confronted with a re-enactment of his crime to make him betray himself. The second, more terrifying dream involved the deliberate torture of a worm 'pricked' in the swollen middle of its body by a boy with a pole, while the head grew away and split into two huge heads, or breasts

with nipples. The more the boy pricked, the more the worm kept
swelling and growing until he burned the wound with a red-hot
poker, and finally tore at it with his hands. The worm was totally in
his power and 'could only suffer the horrible torture going on in its
middle'. Guntrip awoke aghast at such aimless cruelty. But he realised that the 'intensely emotional sadistic rape' of the dream was very
similar in its essential aspect to the Nimrod scene. It occurred to him
that the spear and the pole represented mother's cane, and that he
was wreaking a cruel, sexually-charged revenge on mother for her
beatings. There were four figures in the dream, corresponding to four
aspects of himself: the horrified dreamer, a fascinated boy observing
the torture, the sadistic torturer and the suffering worm. The four
aspects in the dream could also be understood in terms of Fairbairn's
concept of the endo-psychic structure, with the horrified dreamer as
the central ego and ideal object, the fascinated boy and the sadistic
torturer represented by the anti-libidinal ego identified with the
rejecting object, who together persecute the suffering and excited
'worm' represented by the libidinal ego and exciting object. The
aspect that most alarmed Guntrip, however, was the extent to which
he was unconsciously identified with his mother in her sadistic
aspect, as well as with the vengeful victim.

> I am both fascinated and horrified by what I see, and identified
> with both the torturer and the victim. They are me, processes
> in my dreaming self . . .   In fact both the worm and the boy
> were getting more and more excited, and that must mean that
> mother not only both terrified and excited me by the beatings,
> but she herself must have got uncontrollably excited, sexually,
> sadistically excited, and couldn't stop beating me.

This inner turmoil was certainly part of what he risked by 'not
resisting' Fairbairn; and he later recorded his thankfulness both for
his own powers of repression, and for 'this kind of analysis', which
alone could 'help us to understand what goes on in the personalities of sexual criminals and murderers'. He realised that, whereas
he dared not have temper tantrums with his mother, the violence
of the feeling that she could arouse in him had been expressed
inwardly in his high temperatures and fevers, which became his
means, both of suffering his rage inside and also of coercing his
mother to attend to him. Gradually the violent feelings were being
expressed – first through drawing and now, more directly through
dreaming. Even so, the suspicion began to dawn that he was using
this material as a defence against the even deeper risk of an emer-

gence of the depersonalising loneliness of the earliest two years, by means of a frantic struggle to express it all in terms of the emotional storms of the subsequent years, more easily expressed in sexualised dreams, since 'in these sexualised fantasies one is at least in a relationship, however bad, not in a vacuum'.

For a time the discharge of emotional tension eased Guntrip, until he sought to identify himself once more with the suffering martyrish aspect of his mother, in what Fairbairn called 'the Crucifixion Neurosis'. He must not upset her or add to her burdens, but share in her suffering: the sacrificial service of the 'devoted son', whilst inwardly he was secretly preparing to break away – only to find himself tied to her in the depths by 'separation anxiety', that compelled him to identify with her again. This theme was now expressed in a confusion over penis and breast, between what was his own and what was mother's. He dreamed:

I asked Dicks if he could lend me a book on physiology . . . as a refresher. Then I had a penis in my hand, but then it was a denture and when I put it in my mouth it was a soft breast. There was to be a meal, but we didn't get much, a general air of deprivation.

Guntrip felt profoundly understood when Fairbairn said,

That penis-denture was also a breast. You feel you have to have a breast of your own, not enough for mother to have a breast. It's something belonging to mother that you want, but you feel you must have in yourself. On the other hand, what is really yours, your penis, you feel you have to borrow from someone else, Dicks' book. All confusion. It's yours and not yours. You're wanting to find all you need in others in yourself. Then you feel you've got to borrow what is your own. This is a swing between Identification and Differentiation, dependence and independence, being yourself and being someone else.

Much later Guntrip realised that Fairbairn had here taken him down 'to the deepest of all problems, that of the primary differentiation of the growing infant from his original state of identification with his mother'.

With Fairbairn's assistance, he was now able to see more clearly the extent to which he remained identified with mother in his deepest unconscious, despite all his apparent 'growing away', which had really only meant repressing the identification. He saw too how, too

afraid to see his mother as really bad, he had 'taken her inside' and
turned both against her and himself in inner fantasy, switching rôles
and starting a campaign of 'self-crucifixion' – driven to sacrifice himself for mother, and then for 'mother-church', giving himself no quarter, from the time of the 'Devotional Diary' to the Salem ministry,
when he finally collapsed into the hands of the surgeon and then
Crichton-Miller. He recalled with a start, that when Bertha had
recently asked how old he was when Percy died, he had replied, 'Two
when he was born, and died when he was three and a half' – the first
'definite evidence' that he may have felt he should die in order that
Percy should live – 'the crucifixion theme'.

From that point his dreams and thoughts turned decisively away
from the hysterical suffering sacrificial relation to mother – the
'miserable worm' destined to suffer the sadistic attacks of his own
self-loathing. Instead he turned for help to father/Fairbairn with
whom he now felt 'in a real relation', certainly partly due to the
very pertinent interpretations of recent sessions, but also due to a
brief conversation after a session. Another sign of a more real
relation had occurred when Fairbairn spoke directly of his own
worst early trauma when he had been chastised for accidentally
seeing evidence of menstruation in his mother's bed. He had said
this in response to Guntrip's having mentioned that in his dream
of the man robbing and murdering his mother there had been
something about red ink or blood on the bed which made him
think of menstruation. Whatever Fairbairn's intention Guntrip was
grateful that Fairbairn had so straightforwardly revealed himself as
an ordinary human being on his own level, and his growing confidence in Fairbairn as a fatherly person enabled him to see that his
own father, whose help he sought vis-à-vis mother, 'was not unimportant but inadequate', so that he was aware for the first time
that he felt angry with his father for his inactivity. He recounted a
dream in which he 'hung about all morning', waiting for a doctor
to prescribe a spray for his nose. The doctor 'did nothing definite'
but, though he felt angry in the dream, Guntrip knew that protest
would be useless. While reporting the dream to Fairbairn, he realised that he had momentarily put his little finger in his mouth, as
if to recapitulate his early discovery of the nipple he found in
himself when he lost the breast. However, when Fairbairn
reminded him that it was a man he was currently seeking, his
father, he realised that, if indeed he had found comfort in his penis
and foreskin when he lost the breast, it had ceased to be a proper
penis, so that in order to find what he wanted in himself, he had
had to go to father for a penis that properly should have been his

own. Thus he realised that both father and mother had 'held up [his] natural development at the very earliest emotional stages', giving him no means of differentiating from an identified state with one or the other. Fairbairn added a further dimension to this already convoluted situation when he observed that, whilst Guntrip, in dreaming of going to doctors for the insertion of a spray, was expressing a need for a father to 'support and not neglect or depreciate' him, the same doctor could be experienced as the bad mother attacking him by putting things into him. Thus, not only did Guntrip feel identified with both mother and father, but he could not distinguish between them in fantasy for he identified them with each other, so that everything became 'confused and merged' in his inner fantasy. Fairbairn concluded: 'It shows how hard it is for the baby to begin to differentiate himself and other people as separate persons.' That he felt a need to experience a safe identified state with Fairbairn was then expressed in a dream of sitting on a chair beside him while he wrote down what Guntrip said, thereby enabling him to feel that he was taken seriously. However, as soon as he reported this expression of need to Fairbairn, he immediately felt that it was time the session ended, and although he saw this feeling as evidence that he was now able both to identify with and differentiate appropriately from Fairbairn, its suddenness was suggestive of needing to 'break free' and not yet of a natural unforced differentiation. Moreover, although he was now feeling more independent of Fairbairn in writing, and not 'needing his O.K.' for what he wrote, he acknowledged that he was 'not holding this "on the level" relationship very steadily at the moment'. Fairbairn asked him simply, 'What's the difficulty? Why can't you just go on feeling friends, going along together?'

There can be no doubt that this was what Guntrip most wanted and needed, but he was once more assailed by anxiety that in an 'on-the-level relationship' he would unconsciously push Fairbairn down in fantasy, and so be unable to return to the identified state. He was also aware of a danger of engaging in an 'intellectual equality' which 'the child in him' was not yet able to support. But nevertheless he said to Fairbairn, 'I begin to feel that I'm more real now when I feel you're more real': a sign of a supported differentiation, and a step towards the resolution of his main problem – an inability to feel real as a 'person' because of being unrelated, and therefore having to 'base himself' upon others by identification, only to feel a further compulsion to break away by being 'one-up' on them, lest he be swallowed up in them. He knew he needed a new identification with Fairbairn as a foundation for genuine ego-

development. Indeed, he had sensed its beginning, but it seemed so
slight an influence in the face of the bad-object world of his inner
experience. He longed for a magical intervention, a 'surgery of the
soul'. But, as if to emphasise the intransigence of his position, he
had a most disturbing dream in which he relived the feeling of the
terrifying beating mother, and the somewhat inadequate protection
of Mary:

> I went with a woman into a wild, desolate place where some-
> thing very suspicious was going on. There among the rocks we
> sighted a wild, sinister woman. The woman with me then had
> a small child whom she picked up and we made our way back
> to the car, but suddenly we came on the wild woman round a
> boulder. She attacked furiously, a terrific struggle, a flurry of
> flailing arms. I awoke thinking of a flailing human octopus, and
> wanting to duck my head under the bedclothes.

Guntrip felt convinced that this was not dream-symbolism, but
'literal memory', so fully did the atmosphere reproduce his experience of the 'worst beating'. Fairbairn pointed out that the situation
provided the factual basis for Guntrip's 'passive martyr situation'
there being nothing he could do about it. However, while the
horror swept over him of his helplessness in a home that had
become a 'wild place', Guntrip spontaneously associated the bleak
scene in the dream with Jerusalem's 'Valley of the Rocks', where
the city's rubbish was burned, 'where the worm dieth not and the
fire is not quenched, the prototype of Hell'. This in turn brought
to mind his dream of the red-hot poker burning the worm, which
Fairbairn took to represent what he secretly had wanted to do to
mother in retaliation. But, whilst Guntrip accepted that he went
into that sinister place in his inner world in order to hunt mother
down, and turn the tables on her for the cane that 'stung and
burned like the red-hot poker in that worm dream' (the 'Nimrod'
situation), he was clear that, although he had felt she would kill
him and that she 'wouldn't, couldn't give up unless killed herself',
he had been 'helpless to do anything but feel a rage smothered by
terror'. Thus, whilst Fairbairn wished to emphasise a hidden raging
potency, Guntrip maintained that his experience was overwhelmingly one of impotent terror. Accordingly, when he mentioned that
he had suffered an 'acid tummy' (that is, anxiety) that night, Fairbairn countered tersely, 'Heat spots'! (that is, anger). A further
complication for Guntrip was the close resemblance of the contemporary external situation in his home with mother and Bertha to

the inner situation with mother and Mary: in both situations he could not easily help one woman without hurting the other. But most defeating was his sense that the mother he could not cope with externally, but could only internalise and identify with, was endlessly locked with him in a 'mutually destructive, crushing and absorbing . . . death embrace, but never dying'. He said to Fairbairn, 'Your analysis has shown me, in a way I had no conception of, *the terrible nature of the unconscious inner world as both static, unchanging, but also dynamic, exhausting and explosive*. No wonder its eruption makes people fall ill.'

The deepest effect of his own 'illness' was registered some two weeks later when he again experienced the dull, lifeless, mechanical feeling which he felt underlay the inner conflict. Edinburgh seemed 'wintry, dark and cheerless' and Guntrip felt fundamentally alone. He recalled as a boy 'wandering about the house at a loose end, wondering what to do, wanting something, vaguely dissatisfied. Mother in the shop, Mary busy, father in the office, no-one to play with. A lonely child among adults who didn't understand children . . . .Only the Salvation Army had brightness, colour, music, cheerful people. It offset a kind of melancholy at home.' He resented the ideal woman, mother, whom he longed for and could not have, so that he had instead to go on doing his duty and enduring, 'with a stubbornness that concealed . . . suppressed anger, inwardly lonely at heart'. Fairbairn again emphasised the 'martyrish' aspect, but Guntrip sensed in this mood '*the re-emergence of the quality of a lot of loneliness in my early days*'. During the next few sessions he returned to wondering why he could not be content with Mary as mother, and Fairbairn responded with another example from his own experience. He said 'She wasn't your mother. I once saw a small girl for the NSPCC. Her mother beat her cruelly. I said "Wouldn't you like us to find you a home where someone would treat you kindly?" She replied, "No, I want my own Mummie."' As before, the emergence of the human, personal Fairbairn who became in the transference the longed-for good parent, reminded Guntrip of his attempts to find a relating father as a way out of his dilemma, and he recalled something he had not mentioned before, that his father had on a number of occasions come to watch him play cricket, and had talked about his prowess to other people. Once again he felt closer to Fairbairn, and once again he felt himself 'drying up', despite the former's confirmation that he had been 'talking a lot more freely and feelingly' in recent sessions. It frustrated him to find himself clamming up just when he was feeling Fairbairn to be friendly and helpful, and when he himself was able to be more respectful of his own needs and of 'simply being human'. But his previous experience alerted him to the probability that he was afraid emotional closeness would 'lead to something disturbing' and he suddenly recalled a dream:

> An atom-bomb raid was feared. Warning hooters weren't very distinct. People might not notice and be caught unawares. Then I was in a building and our hooters went. I realised it was a real raid warning.

Both he and Fairbairn felt he was afraid that an emotional explosion would result from his asserting his 'proprietary right to possess' mother and Fairbairn; and he noted an important change in his fantasy life: whereas normally his fantasies were intensely active but he never saw the people in them, on the previous night he had mentally seen his wife very clearly, and had wanted her but there had been no action. He was unable to claim the person he needed, and was 'deeply grieved' that his early life had crippled his freedom. Moreover, he felt resentful of the psychoanalytic view that 'You can't alter childhood', but must 'face and accept it and become mature, realistic, and make the best of what you've got', a view which he felt mirrored the giving up of his 'wants and activities', as the only basis for peaceful coexistence with mother, who due to her having become 'an overburdened little mother as girl . . . literally took it for granted that everyone ought to sacrifice themselves for her'. As he surveyed his life, he felt that he had been 'in process of breaking away from situations, moving, exploring' all his life until at forty-five he had found in psychotherapy what he could really do and find satisfaction in. However, as his melancholy dispersed he realised that he had made real gains, and as the Christmas break approached he was aware of 'a very marked improvement in my state of mind and my inner emotional relation to my wife; feeling happy, contented, can make love spontaneously, a real gain from recent talking out'. He also felt more sure of his judgement of his own work, and announced his intention of applying for a Fellowship of the British Psychological Society after achieving his PhD. At this point after two and a half years of analysis, he realised that, especially in the last three months, profoundly repressed emotions had been reactivated, and that he 'certainly had good reason' to feel that his analysis was really getting results, although the question remained in his mind as to how far a start had been made in growing a fundamental change in his inner emotional world.

CHAPTER 10

1952

The Christmas holiday was happy, and on his return to Edinburgh Guntrip experienced the familiar foreboding that Fairbairn's analysis might reawaken 'the terrible early conflicts between fears and rages and the sado-masochistic fantasy relation to mother which dissolved into the hysteric suffering in her stead'. He dreamed of being invaded by someone slowly pushing his consulting-room window open from outside; and contrastingly of being held by an analyst comforting a small child curled up on his lap. The latter dream caused him to wonder if he kept that image of his mother as cold and unresponsive when he climbed upon her lap, as a 'screen memory to blot out mother as an exciting object'. Not surprisingly, Fairbairn regarded this as important, but there is no record of his having responded to the still deeper implication of a further dream in which a business man representing Guntrip's practical everyday self brought one of his male staff and his whole family to Guntrip's rooms for help. The employee's problem was one of *collapse*, the word used for Guntrip's illness after Percy died, and he lay on the couch, very afraid and trembling. But although the man felt he was doomed, Guntrip detected a weak pulse which he felt was 'beating strongly very deep down . . . too deep to be felt by others'. In the dream the whole family was distressed, as had been the case when Guntrip collapsed, and he had a powerful feeling that he must not allow the man to sleep 'or he would never wake up again', even though the collapse had appeared also to suppress very strong emotion deep down. Despite his caution in the first week of restarting analysis, he felt he had 'tapped the hidden emotional volcano inside', and his unconscious reaction was to bury himself in his work, thereby causing Bertha to remark once again that he was 'in his shell'. He had damped down all emotion for fear of another eruption of the volcanic sado-masochistic emotion he had experienced in the dreams about the worm and the wild woman. He would want no woman at all, and he recalled his 'counter-rejection' of mother when, at three and a half to five years, he passed by her tempting sweets unmoved. He now reacted to Fairbairn as in the first dream in which someone was breaking in. He dreamed that Fairbairn was demonstrating a chandelier 'shaped down to a point' which he lowered by means of a pulley. But he felt menaced by it and 'gave it a vicious push' so that it hit the ceiling, smashed, and fell on him – his own reactive fear-driven violence recoiling on him as the tempting glittering penis-breast dangled above him. He remarked to Fairbairn that he had felt a similar dilemma while writing his thesis: a release of creative energy which might become uncontrolled, unbalanced, and recoil on him. Fairbairn said, 'You're afraid of your active imaginative self doing anything that's not obsessionally controlled. You're afraid to let go and drive ahead. Afraid you'll die or kill yourself, or . . . Kill someone else.'

Guntrip's rage at his mother implied a need of her, and he developed 'an important fantasy' in which the Queen had heard him broadcast and sent for him to comfort her in her bereavement. He had to make journeys to London, and they became closely attached. The Queen represented his mother, and he recalled the occasion when he had wanted to comfort Harriet after his father's death – only to be prevented by the consultant, and herself not wanting to be touched lest she break down. But he also recalled that earlier time when Percy died and he had got into the room. Then he and mother had cried together, momentarily sharing their grief, before she sent him away with Mary. He believed the Queen fantasy expressed a wish to re-experience that one time when mother and he had cried together and 'had a human relation'. It also occurred to him for the first time, that his 'collapse illness' might have been a response to that refusal by mother to allow a human relation to develop with her surviving son. The problem was compounded, moreover, by her hostility to anyone with whom he promised to have a relationship, and he felt she would attack him murderously in his fantasy if he got from anyone else, Mary or Bertha, what she herself would not give.

The following week 'a marked change' occurred. Guntrip felt a strong sense of 'internal self-sufficiency'. However, he soon realised that this was a product, not of genuine growth in the therapeutic relationship, but of identification, in order to counteract the experience of 'object-loss'. The lost object was not only his internalised mother, but also Fairbairn, who had had to cancel a session due to influenza, and he dreamed that he was saying things in his mind at the very moment Fairbairn began to mention them, and 'thinking the same things as he was with him'. Ever since his paper on Fairbairn's theory of schizoid reactions Guntrip had been exploring the precise nature of the 'therapeutic factor' in psychotherapy. The subject had become, to a considerable extent, the focus of post-sessional discussions between Fairbairn and himself: so much so that he had absorbed many of the former's ideas without realising he was doing so. The extent to which he was identified with Fairbairn himself was to become a matter of some contention when Guntrip produced another manuscript. But at the time of this dream it was the degree to which he had remained identified with his parents whilst apparently becoming self-sufficient, which preoccupied Guntrip, and his realisation that he had done so to counteract feeling he had no relationship with them. He recalled that he had left their church as early as seven or eight years and thereafter did very little with them, and added 'So far as they were concerned, I developed a private world of my own to retire into'. That private world developed from middle teens onwards into communing with himself in his Devotional Diary, 'Living an "Interior Life" (the title of a devotional book he bought but never read), keeping his deeper feelings locked inside with internalised objects, and not exposing himself to needs for the external objects with whom he could get no sense of connection.

He began to see how he had always preferred 'half-in and half-out situations' – an aspect of his personality that he had never clearly and comprehensively considered before, and which had arisen from his need to 'live inside himself' with his mother always in the shop, father there also when not at work, and Mary busy with the house, so that he could recall 'no home life of leisured evenings to sit and chat and get a relationship' and he added, 'My daughter must have felt the same about me.' Clearly the same had applied to Bertha, for he dreamed,

I heard a voice say clearly 'Can you let your wife have an effect on you and stimulate your feelings?'

and he began to be able to allow a greater freedom to grow in their relationship, realising that he must have inhibited Bertha more than he knew.

A sense of progress was developing. Guntrip gave up cigarettes permanently at this time, made only occasional use of the nasal spray, and was less obsessively concerned with his dentures. His needs became more focused in his personal relationships, and whereas he had felt that Edinburgh was a place to escape to, he now felt lonely there and longed to be at home with Bertha, despite the continuing influence of his mother, who had recently said to Bertha, while reminiscing, 'I used to make them all dance round. A look was enough. I didn't have to say anything.' The thought that he himself might be identified with such a destructive and dominating personality continued to trouble him deeply, and he dreamed that he had left mother in bed and slipped out to a school and met Alf Blows and arranged to call for him. He let himself back in quietly, hoping not to wake his mother, but she was standing there in the dark, gloomy bedroom in her dressing-gown. Fairbairn suggested that Guntrip was afraid that if he really broke free of his mother, by changing from her world to a boy's world, it would be the death of her, alone in the gloomy house. Thus despite his feeling of progress, the tie to mother seemed unbreakable, and he became depressed by the thought that he had come too late to psychoanalysis, and that he would 'fade out in obscurity having been neither a real person nor a real analyst'. However, in his deepest unconscious a glimmer of hope continued to grow, for he dreamed that one of his patients, having ended the analysis after dreaming of abandoning a young man in the grip of an Octopus, had crept back in the night for a session and was 'fumbling in the dark', and he said, 'This must be myself.'

The two big dreams of the tortured worm and the fight with the wild woman seemed to have marked a turning point in the analysis for, after them, both dreams and symptoms steadily lessened and 'instead of going backwards into still earlier infancy, the pre-Percy years', he 'worked steadily forwards'. In the 1970s Guntrip noted that Fairbairn did not return to his very early interpretation about a 'disaster I nearly succumbed to once', but by his steady interpretation in terms of a fairly classic Freudian sexual symbolism 'actually helped' him to keep going on the level of the three and a half years plus period, exploiting 'bad-object relationships' as better than no relationships at all. He felt that Fairbairn failed to see that the physical existence of parents who cannot relate to the child adds a poignancy to that child's isolation: a situation which Guntrip increasingly felt to be reflected in Fairbairn's own non-recognition that the earlier 'disaster' could amount to anything other than castration – the circumcision and its implications. Thus Guntrip concluded that he had moved forward to survey his 'breakaway developments in real life' because he could not move backwards without real help, and 'could not go on marking time on the spot of the sadomasochistic sexualised fantasies of the 3½ to 7 year period'. Whilst he did not overlook the real-life improvements, there was a sense in which they only served to throw into sharp relief his underlying feeling – not of guilt at wanting and needing to break away from his mother, but of 'not feeling at all', because, as he said, 'there is no real relation between me and mother and I can't invent one'. Reflecting upon Fairbairn's scepticism regarding the therapeutic effects of 'pure psycho*analysis*' and his belief that although libido could be drained out of its unconscious structures, the basic personality pattern, once made, is unalterable, Guntrip considered 'cutting his losses' at this point, wondering if Fairbairn himself was sensing that the analysis had become static. In his notebook he posed the question, 'Why am I going on with analysis and what can I get out of it?', and he enumerated his gains as follows:

> In three years I have gained a lot and am a lot better . . . sleep is good and without pills, weight has gone up nearly two stones, nasal congestion has cleared, the transient physical symptoms have faded out, tension has faded out mentally and I have a lot more insight into personality problems and see much more clearly what is happening in my patients. But . . . is it worth going further?

Clearly much depended upon the nature of 'the object-relation to the analyst', and it was at this point that the extent of Guntrip's identification with Fairbairn and his views became more apparent – to Fairbairn at least. In May Guntrip sent Fairbairn the manuscript of an article on psychoanalysis and exorcism, and a paper, 'The Therapeutic Factor in Psychotherapy' (Guntrip 1953, in Hazell 1994, p. 63), which he had read earlier that month at the department's clinical discussion group. In the paper he made reference to a number of ideas which had been discussed in post-sessional meetings with Fairbairn – and in particular, Fairbairn's view that psychotherapy was like a religious experience of salvation by a personal relationship. Another of Fairbairn's ideas he represented was that the free association method was properly 'a method of maximum spontaneity of thought and feeling, but not of action' (personal communication, 18 May 1952). In Fairbairn's view, Guntrip had virtually paraphrased these original views of his, in a way that amounted to 'a stealing of his father's penis', and whilst Fairbairn did not wish to play 'the rôle of castrating father in reality', the transference implications would have to be discussed in sessions. In fact, the letter in which these views were expressed by Fairbairn came only days after a letter of totally unreserved approval and support for Guntrip's paper, in which Fairbairn strongly urged him to send it to Sutherland, as editor of the *British Journal of Medical Psychology* (14 May 1952); and even in the second letter Fairbairn, after his initial objection, devoted himself to detailed comments on matters of style or of unclarity, and taken as a whole the letter shows an extremely painstaking effort to improve the paper for the reader. I recorded my own view in my introduction to *The Collected Papers of H.J.S. Guntrip* (Hazell 1994), namely that Guntrip's identification with Fairbairn and his views was 'evidence of his need to make good the weakness resulting from early environmental failure' (p. 7), rather than a product of the Oedipus complex. Understandably Guntrip made much of Fairbairn's first encouraging letter. He replied, 'You have given me reason to feel that I mean something to you that you value and that is new . . . [It] paves the way to go deeper into my unconscious world.' He made the point that while he felt with Fairbairn a shared sense of the reality of essential religious experience, he had formed such convictions on his own before he had heard of Fairbairn, on the basis of the writings of John Oman, Martin Büber, and John McMurray. The main value for him of Fairbairn's comparison of religious to therapeutic experience was its implication of deep compassion which spoke to his schizoid core. Although he had little in common with Fairbairn in political and broadly social feeling and thinking, he had sensed 'the very warm heart of the man and his deep concern for people'. Thus Fairbairn's recognition of his first efforts at research writing came as a valuable recognition of his 'real self', of a kind he had never received from his parents. Guntrip felt that the fact that Fairbairn's letters were 'in a sense extra-analytical' illustrated the latter's view that it was not 'pure analysis' but 'personal relationship' that was therapeutic. He felt that it broke into his 'internally empty world' and created a situation in which he could feel he 'did really exist as a person', and he told Fairbairn that he was beginning to feel less mechanically driven and 'more like a tree growing with roots deepening in good soil'. It is not clear how or whether Fairbairn responded to such an expression of affirmation. However, a later interpretation suggests that he remained somewhat cautious, for when Guntrip dreamed that a large tree had been cut down and left at a petrol station where he wished to 'fill up', Fairbairn reminded him that in some notes for the further development of the manuscript of his recent paper Guntrip had again used a sentence of Fairbairn's without quotation marks, and added, 'You stole my penis and now can't use it. The tree is cut down and then left.' Maybe Fairbairn felt pushed in the direction of a degree of personal responsiveness with which he did not feel comfortable, but it should also be remembered that the publication of Fairbairn's book, *Psychoanalytic Studies of the Personality* (1952) was imminent, in Chapter 3 of which, 'The Repression and the Return of Bad Objects', the idea of psychoanalysis as exorcism is propounded. For Guntrip, however, Fairbairn's encouraging first letter represented a response to a deeply-felt need for an object-relationship with the analyst as 'The Therapeutic Factor in Psychoanalysis', and he was not going to forget it. A few sessions later, he strove to clarify his relation to Fairbairn, asking 'Am I, in writing, simply stealing your ideas or have I got real ideas of my own . . . Your "Object-Relations Theory" and your view of therapy as saving people from internalised bad objects, devils, has proved to be the key I hoped to find with you, by which I could come to understand what I was myself groping towards, without the psychoanalytical experience to get there clearly.' His deepest need, which he saw with increasing clarity, was for Fairbairn to relate to him therapeutically in an area of experience in which he had no relationship at all – an area which continually brought home to him the sheer impossibility of any genuine contact with his own parents.

During the ensuing eighteen months he made repeated attempts to bring his ultimate problem to Fairbairn's attention. He produced a fantasy of being suspended, 'a naked helpless body hanging in the air' above an abyss, before rushing back to bad persecutory objects to rescue himself from 'that sheer terrifying emptiness': devils with claws to tear him to bits or hidden deep-sea fish to devour him. He appealed to Fairbairn to lower his conscious self on a rope to bring back the part of him suspended in the emptiness. Fairbairn's response was hardly adequate, for he simply observed that the frantic need expressed in the fantasy was characteristic of 'the hysteric' – an area of psychopathology with which he was deeply preoccupied at that time,[1] and one which reflects the extent to which parts of the body become involved in, and later represent, the struggles of the 'libidinal ego' with its internalised bad objects in a 'closed system' of internal reality. Accordingly Fairbairn went on, 'Your basic position is that mother is the castrator and you want a man, father, to free you from her and he didn't' – an interpretation which was true of the later years of Guntrip's childhood, but which failed to account for the basic earliest problem. The needs of this earlier period were expressed simply by a 'wishful' dream in which he slept a full eight and a half hours in and after a session, while Fairbairn allowed him to sleep. In the same dream a woman woke him and showed him 'lovely corals in closed glass water tanks, and one moved as if alive, with a mouth-like action', reminding him later of 'an embryo in utero, a new self waiting to be born'. He explained to Fairbairn his feeling that the dream expressed some part of him that had never yet 'got properly born, and needed to be discovered and brought out' – the only solution, he felt, to his forced activity. He dreamed again of a small mouse which could not manage a jump and fell. He wanted to help the mouse, but it did not realise that. Fairbairn's only comment was 'You're like the mouse, struggling, overcompensating for being castrated by mother.' In spite of his feeling that in his deepest self he felt not 'castrated' but simply unrelated, Guntrip tried to apply Fairbairn's interpretations. His own fear of madness made him desperately anxious for structure. He realised that if he had been swallowed up in that fantasy of suspension in the abyss surrounded halfway down by devils he might have been schizophrenic, and that he was fortunate to be able to control it and keep it as fantasy, and yet he deeply believed that what Fairbairn was interpreting as a hysteric castrated suffering state was his 'deep down, schizoid, sleeping, unawakened, unborn self, never called to life by truly maternal relating, needing to regress to a psychic womb, as in the "sleep dream", to be "born again". Perhaps despairing of this possibility, he became impatient with his lack of progress and told Fairbairn, 'I want to push on with analysis. Is it reasonable to get through in five years all told?' Fairbairn replied: 'You can analyse for ever; it depends on the practical aim you set out to achieve. You put a lot more into analysis than most patients do, and you have no hopeless inertia, you know what it's about. I think you should find another year's analysis enough.'

At this point the six-week summer break intervened, during which the Guntrips made an offer for a new spacious bungalow which would ease Bertha's burden in caring for the now almost entirely bedridden but unremittingly critical Harriet. The inevitable expense of a move increased Guntrip's desire to 'get on with the analysis and reach a useful ending'. He began to fear the emptiness of the new house, feeling a need both to escape and to stay put. It seems likely that Guntrip's sense of inner emptiness was exacerbated by the fact that Fairbairn himself was undergoing a period of great strain at this time, which culminated that September with the death of his wife, after a long illness. Guntrip expressed his sympathy – feeling 'quiet and sad for Fairbairn' and successfully persuading him to postpone the resumption of analytical work. But the ensuing six-week break in sessions together with a projected house-move and the theme of death held unconscious meanings for him, and he dreamed that he was condemned to die by eletrocution in the very room where he had found Percy lying dead on his mother's lap: part of him 'shocked' to a standstill, as if he had died with Percy, though in a later part of the dream 'it seemed that somehow he did not die'.

It seems from his record that he and Fairbairn both retreated from this disturbing level of experience into philosophical discussion, though Guntrip believed that 'real emotional issues can be at stake in intellectual problems', quoting Ernest Jones' view that analysis should not end until conscious beliefs and ideology have been analysed. In fact, Guntrip now believed that he was seeking to bring out his basic problem by means of an exploration of intellectual quests. He noted that whilst his need for intellectual independence had roots in breaking free of mother's domination, he would often come up against a feeling of having only an arid intellectual philosophy, and wished that he could 'feel' more deeply than he could define. He would experience 'occasional awful moments of insecurity, feeling stranded, no orientation, feeling all [his] foundations crumbling' – and he felt sure that in these experiences he was sensing deeper schizoid emptiness of the failure of genuine personal relationship with mother.

The house-removal now intervened, adding considerably to Guntrip's sense of insecurity. He dreamed of having to pay a jeweller dearly for an object he himself had retrieved from a river because he had 'delivered it into the jeweller's care'. He felt it represented both the draper/mother behind the counter and Fairbairn behind his desk, taking advantage of 'any giving' on his part. Fairbairn merely remarked that distrust was a 'great source of resistance . . . a progressive source of resistance which removes more and more things from analysis till there's nothing left they can talk about. A deep fear of exploitation.' To Guntrip this felt like a critical attack, and he noted a strong tendency to withdraw safe within his 'Schizoid Citadel'. In the final session before Christmas he said, 'I feel I'm schizoid to escape being paranoid . . . I maintain some core of detachment out of reach of the bad mother. She inhabits my unconscious and I must retreat even deeper still to get away from her.' But he was also aware that his secret inner isolation in the 'citadel' of his deepest unconscious was so frightening that he felt compelled to return to the bad-mother in his highly disturbing dreams.

Note

1   Fairbairn's paper, 'Observations on the Nature of Hysterical States', was published in the *British Journal of Medical Psychology* in 1954.

CHAPTER 11

1953

When sessions resumed Fairbairn for the first time referred to 'castration-anxiety' as a fear of ego-loss. He said 'Castration is really symbolic of a total personality situation, feeling stopped from being oneself, fear of loss of individuality and personality.' Indeed Guntrip's 'self-expressive' action of choosing a better house had stirred his 'deep original fears of mother's retaliation', from which prospect he withdrew, causing Fairbairn to observe that fear of the loss of his personality had impelled him to withdraw into 'a secret room' in his mind where he could 'get away alone', do things all by himself, as the only way to get away from his mother in the house and, by transference, from Fairbairn himself. He said, 'You feel that if you let me into that room it's the end of freedom for you.' But although Fairbairn recognised Guntrip's need to withdraw to escape annihilation, he never ascribed the same motive to his attempts to turn the tables on the crushing mother. He did, however, make a great impression on Guntrip when he said, 'There are two sides to this: You defend yourself against relationship which you feel to be dangerous by withdrawing and being alone. But also as a creative person you need privacy. You find things out when you're alone, like the Yogi. American psychology lacks originality because they're over-sociable; everything is done in groups, and all activity is extroverted. It can lead to superficiality.' In the light of later experience Guntrip came to differ with this view of 'Americans', but he was much helped by Fairbairn's recognition of value 'and therefore reality' in his withdrawn self. He regarded this as one of the most important moments of the analysis, for Fairbairn had respected his right to privacy and had helped him to counter-act the fear that withdrawal meant self-emptying and ego-loss. Hitherto, he had only been able to maintain privacy at the expense of self-isolation, since he had to save himself from being exploited by mother, with whom a 'relationship' meant to submit to being invaded. He saw that he had lacked the experience of mother being interested in any personal development of his that was beyond the range of her own limited experience, so that he now needed to experience personal relations in which he could be himself and not lose himself.

As he pondered further upon the nature of the therapeutic analytic relationship he began to fear that he would have to 'dissolve away' all relationship with Fairbairn in order to be free, once more transferring on to the latter his imprisoning experience with mother. But again he realised that real freedom could only grow within a free relationship, and that since mother had made him fear relationships as being possessed, he needed to find the experience of personal freedom for the first time with Fairbairn. He also observed that he was dreaming less often, and that he was aware of feeling the extreme importance of a 'here and now' relationship that he could develop with Fairbairn on a mature level. Accordingly the next session was devoted to a discussion of a lecture on 'Psychoanalysis and Religion' which Guntrip had been invited to give at the Victoria Institute in London. Guntrip found great value in these 'on-the-level' discussions, as he had in the earlier philosophical debates, and whilst he was aware that some analysts would question the wisdom of Fairbairn's participation on the grounds that it would complicate the transference, he maintained that although these occasional discussions were intellectual in content, they were emotionally important in value, since Fairbairn gave him a real-life relationship in a way his mother was unable to do, by sharing with him his wider knowledge of psychoanalysis, in a way which actually made it easier for him to recognise openly his purely transference reactions. Indeed it was directly due to Fairbairn's professional encouragement that Guntrip's paper 'The Therapeutic Factor in Psychotherapy', which had been the subject of so much earlier controversial discussion, was duly published by Sutherland in the *British Journal of Medical Psychology* at this time. In the paper Guntrip describes the psychotherapist as analogous to a saviour who delivers the patient from the power of the bad objects by his love and justice, working through positive and negative transferences, so that the patient becomes 'ever more free to experience directly and in more mature ways the reality of the analyst as a mature helper who is enabling him to grow into a mature adult person' (Guntrip 1953, in Hazell 1994, p. 85). Nevertheless, the real feeling evoked by these encounters was unsettling, for the very reason that more than 'transference' was involved, so that, although he felt more openly responsive, Guntrip slept badly. Moreover, he realised afresh the extent of his tendency to keep his emotions inside, 'real but not outwardly expressed', since natural expression of feeling simply had not occurred in his home. Fairbairn said, 'That often occurs in therapy.

Patients can't admit to feeling any attachment to me in reality, or that I could feel any genuine interest in them. That destroys the two main motives for recovery and sabotages the treatment. They can't get well for the sake of our becoming more real persons to each other.' The possibility of open emotional exchange raised the issue of possible 'acting out', causing Guntrip to recall a 'violent outburst' by one of his male patients during a session. But, beyond a general observation that 'acting out' was appropriate to 'children's treatment', and that if adults could not convert action into 'story-telling' they needed 'in-patient conditions', Fairbairn did not respond. Provoked by what he considered an evasion, Guntrip reacted with irritation, whilst at the same time delighting in his ability to feel this normal human reaction to Fairbairn's side-tracking. Indeed, he told Fairbairn that he had a definite impression of Fairbairn as the real person he essentially was, and of the analysis having reached the new point of his getting rid of the mask that had existed between them. For him Fairbairn now had 'a more definitely real human face'. The latter, however, again avoided Guntrip's directness with the seemingly inexplicable remark, 'Don't make too rigid anatomical distinctions such as the face. It might be a penis.'

Despite these evasions, Guntrip felt that his relation to Fairbairn had become much more real than it had been in the early dependent and negative transferences of the early stages of the analysis, and he was delighted when he and Bertha received an invitation to be present at the wedding of Fairbairn's daughter, feeling that it was an expression of faith in his 'capacity to deal realistically with the situation on both the social and analytical level'. Fairbairn, however, was careful not to lose sight of the negative transference, and when Guntrip could hardly contain his fury with his mother's assumption that Bertha was waiting to 'take her place' in his life when she died, as if she was 'number one', Fairbairn was quick to describe 'Hate disposal' as 'the real problem in psychotherapy'. He said, 'Patients insist on having bad objects – must have something to kick against. I think since Glover attacked my views, deep down you feel I'm no good as a supporting father to you.' There really seems to be so little evidence for this view that one is bound to wonder whether Fairbairn – the analyst – was intent upon being a bad object – or at least an inadequate one – for Guntrip to 'kick against'. In March Guntrip had responded vigorously to a negative review by Edward Glover of Fairbairn's recently published book, urging Fairbairn to write to the editor of the *Listener* magazine in which the review had appeared. He was to be equally vigorous in his response to the view taken by Winnicott and Masud Khan (1954) 'that if one could escape from Fairbairn's claim that his theory supplants that of Freud we could enjoy the writings of an analyst who challenges everything, and who puts clinical evidence before accepted theory'. Guntrip pointed out that this was no way to advance the cause of any science (see Guntrip 1961, p. 297). There is no sign of disillusionment with Fairbairn in either case. The fact is that a genuine level of professional collaboration had developed between the two men in external reality. In the contentious correspondence over the 'Therapeutic Factor' paper, Fairbairn had already made it clear that he regarded Guntrip as 'not only an adherent but an active participator' in the development of the Object Relations point of view, and that it was 'a great encouragement' to have his 'active support' in this way, (personal communication, 18 May 1952). Moreover, while he expressed his deep appreciation of Guntrip's support in the matter of Glover's review, he had already written himself to the editor of the *Listener*, claiming that Glover had misrepresented his views, making a travesty of them (personal communication, March 1953). During the Easter break, Guntrip reflected that although disposal of hate aroused by the *rejecting object* was indeed a real problem, it did at least amount to a 'negative relationship', whereas the *exciting object* 'who stimulates the small child's need of her by being there, but does nothing to satisfy it properly, gives only a half relationship'. He felt the latter to be more devastating, causing the child to withdraw, 'regressing into an empty objectless world, schizoid'. Fairbairn's own recent evasiveness must surely have stimulated these thoughts and Guntrip once again played with the idea of 'cutting his losses'. But he knew he was 'up against a hidden core' which he was unable to penetrate, and although he knew he had benefited greatly from the analysis, he still felt that he must secure further changes in himself. Fairbairn seemed to be in tune with Guntrip's thoughts about the 'exciting object' when he suggested that the deep tie to his mother arose from his need of her. Guntrip found that suggestion extremely relevant, and for the first time he clearly acknowledged a persisting deep need of mother, underlying and giving rise to his preoccupation with anger and hate, since she had given him 'only the form of a relationship but not the content'. It seems likely that it was entirely due to his new level of confidence in relation to Fairbairn that he could have arrived at this realisation, for without that, he would have had nothing to compare with and no means of distinguishing 'form' from 'content'.

Fairbairn's increasingly positive inner significance for Guntrip was suggested by another dream in which the former was again 'on the platform of father's Mission Hall', but this time lecturing, actively and without 'mother's hard face', while Guntrip too was

active, albeit at a lower level, and not lying passive as in the earlier
dream. Yet the dream contained frustration, for Guntrip felt
constrained to wait for Fairbairn to finish speaking before he
crossed the hall. Moreover, on a conscious level he was evidently
still aware of a barrier of reserve in Fairbairn, for he said, 'It would
do something for me to shake hands with you after the session,
but I feel you may not like it. If I sat on the chair and talked to
you face to face, you might feel awkward and embarrassed.' He did
not realise that he was attributing to Fairbairn in the negative
transference his mother's 'exact reaction on several occasions' when
he had tried to relate to her. Nevertheless, Fairbairn was quick to
confirm that the dream had marked progress, and that it reflected
a breach to some extent of Guntrip's 'closed system of inner
reality'.

A further development occurred when Guntrip made a plain
statement: 'If I could be a naive child with you, I'd get on quicker',
but Fairbairn's response was again reserved and theoretical: 'Is it
better for psychotherapy to uncover the infantile needs and depend-
encies, or to strengthen the adult ego against them? It appears in
fact that uncovering them does help patients grow.' It was surely
this combination of reserve and understanding on Fairbairn's part
which had helped to bring about in Guntrip a sense of 'the deep
loneliness of childhood' in the waiting-room before the session. He
felt that he could 'hear no sound, a mysterious and deathly silence.
Like going to someone and finding no-one there, discharging love
into a vacuum.' When he described this experience in the session
Guntrip found himself wondering if Fairbairn had been with a
female patient in the consulting-room – a primal scene fantasy – or
one expressive of his mother's wish for him to be a girl. But, upon
deeper reflection, he felt that he had conjured up that bad-object
relation as a defence against losing his ego in a vacuum. Fairbairn,
on the other hand, suggested that Guntrip wanted 'comfort or
excitement' from him, 'but not help to get better . . . It's mother
basically. You're wanting a handshake with me in place of her.'
Guntrip later denied that he had felt any desire for 'excitements of
a bodily kind as a substitute', again asserting that 'it would have
made an enormous difference', if Fairbairn had said 'What you
really wanted was some evidence that mother was really interested
in you, cared about you as you.' At the time, however, he could
not find the words, and in the following session he said simply, 'I
feel I have nothing to say. I feel you prohibited my feeling anything
for you.' Fairbairn again described this as 'the hysteric reaction' of
interpreting his remarks as criticism and 'locking everything away

inside'. Guntrip later noted that although Fairbairn had seen that it was the personal relationship of therapist to patient that was the 'curative factor', he was, 'by nature cautious in exploring the possibilities of the outlook'. He also puzzled over Fairbairn's ability to understand, and help him deal with some particularly dependent and demanding patients, thereby showing himself to be accepting of a measure of 'acting out' that certainly not all analysts would have accepted, and with good results. But the fact remained that Guntrip himself was unable to be as naive as these usually seriously disturbed patients, who 'acted out' with little self-consciousness about doing so. He felt that he, by contrast, could not be naive enough, and was not seriously disturbed enough, to be capable of 'acting out' in sessions. Meanwhile Fairbairn's assumption that interpretations that steadily uncovered the excited unsatisfied tensions of the libidinal ego, would promote regrowth to mature selfhood of the *whole* psychic self did not address Guntrip's feeling of not having or being a 'self' to promote. Nevertheless, his struggle to solve that fundamental problem in analysis 'went on ever more unremittingly from 1953 onwards', despite his belief that Fairbairn did not see that in interpreting 'excited body symptoms' he was only 'analysing', and not 'relating' to the deepest withdrawn infant whose need was to be found, and recognised, not merely explained.

Guntrip came very near to expressing the meaning of his 'resistance' when he pointed out that his deep fear that Fairbairn did not want to accept his dependence on him, meant that if he were to relax, what would emerge would be intolerably painful. He said, 'There's some deep fear in me of being overwhelmed by something utterly frightful that I've no means of coping with. This fear is a constant undercurrent.' Fairbairn saw the importance of this, but did not connect it with 'the catastrophe', nor did it occur to either of them to connect it to Guntrip's amnesia. But Fairbairn did make the penetrating observation that when excitement takes the place of an ego-relation, anxiety and excitement become indistinguishable, so that 'if it comes to an end, it is death'. At this, Guntrip felt 'almost reached' in his psychic predicament, but Fairbairn's attention remained fixed upon the analysing of bodily excitements rather than the feeling of 'death' that might underlie an over-mastering need for them. Thus Guntrip began again to feel that he was obliged to be passive and 'rigid' in the analysis. He said, 'I feel I can't make a move unless you give me a lead', a way of expressing the fact that he had felt unable to be real with mother, because fundamentally she was unreal with him, however much she may have 'excited' him inadvertently in the course of bodily handling.

It was at this moment that Fairbairn, with uncharacteristic directness said, 'Well, come and sit on the settee', and although Guntrip had been aware for the last four years of the small settee beside Fairbairn's desk, he made no move and said, 'Oh! dear, [sic] I cannot. For some reason it scares me. I'm suddenly tense in my tummy and tight inside.'

Fairbairn asked, 'What are you afraid of?'

Guntrip replied, 'I'd see you as a human being. I can sit and have sat on the settee to discuss a theoretical paper with you. But as part of my analysis it becomes an emotional issue.'

Fairbairn pointed out that Guntrip was casting him in the rôle of parents, and especially mother, an interpretation which contained sufficient relevance for Guntrip to avoid his own fear of ego-loss in identification to Fairbairn, and to recall instead how his mother had been 'tense and self-conscious' on the few occasions when she spoke to him 'about anything personal', thereby communicating 'her own unnatural state of mind' to him. He therefore attributed his inability to sit near Fairbairn to a feeling that the latter would find it embarrassing if he did so, and inhibit both of them. This having been said, however, he went straight to the settee at his next session and remained there to talk for the remainder of his analysis, building, as he felt, upon the easier relationship he had had with his father, and ascribing his momentary paralysis to a fear that he was about to be 'drawn out into the world of the frightening and preoccupied mother'. In his review in the 1970s Guntrip emphasised the importance of Fairbairn's having made the first move: 'The move had to come from him if it was to make contact with my deepest ego-split.' And, whilst acknowledging that 'neither therapist nor patient could transcend his natural growth-rate in delving into the deepest unconscious', he formed the view that the analysis would have arrived at 'a critical turning-point therapeutically', if Fairbairn could have seen and interpreted that he was contacting the lost, withdrawn child, left in isolation by his mother's inability to relate, and therefore powerless to take the initiative in relating. At the time, however, in 1953, Guntrip unconsciously countered his conscious adoption of the settee by feeling it would be more appropriate to use the couch when dealing with his deepest needs, and to reserve the settee for discussing transference issues. He could only react to the new physical closeness by distancing Fairbairn, keeping him as a 'transference figure'.

Fairbairn allowed Guntrip to reach his own interpretation of his fears of a good relationship. The fear that the love-starved schizoid might destroy the very object with whom he was primarily identified, and so lose himself, was certainly prominent in Guntrip's mind, for he recounted to Fairbairn occasions upon which two of his own female, schizoid patients suddenly broke through their locked-in immobility by rushing at him, trying 'to strangle, bite and tear' at his breasts. He described how he had held their arms firmly enough to control and yet let them work out their basic tension so that quite soon they had stopped and had returned to the chair and talked about their rage at the mother who had starved them. This was clearly a message to Fairbairn who concurred, 'Some patients can get completely blocked just lying on the couch talking. They may never get any further if there is no acting out.' The indirect nature of this reply ('some patients') was matched by Guntrip's own tentative exploration as to whether he – that is, he as therapist – could have handled a male patient as successfully. He recalled having walked arm in arm with a male patient at the departmental clinic who was 'screaming his head off' while two colleagues waited outside the door, ready to assist if necessary. He was certainly investigating the question of whether Fairbairn could handle a similar outburst in himself – but the issue was not directly addressed by either, and the only suggestion of 'acting out' in this last session before the summer holiday was expressed by a desire on Guntrip's part to take some of Fairbairn's books out of his bookcase and put them back again. Fairbairn acceded to this need and his acceptance of this simple but deeply symbolic action was later felt by Guntrip to be an essential recognition of a need to get something out of Fairbairn which mother could never give.

During the summer, the physical condition of Guntrip's mother worsened, and she was taken into hospital in early September. Consciously Guntrip was mightily relieved, and he and Bertha motored together up to Edinburgh for his second session of the autumn term with a new sense of freedom. The unconscious effect was very different, for Guntrip suddenly and repeatedly saw a mental picture of his mother's face, hard, cold, severe, non-human, and never looking at him. He told Fairbairn that it felt to him like the permanent unalterable background of his inner mental life: 'a sad, empty, embittered non-relation'. Consciously, Guntrip hoped his mother would die, for her own sake, and for his, and Bertha's. He dreamed of a lion or lioness (he was uncertain which) in a large, glass-fronted room. He went in with a large spear to ward it off and then backed out, keeping an eye on it. As he got out, it bounded up to the doors. Then he was in a room with a sleeping leopard sprawled on rugs. He put his hand on its head and kept it there to keep it quiet, while he sidled round to the door and backed out. The glass-fronted room resembled the hospital ward where his mother lay, and the scene reminded him of his wariness of her moods when they visited: she might 'spring' at any moment. The sprawling leopard, he had no doubt, represented his own life-long accumulated rage against his mother, and at bottom his 'object-seeking' libidinal need for her, upon which he must keep a tight hold by means of repression. Although Fairbairn offered a different interpretation in terms of castration fears, maintaining that the leopard was Guntrip's penis which he was holding down[1] – a kind of self-castration – Guntrip was convinced that a more fundamental fear was involved. He had felt in the dream that the lion(ess) would kill him if he gave it the chance, hence the 'Nimrod' spear. For him sex and gender were secondary: he felt his life was at stake, and he was not 'cutting off' the leopard but controlling it, as he had to with his emotion about his mother.

Guntrip was genuinely upset when Fairbairn interpreted several short dreams of his being in Fairbairn's house as expressing a homosexual wish following castration fantasies. He felt that this line of interpretation imposed theory upon the realities of his need to find a good father in Fairbairn at this critical period when his mother was dying. The dreams reminded him of his longing for a good relationship with his father, whom he consciously wished had outlived his mother. Fairbairn's apparent retreat into theory made Guntrip wonder if his mother's impending death had reactivated Fairbairn's earlier emotional disturbance over his wife's death. Looking back at this time twenty years later he felt sure that he would have been helped had Fairbairn simply said: 'You are facing the fact that your mother is soon going to die, and you must have very mixed feelings about that. What are you feeling?' He felt that the current real-life bad-object situation was absorbing all his mental energy, for his mother was getting restive and troublesome in hospital and had to be restrained, while he and Bertha felt helpless to influence the situation. He dreamed of accepting a call back into the ministry, as if he felt the need for a warm family life to belong to, similar to the Salvation Army of his childhood days. But in the dream, he did not abandon psychotherapy, feeling that it represented the only way out of his unconscious isolation, and he withdrew from the church. He longed to be able to summon up real feeling for his dying mother, but none would come. In his unconscious he transferred his initial experience of isolation to

Fairbairn, by dreaming of accepting an invitation to a meal at his house, only to find no-one knew or spoke to him, leaving him feeling alone. His mother's terminal state had exposed his ultimate problem, of being physically with someone, yet utterly without any relationship and unable to make it from his side. The need for someone to reach through to him was expressed in a stark dream:

> I was locked in alone, struggling with something I couldn't get free of and felt hopeless. Would anyone break in and rescue me?

It was a problem he could not solve alone, and yet Fairbairn did not seem to have the key to recognising it and knowing how to help him, for, according to Guntrip, 'he was still interpreting in terms of feeling castrated, wanting father's or mother's penis, being a man or a woman, hetereosexual or homosexual trends'. Thus Fairbairn was apparently unable to see that the deeply isolated schizoid individual, like the very early infant, cannot begin to make a personal relation from his side, but needs the psychotherapist, like a maternal mother, to evoke in him the beginnings of personal-relatedness. Instead of relating in that deeply personal way, Fairbairn appears to have 'commented upon' and described Guntrip's states from outside that area of experience, making such remarks as, 'That's what the hysteric always wants', and 'Locked up inside yourself with the mother who beats you. A perpetual orgasm of suffering and no relief.' Yet it was slowly becoming clear to Guntrip that in the lack of a true recognition of his deepest unmet need, the 'orgasm of suffering' in which he was locked with mother could indeed be no other than perpetual, since it represented all he had known of a 'relationship' with his mother, for he had never been a 'person' to her and she had never been a 'person' to him. It seems that Fairbairn exhorted Guntrip to defy his mother as an internal bad object and 'thus to be himself', whereas the latter knew that to do so would only have ensured the perpetuation of a running battle. It would never have resulted in the development of a naturally secure sense of himself.

In fact the strains imposed by the death of his wife and the recent marriage of his daughter had meant that Fairbairn's private life had undergone a drastic change over the previous twelve months. In late October, when Guntrip arrived for his early session before catching the train back to Leeds, he had to knock persistently at Fairbairn's door before the latter emerged in his dressing-gown, apologising for having overslept. Indeed, he looked unwell, and at the end of that session he said he felt that the early

morning session had begun to be too much for him, and it was
agreed that it should be discontinued. After a week's break, Guntrip settled into a new routine of three sessions a week – one on
Tuesday evening and two on Wednesday in time for him to catch
the Wednesday evening train home. Guntrip felt that this deterioration in Fairbairn's general health and well-being had contributed
to the latter's failure to respond to him as a person. In practice
Fairbairn seems to have assumed that Guntrip could give up the
masochistic struggle to get his implacable mother to respond, once
it was pointed out to him that it was futile. Guntrip, however, felt
that the part of him that was fixed in that struggle had nothing
else, and that to give it up would mean falling into an impersonal
world with the mother who neither saw him nor wanted him. As
it stood, the therapeutic relationship offered no help with that
deeper problem, because it continually fell just short of a security-
giving, growth-fostering, personal relationship. But, as his mother's
illness entered its final phase, Guntrip almost secured from Fairbairn the vital recognition. He described how he felt 'a permanent
blank' where there should be a relation to mother, and a strong
sense of the patient's need for the analyst to be a real good object
to him as a foundation for his personal development. Fairbairn
replied: 'Yes, the patient has got nothing at first in his inner world
to build on. He only has the analyst. Analysts tend to regard the
patient's dependence as a nuisance, a menace, but they need someone to fill the gap, the blank you were talking about this morning.'
Here, Guntrip was able to break through the 'third person' references to the 'patient' and the 'analyst' and say, 'I feel I can build
you in as the concrete foundation where mother left an emptiness.'

At this point sessions ended for six weeks due to Harriet's
terminal condition. As he sat through the night with his dying
mother Guntrip was appalled by the sense of 'a total gulf' which
lay between them as if some part of him 'had simply never come
alive in relation to her and could not now do so'. She died the
following morning while Guntrip was at the department clinic.
Both he and Bertha were horrified by the expression on his mother's face, her 'death mask' as he was later describe it, set in 'a cold,
cynical smirk, an arch superior smile, a look of triumph which
seemed to say, "I've got the better of you all in the end"'. He had
seen this expression many times before, and he recalled a family
photograph when he was about fourteen, in which his mother was
'looking away into the far distance as if she were not part of the
occasion', and he commented, 'She had retained her independence
and her need to get the better of everyone to the bitter end, at the

price of isolating herself from us, and isolating us from herself.' The one sign he was able to detect that there was 'a part of her that still felt human need and dependency, pushed away behind her compulsive "fighting self", was a distracted cry in the hospital: 'Am I in Bertha's house?' Her ashes were buried in Guntrip's father's grave at Benfleet. Fairbairn's letter of condolence illustrates the warmth of his feeling for Guntrip at the time. The letter is a classic example of how deep feeling can be expressed through formal language. Fairbairn wrote:

> These will be sad days for you, with much thought and questioning; but I feel that at any rate you have no real occasion for self-reproach, and that your mother was very fortunate to have so considerate a son . . . It will take you some time to settle down, I expect, after all the distress of recent months, as you watched your mother's health fail under such distressing conditions; but I believe that in the end you will emerge from these dark days with your spirit enriched.
>
> With my deepest sympathy and best wishes for the years to come.
>
> Yours very sincerely,
>
> W. Ronald D. Fairbairn.

The conscious sense of relief at his mother's passing was indeed very great. Guntrip wrote: 'At long last, after twenty-five years, and even thirty-one years, including the University period, we were free from my mother's active and hostile and unremitting interference.' He and Bertha were able to develop their shared interests in music and literature, and they began regularly to spend their holidays in the Lake District and Scotland, often visiting Bertha's mother and aunt in their cottage in Perthshire.

Note

1 Fairbairn's (1954) account of this dream appears in his paper 'Observations on the Nature of Hysterical States' (pp. 114–15) in which Guntrip is given the pseudonymn 'Jack'. See also Hazell 1994, p. 12.

CHAPTER 12

1954

Gradually Guntrip's feelings about his mother began to return on two different levels. Whereas he was consciously aware of feeling a deep sadness and distress at the profound loneliness that he knew lay at the heart of his mother's aggressiveness, his unconscious mind alternated between trying to keep her with him either by being identified or by bad relations with her. When sessions were resumed he reported a severe pain in his right arm near the shoulder which had begun shortly before his mother died, but which had intensified after her death. It had the character of a 'hysterical conversion', by which he was maintaining an internal bad-object relation with his beating mother in his own body, and thereby 'keeping her alive'. However, he was surprised and relieved when Fairbairn examined his arm, testing the muscles and reflexes, and he experienced the same sense of security which his father's presence had always evoked. He suspected that the pain was at the spot where his mother had gripped him with her left arm when she gave him the biggest beating, and it would seem that Fairbairn, at that moment, clearly saw how utterly alone Guntrip must have felt as a child, and still felt inwardly, for he said, 'One patient says she needs me, not as a person, but as "everything", the world, the universe. It's what the mother is to the new born or unborn baby.' Since his health had deteriorated Fairbairn had taken to citing instances of what other patients needed of him, partly in recognition of a growing professional equality between Guntrip and himself and partly as a way of tentatively exploring possible needs in Guntrip. This formal and rather distant kindness reminded Guntrip greatly of his father who, like Fairbairn, was available only at certain times, but whose importance as 'a protector' was out of all proportion to his physical availability. He had always appeared as a good figure in Guntrip's dreams, and the latter now felt that Fairbairn was able to build on the positive experience both in sessions and more especially in the post-sessional discussions, which he experienced as not only professionally and intellectually valuable, but also as slowly making the difference to his unconscious sense of loneliness at home. At this time, Guntrip re-experienced in a dream his profound grief at his father's death, and he felt that his ability to do so was due to his father's having been a good object to him whereas his mother as a bad object gave him no relationship to mourn the loss of, only a sense of perpetual struggle for recognition. Guntrip even realised that part of that struggle had taken the form of caring for his brother Percy during his short life. He had, he felt, projected into Percy the 'self' that he felt his mother gave nothing to and failed to relate to, in an attempt to get a sense of being real after all, so that when Percy died he nearly died with him. Meanwhile, he was coming to feel that Fairbairn gave him far more than his father had. He wrote in his notes,

> Fairbairn gives me far more than I got from father, stimulus as well as an example, but also I am more free to make my own use of that, an objectively stimulating relation of discussion, shared ideas, mutual give and take and mutual respect, the dissolving of mere identification and positive transference; an interaction of two persons.

From the vantage point of the 1970s Guntrip was able to see how close Fairbairn had come to the insights of Winnicott, particularly when the former cited a patient who had convinced him that severe hysterics could be reduced to such a degree of helplessness that when they said 'I can't help myself', the only therapeutic way forward was to believe them and see that it was actually true. Thus, treating them meant being 'prepared to break the orthodox rules, let them ring you up, not stick to a rigid timetable. They need more contact.' However, it was, as Guntrip saw, not only 'contact' that the 'hysteric' needed, but to be seen and related to as a real person in his own right, in a way which the parent had been incapable of. Only this could release the unevoked capacities of his natural self, whereas merely supportive treatment was apt to prolong the patient's basic helplessness. However, Guntrip fairly states that no-one at this date had seen what he believed to be the deepest problem, although Winnicott and Balint were working their way towards it. At this stage he simply knew that he could not by himself remedy the basic initial failure of true maternalism in his first year, and that, despite his genuine feeling for him at other levels, Fairbairn, like his father, could not reach him at that most profound level, where his mother showed no interest in him, and thus evoked no genuine response from him, so that he felt basically ignored, depersonalised and helpless. It was not even *bodily* contact that he needed primarily, but a relationship of personal recognition, specifically related to his childhood situation, in which that deepest helpless part of him could begin to become alive and to grow. At this stage, he could not achieve such clarity and Fairbairn could not see it.

Slowly however, the problem of *feelings of unreality* was assuming prominence in their discussions. Guntrip mentioned a young, female patient, diagnosed psychiatrically as a borderline schizophrenic, who needed to sit close to him in order to feel safe. She had had exceptionally bad mothering, an unwanted child whose father had deserted her mother, and mother had to dump her with an aunt and go to work all day. At first, Guntrip had thought her desire to sit close to him was 'resistance to analysis', but he came to believe that it was 'a genuine feeling of helplessness at a distance' and that the patient felt more related and real when close to him, for as her feeling of safety increased the patient found she could respond to her husband at home. Reviewing this case in the 1970s, Guntrip described how the patient came to see that it was not mere juxtaposition but 'being understood and accepted as real' that brought about the feeling of safety and personal reality. At this stage, in 1954, although Guntrip himself had not reached quite that level of insight in his own treatment, he had come to feel more real since he had 'given up the couch'. However, he sometimes felt that even the small space between the settee and Fairbairn's desk was 'a gulf', which he felt unable to cross from his side: '*not mustn't but really can't*'. He told Fairbairn, 'If I got to feel really isolated, you would have to see my need, and come to my rescue, offer me some physical contact to save me from mental isolation'. Thus the need for physical contact to be initiated by Fairbairn was the only form in which, at this time, he could express his own feeling of incompleteness. He was not angry with Fairbairn as he had been with his mother, nor was he hungry for Fairbairn as with mother. Rather he was *lonely* in the therapeutic setting, waiting for a gap to be bridged. Beneath the aspect of mother that excited his rage was the mother who failed to relate at all. He wondered why his mother had to send him to Aunt Dolly after Percy died. What was wrong with her? Why could she herself not nurse him back to life? Part of him remained 'paralysed in initiative' and unable to know exactly what was needed. Sometimes he longed for Fairbairn to 'invade the region'. Indeed he was at a loss to explain what more Fairbairn *could* do, or what he had a right to expect of his analyst! He said, 'Your careful listening and sometimes taking notes of what I say has been a valuable form of "taking me seriously". Your treating me as a partner in theoretical interests, lending me your papers, reading and discussing mine, has been an invaluable stimulus. I have a firmer self-confidence. You have helped my conscious development as perhaps no-one else has done, and made up for father's rather passive lack of direct interest. But now I need you to be a father who can counteract mother's crushing power who can be active against mother.' Remarkably, Fairbairn saw more deeply. He said, *'Perhaps not that, but you need me now to be a good mother to you'*. This was indeed what Guntrip needed. But it seemed that, despite the penetrating insight, neither knew in experience what being a good mother was like. Guntrip's mother was either punitive insofar as he was active or physically caring insofar as he was passive and ill: 'the cane or the tent-bed. Otherwise she was in the shop absorbed in her own interests.' Sutherland (1989) informs us that 'the family atmosphere into which . . . Fairbairn was born in 1889 was pervaded by the contradictions of devoted loving care, combined with oppressive strictness . . . Most prominent, perhaps, was the fact that his exacting mother maintained an over-intensive supervision of all his activities throughout his early years' (p. 1), forbidding him to touch his penis except when washing or urinating (pp. 66–7). Sutherland also notes that 'the early bad experiences had engendered a continuing strong attachment to his mother' so that he was 'somewhat depressed for a considerable time' after her death in 1946 (p. 134).

As if in acknowledgement of his own inability to conceptualise therapeutic regression, Fairbairn had generously put Guntrip in touch with Winnicott, asking Winnicott to send Guntrip a copy of his paper 'Metapsychological and Clinical Aspects of Regression within the Psychoanalytical Set-up' (Winnicott 1954, in Winnicott 1958). The paper was to have a decisive effect upon Guntrip. At this time, however, it was not about his own needs, but those of his female patient that Guntrip wrote, at some length, to Winnicott, with positive results. Guntrip was quick to spot the relevance of Winnicott's work to his own predicament, feeling that there was 'a maturational process' going on in him deep down, of which he said to Fairbairn, 'I feel I can do nothing to hurry it. It will break surface when ready.' He felt it was in some sense 'positively related' to Fairbairn but he could still only see his analyst as chiefly 'a protector against the crushing internalised mother', and not as the primary facilitator of the infant's 'true self'. As the Easter break approached, Guntrip felt that they had approached 'nearer and deeper towards the ultimate problem in the preceding three and a half months than ever before'. He recalled a pre-analysis dream of being drawn towards absorption into the dead Percy: the catastrophe he nearly succumbed to once, and a possible origin of the deep feeling of fatalistic hopelessness which was always there deep down. He said, *'It's not exactly that mother kills people but rather that she can't keep them alive. She doesn't know how to.* If one can keep alive without her help then she can boss and castrate, but that's a very secondary peril compared with the ultimate one to which I nearly succumbed at three and a half.' In the sense that Guntrip was still in the grip of the deep problem, he could only remain aware of it temporarily, and he was always being drawn back to the repetitive theme of sexualised bad-object relations with a castrating mother. And Fairbairn, perhaps because of similar experiences with his own mother, tended still to make literal sexual interpretations. Thus the stalemate continued, though Guntrip had a penetrating insight, when, in the course of developing a fantasy of mother bursting through the bookcase into Fairbairn's consulting room, he suddenly began to see her turning into a corpse, and then into a ghost-like figure as if she herself was not really alive, but only 'going through frightening motions, perhaps to make herself feel alive'. Indeed it seems entirely likely that Guntrip's mother was exhausted by having been prematurely responsible for the care of her own siblings, and without any real parenting herself, so that her 'energy and determination', which often became vicious in the face of her children's needs of her, were, like Guntrip's own energies, the result of a desperate attempt to function effectively and meet responsibilities which she felt were beyond her. As Guntrip himself commented, it was as if she had only enough mother-wit to know that she did not know how to be a mother, and to send him away to the motherly Aunt Dolly when Percy died. He felt that she was unable to evoke any feeling in him other than an 'unhealthy excitement' when her driven energies were expressed in power over him, by means of suppositories, rubbing spots, the tent-bed, cleaning his penis, or beating him. Thus, any excited feeling tended to become swallowed up in an unhealthily stimulated tension, due to a morbid compulsion on his mother's part to interfere with his body. That gave rise in turn to an equally 'unhealthy' over-excited urge to turn the tables on her, symbolised by the Nimrod scene and the worm dream. Yet beneath that actively negative influence lay the other mother of whom his one clear memory was of her completely ignoring him at eight years old, when he climbed on her lap, so that he slipped off again 'almost feeling "nothing", a blank'. It is unlikely that this event would have been remembered, or have evoked such a strong reaction, had it been an isolated example, rather than a sign of the mother who was herself 'not really alive'.

At this point, Guntrip had been in analysis for exactly five years. He had not envisaged being able to carry on so long, and at fifty-three he was thinking in terms of one further year – mainly because of financial restraints as he planned towards retirement, but also for the sake of his relationship with Bertha which had been so restricted by his visits to Edinburgh. Yet the analysis remained among the most significant experiences of his life, without which he would never have known consciously 'the enormous extent' of his mother's interference in private spheres that do not naturally involve another person – an interference which Fairbairn believed came close to Freud's early view of parental seduction. Even so, what his mother could not do seemed to him more impossible to cope with than what she did, and he wanted to reach a 'real result' in the analysis, notwithstanding his previous realisation that there could be no hurrying of the process. Fairbairn responded by saying that he was now sixty-five and that it would suit him if Guntrip could finish in about a year, as he felt he needed to reduce his commitments – a response which produced a certain ambivalence in Guntrip! Almost predictably, the prospect of ending analysis – albeit at a year's remove, set up separation-anxiety in Guntrip which in turn caused a recurrence of sado-masochistic fantasy. Since Harriet's death, he and Bertha had begun reading to each other in the evening, and at this time he had been reading of the thrashing of Squires in *Nicholas Nickleby*. The night after mentioning this in his session he felt a return of the 'sharp nervy working feelings in my body, and wanting to wriggle and squirm, as I did when mother caned me'. He later believed that this had been 'the first clear immediate recognition of that type of body tension as a re-experiencing of mother's canings'.

As the sessions proceeded, the defensive sado-masochistic emphasis yielded to the underlying problem of a deep inertia, and inability to get down to work or to concentrate. Two stark dreams returned Guntrip to the basic problem: In the first he was 'living in reduced circumstances', and in the second he dreamed simply 'I was going to die.' The thought came to him of lying dying on his mother's lap, and he arrived at a penetrating insight which was to be remarkably confirmed in his dreaming in 1971-72. He said to Fairbairn, 'While Percy lived I had someone to live for. When he died, hope died, and I feel I fell ill of despair.' He saw that although his mother was 'a destroyer' her primary aim was to use the members of the family to keep herself alive, because her own parents had never helped her really to be 'alive'. She had felt betrayed by Henry and Mary dying on her, and Guntrip believed that he himself would have died before her had he stayed with her in the business as she had wished, only to be 'frustrated and used up by her'. And, although he had got away, if only with his conscious self, thus holding open the chance of growing free of her at deeper levels, his real unconscious fear of destruction was borne out by an odd dream:

> Someone called out loud in the night several times 'Murder'. But I hadn't heard. I'd been asleep.

The dream demonstrated the extent to which his conscious mind had shut off from his inner trauma. But he was equally afraid that, by shutting off all feeling, he would be unwittingly destructive. Thus he dreamed again:

> I was alone and made a terrific hit with a baseball club . . .
> The ball soared out of sight. It was not so much strength as skill and timing. I wondered if it would hurt anyone in falling.

The dream seemed to refer to the period when he was 'growing away' both from mother and from his conscious need of her, and Fairbairn observed: 'This is narcissistic activity, all by yourself. Narcissistic activity is not a real relation with anyone. Hence your fear that it might have a destructive effect and hurt someone if it gets loose.' Guntrip had thought of the ball he hit as tied to the bat, 'like an umbilical cord, and if it breaks, the ball, the baby, flies off into space, terrified. That's the result of trying to break away from mother.' But, as he saw, he was in no better position when tied to her because he still would have no genuine relationship. He felt acutely aware of the futility of his existence, not so much in his analysis or professional life, and not in his marriage, but deep down within his personality, a sense of something static and unchanging.

The feeling of stalemate lasted through the summer break, despite an invitation from Fairbairn to Guntrip and Bertha to have tea with him on their way through Edinburgh to visit Bertha's mother and aunt. Perhaps this was in part an attempt on Fairbairn's part to phase out the analysis, or to extend the limits of psychotherapy, as he felt to be appropriate for some hysteric patients. But despite its benefits on the human, social and professional level, this acceptance of Guntrip as 'a person in his own right' did not by itself reach the unrelated child in the unconscious: it needed somehow to be 'explicitly interpreted to the child-who-could-not-get-a-relation with mother'. Reiteratively identifying the sado-masochistic bad relations between Guntrip and his mother could not in itself achieve this end, and Guntrip recognised that his feelings for Fairbairn were not as strong as the latter's generosity warranted in realistic terms. Neither man knew how to proceed when Guntrip dreamed, 'I was in a shut-in space, no air, couldn't breathe.' He said to Fairbairn, 'I need you to get me out of this. I can't get out by myself.' Somewhere in him he felt 'dead with mother and one with Percy', buried in a complete amnesia. So unchanging was this sense of part of him 'buried alive', and so oblivious to the clear benefits of the analysis in other respects, that he wondered if he was sabotaging his own treatment. He scanned his life-story in vain for evidence of self-sabotage. But, as he did so, he suddenly felt a conviction that he would in the end achieve a successful result which would have its roots in his experience of having come to feel 'more real and solid in himself in relation to Fairbairn', and that this would play a vital part in enabling him to face whatever lay behind the amnesia for Percy's death. He also saw the tomb-man dream in terms not of 'castration' but of a total personality problem, for whereas he was unable to stir when he 'lay there all alone', as soon as 'someone' (the 'I' of the dream), came in, the tomb-man became able to move. Personal relation had restored life and it was only a fear that the tomb-man's emergence would mean illness that caused the 'I' of the dream to threaten him with the doctor and nurse, repress him and rush out, as if being active depended upon the continued repression of his paralysed natural self. He recalled how in the dark times at Salem he would have to retire exhausted to bed in the evening, his body quite dead and absent, leaving only his 'mental self, a bare point of existence, doing nothing, queer, like that tomb dream, buried alive in an emptiness'. The need for a parent with whom to be reborn was simply expressed in a dream:

Dicks sent me a letter simply to say 'Freud has a son'

and he said to Fairbairn, 'Freud must be you. I'm reborn with a new parent.'

Fairbairn had made hardly any interpretations since his statement in the summer about ending analysis after a further year. It seemed to Guntrip that he had come to realise that the old internal bad-object terms were no longer relevant to his problem, and that he was waiting and watching to see its deeper signifance. Guntrip appears not to have noticed any significant connection between Fairbairn's having introduced him to Winnicott's work so soon after his perception that he needed to be a 'good mother' to Guntrip, and his announcement shortly afterwards of his wish to retire. At any rate, Guntrip proceeded to develop the theme of 'rebirth'. He observed that he was unable to resolve the problems of the internalised bad-object mother, 'on the analytical way down', until he could 'reach some point of stability in a "good-object experience" as a base to build on and resolve them on the way up again'. He had found with his own most ill patients that at the deepest level they encountered not simply 'a hell of bad-object experiences', but 'a vacuum of good-object experiences' and thus had 'nothing with which to work towards recovery'. At this point in his analysis he was encouraged to feel in a 'stronger strategic position' to face his deeply repressed traumatic experience. He dreamed of clearing a garden and noticing some small late-blooming hydrangeas, which he thought would do better still next year, and produced a fantasy of a woman, whom he felt to be Aunt Dolly, putting him to bed with her own children, rescuing him from his antilibidinal mother and, most importantly, bringing him to life again. He felt that the fantasy contained a real element of memory. However, he felt and expressed genuine anger at Fairbairn's failure to co-operate with his new conviction, or to clarify for him the significance of his schizoid symptoms. He felt 'stuck and angry', and when he felt a resurgence of his boyhood state, wandering about aimlessly in an empty world, so that bodily contact seemed suddenly very important, Fairbairn merely replied, 'That's typical of hysterics.' Similarly, when Guntrip mentioned marked feelings of being 'worn out, lifeless, drained of energy' so that he could only slump in a chair, Fairbairn simply commented, 'Therapeutic regression' – almost, it would appear, as an 'aside', for, as he later told Guntrip, he had never been able to fit 'regression' into his scheme of endo-psychic structure, and so could not interpret it. The frustration which Guntrip felt was compounded by his own incomprehension. He said, 'I can't ask for what I want because I don't know what it is. It's never been given to me.' Towards the outside world he felt 'a sort of lifeless despair and rejection of it' and had fallen back into himself, in a way which had been noticed by Bertha at home. Later it seemed to him that he had been near to breaking the amnesia for Percy's death through reliving the illness that followed it. At the time he said, 'On last Sunday morning I felt like a child of one year old, and can't get them to understand what it is I need. I'm lonely, cut-off, out of touch, because they are inaccessible and they don't understand. I'm puzzled, hopeless and helpless, can't find a way of opening their eyes to the fact and they haven't got the human intuition to see it. I don't even know what it is I need. If mother had been a real mother she would have met that need without my needing to know what it was. I feel I may end the analysis no better, in a deplorable state, suicide and writing to you and saying, "sorry", I've done my best but can't go on like this.' He later felt that by 'suicide' he had meant a reliving of his near-death experience with his uncomprehending mother, simply fading right away. This was, undoubtedly, the nadir of his analytic experience with Fairbairn, for it was accompanied after five and a half years and 736 sessions by a return of all his old symptoms 'as bad as ever, bad sleep, blocked nose, acidity, feeling physically jaded'. He said, 'I feel mother gave me *things*; she didn't give me herself as a person.' Fairbairn interpreted: 'You feel she didn't give you her body', which represented a complete inability to comprehend Guntrip's state, similar to his mother's incomprehension, for the body, the breast, was all his mother could give. Guntrip's problem was that she could not give herself. As Guntrip later realised, at this time in 1954 Winnicott's work on therapeutic regression and its relation to the early stages of ego-development was only just emerging in print, while Fairbairn himself assumed the baby to be a whole individual at birth and simply did not think in terms of bad mothering causing an initial failure of ego-development, an experience of emptiness and non-relationship. He therefore continued to interpret the bad-object world as primary and causal, and Guntrip's preoccupation with it as due to a fear of the emergence of incestuous wishes and acts in fantasy. His assumption was therefore that the therapeutic relation-ship with himself should be adequate to enable Guntrip to release his incestuous 'clinging to mother very deep down', because he recog-nised Guntrip as a person in his own right. Guntrip, however, could not proceed unless and until Fairbairn could see and relate to his unmothered core, that was too undeveloped to take the initiative, and the reaction of his adult conscious self was one of angry desperation. He said, 'I feel in real danger of reaching the end of my ability to go on with analysis . . . Though my health has improved so much, *it is now worse than at the beginning.* I feel in a bitter, disillusioned mood. I feel your views on analysis are after all bankrupt and useless as therapy'. Fairbairn again replied that Guntrip felt compelled to sacrifice both himself and his cure in analysis to his secret inner fantasy life. However, what really compelled Guntrip to cling to his inner fantasy life was a dread of the emptiness and weakness which he felt was the only alternative. He felt he had nothing and no-one basically to cling to and no ego to cling with. He did not feel he was enjoying a secret world of hidden satisfactions, but that he was lost in a vacuum of non-relationship. Fairbairn's insistence that Guntrip was secretly so enjoying possessing his mother as an internalised bad object, that his own therapeutic interventions were resisted as an 'encroachment', found expression in his paper 'On the Nature of Hysterical States' in that same year, where he demonstrated how the hysteric maintains a 'closed system' from which he feels the analyst must be excluded. But neither in this paper, nor in his later clinical paper on 'On the Nature and Aims of Psychoanalytical Treatment' (1958) did he consider the possibility that the closed system of internal reality may be maintained as a defence, not only against therapeutic intervention, but also against an undeveloped ego in the unconscious. For Fairbairn the ego was a unity at birth, possessed of active libidinal object-seeking energies. He therefore assumed that Guntrip maintained a deep hidden and continual possession of his 'original simple primary enjoyment of mother', as if he was unable to conceive of a 'seriously non-maternal mother'.

Two weeks before the Christmas break Guntrip dreamed of the last session before Christmas. He delayed the ending of the session in his dream, fumbling with some notes, trying to find something he wanted to show Fairbairn, but could not. Eventually they left together in a taxi. But suddenly they were back in Fairbairn's rooms and the session was ending again, whereupon Fairbairn looked Guntrip full in the face with an easy kindly smile and put a hand on his shoulder. It seemed to Guntrip that the dream was an expression of his faith in Fairbairn, which was fully justified at the adult level in terms of the latter's reliability. He felt safe to leave because there would be no breakdown of relations behind his back, despite his having been unable to get his deepest need across to Fairbairn. He felt that the last three and a half months had been a critical turning-point in the analysis, having brought him steadily to the point where he had almost succeeded in getting the amnesia for Percy's death into consciousness, and the illness that followed it. He had felt as near a return of his previous exhaustion illness as was possible without becoming too ill to work or travel, and he determined to continue.

Transition

CHAPTER 13

1955–62

The year 1954 was effectively a turning point that marked the start of a period of transition, leading in 1962 to Guntrip's decision to enter analysis with D.W. Winnicott in London – involving a journey as far to the south of Leeds as Edinburgh was to the north. The framework of analytic sessions with Fairbairn continued, albeit at a reduced frequency, but the discipline of analytic neutrality had been relaxed, and while the therapeutic relationship never reassumed its previous formality, neither did it quite penetrate to the deepest layer of Guntrip's pathology. As already mentioned Guntrip had followed up his introduction to Winnicott with a lengthy correspondence concerning his own treatment, by a controlled therapeutic regression, of one of his own borderline patients,[1] whose deepest needs could not be met by the giving of interpretations at the right moment. Winnicott had affirmed the rightness of moving beyond interpretative technique to a nurturant holding of the more severely ill patient: 'In the more severe cases, this probably becomes the main thing over a phase. Some people think analysis has been abandoned when the analyst acts so, but I am sure that these people fail with analyses that could have succeeded' (personal communication, August 1954). But he had also warned Guntrip that the analyst's 'survival' could become an issue as the patient emerges from regression: 'You have been able to follow the patient's regression to dependence and to be in the place of an early mother-figure. I would think that there might be very great hate of you because of this position that you have taken as the patient emerges from the regression and therefore becomes aware of the dependence. If one is not expecting this, one may be puzzled at the tremendous hate which turns up within the love relationship in these more regressed states' (ibid.). The subject of the inevitability of the patient's hate of the analyst remained unsettled eight years later when Guntrip entered analysis with Winnicott. He himself believed that the dissolution of unconscious dependence, when not frustrated but facilitated by the parent/analyst, did not inevitably involve hate, but could give rise to vigorous and enthusiastic 'healthy rivalry' –

even though this could 'become hate' to whatever extent the parent/ analyst failed to survive the patient's energetic interactivity. However this may be, the fact of overriding importance for Guntrip was Winnicott's recognition of the need for nurturant holding which he sensed within himself, and when his sessions with Fairbairn were resumed in 1955 he made a private note in his record that he felt Fairbairn could not do much more for him, and he wondered about going to Winnicott, though noting that he 'would not seriously have made such a move at that date'. Nevertheless, a point of no return had been reached. Fairbairn had published his paper 'Observations on the Nature of Hysterical States' in the same year as Winnicott produced his paper on regression, 1954. Whereas the former deals with the problem of how 'libidinal charges become . . . damned up in organic systems' (p. 124), as with Guntrip's own psychosomatic symptoms of congested sinus, anal retentiveness and acid stomach, the latter addresses the more profound question of the patient's feelings of non-existence, the very problem to which Guntrip had been trying to draw Fairbairn's attention. In his paper, Fairbairn, referring to Guntrip under the pseudonym 'Jack', claims that the congested sinus improved markedly in response to his interpretations in terms of internalised libidinised and antilibidinised bad-object conflicts, an improvement confirmed by Guntrip in his record. But Guntrip also makes the point that this 'real gain', though it 'represented a genuine psychoanalytical breakthrough in a whole defensive area' had 'come to be treated as an end in itself and not recognised as a defence against something deeper to which such terms as "schizoid" and "regression" pointed me'. By comparison Winnicott's paper must have come as a revelation to him at this point, when he and Fairbairn were thinking in terms of one further year of analysis and settling for an incomplete result. Even so, in correspondence with Winnicott, who had invited him to 'have a look into the matter of [his] relationship to psychoanalysis' . . . so that he could 'have [his] relationship and not Fairbairn's' (personal communication, 13 August 1954), Guntrip made it clear that his attitude to Freud had been formulated before he met Fairbairn or read his papers, and that he independently regarded Fairbairn's theory as a 'simple, accurate, and strictly scientific' statement of 'endopsychic development by splitting in reaction to a bad object environment which has been internalised (or magically incorporated) to master it' (personal communication, August 1954). He did, however, relay Winnicott's views to Fairbairn, who replied that he found Winnicott's attitude to his theories 'rather tiresome; and I think it is a pity that he is so obviously desirous to wean you from them'. While he expressed interest in Winnicott's support of 'active psychotherapy in regressed cases, and that he does not regard this as involving an abandonment of the analytical method', Fairbairn agreed with Guntrip that Winnicott had not really grasped the fundamental principles involved in the object-relations theory of the personality and the theory of the dynamic structure. In particular Fairbairn felt that Winnicott, following Melanie Klein, failed to distinguish between introjection of good experience, the effects of which are registered in satisfactory ego-development, and internalisation of bad experience, which results in the establishment of internal objects as differentiated structures.[2] In his letter to Guntrip, Winnicott had suggested that Fairbairn, in stating that only bad experience was internalised to form internal bad objects, was implicitly denying the original introjection of the good object on the basis of which the inner world is built up. Such confusion of 'processes that are logically distinct and speaking of them as identical' wrote Fairbairn, was really due, in his opinion, 'to faulty and slovenly conceptualisation' on the part of Winnicott. He was clearly nettled, and concluded, 'It is interesting, in view of the fuss which Winnicott makes over my emphasis on the original internalisation of bad objects, that he should go on to complain that, in doing so, I am spoiling my good work "by making a point of disagreeing with Melanie Klein over an *unimportant matter*". If it is so unimportant why make such a fuss?' (personal communication, 30 August 1954). As mentioned earlier, Guntrip had himself made a stand on Fairbairn's behalf against Winnicott and Khan's review of *Psychoanalytic Studies of the Personality*, on the grounds that he believed their criticism to be incompatible with a scientific approach. He had a great admiration for Fairbairn's pioneering work, and he was aware of how isolated he was in Edinburgh, where he had little support from the psychiatric and academic community. On the other hand when he heard that Winnicott and Hoffer believed that his frequent quoting of Fairbairn in print covered an unresolved negative transference, Guntrip himself attributed a new emphasis by Fairbairn upon aggression in the analysis to the latter's use of him as 'a model experimental subject for the analysis of aggression', even claiming that Fairbairn was crucifying him on the cross of analysis! Why did he remain in the analysis? It would seem that despite Guntrip's feeling that he himself was turning psychoanalysis into 'a study of psychodynamics and a spur to writing', Fairbairn's basically warmhearted attitude continued to give him hope, especially when his analyst could allow that quality to guide his interpretations, as for example when he said early in 1955 'Some patients feel they can't "do" anything unless they are allowed to "be".' For although terms

such as 'some patients' were too general for Guntrip, whose need, as
he pointed out, was not to be 'allowed' but to be enabled to 'be'. It
was surely his feeling that Fairbairn 'had it in him' to meet this
deepest need that was chiefly responsible for keeping Guntrip in
analysis. He could not let go while hope remained. Two stark dreams
of this period illustrate how profound was Guntrip's insecurity. In the
first, he saw 'The whole earth pitching and tossing amid angry
clouds', and he, the dreamer, was clinging desperately to it, feeling he
would be jolted off. He felt the dream referred both to his need to
cling to his mother in her stormy volatility, and also to the analysis
itself, which had become unreliable. Fairbairn replied with some heat
that Guntrip was showing a marked obsessional defensiveness. He
told him 'Either you don't let me get a word in, or you go into
unnecessary detail and give too complete a description and take all
the time.' Guntrip did not deny the obsessionism, but argued that
Fairbairn gave him nothing else to cling to: he was controlling the
sessions because he had lost faith in his analyst. The second dream
brought out vividly the deeper reason for Guntrip's obsessionism. He
dreamed:

> I was going home from Edinburgh by train and had a lifesize
> dummy of a man left with me, made of flesh, human but with
> no bones in it. I put it in the Guard's van to get rid of it, and
> propped it up as it slumped limp. I hurried away so the guard
> wouldn't know it was mine. Not that I was doing anything
> wrong, but I didn't want him to know I had any connection
> with it. I met the guard in the corridor, and suddenly heard it
> shambling up after me, calling out. I felt a queer horror, as if it
> were a sort of fleshly ghost, and said to the guard, 'Quick, let's
> get away. It's alive. It'll get us.'

The dream astonished him by its clarity, and he told Fairbairn,
'This is my passive self that I am afraid will emerge into consciousness. You are the guard. I want you to see it because I fear
it. It's the part of me I've spent a lifetime trying to keep suppressed. It would undermine me.' Fairbairn noted the importance
of the dream, but only in terms of Guntrip's repression of the self
that his mother had crushed, not as the part of him his mother
had never recognised, related to, or called to life.

   Both Guntrip's periodic lifelessness and his obsessionism had
been noted by Bertha, and by his daughter who had completed her
thesis at the London School of Economics the previous year. The
correspondence between Gwen and her father throws an intriguing

light on Guntrip's state at the time. It is also evidence of an extremely lively father–daughter relationship. As mentioned already, their relationship had been somewhat stormy since Gwen's adolescence, when Harry had noted certain temperamental similarities between Gwen and his mother: 'as a fast developing adolescent, she never gives way, always right, wants to be boss, provokes me to assert some parental authority at times and is very resistant, won't be told anything, can't accept criticism'. Harry and Bertha had discussed this often and had decided that it was wisest to avoid too many head-on clashes, and better to give Gwen time to come round. However, the matter came to a head in Christmas 1954, after a visit by Gwen and her husband, Denis. The atmosphere in the household had become so tense that Guntrip wrote to Gwen, after their return, suggesting that she should air some of her grievances, which she did in no uncertain manner. In a seven-page letter she expressed her keen disappointment that her father, with whom in her teens she had enjoyed spirited and stimulating discussion on a wide range of subjects, had become so obsessed with psychoanalysis that he reduced everything to psychoanalytic formulations, upon which he was the ultimate authority. In his letter to her Guntrip had remarked that Gwen had a tendency to be dogmatic. Her reply was as follows: 'Despite your analysis you don't seem to have got any less dogmatic and pontifical . . . If I am [dogmatic] in your presence, it is a long habit of self defence, without which, during my years at home with you, I should have lost all confidence in my own powers of thought . . . You can never conceive of having made a mistake yourself, even in silly little things . . . .' Acknowledging that she had felt stung by Guntrip's apparent lack of interest in her thesis, she nevertheless ended her letter by telling him that those friends in whom she confided 'all said with one accord that they envied me my relationship with you, in that it was even possible to discuss such things openly with my father'. In his reply, which ran to ten pages, Guntrip wrote, 'I feel that quite the most important thing in your letter is what you say about having needed to defend yourself against me or you would have lost all confidence in your own powers of thought. I accept primary responsibility for your having that problem. I've known about it for a long time and pondered on it sadly . . . I always hoped you would get to a stage where you could bring it up yourself when you were ready, and give me the chance to do what bit I could to ease the situation.' He made the point that while Bertha and he resented the infringement that analysis imposed on their life together, they had discussed it at every stage, and both felt it imperative that he carry on, for his symptoms had worsened dramatically during the last months of his mother's life, until, in the previous September, everything seemed to have flared up at once: 'Sinus trouble, tummy acidity of a kind I never remember . . . almost complete insomnia, a constant depressed state, revival of symptoms I had as a child – for three weeks I was covered with "heat spots" I remember having at the age of five.' He added 'At times it's been about as much as I could manage to cope with all that and do my work, and I owe a terrific lot to Mum for her help.' Pointing out that these were the circumstances underlying his 'obsessionism' with psychoanalysis, Guntrip suggested that psychoanalytic insight might help with their problem over dogmatism: 'It's a good thing that you did keep your end up, but it's not a good thing that I should have made it necessary for you to develop a counter-dogmatism of defence by counter-attack. Naturally I feel sad about this, but not consciously guilty, because I know that you and I were both together caught up in something not originally of our making. It was my pattern before it was your's, and my mother's pattern before it was mine, and her father's pattern before it was her's, and must go back further still.' He pointed out that in defending himself against his mother he had been obliged to fight her with her own weapons, thereby taking on some of her characteristics, and that in defending herself against him, Gwen had had to do likewise. He had avoided imposing upon Gwen the physical beatings his mother had given him between four and eight years, though in several of his dreams when Gwen was about the same age, his hand had been arrested by 'an invisible force' about six inches from her body as he was about to strike her. But he had been unable to avoid his mother's 'mental aggression', some of which broke out in his letter: 'For heaven's sake don't accuse me of being psychoanalytical. What's the use of trying to understand a problem of this kind and ruling out the only facts that throw any real light on it . . . If I'm analysing, then I'm analysing both myself and you, our relationship . . . the old pattern in reverse is hardly the solution we want, but rather a mutual growing beyond it . . . with respect for and acceptance of our differences . . . You can help me, perhaps in part by realising that you can afford to tolerate my idiosyncrasies more now than when you were a child. I can help you by being prepared to be open about the whole issue, and not wanting any other than an "on the level" relationship.'

If this letter serves to illustrate Guntrip's tendency towards dogmatism, it also brings out clearly the deep love and sincerity which characterised his relation with his daughter, and his determination to do all in his power to foster it. Gwen's next letter shows that his disclosures marked the beginning of a healing of the rift. She sympathised greatly with his sleeplessness, and recognised that he had no choice but to continue with the analysis, and, with characteristic frankness, looked forward to the time 'when you have got over all this and are yourself again'! Moreover, she showed a healthy scepticism about analysis, pointing out that while for Harry psychoanalysis was a 'religious ministry', for Denis and herself it was 'one of several methods of tackling mental illness', and adding that they did not feel as he did, that 'almost all problems are reducible to this kind of approach'. With regard to the generational repetitive pattern, she rightly pointed out that just as Harry had modified his mother's pattern 'terrifically', she would probably modify his, 'so that the outlook isn't too bad! At any rate, despite the traces of your mother's pattern that we can see in your relation with me, they haven't been serious enough to produce a neurosis.' She then added, what must surely have come as a great relief to Harry at that time, 'In many ways, in our particular culture, my rivalry with you in certain spheres has helped me to be fairly successful, which is always rather a reassuring feeling. Although in my early years and up to adolescence I did feel your personality as a threat, I never felt that the threat was realised; i.e. I didn't ever feel "squashed" by it.' It is clear from the tone of the correspondence that father and daughter had missed each other when Gwen left home for the LSE. Harry was surprised by the force of his depression when she went. The 1955 letters, all of prodigious length, were a fruitful 'rapprochement', for subsequent letters bear witness to a strong and mutually satisfying relationship. One of the results of their estrangement had been a feigned disinterest in each other's writings. Gwen's letter ends with the promise of an exchange of theses! The break with home having been achieved, father and daughter corresponded as emotional equals, and a deep and lasting friendship developed also between Harry and his son-in-law Denis, who like Gwen had qualified as an Educational Psychologist.

Bertha Guntrip seems to have remained in the background during this correspondence, though Harry, in his long letter, makes reference to her support during his illnesses, and her understanding and forbearance of the limitations the analysis imposed on their life together: 'Often I have said to Mum, "I'm sick to death of psychoanalysis." This sort of life isn't worth living, 5 days with patients 12 hours a day and the other 2 days with my own analysis! I've no time for attending to necessary things at home and I long for the completion of this programme so that I can slacken off and broaden out again . . . What little we can do at the moment, we do by enjoying an hour's reading of English literature four nights a week and planning the garden.' Although Harry seems to have been the main letter writer to Gwen and her family, his letters invariably included some news 'from Mum'. In the final part of her letter cited above, Gwen conveys her delight that Bertha had enclosed a letter with a cutting Harry had sent: 'We were thrilled to get one from you!' Because of her quieter nature it is possible that some may regard Bertha as 'eclipsed' by Harry's personality – especially in view of Gwen's need to defend herself against his dogmatism. However, the correspondence is more suggestive of a quiet contentment with their common life, in which they withstood strains which would certainly have defeated a more troubled relationship, with a fortitude that drew from deep mutual regard. By May 1956, Harry was able to express his delight that Gwen 'had written to say we were nice parents, didn't interfere', and that Bertha had passed her driving test first time. He was happy to conclude, 'I am thankful that my daughter and I have been able to form an incomparably better relationship than mother and I ever had, which I'm sure we both agree owes a lot to psychoanalytical psychotherapy . . . .'

After the Dummy dream, as if in confirmation of the kind of obsessional personality he had to become in order to overcome his passive self, Guntrip dreamed of a Jewish man: 'a tense obsessional kind of man, assertive, though not in a bad way, but determined, as though all his life he'd had to keep his end up. He had good characteristics and had good things to say, but said them in too dogmatic a way.' Guntrip recognised the man as himself, for both Gwen and Bertha had said he was too dogmatic in conversation, and moreover the Jew represented his feeling of having been an outcast with no home, having to fight for existence and recognition.

Guntrip's exasperation at being unable to relax his obsessional controls in the analysis was expressed in a letter to Fairbairn in which he described how the deeply disturbed patient about whom he had contacted Winnicott, had acted out 'in miniature, stage by stage the whole process of growing up', once he had 'accepted her deep regression'. The process had taken place over an eighteen-month period, and he wondered about the chances of his doing likewise with Fairbairn, adding that although Bertha encouraged him to continue in analysis for another couple of years, he feared that 'the ruthlessly determined prosecution of systematic analysis' would only produce more damage than advantage in terms of their life together and financial provision for old age. In conclusion he urged Fairbairn to exercise his authority against the internalised bad mother, and thus release him from his fear of her so that he could 'be something in his own way' (personal correspondence, 8 June 1955). In a characteristically prompt reply Fairbairn pointed out that if he were to intervene every time he thought Guntrip was being obsessional he would be intervening the whole time; in which case he feared that Guntrip might 'find it too disconcerting and become almost afraid to say anything at all'. Fairbairn made the further suggestion that due to a homosexual attachment to his father, and therefore in transference to Fairbairn as a 'super-ego figure', Guntrip may be harbouring a hidden libidinal satisfaction at the prospect of being beaten by the 'Fairbairn super-ego', as a source of gratification as well as anxiety (personal communication, 15 June 1955). Guntrip replied, by return of post, that his 'need to be touched' was for neither erotic nor punitive bodily contact, nor yet for Fairbairn's medically investigative touching, since that was remedial and not purely affectionate. He pointed out that his mother's unnatural attitude to him had made it impossible for him to feel centred in his own body so that he strove to become an unreal being which she both admired and despised. Thus his need was to discover that he was not 'bad and untouchable in body', and that the 'self' that included his body was acceptable, as he was not to his mother and father. He wrote, 'I feel I want to say to you, "For God's sake don't leave me with this problem unsolved; otherwise the real raison d'être of my existence, what I've both blindly and consciously, but with all my determination lived to get at, will disappear"' (personal communication, 16 June 1955). The pathos of his appeal was emphasised by the fact that, at the end of this letter, Guntrip accepted Fairbairn's somewhat tetchy remarks about the likely effect upon Guntrip of active intervention, as evidence that Fairbairn took him seriously as a person, and of 'how concerned he was to find the right way' to help him – a view hardly supported by a dispassionate view of Fairbairn's letter.

No series of sessions had been so lacking in any sense of new direction. Bertha had declared that she would be glad when he had finished at Edinburgh and, by the end of 1955, Guntrip had concluded that psychoanalysis led to very small gains, for whilst it afforded 'a lot of insight for professional and research aims' there was 'not enough personal gain to justify seven years time, money and disruption of domestic and social life'. He felt the truth to be that Fairbairn's acknowledged 'suspicion of regression beyond the

Oedipal level' was blocking his need, and in the last session before Christmas it was agreed that the frequency of sessions should be reduced to one a month in the New Year.

Despite this reduction in the number of sessions, Guntrip remained curious regarding Fairbairn's failure to deal with his need for therapeutic regression. For one thing, both men were agreed that psychotherapy was sterile unless it was conducted from 'a religious point of view', that is 'one which makes the value of the "person" central' (personal communication, 1 February 1956), and to deny the need to regress seemed to denote a lack of tender concern for the person. Moreover, although Fairbairn acknowledged that tenderness could develop as 'an independent factor in it's own right, not only as Freudian aim-inhibited sexuality' and that tenderness could therefore develop 'distinct from sexual feeling by the parent being interested in the child for itself as a person', he continued to insist that Guntrip's 'real problem' arose not from his mother's failure to evoke tenderness in him but from her active crushing of his libidinal ego. For Guntrip, who at this time was working on his book *Mental Pain and the Cure of Souls* (1956), Fairbairn's insistence on an Oedipal diagnosis was inexplicable. Indeed he regarded his psychotherapy as a religious calling, as he wrote to his daughter (13 January 1955): *'To me, psychotherapy is a ministry, a dedicated vocation, as much as ever a religious ministry was*, and in my heart, I believe the two are one and the same thing; and psychoanalysis to me is the indispensible, significant part of my own search for answers to basic questions about human nature and human life, largely because, having explored philosophy and theology and other such matters, I see how the usual cultural answers misfire and deal with false issues for lack of knowledge of what really goes on in human minds.' Moreover, four of his own patients were making good recoveries through therapeutic regression. But when he told Fairbairn of this the latter merely replied that he could see that Guntrip was trying to get him to treat him like he treated his own patients, thereby regarding it as 'hysteric dependence on and exploitation of the analyst' (reported in a letter from Guntrip to J.D. Sutherland, 24 March 1973). Guntrip concluded, 'whatever regression meant (and it does not mean the same thing for every patient), Fairbairn was not prepared to risk it with me. Once later I went back to the couch and lay down and said "I need to regress to get at something", and he became very agitated and said, "Regression is terrible", so I got up and went back to the chair, and knew that whatever was involved I would never solve it with him.' Guntrip later acknowledged what he had not fully realised at the time, that Fairbairn had been in deteriorating health with Parkinson's disease ever since the death of his first wife, and that he had, when younger, treated a regressed patient with complete success, conducting sessions at her hotel when she was too ill to leave it. There is reason enough here for Fairbairn's reservations regarding regression, and for analysing Oedipal problems as Guntrip believed, 'in such a way as to prevent regressions'. Like any professional analyst, Fairbairn felt obliged to expose in his patient only those needs which he felt confident of being able to contain, and to avoid adding to them by imposing on his patient the burden of his own anxieties. There was, of course, the additional complication of how a regression could be managed at such a distance, especially if it came to involve 'apparent dying'.

In marked contrast to such grave matters was the manner of Fairbairn's correspondence on the occasion of the Freud Centenary Celebrations in London, to which Guntrip had hoped to gain admission as a non-member of the Institute of Psychoanalysis. Fairbairn wrote (26 February 1956) inviting Guntrip and Dr Markillie, a new Institute-trained colleague in the Leeds Department, to dine with him at his London club. In the event Guntrip could not attend the celebrations which were confined to members only, but this extramural expression of friendliness would surely have been welcome at such a time. It is a mark of Guntrip's respect for Freud – and probably also of his determination to participate in the 'Celebrations' in some way – that he produced a fine paper, 'Centenary Reflections on the Work of Freud' (Guntrip 1956, in Hazell 1994, p. 115), which appeared in the Leeds University Medical Journal. The paper also demonstrates Guntrip's determination that the cause of psychoanalytical psychotherapy should not become overlaid by the organic and behavioural bias in the University Departments of Psychiatry and Psychology. In the letter quoted above Fairbairn referred to two theoretical propositions which Guntrip questioned and which arose out of Fairbairn's paper on the Schreber case.[3] The first was his contention that 'the Oedipus situation is central for therapy, but not for theory', which Guntrip contested on the grounds that true theory is the theory of therapy (Guntrip 1975, in Hazell 1994, p. 354); and the second was an 'observation regarding the separation of the horror and the pleasure factors in the primal scene'. Indeed it was the 'primal scene' which now took precedence in Fairbairn's conceptualising as 'central for therapy', and to such an extent that Guntrip found himself under a compulsion to re-examine 'every activity of his life' in terms of unconscious expression of primal scene involvement, even attributing a clicking right thumb to a possible 'conversion symptom of castration anxiety'. However, the thumb was diagnosed as due to a nodule on the tendon requiring surgery, and Guntrip became frustrated by the feeling that Fairbairn was fitting him in a 'new twist in his theory', just as he had during the latter's interest in hysteria. In his deepest conviction Guntrip felt that he was so 'unawakened to real self-experience' due to his mother's inability to love him, that he had had 'a great need to make use of anything at all going on around him' – whether things seen or heard at night in his parents bed-room 'or at any time of the day or night when awake', in order to have something to experience himself with, and 'any sexual or somatic tension would have been grist to the same mill'. Thus, he did not deny primal scene phenomena as such, but only their 'centrality' in Fairbairn's view of him.

Guntrip's longing that Fairbairn should recognise his unmet need for simple, uncomplicated relation was expressed in a dream shortly afterwards. He dreamed:

> I was having analysis with a middle-aged woman who was a child analyst. She was cheerful and pleasant, understanding and with no tension. I said, 'You must love children or you couldn't deal with them as you do.' I kissed her and she smiled happily, saying, 'I wanted you to do that.'

Fairbairn pointed out that whereas a bad-object analyst merely repeats the original traumatic situation, if he is too good a good object, he smothers the patient's guilt and aggression so that nothing happens. Guntrip's concern, however, was less with his analyst's goodness or badness, than with his extreme neutrality when it came to emotional issues. This was highlighted by Fairbairn's reaction to a very anxious fantasy concerning an air-trip taken by Guntrip's daughter and son-in-law as part of a Himalayan climbing expedition. Not only did Guntrip fantasy that their plane crashed and they were killed, but that, in trying to tell Fairbairn about it, he was unable to speak or to show any feeling. In the session he said to Fairbairn, 'For God's sake touch me. Do something to make me feel less cut-off. I'm terrified of this isolation and apartness ... Rescue me from it.' Although he was well aware that he was using his anxiety over Gwen's safety to draw Fairbairn's attention to his emotional isola-tion, he was nevertheless disheartened by Fairbairn's reply, which he recorded as follows: 'A patient, speaking of the loss of her home said, "I didn't know it was possible to want something so much that I could feel its loss so frightfully."'

At this point in June 1956, the operation on Guntrip's thumb necessitated a break in sessions, and in writing to inform Fairbairn of this Guntrip raised the question of fees. It appears that Fairbairn, in proposing a fee increase, had been influenced by the fact that Guntrip had recently bought a new car, and whilst Guntrip made it clear that his inability to meet the increase until September was unaffected by his recent purchase, Fairbairn made it equally clear that he could not afford to buy a new car himself, and that as he was getting older he was able to see fewer patients with a consequent reduction of income. Moreover, he added 'in consequence of my views about object-relations, etc., I have felt it my duty to give my patients (including you, of course) longer time when possible'. Guntrip, for his part, whilst he acknowledged Fairbairn's generosity with both time and fees, pointed out that the analysis was exceeding the time expected, so that an endowment insurance he had purchased to give Bertha security was straining their resources. He added that, what with the financial and time constraints imposed by the long analysis, Bertha 'had ample justification for beginning to feel we were hardly married as far as a life together went'. This rather genteel wrangling, on either side, culminated in an admission by Guntrip that he had made an automatic assumption, based upon a phantasy of Fairbairn as a paternal superman – which had first been suggested by a remark by Professor MacCalman over seven years ago that Fairbairn had independent means and only took a small number of patients for research purposes. Fairbairn wrapped the matter up by observing that Guntrip's conception of him as a paternal superman provided 'an interesting example of the influence of phantasy upon the assessment of reality even in those who might be expected "a priori" to be less naïf than the average patient', adding, 'It's certainly news to me that I only took a few patients for research purposes. If that had been so, it would have been my own phantasy come true!' (27 June 1956). In the event, Guntrip must have realised that although Fairbairn was unquestionably better off than he financially (having acquired a private income after his mother's death in 1946 and another after his wife's death in 1952, and being able to afford membership of a 'London club'!) his analyst was under considerable strain and worried about the future. An additional factor, of which Guntrip was unaware, was that Fairbairn's younger son, Nicholas, having switched from studying medicine to train as a lawyer, was going to be financially dependent on Fairbairn for longer than originally expected. Guntrip made his cheque out for the full fee for July: two guineas – and it was in the new car that Bertha passed her driving test!

The above exchange seems to have had a liberating effect upon the analysis. In the run-up to the argument about fees, Guntrip had almost reached the decision to abandon the analysis, but in the last quarter of 1956, despite a five-week period when Fairbairn's deteriorating health made it necessary for him to enter a nursing home, he appeared to develop a new insight into the origins of Guntrip's mental state. For example, when Guntrip described a mental picture of himself as a small child in the Goose Green shop, totally ignored by his mother and feeling real hate for her, Fairbairn replied, 'It's being ignored, unloved, treated as a nuisance, not an end in yourself, and as clay to be moulded. The problem it makes is that you can't begin to be able to love, and then begin to have only hate to make a relation with.' Again, just before the Christmas break, Fairbairn drew nearer to his stranded patient, when he said, 'The basic trauma is the mother ignoring the child and its needs. The child only gains a feeling of being a real person through mother's attention to it.' However, although these are accurate comments, they are really statements about Guntrip, rather than direct communications: more the observations of a sympathetic observer, who can sense the child's distress, but who feels unable to influence him directly. Fairbairn was a sympathetic man. Sutherland once stated simply: 'It mattered to Fairbairn if a patient suffered', and it must have pained him to be unable to reach the heart of Guntrip's suffering. And yet, it was surely more excruciating for Guntrip to sense Fairbairn's warmheartedness and yet remain unreached.

In the meantime, the two men corresponded about theoretical and professional matters. Guntrip made full use of Fairbairn's experienced advice in the matter of his lectures to would-be psychiatrists preparing for the Diploma in Psychiatric Medicine, and Fairbairn commented enthusiastically and pertinently upon the manuscript of Chapter 7 of Guntrip's projected book *Personality Structure and Human Interaction* (1961). As a major part of his preparation for the book Guntrip published the paper 'Recent Developments in Psychoanalytic Theory' (1956, in Hazell 1994, p. 89), in which he attempted to assimilate Fairbairn's views of endopsychic structure with those of Winnicott regarding the psychesoma, which, as he points out, is 'not an impersonal id but the primary, natural self, the libidinal psyche, and . . . "true self"' with which the patient seeks to recover contact through therapeutic regression.

As the analysis entered its eighth year Guntrip felt a new sense of security in relation to Fairbairn. He said, 'It has taken me seven years to feel sure you take me seriously as a person and are genuinely concerned about me, and that professionally you treat me as a colleague.' And even more importantly he could say, 'I feel my relation to you is a permanent unchanging mental factor, not lost by bodily absence': a therapeutic result which, one might think, any analyst and patient would be proud of having achieved. Guntrip thus concluded that his inability to make full use of the therapeutic relationship that Fairbairn 'quite genuinely gave' was due to the latter's belief that regression to the infancy year involved a dangerous over-dependency against which both analyst and patient must be protected 'by ever more pressing analysis of the oedipal phenomena'. Guntrip felt that Fairbairn's belief that regression would involve the patient in helpless infantile dependence upon the analyst (surely impracticable for him and Guntrip in the prevailing circumstances) was encouraged by Winnicott's views that a 'management' stage for regressed patients should lead on to 'psychoanalysis proper' at the Oedipal level. By contrast, Guntrip believed that 'management', an empathic relating with the patient as an infant-person, should be accompanied by and implicit within 'analysing' in order 'to make clear to the patient the real significance of what is going on', so as to avoid the danger of 'cultivating permanent dependency' and exploitation of the analyst, which he believed Fairbairn feared – though at that time he knew nothing of Fairbairn's own suffering at the hands of a regressing patient.

Guntrip later believed that what he needed from Fairbairn was not 'nursing in a state of helpless regression' (though the example he gave Fairbairn of his own work with a regressing patient seems to have come close to this), but 'a certain type of analytical "interpretation" of the need to regress, an understanding of the need to go back to where mother had originally and most seriously failed him'. Thus assisted, Guntrip believed that he could have 'managed' his own regression without collapse, although his original trauma, as well as its later manifestation during the Salem crisis, had certainly involved debility.

In general, the analysis seemed to be moving towards an acceptable compromise. Guntrip felt more inclined to accept the intransigence of Fairbairn's theoretical view of the ego as an unmodified unity at the start, whose original unity could be restored by analysis of its 'splits' as represented in the Oedipal internalised bad-object world – even though this view failed to conceptualise the ego as a product of the mother's recognition of the infant as a person, or the consequent need for a patient lacking this experience to regress in search of belated recognition from his analyst, in order to rediscover his 'latent infantile aliveness'. For his part Fairbairn was moving nearer to a recognition of the importance of the total relationship between the analyst and patient. In correspondence with the American psychoanalyst Thomas Szasz, Fairbairn stated his view that 'the relationship with the analyst is not just what springs from the transference, but the total relationship between the patient and analyst as human beings' (personal communication, 1957), and, at Guntrip's instigation, he refined this view still further in his paper 'On the Nature and Aims of Psychoanalytic Treatment'[4] (1958), where he stressed the need for the therapist to become a 'real good object' in his patient's experience, so that the latter might discover an inner incentive to emerge from the closed system of his internalised bad-object world into an open system of emotional equality with the analyst. It was thus in a context of growing rapprochement that Fairbairn sought once more to free Guntrip from his inner struggle to get his mother to relate to him. Doubtless encouraged by Guntrip's having dreamed that Fairbairn came to his home for a session, the latter responded to a further dream in which Guntrip was involved in an oral sadistic attack on his mother, who was 'probably responding a bit' by saying, 'You've got to accept the facts. Mother was like that and there was really nothing to be done about it. Hard for children to accept facts.' It seems that Guntrip had a momentary experience of 'quietus', for he replied, 'I feel I could drop analysis now.' Moreover, despite a familiar flight back to bad relations in the form of a dream of an attack 'by a sinister creature, half bird and half bat, a vampire', recalling the dream early in his self-analysis of mother as a destructive black bird, his new sense of ease and calm remained, and was remarked upon by Bertha. He was able to confirm that his rapport with his real world had definitely improved, and he told Fairbairn, 'I feel you are more a human being to me now, and less an idealised imago, a second Freud.'

This 'movement in the direction of an open system' was further helped by Fairbairn's move from his Edinburgh house to an old and beautiful house with a small lovely garden in the historic village of Duddingston, and it was in this new setting, looking out from the consulting room on to the beautiful walled garden, with the Pentland hills on the skyline, that Guntrip had his last two sessions before the summer break. In this new security he related a dream which shed some light upon the inner meaning of his ceaseless activity:

> I was being analysed and said I realised I was schizoid at heart and didn't show much emotion. The analyst said, 'You run everywhere, dash along at high speed.'

The theme of how the manic defence served as a counter to a devitalised schizoid core was soon to be worked out in detail by Guntrip in his paper 'The Manic Depressive Problem in the Light of the Schizoid Process' (1962, in Hazell 1994, p. 187). At this stage, however, the full significance of the dream remained obscure.

Regrettably Fairbairn's health continued to deteriorate. From August through to October there were no sessions. But whenever Harry and Bertha went on climbing expeditions in the Cairngorms Fairbairn would invite them to tea at Duddingston. Guntrip himself was overstrained and he took advantage of the break in analysis to take a complete day-off each week, when he and Bertha would walk together in the Yorkshire Dales. Those days off, so long overdue, were among the happiest times that he and Bertha could remember, and it would seem that recovery was underway. However, circumstances were to determine otherwise, for in the autumn of 1957 Guntrip heard that his old college friend, Leslie Tizard, had succumbed to a fast-acting lung cancer. After visiting his dying friend Guntrip found himself withdrawing in fear of the external world, with a powerful need to escape to his home, away from the demands of his patients. What threatened him most was a feeling of becoming absorbed into his dying brother-figure, as if he were once again 'dying with Percy'. He felt 'endangered' within and without, and had a vivid nightmare, very similar in tone to his pre-analysis dream of 'the pale passive invalid'. He dreamed:

> I was visiting some historical place with a woman not unlike my mother. She said, 'Some little creature was buried here.' I thought he had 'faded out' now and we went in. Suddenly a ghostly force or magnetic pull seized me. The invisible force swept me irresistibly up the stairs and rushed me irresistibly across the room as I uttered a long moaning cry.

Fairbairn made no comment. Doubtless he had in mind his own failing health, for when Guntrip mentioned a feeling of being 'sucked into someone dying' he quietly commented, 'I'm somewhere in this.'

Tizard died on 22 December 1957, and for the next year Guntrip held on to the 'living Tizard', so to speak, by completing two books, *Middle Age* and *Facing Life and Death* (both 1959), on which he and Tizard had collaborated. Guntrip wrote a biographical introduction to the latter book, and an epilogue of deep appreciation and compassion. But the additional work on top of a mountainous clinical load eroded his improved physical health, and no sooner had he posted the manuscripts of both books to the publisher, Allen and Unwin, than he collapsed, totally exhausted, with a powerful feeling that he had no future. Living seemed 'futile, pointless, a nothingness'. He dreamed of standing aimlessly in his accountants' offices, above which he had new consulting rooms, his old ones having been demolished for road improvements. In his dream the accountants had gone out of business and the rooms were empty, so that he 'just stood looking'. Tizard's death, like Percy's, had left him feeling alone in an empty house. Fairbairn made no attempt to interpret the deeper significance of Tizard's death, probably because his own uncertain health meant that he could not be confident of managing the probable consequences. Guntrip dreamed, significantly,

> I was in session with Fairbairn. He had a small mentally-deficient child there who could not speak and he had no-one to leave him with. There was a lot I needed to talk about and couldn't because of this child, and Fairbairn couldn't provide for him in time for me to have a session.

Much later, in the 1970s Guntrip saw that he was bringing his schizoid self to Fairbairn in this dream: the part of him he needed someone to recognise before he could respond and experience himself as fully alive. At this time in 1958, he could only fantasy the kind of 'mental convalescence' he needed, 'Living in rooms, over the garage at the bottom of Fairbairn's garden.' In fact Fairbairn's younger son, Nicholas, was living in the rooms at this time and it is probable that Guntrip knew of this. However that may be, he was finding that Fairbairn's 'non-interpretative supportiveness' was enabling him to 'inch his way' slowly back to the deepest problem and he dreamed,

> I was going to Fairbairn's house very disturbed and I arrived very poorly. He held me while I talked. I said I felt much more ill than I'd ever done before, but I wasn't worried about it. I felt it was a stage I had to go through.

He began to feel he must be 'schizophrenic at bottom, disintegrated', that Tizard's death, reflecting Percy's, had sparked 'a very early disillusionment with life in the family', so that he felt in a very disturbed state of mind with no energy or drive, feeling that death would be 'a welcome release from the strain of living'. In retrospect Guntrip believed that if Fairbairn had interpreted specifically that he was on the point of re-experiencing the blank terror of his isolated state after Percy's death, he could have coped with it himself 'and remained operative', so that it would not have involved 'being seriously ill on him'.

In fact it was not Guntrip, but Fairbairn himself who became seriously ill, with influenza, after the Easter break, and apart from a few sessions in June, he was ill for six months, so that it was not until the end of January 1959 that the analysis was resumed. Guntrip wrote in May, saying that he felt 'more normal despite a background of mild anxiety still', and his record suggests that Fairbairn's quiet supportiveness had given rise to a number of 'positive transference' dreams in which Guntrip's father appeared 'tall, smiling and very impressive'. Indeed Guntrip felt that Fairbairn and his father shared 'a similar quality of integrity, trustworthiness', which he also found in Bertha and which represented to him '"objective good" in the outer world, like a religious faith'.

The strength of Guntrip's conviction regarding reliability of human love at this time was vividly illustrated in his response to J.C. McKenzie, Professor of Theology at Nottingham University, who claimed that only God in Christ, and not the psychotherapist, could love and free the patient. Responding through the correspondence pages of the Congregational Journal, *The British Weekly* (1958), Guntrip wrote:

> The child grows up to be a disturbed person because he is not loved for his own sake as a person in his own right, and as an ill adult he comes to the psychotherapist convinced beforehand that this 'professional man' has no real interest or concern for him. The kind of love the patient needs . . . involves taking him seriously in his difficulties, respecting him as an individual in his own right even in his anxieties, treating him as someone with the right to be understood and not merely blamed, put off, pressed and moulded to suit other peoples' convenience . . . showing him genuine human contact, real sympathy, believing in him so that in the course of time he can become capable of believing in himself. All these are ingredients of true parental love (agape not eros) and if the psychiatrist cannot love his patient in that way, he had better give up psychotherapy.[5]

Guntrip's only option in the face of Fairbairn's long illness was to 'reinstate repression', and to intellectualise the problem which he could not work through with Fairbairn in person (see Guntrip 1975, in Hazell 1994, p. 360). It was not, however, purely a process of deliberate intellectualisation for 'spontaneous insights kept welling up at all sorts of times', and he 'jotted them down as they flowed with compelling intensity'. These insights prompted him to begin work on three major interrelated themes which preoccupied him, namely, ego-weakness, how to retain conscious control of regression, and the way that 'devitalisation' – a deeper problem than 'depression' – gave rise to a 'manic defence'. His deliberations, which were later to assume the form of three seminal papers, clearly reflected his own struggle over his own need and fear of regression, and his 'manic' efforts to overcome his anxiety and inner weakness at a time when his analyst was unavailable. As if this were not enough, Guntrip was in the process of finalising his first major psychological book *Personality Structure and Human Interaction* (1961), and in May, before Fairbairn's illness had become acute, he sent the whole manuscript to Fairbairn for his consideration. He also mentioned a feeling that he had worked through something decisive, and that he felt some benefit. It was clear from Fairbairn's reply that he too felt frustrated at having to discontinue the sessions, for he wrote, 'I am extremely sorry to have to put you off, particularly at the present stage . . . I hope we shall be able to bring about further movement in the next session' (personal communication, 17 May 1958). Fairbairn was generally enthusiastic about Guntrip's manuscript and he did all he could to make available his latest paper 'On the Nature and Aims of Psychoanalytical Treatment' (1958), allowing him to read it in draft form in case it was not published in time to be referred to in the book, and even suggesting that Guntrip might prepare a passage on the paper in advance, to be rushed to the publishers as soon as 'Nature and Aims' was published. In the event, this probably happened, for 'Fairbairn's views on Object-Relations Theory and Psychotherapy' appears on page 413, right at the end of the book. However, Fairbairn was not entirely uncritical. In particular he singled out Guntrip's analysis of the basic forms of object-relationship in terms of his own structural theory (1961, p. 375), observing 'Jung's "psychology of Types" bored me to death; and when it comes to reading details about the differentiating characteristics of fourteen types of relationship, I am afraid I found it difficult to sustain interest . . . However, I feel that, if you feel disposed to write about types of relationship at all, your typology is founded on a sound basis.' Fairbairn also could not resist a crack at Winnicott, whose 'views on therapeutic regression' occupy the section preceding those of Fairbairn (1961, pp. 396–413). Referring to Guntrip's citation on p. 409 Fairbairn wrote: 'I have had a glance at Winnicott's short paper on "Transference",[6] . . . What a pity he is not a more clear-headed writer, and more capable of formulating his insights coherently. Personally I don't like the concept of "The intact ego" . . . If my views on mental structure are correct, the psychoanalyst never has to deal with anybody with "an intact ego", since splitting occurs at such at early stage.' On the other hand, 'the idea that there is no ego present at birth, and that the ego is some sort of special creation who has difficulty in learning to tolerate id-impulses, which are really his own impulses, seems to me fantastic as a piece of conceptualisation. At the same time Winnicott's clinical insights are very impressive' (personal communication, 17 May 1958). Perhaps this last letter before Fairbairn's major illness was in some ways prophetic. For it was precisely this question of the unity or otherwise of the ego at birth that was at the centre of Guntrip's investigation, both in the area of his own psychopathology and in his theory-writing and it was to the impressive clinical insights of Winnicott that he felt himself increasingly drawn.

Fairbairn's illness was so severe that he wondered if he would ever recover, and he thought seriously about retirement. In September 1958 Guntrip and Bertha stayed at the Royal Hotel, Portobello, and called to see him, bringing him some sweet-smelling 'Doreen' roses, which delighted him, for he was a keen gardener. But he was still unable to predict when he would be able to resume sessions. However, when in October Guntrip wrote summarising his position and raising the question of terminating the analysis, with a suggestion that he might transfer to either Sutherland or Winnicott, if this would be a help to Fairbairn, the latter replied, 'I think it would be a great pity if you had to "change horses" at this stage; and it would be very unsatisfactory for you if such a course were adopted except as a last resort.' He added, 'I agree with you that great developments have occurred latterly in your analysis but that an opportunity for further development is very important to enable the analysis to reach a closure. I also agree that there is no longer any indication for intensive analysis' (personal communication, 11 November 1958). Fairbairn then stated that he hoped in due course to continue sessions with theoretical discussion at three-weekly intervals. By December he was coming back to his old form, having resumed sessions with one patient 'owing to a "crisis" which has revealed the basic ego weakness which we have recently discussed – a most illuminating revelation, which I daren't allow to become obscured'. A further sign of returning vigour occurred when, in the same letter, he took spirited exception to a reference made by Marjorie Brierley, in her draft review of Guntrip's new book, to 'instinct as the stimulus to psychic activity', stating his own view that 'the term instinct means nothing if it does not mean "the primitive pattern of psychic activity"', and is thus not a stimulus, 'but a form of psychic activity'. He continued, 'She is really saying . . . that the id is a stimulus to the ego – which from an ultimate point of view is rubbish. I really don't know what one can do with people who can't see this point' (personal communication, 2 December 1958). From this one might deduce that Fairbairn was on the mend – a recovery aided by the fact that his secretary, Mrs Marion MacKintosh, had obtained a divorce. They were to be married the following April.

When sessions were resumed on 27 January 1959, Guntrip reported general progress, despite the persistence throughout the year of a feeling that he was 'inescapably tied to a frightening situation, a fearful apprehensive little child'. He was amazed to hear Fairbairn make an entirely new interpretation: 'I think your emphasis on Ego-weakness is right. It yields better results than interpretation of libidinal needs.' This new emphasis which represented a major change in Fairbairn's clinical theory, was confirmed the next day when Guntrip reported a dream in which he felt friendly to a little boy whose penis would 'grow adult in its own good time', for Fairbairn replied, 'That's a good attitude. The penis is a symbol of the Ego.' It seemed to Guntrip then that the long break in sessions had had the dual effect of triggering off his deepest infantile fears, whilst also enabling Fairbairn to recognise them. But the emergence into consciousness of the weak infantile ego brought home to him forcibly the accumulated strain of 'having to be adult'. He felt weary to the point of exhaustion and began to doubt that he could keep going. His anxiety during the period of Fairbairn's illness had resulted in the excessive rate of work referred to earlier, in which he was seeing twelve patients a day, five days a week and writing on the other two days. He longed to sell up and move into a small house and retire – which at 58 was hardly a viable option. Gradually he became more accepting of his weaker nature and less identified with his mother as a rejecting object. He had fantasies of being the only good guard in a concentration camp, protecting a suffering girl from oppression: which he felt to be an important development, since it represented a new respect for his basically denied nature, and a further dissolution of the identification with his rejecting mother, who had previously been his only effective active model. That he could now let this model go and develop his own nature was, he felt, due to Fairbairn's recognition of his ego-weakness, in which medium he could outgrow the necessity to 'live by identifications', and begin to grow as a 'self' which could function distinctly in its own right. He noted, 'I did feel that Fairbairn had played a genuine good father rôle in inspiring a son, and then leaving him free but supported in following his own line.'

Gradually, of course, the fear began to grow that Fairbairn himself would die before this new growth could be consolidated. Fairbairn put it succinctly: 'Your problem with me now is not so much a father–son relation. We are more brothers. If you live, I may die like Percy.' Guntrip himself felt that if Fairbairn were to die, he would lack the strength to go on living, and would fall back instead into identification with his internalised mother as rejecting object. In fact, this happened anyway, while Fairbairn lived, for Guntrip developed severe arthritic pains, which the former interpreted as 'no doubt a deep unconscious self-punishment on behalf of mother for struggling to get free of her', and indeed Guntrip felt sure he derived 'a secret reassurance in "having symptoms"'. However, an even greater dilemma occurred when he saw that he could never solve his problem *with* an analyst, since, once the analyst had become his brother in transference, *losing him*, whether by ending analysis himself or by staying with him until he died, would represent the death of Percy, leaving him with 'a full-scale eruption of that traumatic event', and no-one to help him with it. Terrified by this prospect he wrote a letter to Fairbairn explaining his dilemma. The letter was never sent, however, because Guntrip felt that Fairbairn, in his precarious health, could not have helped him with his problem in transference analysis.

Ever since Tizard's death and Fairbairn's illness Guntrip had felt exposed to something 'even worse than Ego-weakness ... a "fading out into unreality"' and compared to that state, he believed 'any kind of experience, whether aches, pains, guilts, angers or libidinal needs is far preferable'. His condition caused him to see an Edinburgh consultant physician who confirmed that he was fully physically fit except for some arthritis which was not serious. There had, however, been a significant change in his reaction to Fairbairn's illnesses, for whereas he had formerly exploited them to feel 'one-up' on his analyst, he now felt undermined by them, as indeed by any separating influence, even wondering whether Fairbairn's recent marriage might have 'preoccupied' his analyst so that he would be 'hardly in a position to follow up closely my bringing up of the basic Ego-weakness problem'!

During the August holiday, Guntrip began to feel that he should not burden Fairbairn any further. But knowing that Fairbairn was professionally isolated, he believed that his visits were important to them both, and after discussion it was decided that they should continue to meet at the rate of two sessions on each visit. In the event, Guntrip had only twenty more sessions in the next ten months, during which the theme of emotional withdrawal appeared with new relevance. He saw that the urge to 'bury himself', whether in work or in retreat, had been his deepest reaction when Percy had died and he was left with mother, deeper than his psychosomatic symptoms or the sado-masochistic battles. He saw that when Percy was born he had devoted himself to him because he needed a love-object, in order to keep himself in being, and that when Percy died, his world and his 'self' had collapsed, since he had no real attachment to anyone else at that age. Thus he had lost interest in living, and collapsed into schizoid apathy, a state which had persisted beneath the surface ever since. He saw that although he had recovered briefly with Aunt Dolly's children, his libidinal attachments to the adults in his own family were too weak to evoke life in him – Aunt Mary having been a 'colourless personality', though she had partly filled the gap, thereby giving rise to the 'pale passive invalid' in his dream. Thus Guntrip realised how, ever since Percy died, he had had to fight to save his active ego from being sucked down into that schizoid withdrawal, because he had been compelled to withdraw from the actively persecuting mother into the worse situation of her non-relating which underlay it. He remarked to Fairbairn that, like Schopen-hauer's porcupines, he felt obliged to establish a mean distance out of reach of his bad objects but not so far removed as to lose himself: an insight which later found expression in his description of the 'schizoid compromise'. In this same session on 4 November 1959, Guntrip first clearly outlined his view that Fairbairn's theory of endo-psychic structure implied a still deeper split, in which part of the hungry, angry, clamouring 'libidinal ego', in addition to turn-ing against itself by identifying with the rejecting object, 'gives up the struggle and just withdraws from pressure and deprivation, and becomes a Regressed Ego, detached and schizoid'. Thus the main inspiration of Guntrip's extension of Fairbairn's theory of endo-psychic structure originated from his own psycho-pathology. At that time Fairbairn could not conceive of a baby withdrawing because he could find no-one capable of relating to him. For him with-drawal was always provoked by an active threat, like castration, and he quoted a patient who said, 'If I come out, Mother's there with a knife.' It is not clear whether this is the patient referred to in his letter as suffering 'ego-weakness'. But if so his weakness was presumably due to a withdrawal resulting from an impingement.

On his next visit Guntrip returned to the couch in the hope of experiencing more directly his 'regressed ego'. He expressed a faith that with Fairbairn, that lost part of him could 'begin to grow and become born, perhaps for the first time', and he added, 'I've always felt a part of me was missing. I've never felt as deeply as I should.' But he had reckoned without Fairbairn's frail physical health, for under the pressure of this heartfelt appeal Fairbairn would seem to have reached the end of his resources, and he said in an agitated voice, 'Regression is terrible. Patients become too ill. Who's going to pay the analyst's fees?' In recording this outburst, Guntrip added, 'That was not the true Fairbairn, but the man whose health was failing more seriously than I knew.' Much later Guntrip related to Sutherland what he had not known at the time, namely that Fairbairn had suffered grievously from 'the destructive pressure of a long-standing patient who would insist on two-hour sessions, and then, as soon as she got home would ring him up and keep him on the phone for an hour; till one day, Marion [Fairbairn's second wife] got anxious because he was so long and went and found him slumped unconscious at the phone. She wrote to the patient and forbade her to come to her house again and she left Edinburgh' (personal communication, 24 September 1974). Nevertheless Guntrip did return to the couch for the second of the day's sessions, feeling more able to relax and allow his nature to grow in peace, as distinct from 'trying by active effort to make things come right'.

Just before the Christmas break, Fairbairn was again incapacitated by illness, but recovered sufficiently to send a telegram on the day before the session was due, saying 'Come'. Thus Guntrip was able to attend his 1000th session and the last of 1959. The year had seen the final revision of his first major research work, *Personality Structure and Human Interaction*, which was read in manuscript by Leonard Woolf and accepted for Hogarth Press with a foreword by J.D. Sutherland, Fairbairn having declined to write one, feeling he would be seen as 'too propagandist' by some critics (personal communication, 2 December 1958). By this stage Guntrip was aware of a need to protect Fairbairn. Furthermore, he was by now inclined to feel that the long period of analysis of the internal bad object 'three person relations level' had been necessary in order to enable his 'Central Ego' (or everyday conscious self) to grow strong enough in relation to Fairbairn, to be capable of accepting the emergence of his schizoid regressed ego. But he realised that, because of Fairbairn's uncertain health, and in return for the latter's willingness to continue accepting his need so far as he could, he now had to manage the situation in such a way as to take the strains on himself.

Between January and July 1960 Guntrip attended only fourteen sessions, followed by two in September, which were the last. During the Christmas break he began systematically to work out his new insights, culminating in the next two years in the production of three papers on the themes mentioned earlier of ego-weakness, the need and fear of regression, and the manic defence, and which later became the basis of his book *Schizoid Phenomena, Object Relations and the Self* (1968). In the first of these papers, 'Ego Weakness, the Core of the Problem of Psychotherapy' (1960, in Hazell 1994, p. 127), Guntrip wrestled with the intractability of the schizoid problem, in which 'a weak, undeveloped, fearful and therefore "infantile dependent" ego' remained buried in the unconscious and made no progress towards maturity (p. 136). Acknowledging that the need for regression presented 'the most difficult problems of all for psychotherapy', he maintained that in regressing, the child was not merely taking flight from a harsh or remote environment, or from the destructive intensity of his needs, but was seeking a revival of identification based upon an original experience with the mother of very early life, or even in the womb. The secret purpose of this regressive search was thus the restoration and development of the true nature of the self, and it was the therapist's task to 'reach the profoundly withdrawn Regressed Ego, relieve it of its fears and start on the road to regrowth and rebirth, the discovery and development of all its latent potentialities' (p. 155). These insights, derived from Guntrip's experience of both his own and his patients' needs led him to propose a final extension of Fairbairn's theory of endo-psychic structure, to the effect that, underlying the inflamed and exaggerated active oral, anal and immature genital needs of Fairbairn's libidinal ego, there was to be found a passive regressed, but still basically libidinal, ego 'in profound fear-driven retreat from life'. Furthermore, he believed that this 'regressed libidinal ego' held the secret of the patient's innate capacity to live and love to the full, which he believed was every person's birthright. Guntrip saw that his regressed libidinal ego had much in common with Winnicott's 'True Self in cold storage', which the latter had described that same year in his paper 'Ego-distortion in Terms of True and False Self' (Winnicott 1960). Indeed, Winnicott wrote to ask whether the regressed libidinal ego was withdrawn or repressed, and Guntrip replied 'Both. First withdrawn and then kept repressed.' The clarity of Guntrip's conceptualising of his own and his patients' schizoid experience, and the fact that it constitutes a logically consistent development of Fairbairn's existing theory,

represents a genuine advance in psychoanalytic theory which has yet
to be fully recognised; and the fact that the concept was derived
directly from his own experience, both as patient, and as psychotherapist, makes his contribution all the more estimable. One of the
most valuable aspects of the concept is that it reconciles the apparently incompatible notions of withdrawal and renewal by including
both regressive and 'libidinal' (that is, person-seeking) capacities, thus
making it possible to see a positive aspect in schizoid withdrawal: the
schizoid withdraws in order to preserve his personal and social potential. Guntrip was later to identify a still more profound phenomenon
than withdrawal, namely 'dissociation' – a state in which the innate
libidinal quality of the individual had never been evoked, remaining a
latent potentiality in the psyche (see Guntrip 1968, pp. 249–55).
Nevertheless he maintained that this withdrawn or dissociated heart
of the self was always potentially recoverable if the psychotherapist
was equal to its demands, first for a mental convalescence and then
for a growth-fostering relationship of genuinely mutual significance.
On 14 January, Guntrip received 'a very important letter' from
Fairbairn:

> I now return your M.S., which I have enjoyed reading very much
> . . .   The formulation that 'the entire world of bad objects is a
> colossal defence against the loss of the ego by depersonalisation'
> seems to me extremely important . . .   I consider your concept of
> the splitting of the Libidinal Ego into two parts – an oral needy
> ego and a regressed ego – as an original contribution of consider-
> able explanatory value. It solves a problem which I had not hith-
> erto succeeded in solving. Your emphasis on the 'purposiveness' of
> regression is, if not entirely original in view of Winnicott's work,
> at any rate extremely good. Your statement that 'the cause of
> psychopathological developments would thus seem to be, not
> sexual and aggressive instincts, but fear and flight from a bad-
> object world' is most impressive and arresting. I also like your
> formulation of 'the troubled dream world lying midway between
> the Regressed Ego "in the womb" and the Central Ego dealing
> with outer reality', as also your statement about bad object rela-
> tions safeguarding the separate identity of the ego when good
> relations come to be felt as smothering.

However, Fairbairn remained extremely cautious regarding the practical implications of 'therapeutic regression', and he was uncertain
whether, but for his very considerable insight, which most patients
lacked, Guntrip himself could have carried on if he had undergone

a full-scale regression. Thus, in the same letter he reminded Guntrip that 'these difficulties in the case of one patient gave Winnicott a coronary thrombosis' and he suggested that regression should be managed in hospital. He continued, 'The trouble is, of course, that this would involve [patients] giving up their work and their other responsibilities; but there seems to me a risk of this happening, even if they are being analysed in the ordinary way. You know from your own experience how you passed through a phase in which you lost interest in your work and wanted to just stay at home with your wife and do things in the garden, and also entertained ideas of giving up your present life and going to live in a remote cottage and bury yourself in the depths of the country; but you have insight and knowledge and inner resources lacking in most patients who regress; and you were able to keep going.' He added that in his opinion the struggle to preserve an ego was 'really a more well-informed version of "the instinct of self-preservation"'. Guntrip's own view was that 'ultimately the dangers of regression in real life fade out as it is brought constructively into the treatment, into an accepting object-relation with the analyst. Only that converts it into a healthy regrowing and rebirth process.' Moreover, more of Fairbairn's other patients were beginning to impress upon him the importance of recognising ego-weakness as a deeper problem, with which they would be faced if they gave up their libidinal attachment to internal bad objects and he read to Guntrip part of a letter in which a patient had described a condition similar to Guntrip's own: 'School was life. Weekends and holidays were death. No integrated "I" is perceptible to me except as a feeling of lack. Instead I feel contradictory impulses from split selves which I can't identify. I resort to a pseudo ego to hold me together.'

Guntrip realised that his own chosen strategy for 'keeping possession of his ego' was to devote himself to others 'starting with Percy and going on in religious, social and psychotherapeutic work' and that his compulsive working, talking and thinking were his own defence against 'falling into a gap, a mental emptiness'. In response, Fairbairn made an interpretation which Guntrip later believed to be the nearest he came to that all important 'interpretation' which Balint was to call 'Recognition'.[7] He said, 'You also kept your ego by devoting yourself to spreading my views too, because you believed them; and now you've reached the stage where you can have real thoughts of your own.'

Through February and March, the recurring menace of influenza struck Fairbairn again, causing Guntrip once more to resort to his 'chosen strategy' of overworking. By the time he saw Fairbairn in

April he said he felt inside his own body 'like a castle, looking out at the world through my eyes: my withdrawn self'. He felt an undercurrent of tiredness within all the time, so that if he rested, 'a peculiar heaviness of the body, especially the legs' made him feel that his 'lower part' could not carry the superstructure, a state reminiscent of the 'Dummy' dream. The combination of these feelings with the clear realisation that Fairbairn, despite his desire to see him through to a 'final result', could not go on much longer, caused him to develop his concept of the 'schizoid compromise and the psychotherapeutic stalemate',[8] in which patients are obliged to mark time if regression is ruled out. When Fairbairn asked him 'What is the therapeutic process?', he replied, 'So far as I can see it is the natural growth in security and reality that the Regressed Ego makes when it is understood and accepted.' He added that in his own case such a development had always been opposed by his 'Antilibidinal Ego' modelled on his hardworking mother, with whom he had been driven to identify as the only means of mastering his 'collapsed small child self'. He continued, 'If the Anti-Libidinal Ego is outgrown, the unmothered child can emerge, but if no-one relates to him, he must be buried again and the old anti-libidinal defence revived.'

On his next visit in June, Guntrip found that Fairbairn had seriously deteriorated, and was unable to maintain the quiet supportiveness of more recent sessions. Instead he was talking garrulously and irrelevantly, 'repeating the same thing over and over, and talking about people never acknowledging letters and publishers are frightful. Then he fastened on the castration complex again and went on about that', so that Guntrip felt his analyst was 'falling back from ego to penis, from Fairbairn to Freud'. On his next visit (session 1013) it was clear that the long analysis would have to end, for he found that Fairbairn had fallen asleep during the session and was snoring loudly. The next day, 27 July 1960, Guntrip told him that he felt he must, for practical and financial reasons, bring the analysis to a close. He explained that the devastating effect of Tizard's death had led him to continue the analysis longer than he felt was reasonable in view of Fairbairn's worsening health. Inevitably the prospect of finishing carried an echo of the former dilemma, for whereas Fairbairn had indeed become more of a brother-figure than a father, so that leaving had come to feel like the emotional equivalent of letting him die, it was equally clear that continuing in analysis would come to feel like the emotional equivalent of trying to keep his analyst/brother alive: clearly a wrong basis for therapy. Guntrip had realised for a long time that their sessions were mutually valuable, and that he must 'break it gently' to Fairbairn. As he walked to the door to leave, he realised that they had never once in all those years shaken hands, and, as so often before, he saw 'that element of reserve that hid the true man' in Fairbairn. Determinedly, Guntrip held out his hand and as the other took it a few tears trickled silently down his cheek. Guntrip later recorded, 'I saw the warm heart of this man with a fine mind and a shy nature' (1975, in Hazell 1994, p. 357).

A few days later a sad letter arrived from Fairbairn in which he stated his belief that his illness and not financial pressure, had been the true reason for Guntrip's departure, and adding that he would like Guntrip and Bertha to join him for tea on their way to visit Mrs Kind. They did so in September and Fairbairn was a generous host, inviting Guntrip to write to him if anything arose in which he could be helpful. Such an opportunity arose shortly afterwards when Fairbairn was able to write in support of Guntrip's successful application to become a Fellow of the British Psychological Society.

It is important to mention that all through his time with Fairbairn Guntrip's attention to his work at the Department of Psychiatry in Leeds was as assiduous as ever. His interest in his students as they prepared for their DPM examinations was as genuine as was his concern for his regressing patients. At a time when 'organic psychiatry' was almost universal, and when 'experimental behaviourism' dominated academic psychology, his isolated and anomalous position as 'research psychotherapist' in a University Department of Psychiatry, must have demanded great courage and perseverance. At this time in 1960 Fairbairn was describing a typical psychiatric attitude when he wrote to Guntrip of a 'Medical Superintendent of a Mental Hospital' who had reported that 'the younger psychiatrists are just not interested in the personal problems of their patients . . . all they are interested in is to decide whether to give their patients Shock Therapy, Insulin Coma Therapy, Tranquilliser Therapy or Prefrontal Leucotomy' (personal communication, 4 November 1960). Guntrip himself was indeed fortunate to have found an ally in the Medical Superintendent of Scalebor Park Psychiatric Hospital, Dr Valentine, who supported his treatment of regressed patients there, despite considerable criticism by many of the staff. He once told me of one such patient who entered Scalebor very regressed. He was unable to talk and hid in the bedclothes. Guntrip simply sat with him and held his hand beneath the blankets. Not a word had been spoken, but the patient later said that he felt that this had been the turning point, at which he began to recover. It would appear from this that Guntrip had taken to heart Fairbairn's caution about the strains imposed by regressing patients. Indeed, in the second of the three papers of this period, 'The Schizoid Problem, Regression and the Struggle to Preserve an Ego' (1961, in Hazell 1994, p. 157), Guntrip considered not only the demands placed upon the analyst by regression, but the cost to the patient himself. As in the ego-weakness paper, he was attempting to explore for himself as well as the patients, the possible consequences of the therapeutic regression which he knew he needed. In particular he was concerned by the prospect of 'the appalling risk of the definite selfhood' involved in a deep regression (p. 163), and he was inclined to the opinion that in the absence of skilled understanding of a kind that would enable the patient to outgrow his fears of a good relationship as engulfing, 'a compromise solution' could often be the best remedy. Such indeed was Guntrip's own position at the time, stranded between analysts, having made important gains but with the core of his problem unreached. Nevertheless, he ended the paper with some promising examples from his own work with patients who were able to 'develop a constructive faith that if the needs of the Regressed Ego are met, first in relation to the therapist who protects it in its need for an initial passive dependence, this will not mean collapse and the loss of active powers for good and all, but a steady recuperation from deep strain, diminishing of deep fears, revitalising of the personality and rebirth of an active ego that is spontaneous and does not have to be forced and driven' (p. 186). There were also further signs in the paper that Guntrip was looking towards London for the continuance of his search for understanding, for he again made reference to the work of Balint and Winnicott, and suggested that his 'Regressed Ego' was 'identical with Winnicott's "True Self in Cold Storage".

In the early half of 1961 Fairbairn's health worsened, and he wrote in January: 'I am afraid I feel now that I have shot my bolt, as my health has not really been satisfactory since my illness in the autumn of 1958. So I shall have to rely on you to carry on.' In July he wrote, 'How far post-influenzal depression is somatic I don't know, but I can't help feeling that the theme of your paper (on Ego weakness) has some relevance to my state.' However, his critical edge was not diminished, as his detailed and congratulatory letter to Guntrip on the manuscript of his third seminal paper of this prolific period, 'The Manic Depressive Problem in the Light of the Schizoid Process' (1962, in Hazell 1994, p. 187), demonstrates. Fairbairn wrote:

I myself think it is your profoundest paper so far; and I
congratulate you whole-heartedly. Your idea of a split in the
Libidinal Ego has proved very fruitful; and, as I have already
indicated, it is quite original. It is your idea, not mine. I consider your relating of Freud's id–super ego conflict to the ideas
of Plato and Saint Paul most illuminating. Freud obviously took
over uncritically the universal idea of 'Impulse and Social Controls' but it took you to point out the significance of his doing
so ... I think your idea of depression being the result of
failure to put up a defence against regression extremely good
and very well worked out. The same applies to your conception
of the rôle played by the manic defence. I also like your 'Fight
or Flight' idea, and your contrast between love and fear of relationships – also your description of the Oedipus Complex in
terms of defence against regression. Then, I like your thesis that
depression arises out of an attempt to fend off depersonalisation
by internalisation of the lost object as an accusing object.
Altogether, I think your paper is magnificent ... I think your
paper ought really to go to the *International Journal*. It is a bit
wasted in the *BJMP*.[9] (1 July 1961)

The paper was duly published in the *International Journal of
Psycho-Analysis* the following spring, by which time Fairbairn's
health had improved greatly. He wrote again congratulating Guntrip, and noting some differences from his own views:

You have rather departed from my formulation in 'A Revised
Psychopathology' to the effect that schizophrenia and depression
were two ultimate psychological disasters against which all other
pathological states represented defences. Apparently your view is
now that depression is bound up with a defence against schizoid
withdrawal. That leaves only one ultimate psychopathological
state, viz. schizophrenia. You may well be right. Certainly many
of the phenomena described in cases of depression are really
schizoid, – apathy being one, I should say. I gather that you
regard mania as a another defence against schizoid withdrawal,
rather than as a defence against depression. Certainly you are
right in regarding hyperactivity as the characteristic manic
symptom.

When Guntrip sent Fairbairn a copy of *Personality Structure and
Human Interaction* the former replied that he was 'more glad than
he could say' that Guntrip had produced a book that had been

accepted for the International Library of Psychoanalysis, and that 'both expounded and expanded' his own ideas, and he added once more that he looked to Guntrip to carry on his work. He had, he said, 'rather naturally' regarded Chapters 10–16 as 'quite the best bit of the book', which he did not think was 'altogether because they are concerned with Klein and Fairbairn'! (10 August 1961). The book, which was reviewed by Marion Milner, effectively marked the beginning of Guntrip's international career as a psychoanlytic writer, and his reputation was further enhanced when he attended a reception at Fairbairn's house for participants at the Twenty-second International Congress of Psychoanalysis.

It is unclear how Guntrip felt about carrying on and developing Fairbairn's work, although he did so with great determination. When Fairbairn said in a letter that his wife, Marion, thought of Guntrip as 'an evangelist' the latter replied that he felt he was 'an evangelist with no good news to preach' (personal communication, January 1962) – a response which probably reflects more his underlying weariness than lack of conviction as to the value of the work. No doubt he was missing his regular access to Fairbairn. The tone of their correspondence suggests that whereas Fairbairn was recovering somewhat, and, with a greatly reduced number of patients, was deservedly enjoying a sense of accomplishment, Guntrip, having lost his analyst short of the breakthrough he had hoped for, was feeling less than confident of his ability to 'carry on the good work' despite Fairbairn's admiration of his 'tireless energy' (personal communication, 15 December 1961). The problem was that the energy concerned was intellectual energy achieved at great cost to Guntrip's underlying weak ego whose state he was having to conceptualise through his own theory writing.

A flurry of correspondence with the educationist and poet David Holbrook may have served to cheer Guntrip at this period. Holbrook was much in tune with Fairbairn's views, but could not resist an amusing comment on the use of abbreviations to describe the dramatis personae of the inner world. He wrote, 'I can see the difficulty, which arises out of complexity. But it gets somehow inhuman and even risible, when you speak of the Anti-L.E. persecuting the weak, infantile L.E. As a personifying drama of the inner life, it invites me to see characters with their initials stamped on their backs . . . as a system it explains many things: but somehow at a cost, of seeing the inward life somewhat like an awkward squad of directors. 'Old I.S. (internal saboteur) was a damn nuisance this morning.' 'Well, C.E. was half asleep, you know.' (26 May 1961)

During this period, Guntrip's awareness of his own needs was inclining him ever further towards an analysis with Winnicott, whose paper on regression, secured for him by Fairbairn himself, seven years earlier, had made such a profound impression upon him. He eventually entered analysis with Winnicott in March 1962, after his own researches had led him further in the direction of 'therapeutic stalemate' (*The Schizoid Compromise and the Psychotherapeutic Stalemate*, 1962, in Hazell 1994, p. 215). Fairbairn meanwhile continued to be fascinated by that aspect of Guntrip's problem which his own theory could not encompass. In the same month that Guntrip began analysis with Winnicott, Fairbairn wrote him a long letter in which he described two male patients, whose situation was markedly similar to that of his former analysand. In both these cases separation anxiety had become 'a prime factor in promoting a schizoid attitude'. The first involved early separation from his mother and removal to an aunt, which triggered an earlier weaning problem, making the patient afraid to risk much needed relationships lest the separation trauma should recur; and the second referred to a weaning trauma, reinforced by the trauma of the primal scene, to allay which the patient had become addicted to infantile masturbation as a substitute for suckling. Then he was circumcised, and the circumcision had the effect of reviving the separation anxiety . In the letter Fairbairn emphasises, more than once, that it was a very long time 'before the basic traumatic situation underlying these symptoms (i.e. separation anxiety) emerged into analysis' (personal communication, 16 March 1962). Although Fairbairn made no reference to the close resemblance between these patients' circumstances and Guntrip's own, he surely intended a reference to the latter's feelings of fading away into non-existence when he wrote two weeks later that separation anxiety, which could begin at birth, is felt by the child 'to involve a threat to his very existence – a threat of death' (personal communication, 30 March 1962). Despite the fact that this belated recognition by Fairbairn of the core of Guntrip's psychopathology arrived – albeit by reference to 'other patients' – when the analysis was over the signs continued to increase that Fairbairn was moving nearer to an acceptance of ego-weakness as the basic problem, and of 'separation anxiety' as the primary cause. In April he referred again to one of the patients he had mentioned, who became afraid of his desires and wishes, not because they were 'incestuous' but because he would make 'a fool of himself by expressing infantile needs' which were unacceptable to his mother, 'that is, a fear of Ego weakness' (3 April 1962). Although he did not say so directly, further references by Fairbairn to separation anxiety as presenting itself to the child as a threat of death suggest that he had finally come to associate Guntrip's deathly feelings with a failure in the maternal relationship, rather than a defence against 'incestuous drives'. There is no record of Guntrip having regretted his decision to leave Fairbairn when the latter's health and insight improved so greatly, but one cannot help wondering about the effect upon him of frequent references by Fairbairn to 'two patients of special interest . . . both of long-standing' from whom he had learned 'how long it takes to get down to really basic issues in analysis' (personal communication, 24 May 1962). Perhaps he had come to regret his earlier remarks to Fairbairn about the undue length of his own analysis. However, there is little evidence of need in his letters to Fairbairn beyond a grouse or two over practicalities, such as having to move consulting rooms, and see patients in his own home.

Of course, it is possible that Fairbairn was unaware that Guntrip had already begun his analysis with Winnicott at this stage, and that he was hoping to draw him back to Edinburgh. For he had in an earlier letter (4 November 1960) written 'I am glad that you did not transfer to somebody else (e.g. to Sutherland or Winnicott) as I wanted to see the enterprise through.' At any rate, it would appear from a letter dated 7 July 1962 that Guntrip had not revealed to Fairbairn the full import of his analysis with Winnicott, which was into its fourth month by then, for Fairbairn wrote, 'I am glad you managed to have a fruitful talk with Winnicott while you were in London.' The reference was not to an analytic session but to an occasion when Guntrip read a paper to the Medical Section of the British Psychological Society. However, when, later that same month, Guntrip had his first difference of opinion with Winnicott over the supposed 'innate ruthlessness' of the infant, he promptly wrote to Fairbairn about it, surely knowing that Fairbairn would support his view that a baby's nature is innately social. Perhaps Guntrip was 'keeping his options open' by omitting to inform either of his analysts fully about his dealings with the other. Nevertheless, there are signs that Fairbairn detected a change of allegiance, so to speak, for when in 1963 Guntrip paid considerable tribute to his theoretical revision in a paper[10] which formed part of a special issue of the *British Journal of Medical Psychology* honouring Fairbairn's work, the latter commented, 'I think there are fewer references to my work than one might have expected in a contribution to a "Fairbairn" issue of the *BJMP*' (personal communication, 4 August 1962). In the section of the paper dealing with psychotherapy (which was drawn from his

address to the Medical Section of the British Psychological Society)
Guntrip had written enthusiastically about his own and Winnicott's
work with regressed patients, which aimed at 'the rebirth of the true
self', making scant reference to Fairbairn. Although Fairbairn's letter
ended with a cordial invitation to Guntrip and Bertha to visit him
that summer, Guntrip was alarmed by his mentor's note of pique,
and he wrote at once explaining his difficulty in offering 'a direct
expository and critically evaluatory paper' on Fairbairn's work, without repeating what he had already dealt with fully in Chapters 10–16
of his book and in previous papers. Fairbairn was not fully assuaged
by this explanation. Indeed he strongly suggested that whereas he had
been amazed at Guntrip's productivity in the past, he was now
inclined to think he too may have 'shot his bolt', with nothing new
to say! – adding, 'What you need now is a let up . . .   Your regressed
patients must have been a great strain.' And he reiterated 'As I expect
you know, one of Winnicott's regressed patients was responsible for
his coronary thrombosis' (personal communication, 11 August 1962).
Fortunately for Guntrip and for psychodynamic theory, this bitter and
rather gloomy prognosis proved unfounded. In time Fairbairn's disappointment over Guntrip's omission of references to him eased.
Both Dicks and Wisdom had written good papers for the special
'Fairbairn Issue' and, in fact, Guntrip himself had paid considerable
tribute to Fairbairn in the first section of the paper, as 'the only
analyst who has taken up the overall revision of theory' from the
point of view of the ego *as a unique centre of meaningful experience
growing in the medium of personal relationships*' (1963, in Hazell
1994, p. 242). When Guntrip wrote a masterly exposition of Fairbairn's object-relations theory for Volume 3 of the *American Handbook of Psychiatry*, Fairbairn was delighted and the rift was healed.
He wrote to Guntrip:

> I am deeply indebted to you for the furtherance of my work. I
> feel I have passed the ball to you now; and I feel I could not do
> better. (Personal communication, 22 March 1963)

As his analysis with Winnicott began to gather momentum, Guntrip
started work on his second major book. Encouraged by good reviews
of *Personality Structure and Human Interaction* in the *Times Literary Supplement*, the *Spectator* and the *Lancet*, he planned to base the
new book on his clinical work, using the three papers that he had
worked out between 1960 and 1962, when Fairbairn's declining
health obliged him to end the analysis. He wrote to Gwen and Denis
Greenald that he wanted to get on 'with what I think will be my

most important book, *The Schizoid Problem and Psychotherapy*[11] for which *Personality Structure and Human Interaction* was a theoretical preparation. I've got the plan of it matured and the enclosed papers, along with the "Ego Weakness" one will form the basis of it. New material is what is wanted, and I've got this in my cases of successfully treated regression . . . This is the kind of material I want to sift thoroughly and write up, and then I'll feel I've done my job and made my contribution' (personal communication, 21 February 1963). Bad weather had prevented him and Bertha from visiting Gwen and her family where they had settled across the Pennines in Cheshire, and the letter ends 'T.T.F.N. and pray for the snow to go. Love to you all – Dad.'

In the summer of 1964 Fairbairn's health deteriorated once more. Guntrip kept him supplied with papers and letters, in an attempt, as he later wrote to Sutherland, 'to keep the real Ronald, the thinking analyst alive in him almost to the end . . . not senile and out of touch, but still reading and thinking psychoanalytically, and actively supporting me in my further development of his basic views' (24 September 1974). In June, Guntrip sent Fairbairn a copy of his book *Healing the Sick Mind* (1964), and the latter expressed 'great interest', adding 'I am glad to hear that you have had a message of congratulation from Winnicott, whose opinion is worth a great deal' (21 June 1964). In fact Winnicott had dined with Fairbairn when he visited Edinburgh that summer to lecture at the summer school of the Davidson Clinic, and Fairbairn wrote to Guntrip that the lectures were very good. In the same letter he recorded his gratitude to Guntrip for his review of Segal's *Introduction to the Work of Melanie Klein*: 'Needless to say, I am very interested in the contrast you draw between Melanie Klein's views and mine. But at the same time you bring out my indebtedness to her, which is, of course, very great' (personal communication, 6 August 1964).

Guntrip and Bertha saw Fairbairn for the last time at the end of September during their annual summer holiday in Scotland. Guntrip was due to lecture at the Davidson Clinic in February, and in his last letter to Guntrip, on 16 November 1964, Fairbairn, with the generosity so typical over the years, offered him hospitality during his forthcoming visit. He was also, he said, looking forward to reading the manuscript of Guntrip's latest paper 'The Concept of Psychodynamic Science' (1967, in Hazell 1994, p. 251). Fairbairn died on 31 December 1964. He was in his seventy-sixth year. However strong Guntrip's reservations may have been about the therapeutic value of the analysis itself, there can be no doubt that his regular correspondence and

discussions on clinical and theoretical issues with Fairbairn, together
with the latter's professional support, made a very great contribution
indeed to the establishment of Guntrip's standing in the psychoanalytic world. Earlier, in August, Guntrip had delivered an address
in response to R.D. Laing's paper on 'Psychotherapy' at the sixth
International Congress of Psychotherapy in London, of which Fairbairn had been made a vice-president, but which he was too ill to
attend. There is a strong sense in Guntrip's address (which later
formed the basis of Chapter 13 in *Schizoid Phenomena, Object Relations and the Self*) that he felt increasingly secure in his profession.
He told Winnicott, 'I felt I was there by right of my own work; my
paper was well received, people from Europe and America, and a
Maudesley lecturer, told me that they appreciated and used my book.'
The views expressed in *Healing the Sick Mind* were also taken up
enthusiastically by David Holbrook, who, in his book, *The Masks of
Hate* (1972), sought to expose 'unconscious themes of hate and false
solutions in the wider culture of children's comics, "pop cults", folk
song and modern literature, as well as in the fashionable adherence
to instinct theory in the psychoanalytical world'. Perhaps it is a
measure of the die-hard resistance to the new 'object-relations' perspective that the manuscript of *The Masks of Hate* was rejected by
Tavistock, after a very long delay, with the strange explanation that it
was considered 'reactionary' as compared with the so-called 'liberalis-
ing' effects of Laing's phenomenological approach. Holbrook was
baffled and furious. He replied that he found it 'shocking' that the
phenomenological approach had become an 'intolerant orthodoxy',
unable to tolerate any criticism of its position. The book was published elsewhere however, and Guntrip was greatly encouraged to feel
that his work was reaching a wider public in the world of education.
Holbrook, for his part, wrote that he found not only Tavistock
Publications, but the University people at Cambridge 'so hostile to
creativity, to "inner reality", to ideas and life' that he wished strongly
to live in Leeds, ·where he could discuss Guntrip's ideas and those of
Winnicott, and their relevance to literature, more freely!

Notes

1   This case is summarised in *Personality Structure and Human Interac-
    tion*, Guntrip 1961, pp. 416–17.
2   In my view the respective terms 'introjection' and 'internalisation' are
    still subject to confusion. In discussion, Guntrip said he felt that
    'introjection' should be used to denote the absorbtion or 'imbibing' of
    good 'ego-promoting' experience, retained as 'pleasant memory',
    whereas 'internalisation' should represent the process whereby

'indigestible' bad experience remained stuck like a foreign body in the psyche. (See Guntrip 1968, pp. 21–2.)

3 'Considerations arising out of the Schreber Case', *British Journal of Medical Psychology* Vol. 29: pp. 113–27.

4 *International Journal of Psycho-Analysis*, Vol. 34, pp. 374–83.

5 The whole correspondence is in Hazell 1994, p. 399.

6 D.W. Winnicott, 1955, 'Clinical Varieties of Transference', *International Journal of Psycho-Analysis*, Vol. 37, p. 386.

7 M. Balint, 1968, *The Basic Fault*. London: Tavistock, p.144.

8 This theme became the subject of a major paper (1962, in Hazell 1994, p. 21) and was eventually revised as Chapter 11 of *Schizoid Phenomena, Object Relations and the Self* (1968).

9 *British Journal of Medical Psychology*, in which Guntrip's papers had been published hitherto.

10 'Psychodynamic Theory and the Problem of Psychotherapy' (1963, in Hazell 1994, p. 235).

11 This was a working title for *Schizoid Phenomena, Object Relations and the Self*.

The Winnicott Analysis

CHAPTER 14

1962

Guntrip began his analysis with Winnicott in March 1962, 'moved consciously' by feeling he 'needed guidance from someone expert in the treatment of regressions', as well as by his need to finalise his personal analysis. He wrote to Winnicott as follows:

> To give you some idea of what I want to do, I may mention that the focal trauma of my childhood was pretty certainly the death of my brother Percy at the age of 2 years, when I was 3½ years. My mother was a business woman, who often said she ought not to have been a mother, who returned to business when I was one year old, and didn't want her second pregnancy quite definitely. I understand that I devotedly 'adopted' the baby, I expect to make up for the considerable loss; and when I lost him too, I understand I suddenly became so ill and lifeless I was thought to be dying.
>
> When Fairbairn had his serious illness four years ago, I knew I had been dealing with the slowly emerging effects of all that for about the previous twelve months; and I was seeing a new significance in several major dreams and events at earlier periods of my life, in the light of this. Then the analysis had to peter out.
>
> Not that I myself stood still in the matter. I feel sure it results in my conceptualising in theory what I could not communicate in an analytical object-relationship. But I feel this carries the risk of the theoretical ideas having to operate as a defence and congealing into a rigid form that blocks further progressive insights. I feel now a need to 'open out' what has gathered up in me about this, not on paper but personally to someone who will understand what I am getting at.
>
> The enclosed paper (manic depression etc.) presents my ideas as far as I have been able to take them. I think it is the most important thing I have done . . . I have one further paper on the stocks and perhaps it is significant that the subject is 'The

Schizoid Compromise and Therapeutic Stalemate'. I have described this compromise to some extent, as I see it on pp. 228–32 of the current number of the *BJMP*. Beyond that point I don't at present see clearly and I feel sure that some sessions with you will set things moving again, to the benefit of both myself and my work.

Time constraints and the long journey between Leeds and London meant that analysis could proceed at the rate of only two sessions once a month, on Tuesday evening and Wednesday morning respectively. Guntrip had 160 sessions in all, usually managing a couple of dozen sessions a year during the first six years, tailing off in 1969. Towards the end of their first session Winnicott suddenly broke in with 'I've got nothing particular to say yet, but if I don't say something, you may begin to feel I'm not here.' Guntrip replied, 'I feel there is a part of me that withdrew and regressed, though I don't really know what that involves, but I need to get that part of me accepted.' Although Guntrip had conceptualised that part of himself as 'the regressed libidinal ego', a term, however, which he did not wish 'to define too clearly', he now needed to move beyond intellectual perception to emotional experience. Thus at their second session, he referred again to the part of him that had withdrawn from the world, and he said, 'I realise I did ask the date of a paper of yours because I needed to hear your voice and place you.' It is of interest to note that whereas Fairbairn had adopted a practice of sitting with his patient in adjacent chairs, Winnicott sat on a wooden chair by the couch, out of the direct sight of his patient, a practice he maintained until near the end of the analysis. Accordingly, Guntrip sat sideways on the couch at first, where he could see Winnicott. In his reply Winnicott identi-fied the core of the problem. He said, 'You know about me but I'm not a person to you yet, and you may go away feeling alone and that I'm not real.' He continued, 'You must have had an earlier illness before Percy was born, and you felt mother deserted you and left you to look after yourself. You accepted Percy as your infant self that needed looking after and when he died, you had nothing and collapsed into the ill child.' Guntrip noted, 'That was the first interpretation of my illness when Percy died that really made some sense to me. I had felt Percy's death as the death or loss of the "inner" me.' He was astonished at the rapidity with which Winni-cott went to the heart of the matter – 'not the actively bad mother of later childhood, but the earlier mother who failed to relate at all' (Guntrip 1975, in Hazell 1994, p. 362).

Guntrip linked this insight to his ambivalence over treating regressed patients. He saw that although Percy had saved him from loneliness, looking after both of them had been a heavy burden, which was replicated by the strain of holding regressed patients. He saw that the exhaustion was an ever-present danger lurking all the time, to break out if anyone representing a brother should die. Winnicott observed, 'Your interest in regressed patients comes from this. Analysing is an active thing but you are more concerned with caring for the regressed ill child who is dead, or dying with Percy.'

This was the period when the corporation were pulling down the building where Guntrip had his consulting rooms and he had mentioned to Winnicott that the problem had brought a return of his 'old bodily tensions', which had all but faded out in the Fairbairn analysis. Winnicott's response was sympathetic and direct. He said, 'I'm sorry you're so worried about your consulting rooms. That's a nasty business.' That night Guntrip dreamed:

I was in session with Dr W. and had a powerful emotional experience as if for the first time I could let my emotions mount up to feeling peak of tension and then quietly relax. That had become possible because Winnicott was there.

The dream was totally different from any he had ever had, and he said: 'I could let my tension go and develop and relax because you were present in my inner world. I feel that's close to my main motive now for analysis, to become a more fundamentally relaxed person beneath all my activities.' Fairbairn's *written* (May 1962) expression of sympathy over the consulting-room problem had been equally sincere. But it's impact was less effective, presumably because of its 'indirectness'. Winnicott replied: 'I think that internal explosion was a sort of orgasm, an experience of love in your body. You were free to be yourself and with me present. You were being active in feeling.' This raised a new important issue for Guntrip. He had always loved his father, but had been unable to show it because of his father's reserved nature and his mother's jealousy, whereas he had admired his mother's efficiency, but had been unable to love her. He saw that both Fairbairn and his father had only been able to show feeling spontaneously in 'terminal situations': Fairbairn at their last meeting had responded to Guntrip's handshake with tears in his eyes, and Guntrip's father had died in his arms with a smile of recognition, saying 'Goodbye'. He wondered whether he himself had been afraid to feel lest, if a real relation occurred, that would mean the end of the relationship, 'death'. Winnicott concurred, 'Yes, you may actually feel that. You were ready for a feeling relation, but it was something your father and Fairbairn couldn't give you till the end. It wasn't your inhibition, it was them. You were in tears just now telling me of your father's death. You can show feeling now with me evidently.' Guntrip felt a new deeper relaxation at the end of that session, and expressed his gratitude to Winnicott for the natural unselfconscious way he shook hands and smiled at the end of a session.

Significantly, it was after this spontaneous expression of gratitude that the dispute over the infant/patient's ruthlessness arose, about which Guntrip had written to Fairbairn. Fairbairn had attributed Guntrip's over-active drive to rivalry with father and therefore with himself. But when, at the next session, Guntrip mentioned that 'some roaring motor-cars stirred some odd kind of fears' in him, Winnicott saw a deeper significance. He said. 'You fear being destructive. It's not rivalry with father or Fairbairn or me, but destructive in some deeper sense, more primitive. You fear destroying him in the process of using him up, being destructive in the process of getting the help that you want. You want to know whether I can stand your needing my help.' As if to confirm Winnicott's interpretation Guntrip was disturbed the following morning by a feeling, while visiting the National Gallery, that he might damage the pictures by looking at them, 'as if I wanted to get their value into me, absorb it'. He said, 'I'm sure mother reacted against any vigorous breast-feeding on my part, because she didn't like physical contact and only breast-fed me, so she said, to protect herself from another pregnancy.' Thus he felt that, as a baby, he had been unable to feel destructive when feeding because of his mother's rejective reaction. Winnicott demurred: 'There's something less civilised than eating, primitive tearing to pieces. You wanted to tear Fairbairn's theories, to see if they stood up to it. You weren't given a chance to do that with mother.'

Guntrip later recalled that this was the first point where he felt Winnicott's interpretation failed to feel 'real' to him. One might suppose that this retreat into debating the origin of destructiveness reflected a fear of 'using the object', after that first vivid experience expressed in the orgasmic dream: an example of how the schizoid person moves 'in and out' of relationships due to his alternating and conflicting need and fear of them. A similar 'retreat into theorising' was to become a feature of the analysis whenever the question of 'innate destructiveness' arose. Moreover, as mentioned earlier, the difference of opinion with Winnicott caused Guntrip to renew his correspondence with his former analyst over this very issue, and, perhaps because he had sought refuge through their correspondence, he now felt a need to talk about Fairbairn 'in order to get free'. He described how Fairbairn gradually, after his wife's death and his influenza illness, had reverted to early Freudian ideas, in which everything was seen in terms of libidinised sexual tensions so that he seemed to have forgotten 'personal relations'. He felt that whilst Fairbairn became afraid of the far-reaching implications of his own theory as his health declined, he nevertheless tried to do more therapeutically than he was then capable of, until finally Guntrip saw this and broke it off. Winnicott supported his patient's need to talk about his former analyst. He said, 'Once you began protecting Fairbairn, you couldn't discuss it with him. I've had other patients come to me to talk out their relation with a very good but failing aged analyst of great reputation. If it's not discussed beforehand, it can't be discussed after you leave him. You've got to talk it out with someone else. You might have the same trouble with me unless you talk it out beforehand. Otherwise it gets intolerable to go on, but also difficult to stop. You pay him for protecting him. Fairbairn at the end was probably repeating his own analyst, the old things he said about "castration complex" etc. That was the way they talked in those days. Fairbairn as a revolutionary thinker probably went beyond himself, and when he began to fail, he fell back on the earlier things, quite uncharacteristic of Fairbairn. You have a few years advantage of me and you must be prepared for me to deteriorate; not that I feel like it, but it must always come – Probably something in Fairbairn's nature held him back from you, as well as his failing health.' Guntrip concluded that he and Fairbairn were really very different types of person, apart from their basic philosophical agreements, a factor which he believed must play a larger part than was generally recognised in all analyses especially if 'psychoanalytic technique' was regarded as all-important.

There was no session during August, and on resuming in September 1962 Guntrip returned to the theme of identification with father, Fairbairn and Percy, all of whom had become inactive. He was then sixty-one and feared that he might die, like father, at sixty-three. Moreover, Fairbairn had written (11 August 1962) 'I myself feel that I have shot my bolt. A point can be reached at which there is nothing more to be said apart from repetition.' It was the same letter in which he had reminded Guntrip that a regressed patient was responsible for Winnicott's coronary thrombosis. On the other hand, Guntrip felt that, since Winnicott was not bound by the 'activity tied to inactivity pattern', the latter could, in turn, free him from it, 'just to be himself' because Winnicott 'knew' him not by intellectual analysis but by sympathetic understanding. Winnicott's courageous attitude encouraged him to confide his deepest problem, the death threat that had 'vaguely haunted' him all his life. Winnicott commented, 'People spend their lives fighting this fear of breakdown and when it comes it may last only a moment, rarely more than a few months or a year. You fear that if you go back to infancy, you'll come on things like illness and death, and you can't afford to risk that now in real life. You're coming to me because you think I might be able to provide a way out that doesn't involve being ill.' Guntrip at this time was himself heavily involved with regressing patients. He was overloaded with extra sessions and phone-calls from these patients, and he felt a strong underlying urge 'to get out of it all', only to feel blocked by a lifelong feeling that some force he did not clearly know would restrict him and shut him in, and tie him down to a living death. Winnicott believed that the force was not external, but mother's repressed hatred of males, internalised by Guntrip, which made him afraid to regress to her, despite a longing to do so, lest he come upon something destructive in her, and die. Thus he dare not relax and fall asleep, but must identify with his mother's forced activity in order to compensate 'for something dead in the background'.

Guntrip was disappointed by the emphasis upon his mother's hatred of men. He felt certain that it 'barred the way to seeing "the mother who failed to relate at all"'. Winnicott, however, continued with his line of interpretation that it was his mother's possessing herself of his sadism, leaving him feeling empty and helpless, which prevented Guntrip's 'timid self' evolving into his 'brave one'. Sensing Guntrip's resistance, he said, 'You bring your timid infant self to me and here you really do depend on me. If you couldn't get me to see and understand your timid self, the little child, then you'd have to have a regressive illness to make me understand it. But there's no absolute split between your timid child self and your brave active self, and the latter can accept the former. You don't "cure" or alter the timid child self. You first of all accept it. To adopt the attitude of "curing it", would mean disapproving of it, seeking to alter it. The patient must come to accept himself for what he is, basically a timid little child, or a cut-off person, and not seek to deny himself but be prepared to grow, evolve, beginning with what he is.' By this Guntrip felt truly reached, feeling that Winnicott had 'saved the day' for him, by speaking of seeing and understanding the frightened child.

CHAPTER 15

1963

Over the Christmas break, Guntrip had two dreams in which he was with Winnicott, 'feeling very secure'. However, Winnicott's terms 'timid' and 'brave' did not ring true with him. His inner child self felt more *lonely* than timid, because his mother could give no relation, and not so much brave as *determined*, to get away from mother and 'find Percy', while simultaneously keeping himself active to stave off collapse. He said to Winnicott 'Whatever my collapse illness really meant to me in emotional terms, I clearly didn't succeed in getting to where Percy was. It must have been, and remains, a retreat into myself, a withdrawal from mother, a mother who couldn't keep her baby alive. That bit of me must feel all alone inside, and accounts for the occasional quite schizoid transient feelings I discussed with Fairbairn.' Winnicott replied 'I think we could say your mother conceived the idea of a dead child, not a really live one, a kind of marionette she could make do whatever she wanted. You had to get yourself alive before you could do anything. So now you have to keep yourself alive, talk all the time, mustn't let up the effort to keep yourself in being. You need me to be a mother who can give life to you.'

Guntrip felt that to be the most significant response yet made to him. Its effect was to free him for spontaneous action. He abandoned his 'sideways' position and swung his legs on to the couch and lay down, feeling that it was the right time to do so. He said, 'I don't need to see you now, in order to know you are there. And I don't need to talk so much. Silence seems safer now.' With a nice sense of balance, Winnicott replied, 'There's a lot to talk about, especially with two sessions a month, but silence is also valuable, though you feel some risk.' The sense of risk was registered by Guntrip in a dream:

I was carrying a hare by the back legs so it couldn't jump.

Winnicott commented: 'A hare is a timid creature, but alive and can jump. A new self growing out of your earlier "lost child" self, but you're afraid to let it jump. You don't know what may happen. You fear you may lose it, lose yourself. The repression of your earliest self had a kind of stability and you fear losing it.' However, despite the feeling on Winnicott's part that Guntrip would lose the new sense of relation in the monthly interval and would 'have to fall back on self-support', the latter continued to experience a new sense of life and purpose, which he saw reflected in a further dream.

> I was looking down from a bridge at a large sweeping bend in a river where it flooded a marshy area, and I realised that the land was being reclaimed, gardens were growing there, and the river was flowing now in its normal course.

He felt it to be 'a most important encouraging dream, of a quite new kind' for him. He said, 'I feel that marsh represents my very earliest experience that never got formed or grown into a definite self, and is now beginning to be "reclaimed" from that formless state, into a definite course.' Nevertheless, the feeling of risk appeared a few nights later when he dreamed that Winnicott had casually invited him to stay after the session, and whilst Winnicott slept quietly he could not get to sleep, until as dawn approached, Guntrip quietly looked over his notes, reminding himself of what Winnicott had said. Only then could he doze off and sleep.

That the new sense of inner security was only precariously held against a fear of losing his independent adult self was shown in a further dream:

> I lost my car and my brief case with all my thesis papers in it, but after a time I found them again.

Winnicott reminded him that his car and briefcase represented all the good aspects of his independent active self that he naturally did not want to lose. This calm acceptance of the 'sweet reasonableness' of his fears of regression enabled Guntrip to relax again. But the precarious balance between a patient's need to regress and his desire to preserve his independent status was again vividly demonstrated when Winnicott gave Guntrip a paper he had written. The initial feeling of pleasure at being given the paper turned suddenly to an anxiety over being expected to be adult. As the next session approached Guntrip felt he was 'keying up' and not 'depending'. Winnicott at once replied, 'Yes, I was worried about that afterwards and wondered if I should have done it. I can't find the little child to talk to now.'

Guntrip realised that his reaction had been exacerbated by a spate of professional recognition and consequent demands in the spring of 1963. It is also noticeable that the dates of his letters to and from Fairbairn correspond to periods immediately after his monthly sessions with Winnicott, though he does not appear to have referred to them. The letters are mostly concerned with 'adult' professional matters, and he was always addressed as 'My dear Guntrip'. But thanks to Winnicott's readiness to see the matter from the point of view of 'the little child in him', he was able to see that he needed, and could have, 'both relations . . . the child and the adult that you help the child grow up to'. It was not only pressure arising from his growing reputation as a writer that tied Guntrip to his 'professional self', but the needs of his regressed patients. In the April session he reported having awakened one night to see 'a clear image of baby Percy in the air and in the dark', as he had imagined him laid on their mother's lap, and had 'felt tied to him'. He explained to Winnicott his feeling that this 'night vision' was a reaction to a fear that two of his regressed patients would wear him out, even though both had made good progress – and especially one – a male – who had acted out what he felt 'in a quite naive unselfconscious way by flinging himself on the ground and clasping Guntrip around the knees, shrieking, "I'm desperate. I'm clinging to you as my last hope!"' Winnicott replied, 'I feel I hate those two patients. I sympathise with them and understand that you couldn't do anything else but stand by them through their crises, but they come between you and me and I can't talk to you . . . There is a pathological element in your sympathy for them which might destroy you.' Clearly Winnicott still felt that the monthly intervals were too long for Guntrip to sustain the sense of their relationship, which he felt to be in need of 'more immediate renewal'. He said, 'You use geographical distance to protect yourself from realising your needs to make demands on your analysts. If you lived next door, you'd feel you needed to see me every day. Mother's illness, shown in her hate of men which protected her from your destructive demands, inhibited you. You got to the point with me two months ago where you could express excited need of me and move forward to the next phase of object-relations. But you are worried about the destructive element in relations and can only become inhibited.'

In the next session a month later, Guntrip himself reported having felt ill during the gap, and on one occasion, feeling 'strange in bed, as if lying in bed was like lying on mother's lap, as I had seen Percy there'. Winnicott interpreted: 'Your depressed self in bed reliving Percy's death, is depressed with mother. If she hadn't sent you away from her you might have died. You felt something destructive in her.'

In the 1970s Guntrip was in no doubt that, analytically, Winnicott had 'got onto the wrong line' by his emphasis upon mother's destructiveness, but he recalled that its ill-effects had been offset by an accidental overhearing of Winnicott's sensitive handling of a distressed little girl patient as she was taken away at the end of her session. His kind, patient supportiveness and intuitive understanding had made a deep impression on Guntrip especially when, in their session the following morning, he learned that Winnicott had visited the child on the previous evening. Thus encouraged he was again able to stress that his deepest fear had not been that his mother would actively destroy him, but that she would let him die as she had let Percy die. Winnicott's response removed any further doubt. He said, 'In some sense a part of you did die. You had an experience of death, and need to relive it to find out that there is a way out with me, from having to be one of mother's dead objects. Your mother couldn't help you through that experience.'

The next session, the twenty-eighth, fell on Guntrip's sixty-second birthday, and he reported two dreams, relating to the problems of ageing. In the first, his car got burnt out and at first he felt hopeless, unable to think how he could manage without it, but then he remembered that the insurance would replace it and he had nothing to worry about. He awoke feeling that analysis was renewing his 'burnt-out' self, and that it was a good insurance against his fears of 'losing capacity' to live. In the second dream he pacified a cantankerous old neighbour in Leeds who was quarrelling with him and his wife, saying that they had a bigger place than he had. He wondered if the dream reflected a feeling that he had no right to go on living after Percy and father had died, and Fairbairn was failing. Winnicott's reply startled him. He said, 'You've been carrying this about all your life, feeling that you had no right to outlive Percy. But you've kept yourself going in spite of it. Now you can let it go. You're not drifting into a decrepit old age, but your dream about the old couple being jealous at being put in the shade by you shows that you are afraid to accept and enjoy your new life. If you have a vigorous old age, you fear you'll be outstripping Percy, father and mother.'

The mention of his mother led Guntrip to recall how jealous she had been of his success, how she had grudged his having a car and a large church. But Winnicott positively affirmed the value of his work and his right – despite his fears – to be successful. He said: 'You may also feel anxious about outstripping Fairbairn, and possibly me too, and that you have no right to succeed. You are for some reason that no-one understands at the centre of the growing point in psychoanalysis. You've written an important book and some important papers, and are doing good work, and you may well go on and do better work than Fairbairn and me, and you are anxious that you may be injuring us, if you go on being alive and enjoying it. Because of mother, you fear that those you surpass will be jealous and paranoid and attack you back.' After pondering this for a while, Guntrip said, 'If I can have a creative ageing period, it will be because of Fairbairn's and your help.'

On 25 and 26 June, in sessions twenty-nine and thirty, the theme continued of Guntrip's need for a loving relationship with his father and the way in which mother's jealousy had prevented this. Winnicott said, 'You were starved of normal homosexual satisfaction with father, no proper love relation. You might be afraid now that in a gap of silence, you would want to say "I love you" or "Do you love me?"' Guntrip replied, 'I do need to be able to be silent with you without feeling you are not in contact with me. If neither of us speaks, I might still find I'd feel lost. I've no feeling of "object-relationship in silence". If mother was silent she was mentally miles away.' Seeing its relevance to Guntrip's state Winnicott took the risk of lending the latter his paper 'On Communicating and Not Communicating' (in Winnicott 1965). Perhaps predictably it gave rise to a mixed response. At their next meeting the following morning, Guntrip took issue with Winnicott. He felt the need for a third term between 'verbal communicating' and 'non-communicating', namely *silent communicating*, which he claimed Winnicott confused with 'non-communicating'. Phrases such as 'the permanent isolation of the individual' and the 'non-communicating central self, forever silent', had 'sent a chill' through Guntrip, for his own experience pointed to the fact that 'the isolate in a solipsistic vacuum cannot exist as a person'. Thus, despite Winnicott's reference to 'communication that is forever silent' in the paper, Guntrip had to be clear that Winnicott distinguished between 'natural' and 'pathological non-communicating', for whereas 'natural not-communicating' could be restful, 'pathological not-communicating' was schizoid withdrawal into isolation, in which state rest, sleep, relaxation would be impossible. On the other hand when silent contact and silent communicating are adequately experienced, he may safely withdraw into inactivity and sleep. This was far from being a semantic argument, for Guntrip's extreme experience of isolation in his early life compelled him to examine exactly the meaning of terms, especially where 'communicating and non-communicating' was concerned. Having heard him out Winnicott replied: 'Because you had no real object-relation to parents, you had a gap where human relation should be. You could have remained a parson, if you had a real object-relation to parents.' Guntrip replied: 'Maybe. I got to the stage where I knew that God was only an idea or an unrealised wish, so long as I had not found the deepest human relations.' Winnicott added: 'You need to know I'll do the job properly when you are away. That I will think of you when you are absent. Do I really care?'

In July the fear of falling out of relation with Winnicott into an abyss continued to preoccupy Guntrip. He said, 'I've got to the schizoid part of me which as yet I can't communicate. You say silence can be the best communication then, and the analyst must wait. I felt last time and this time that, on that level, I've nothing to say, and most need to be silent with you, but I'm afraid I'll drop into an abyss of isolation, out of touch with you.' Recalling how he had needed Fairbairn to help his 'in-touch self' to reach his 'other self suspended in a horrible abyss', he said, 'I need to feel you can keep in touch with me. I need to talk about the need to be silent so that silence can become meaningful between us.' His fear that the failure would be on his side – by his own blocking of the analysis – was expressed when he dreamed of discussing with a colleague a difficult patient of his who 'acted out' his twin fears of isolation and closeness and blocked the analysis:

> What should we do with him? Then I found he was in a nearby room and could hear us and was furious. I arranged to meet him and put it to him that something must be done about his behaviour.

Guntrip was quick to associate the patient in the dream with his schizoid self, which he 'discussed' with Winnicott in order to keep it repressed, thus provoking its 'fury' at being left out. Of that part of himself he said, 'He can only be allowed to show up if he conforms, so he can't really be allowed to show at all. I could never show my real self to mother, only conform to her demand that I should not be a nuisance and want mother-love.' When he considered whether he might be feeling obliged to 'conform' to what he assumed to be Winnicott's expectations, he recalled the interpretation of his fear of injuring his father and mother and his analysts by being active. He wondered if he was unconsciously wanting to 'tear up and digest' Winnicott's paper, as if he were 'tearing at the unforgiving breast of mother'. Whether or not that

were so, he felt that 'the schizoid little child who had never been
related to at all' underlay everything else, and that Winnicott's
paper about the 'ultimate core of the self having to be permanently
incommunicado' had stirred a fear that there was no hope of Winnicott finding his unrelated core. Thus he felt that by dreaming of
making his 'patient-self' conform he was 'fantasising bad-object
sadistic relations as better than none', lest he should try to 'tear
recognition' out of Winnicott. Viewed from a purely objective
standpoint it may be clear that by 'incommunicado' Winnicott
meant protected by 'silent communication', both from impingement and isolation. But his imprecise terminology aroused the fear
in the 'ontologically insecure' Guntrip that Winnicott might not
yet fully comprehend the extent of his terror of falling out of
relation.

And yet, despite this powerful reaction, a further dream showed
an alive though uncertain hope that Winnicott 'knew the region'
where his problem lay: 'I was lying on a couch and a small child
wanted to play with me. I said I was tired but then presently I
said: "We must find that little child in you, mustn't we?"' With
great sensitivity Winnicott reminded Guntrip 'You may feel not
sure whether it's safe for that child to be found, though your
biggest fear is of not being found.' Sensing that his anxiety was
safely understood, Guntrip produced a fantasy of Leeds like a cart-
wheel pattern of roads, which he set out to cross round the periphery only to find he had gone to the centre. Winnicott interpreted:
'The periphery is your intellectual life where you've got everything
card-indexed. That's useful and has to be carried on, but you're
also needing to get to the centre, to your spontaneous life of feeling
and impulse, the living you.' At this, Guntrip felt reached, for he
replied, 'I feel now I've got my central self in touch with you.
You've understood and accepted and no need to talk now. I can
relax and be quiet.'

A projected visit in August had to be cancelled when Guntrip
had an operation for the removal of a cyst which proved to be
benign. Although his relaxed state of the July session gave rise to
better sleep during the break, the operation stirred deep fears associated with the loss of active powers, and anxiety reactions to the
previous operations on his sinuses and mouth, and the early circumcision operation. In September he dreamed of 'Fairbairn trying
to give a paper in public, being slow and halting, and having great
difficulty in getting through it', and of himself as an older man
invited by younger men to play cricket, and going in first. His fears
regarding Fairbairn's health were partly objectively founded. In July

he had telephoned Fairbairn to enquire after his health and was not reassured. Fairbairn's letters, though still cordial, were now much shorter, and showed signs of weariness.

In October Guntrip's somewhat depressed mood deepened despite a late September climbing holiday with Bertha. An old friend had a stroke whilst they were with him and another friend had recently been bereaved. Old age seemed a sad and lonely time. With characteristic forthrightness Winnicott suggested that Guntrip may be afraid that by bringing his depression into the analysis he may cause his analyst to have a stroke and die. Guntrip recalled that he had felt 'a kind of hopeless reaction', when he heard of his friend's stroke, with a feeling that there was nothing he could do to save the situation. It made him think of Percy dead and his feeling of being unable to save him. He said, 'After Percy's death I gave up the struggle but then took it up again for sixty years, and now once more feel that underlying sense of helplessness to do anything, . . . I must feel that the deep down me that was helpless to save Percy must be bad for people. If I can't help them I shouldn't burden them; bad for you [sic].' He added that he had dreamed the previous night that he was telling his mother and father that he was settled and didn't need them to support him, and that they should now retire or reorganise the business in their own interests. He said to Winnicott, 'I think I'm telling you, you shouldn't carry on for my sake if you want to retire.' Winnicott made an important intervention 'You cracked when Percy died. People don't crack in later life except to repeat an earlier breakdown, which they spend years trying to avoid. If I couldn't or didn't see you crack, you'd have to crack again to make me see it. You broke down on mother's lap before, to force her to see it. Also, mother said Percy had gone away to be with Jesus, a manic defence, her denial of reality. You have got to face your real knowledge that he went dead, and you feel you, or a part of you, died with him. These feelings of dying are feelings of insanity; not neurosis but more primitive, deeper than castration fears. You also cracked on mother to pay her out, and fear cracking on me, and need to know that I can cope.' In retrospect Guntrip realised that this session in October 1963 and, in particular, this last interpretation, predetermined the whole future course of his life. Not only had the first sentence of the interpretation enabled him to accept his 'early breakdown self' in a constructive way, but the interpretation as a whole had opened the way to the deeper significance of his 'exhaustion collapses' and his eighteen months of psychosomatic illnesses after Percy's death. He began to see that he was not merely trying to get his mother out of her shop to get more attention, but rather he was testing mother out fundamentally to get proof that she could prevent him dying like Percy. As Winnicott had pointed out the feelings of dying were feelings of insanity, belonging to the pre-Oedipal, two-person relation where basic ego-strength is formed or not formed; and not to neurosis which belongs to the later Oedipal three-person situations. Guntrip later observed that 'more than likely' he could not have got so close to that deep trauma with Winnicott in only thirty-six sessions at monthly intervals, had he not first cleared thoroughly with Fairbairn the area of the 'internal bad-object world', which functioned as a defence against this more primitive and deadly fear.

When in November Guntrip returned to the feeling of hopeless failure at being unable to prevent Percy from dying and a 'terrible disillusioned sadness at the bottom of me', Winnicott replied 'That illness is there and in a way it always will be. You can't be as though it had never happened. When it stirs you can feel as ill as ever. But you can grow strong enough to live with it. Patients go on nicely and then suddenly feel as ill as ever, and think that they've made no progress, though in fact they've changed a lot.'

The same theme continued the following morning, when Guntrip became acutely aware of how isolated he felt in Leeds, recalling the lonely struggle to stand by his severely regressed patient in hospital, where the staff were critical and only the Superintendent supported him. Moreover, in October Dr Max Hamilton had succeeded Hargreaves as Professor of Psychiatry in Leeds and Guntrip felt that no-one in the department was really in sympathy with his views on the need to treat the underlying regressive factor. He had dreamed the previous night that he was caring for a baby boy, whom he took to represent both Percy and himself. Winnicott replied, 'You may at times fear I'll tell you to pull yourself together, like the doctor who diagnosed your regressed patient as hysteric. Patients regress with the analyst to find security and become strong enough to re-encounter the illness, the original illness and get over it. Patients suffer acute pain in regression. You want to know if I can help you with your illness and not just make you push it away. You may fear I might need to make a success of your treatment instead of helping you to be ill and get over it.'

In his thirty-ninth session on 3 December Guntrip was feeling clearer about how a sense of failure over Percy's death had made him over-anxious about his patients' recovery. But when he had heard the news of the death of the President Kennedy, he had felt

'like a man with a secret grief unrelieved; the dreadful blank,
Kennedy simply not there; what the disciples must have felt after
the Crucifixion, and I felt after Percy died. My life centred on him,
then suddenly he was dead, gone, disappeared. Part of me withdrew
from life, as if it's too horrible to be close to.' Winnicott replied,
'You put your patients in Percy's place to make life meaningful and
worth living. You're streets ahead of nearly all analysts in your
methods of treatment, and what you write will go on and have
influence after you've gone. But there's another side you find hard
to accept. Your reaction to Percy's death was sheer grief, but before
that you hated him as a rival. You were jealous of the brother who
had mother's breast.' There is no record of Guntrip's reply, if any,
and the next session session 'brought nothing of importance'. Writing ten years later, however, he expressed disappointment that
Winnicott, for all his profound intuitive understanding, had thus
far been unable to clarify for him the basic problem that Fairbairn
also never saw, that in the end his worst problem had been 'the
blank emptiness of experience with a mother who failed to relate'.
At that time in December 1963, however, that experience was still
partly repressed and he could only assume that he had omitted to
inform Winnicott (because of their infrequent meetings) that his
mother had refused to feed Percy, so that he felt that Percy had no
more of her than he had himself: they only had each other. Sibling
rivalry, insofar as it featured, had not been the main issue for
Guntrip. But it is certainly possible that Winnicott was making a
further attempt to commend to Guntrip his right to have his own
therapy instead of devoting it to Percy/patients. Whatever the truth
of that, Guntrip felt at the end of 1963 that he had gone much
deeper than ever before in any analysis that he had undergone.

CHAPTER 16

1964

One advantage of the monthly meetings was that there was effectively no Christmas break. In the next session, which occurred on 7 January, Guntrip worried about the extent to which his 'Percy problem' was involved in his motivation for doing psychotherapy, for he was expressing not only weariness, but also some resentment, at the strain of being tied to patients, though he could think of no other work he would rather be doing. Nevertheless, waking in the early hours whilst he and Bertha were looking after his grandchildren when their daughter was unwell, he had felt the burden of his patients was too much for him, and he told Winnicott, 'In some ways I could say I hate patients and Percy behind my love for them.' He even dreamed of an analyst lying on a couch in great emotional distress, broken down, while two of his ex-patients sat behind him, laughing at him! He felt he must get the analyst out of this, get him to see he was being taken advantage of. Evidently he feared seeing patients cured and well, and himself worn out. Winnicott's exasperation showed in his reply: 'Your whole life has been based on a reaction-formation, the opposite of hate which is repressed. If you'd been analysed at four, you might not have become a therapist at all, but something more aggressive. You're afraid that if the Percy problem is cleared up, you'd be left with no motivation to go on with your work, and you'd lose everything. So you're on guard to prevent the real Percy-hate emerging from behind your resistance to patients.' The devastating impact of the suggestion that his 'whole life' had been reactive and not genuinely responsive brought home to Guntrip the extent of his ego-weakness, and he recalled having woken early one morning 'feeling unable to move or stir, exhausted'. He had dreamed:

> I was to have an operation and phoned the doctor, but then a revolution broke out ending a long period of enforced stability, like the Picts and Scots breaching the Roman wall. Then I was

with the doctor again and there was some discussion of my
having E.C.T. to put a stop to the trouble. I thought: 'The best
way. Years of analysis wouldn't produce such a result.'

In pondering on the dream Guntrip had seriously considered
whether his problem might not be fully schizoid after all, but
mainly repressed aggression and hate of Percy, making loving service a guilt-ridden compulsion. But he concluded that because he
was really too weak, between two and three-and-a-half, to help his
unmothered self in Percy, any hate he experienced was not just
resenting him, but was really a desperate way of 'trying to feel
something' to stop himself breaking down. When Winnicott per-
severed with the hate theme Guntrip conceded 'No doubt I did
hate at times, but I feel it was part of my struggle to keep going
with no-one behind me. I feel now that I have you behind me in
an understanding way that I've never had an experience of before,
in relation to my ultimate problem.' He therefore told Winnicott
that his explanation of his work as 'a reaction-formation to inhibited rage and aggression' simply failed to 'click home' in the way
his other interpretations had, and that he felt his work to be an
all-out attempt to 'mother' both Percy and himself at an age when
he lacked the strength to stand the strain. Indeed he wondered
why, when Percy died, his resultant breakdown had not resulted in
schizophrenia. He was doubtless recalling Winnicott's profound
observation of the previous October that his 'feelings of dying' were
'feelings of insanity', which he had experienced as a recognition of
his 'early breakdown self'. Taking full account of the threat of
madness, Winnicott replied, 'Possibly because mother sent you
away to your Aunt's when you broke down. That gave you the
possibility of feeling that there was an escape from her influence.'
Guntrip was greatly helped by this explanation, feeling that he
could be free to develop a non-anxious mothering capacity on the
basis of his experience of the reality of Winnicott's concern for
him. He added that an analyst had once described Winnicott as the
only genuine male mother-figure he knew: a description which the
latter enjoyed. Guntrip now felt sure that his compulsion to
'mother Percies' was not a reaction to repressed hate, but an all-out
attempt to stave off the weakness resulting from inadequate
mothering. He said, 'I'll need time, probably a lot of time, to
regrow sounder foundations, but at least I now have a genuine
relation to a genuine "mothering person" in you' – the beginning
of an answer to the need which had broken out in a big way in his
illness after his Salem colleague left, but which was then 'locked in

the "tomb-room dream" for twenty-five years'. Guntrip felt that he had 'only now really begun to get that tomb open again'.

In March Guntrip reported a dream which he felt implied a growing reconciliation of the loving and hating aspects of his personality. He dreamed that he was looking at a cupboard like his old toy-cupboard, when he saw a movement inside and thought it was a rat. But on inspection he discovered it to be 'a beautiful velvety big kitten, rosy-brown coloured, quiet and gentle but alive'. He commented, 'I'm becoming strong enough to feel the anger I felt but had to hide, over mother forcing such strains on me.' He felt that the aspect of him associated with his gentle father had 'emerged from the tomb' together with his murderous 'Spanish ambassador' side, allowing his affections and legitimate angers to come out together, a feeling which seemed to find expression in the following dream.

> I was in a large room with Winnicott and a company of people. A married couple sang a duet and I had sung with them while I was quite unconscious and Winnicott held me. Later he told me I had done it quite well and acceptably. I said, 'I must trust you completely or I'd never have been able to let myself go unconscious with you like that.' He smiled reassuringly. I had done something, expressed myself with his support, though unconsciously. Then he brought a chamber-pot and I sat down over it and tried to pass faeces. I felt I had something there and it would come out at any moment but could not quite manage to get it out. But he was there to help me do this.

Guntrip believed that this dream was 'a clear reference' to his inability either to eat or to defecate after Percy's death. Winnicott said, 'Your active self was dissociated, cut-off inside with mother. You are needing me to help you find yourself inside and let your active self come into expression spontaneously.' Guntrip assented. His mother had tried to force him with suppositories, whereas Winnicott waited and supported encouragingly. Next day, in the last session before the Easter holiday, Guntrip returned to the theme of letting go the essential structural defensiveness of his innermost personal self. He felt that his dream showed a deep confidence in Winnicott's ability to enable him to stand the 'letting out' of his 'inner psychic reality'. Winnicott commented that the dream related to two problems: 'functioning' and 'product'. He pointed out that although in the gaps between visits Guntrip could experience him as the bad mother who would force him to produce something, he had nevertheless been able to dream of Winnicott as a good-enough mother who waited and helped and did not interfere, so that both function and product were good. For his part Guntrip felt that for the first time in that dream he had moved beyond 'the Percy problem' to what was really his original deepest unmet need: to find security with a parent, and to be accepted for himself so that he could be his own properly fulfilled self.

During the Easter break both Harry and Bertha were unwell and Harry had minor surgery for a blocked tear-duct. Although they managed a short holiday, the analysis 'seemed to have been distanced', and Guntrip was conscious of holding back. However, Winnicott supported his 'right to withhold' whilst also making it clear that he valued his facility in talking, which had 'both something defensive and constructive in it', so that Guntrip felt that he could be equally real and 'himself' in relation to Winnicott whether actively talking or passively relaxing. In his reply, Winnicott confirmed that his interest in Guntrip as a person made such considerations secondary. He said, 'When you're not talking, I'm thinking, not of the words you've said, but of you; as being in the nursing home, having an operation, being tired, being on holiday and seeing five white hares, and so on. Perhaps in bed you think about your thoughts, not about your breathing, heart, body; and so have to keep your thoughts active, instead of enjoying being in your body.' Unfortunately, however, the beneficial effect of this generous communication was not fully registered by Guntrip. Perhaps because he had been for so long and so radically dependent upon activity, mental and verbal, to generate self-feeling, he appears to have been alarmed by the thought that Winnicott was 'not thinking' of the words he said. He reported having dreamed that he was in a nursing home a week and the surgeon was too busy to operate and then said, 'We'll leave it for six months.' Winnicott's reply, despite its accuracy, did little to relieve Guntrip's alarm! He said, 'It's probably me saying I'd best not interfere, might be better if I did nothing and left you free to do nothing. You may be raising the question of ending analysis.' Guntrip took Winnicott to be suggesting that he should finish. He said: 'I think your suggestion that I end analysis disturbed me. I cannot stop analysis till I can not only feel free to say "No" and withhold, but also to give out, to co-operate, to be active, not defensively to keep myself in being, but just to be really "me" . . . Something [has] been buried alive in me, some part of me mother never really allowed to come alive. I still feel there's some blocked-in part of me that needs a way-out to be cleared.'

In May Guntrip described a weekend of impossible pressures, which bore heavily upon his indifferent physical state until he felt a 'paralysis of the wish and will to do' and a longing 'to stay regressed in a womb-state'. He was more conscious than he could ever remember of the 'split' between his active adult self and his regressed passive self. He felt himself shrinking once again from having to stand the emotional strain of patients, and had felt obliged to decline to treat the wife of a colleague, and a former patient. Winnicott commented: 'You couldn't escape mother's pressure. It was important that you could say "No" to taking on your colleague's wife. I was wondering at what point you could say "No" if more pressure piled on. It's not easy once you're involved but you can say "No" to a new patient. But you feel some need to turn the tables on mother. You value having me to understand what you have to talk out, but also to unload it on. If I identified too much and couldn't forget you till tomorrow morning, I might have a thrombosis. You too need to be able to throw off patients' troubles.' It would seem that Guntrip profited from this 'realistic and valuable example' for next morning, he described how he had seen 'a really beautiful painting . . . of a peaceful meandering stream and silver birches by an Italian, Cirano',[1] and he declared his intention of buying it. The painting seemed to 'light up' in a way which reminded him 'of Home's paper on "scientific" and "humanistic" thinking, the dead thing and the living person'.[2] Winnicott said: 'We differ from Freud who was for curing symptoms. We're concerned with living persons, whole living and loving, like your love of that picture. You buy it because you want it, not because it may be worth more later.'

Perhaps alarmed by the spontaneity and joyfulness of Winnicott's response, Guntrip reverted sharply to the subject of his anxieties of the previous day concerning pressure from his mother. It was, he said, the 'top' problem that he could not escape her pressure, whereas he now needed, not a reworking of that, but a recognition of the deeper problem with mother: her failure to relate to him as a person. He said: 'I feel my reaction to mother was twofold, fight and flight, but there's something else, not being able to react at all, nothing to react to . . . Mother broke down helplessly over Percy. I said, "Don't let him go" but she was powerless and had to send me away.' Winnicott added: 'A part of you got stuck in the tomb: your inhibited egotism that you probably experienced for the first few months but never afterwards.' Although Guntrip reacted by pointing out that he had said 'No' to nine prospective new patients in the last three months, knowing that he simply could not take them, Winnicott persisted: 'You have intellectual reasons for saying "No", but you lack emotional reasons. You feel if you took another ninety-nine patients, you might then possibly not feel guilty if you release a bit of your ruthless aggression and egotism. It's the you that you draw energy from.'

It would appear from his sessional record that Guntrip made no reply, but his commentary of the 1970s reveals his profound dissatisfaction with Winnicott's suggestion that his 'energy' came from 'ruthless aggression and egotism'. For him it was a throw-back to Freud's concept of the rational ego drawing its energy from the 'id'. He wrote, 'If indeed all our energy for living came from ruthless sexual and aggressive instincts, then therapy and civilisation would be impossible', and he expressed the view that just as Winnicott had regarded Fairbairn's emphasis upon castration as a repetition of his own analyst's interpretations, so Winnicott's interpretations in terms of hate, egotism and aggression proceeded unmodified from his own classical Freudian analyst, James Strachey.

Guntrip, by contrast, had no doubt that it was a serious intellectual error to assume that destructive aggression was identical with our 'natural bodily assertiveness' or 'innate *energy* for living even on the biological level'. Instead, he held that on a truly psychological level destructive aggression is "an ego reaction to the threat" and as such can only develop as the ego develops, and is preceded by the more primitive reaction of fear'. He concluded, 'I was still waiting for Winnicott to clarify what happened to me as a result of my mother's failure to relate, which I would now say left me, not with inhibited egotism, but with some unevoked capacity for feeling which had never been able to come alive.' Consequently, Guntrip recorded that he reacted to Winnicott's interpretations by feeling an increase 'during the following month of feeling schizoid and apart', and in the next session all he could do to draw attention to his deepest need was to make a long rationalised statement of his predicament and his need to regress with Winnicott in order to recover his lost psychic potential. This statement, which clearly proceeded from Guntrip's 'intellectual self', was far from the 'child' with whom Winnicott was most concerned and Guntrip records that Winnicott fell asleep for twelve minutes – surely an eternity for Guntrip. When he awoke, Winnicott said he was sorry, that he was very tired, had had a heavy day, and was keyed up. He took a bit of luminol to reduce tension, and said that he had felt pressure from Guntrip right at the start of the session. Guntrip was reassured by this openness, and by what he managed to regard as a measure of trust in him on the part of the sleeping Winnicott: 'I felt he trusts me, or he wouldn't go to sleep in my presence.'

Further repercussions of this experience occurred the next morning. Winnicott's sleep had aroused the earlier problem for which the Percy problem had provided a 'screen', a problem not primarily of anger but of 'hopelessness'. Guntrip said, 'I'm sure I grew hopeless about mother long before Percy was born, which was why I fell ill when he died and left me alone with mother.' He continued, 'Her sending me to Aunt Dolly saved me, but completed my disillusionment with her . . . It occurs to me now that my not eating and not defaecating with mother after Percy died are significantly related. I must have felt I got no real response from her to take in, and if I gave out I'd be left empty.' Winnicott, however, continued to interpret the problem as one of repressed anger at mother's lack of response. He said, 'My falling asleep must have been traumatic, though you were able to make use of it. I was the mother you could get nothing out of and you were frightened and angry, but not now. You need to be able to let out your anger at the mother you got nothing out of, and I must be able to take it.'

A month later the hopeless sense of sucking on a barren source persisted when Guntrip dreamed of examining a huge plant-octopus on land. It's tentacles ended in small sucking mouths fastened on the earth. But it was clear to him, if not at that time to Winnicott, that his analysis was drifting back into the Fairbairn pattern of the struggle with internalised bad objects. He even found himself using Fairbairn's terminology, regarding mother as an 'exciting and rejecting object', and describing how, as a child, his alternating libidinised and de-libidinised states of nose, mouth, and excretory organs had kept hope alive in an otherwise dead world.

It is possible that both men were retreating on to 'familiar ground' from the demands of the primary need. Guntrip felt unconnected, and identified strongly with his own patients who were always looking for something to meet an unmet need; 'never knowing what it is, turning from people to things, books, records, food, cigarettes, pills, situations in life'. Both he and they were 'wanting something from life itself'. One can imagine his relief when Winnicott said, 'You talk of "wanting", sucking at the breast of life, but if you got everything you want, it still wouldn't meet your need. The more fundamental thing is not to have, to get, but to be. Possibly your difficulty with sleep is that sleep is just being, not doing or getting anything. Probably you keep awake to go on thinking things out, working.' Guntrip at once felt that Winnicott had 'struck the right note' and that they were 'back onto the real problem'. He had been impressed by Winnicott's view that a fantasy period was needed between sleeping and waking, and wondered whether his desire for 'a drug to put me straight off, and once awake to stay awake' was due to a fear of encountering his early disturbance during the fantasy period. Winnicott made an important interpretation: 'I want to say you are afraid to "be" because it means having again your early experience of "dying". As if to "be" has come to mean for you "to experience dying". You have experienced dying and remained alive to know it. You were alive and something in you died because mother couldn't give you what you needed to stay alive within that part of yourself. You used Percy's death to get at your experience of dying, and partly to disown it and mask it. You know what death is. You experienced it while you were alive. It's the only way you can know death. But now, if you want to come alive in that dead part, you have first to experience yourself as dead, and then you need me to understand and be someone you can come alive with.'

Guntrip felt this to be the most important moment, so far, in his analysis. Winnicott, 'using no "theoretical formulae"', had shown him that he recognised and was in touch with the dead, lost part of his personality that must have been the source of the occasional quite schizoid moods that he had experienced in his analysis with Fairbairn. This was undoubtedly the area of the deepest trauma to which he had tried to draw Fairbairn's attention, and which was amenable not at all to a theoretical technique, but only to the intuitive response of another person who related to him in a way that his mother could not. He said, 'Perhaps I often talk in sessions because I am afraid that saying and doing nothing will allow my "feeling dead" to emerge. I only related to mother with my superficial conscious self. I had little opportunity to relate to father in any meaningful emotional way. My "internal bad-objects world" that Fairbairn analysed must have been my defence against the emergence of my experience of dying, both with Percy and deeper still, before Percy came, with mother.'

The therapeutic effect of this new insight pervaded the summer recess. Guntrip enjoyed an invigorating holiday with Bertha, free from symptoms, and they were both fit enough to climb together in Scotland. In August he attended the sixth International Congress of Psychotherapy where he responded to Laing's paper on Psychotherapy. His paper, which he later developed as part of Chapter 13 of *Schizoid Phenomena, Object Relations and the Self* was well received and he told Winnicott that he felt part of 'a widespread community of like-minded people' which compensated for his sense of professional isolation in Leeds. He also had the satisfaction of knowing that Fairbairn and Winnicott had dined together at the former's invitation when Winnicott lectured at the Davidson Clinic. When sessions were resumed in September he began to associate his lifeless feeling on waking with Winnicott's statement about his 'having been alive to experience dying', and with his need 'to come alive' with Winnicott. He felt an inner conviction that he was no longer isolated in the dead part of himself that Winnicott had recognised, and he had, in fact, begun to re-experience the bleakness of his unrelated state during the summer break in a dream in which he was deserted by a woman and felt in despair. He felt sure that the woman was mother, and that he was re-experiencing the feeling of having died with her. Two weeks after that he had a more positive dream in which he was lying in bed feeling dead to the world, but after a time his mother came in and sat with him, explaining to some people that he was not well and couldn't make himself stir. In the dream he felt content to let his mother explain while he lay there barely conscious of it all, but he said faintly, 'The second film, not the first, bears on or illustrates my trouble.' What had seemed at first a crowded scene of violence, on closer inspection proved to be a crowded and lively social scene, in which he was able to emerge and participate. Winnicott believed that he himself was represented by the mother who understood and sat by Guntrip's dead self till he could feel alive, whilst the second film probably stood for his second analysis, and second analyst. Guntrip felt 'absolute certainty' that this was right. In the 'dead part' of himself he was waiting for this vital contact, and knew instantly whether or not it occurred, or seemed likely to do so, via an effective 'mutative interpretation', and the effect was immediately registered in his consciousness. He took it as a sign that his dread of being undermined by his dead self was diminishing when he dreamed:

> A young man I know (not a patient of mine) who has had a 'nervous breakdown', was in a car with me. He was driving and letting it slide backwards. I said, 'Pull on the brake.' Then he was outside the car and I was inside and saw it was still sliding back and I leaned out, got hold of a post and halted it. He seemed helpless.

He felt that he was coping with his long repressed 'dead self' coming alive as weak and helpless.

By the end of October Guntrip was inclined to feel that Winnicott's recognition of the 'dead child' in him had facilitated the beginning of a 'self' who could experience 'hate'. He said, 'Mother left me only three possibilities: stay and be crushed; kill her, which I can't do, even in fantasy (though I nearly did in some dreams with Fairbairn); or get away.' Winnicott observed: 'Many get away as you did and are content to leave it at that. You are not content. You want to save the crippled part of yourself, which is ultimately your real self. You had no normal oedipal phase. You've done wonderfully well to make so much of marriage without it.' Guntrip recalled once again his fascination with the Nimrod story and how he had made his mother read the story while he gazed at the picture of Nimrod about to plunge his spear in the lion's throat. Winnicott said, 'It can be looked at in two ways. Mother saw herself as Nimrod and you and all males as the lion. You were seeing yourself as Nimrod and mother as the lion.' Guntrip affirmed, 'Yes. That's definitely how I saw it.'

Next morning Guntrip reported a dream which was clearly a fearful reaction to his definite identification with Nimrod, the mighty hunter! He dreamed:

> I was in a meeting of organically-minded psychiatrists, all mechanists who were hostile to my views. I found they were planning to get me drugged and reconditioned and at the crucial moment one of them said, 'You'll be harmless after this.' But I had suspected this and had arranged for the police to be secreted with tape-recorders and cameras, and expose them. There would be an outcry, but I had a twinge of feeling: 'Poor chaps, what will they do with families to support!'

Guntrip noted that although the dream showed evidence of internalised surveillance of his 'bad-object situation' and support for his 'revolt to independence', the same basic dilemma over how to deal with his mother remained: let her crush him, turn the tables and crush her, or get away. He pointed out that a major part of his problem had been that as a child he was more alive outside the home than inside, so that 'getting away' seemed his only option. He said, 'From 3½ to about 6 I mooned about indoors, lonely, not eating or defaecating, and sleep-walking. Then I set about steadily developing my life away from home . . . .' Winnicott pointed out the lack of an active fatherly influence to help him. He said, 'You have no real negative transference. No ambivalence of loving and hating to help you keep your masculinity, no real rivalry with father.' But whilst Guntrip accepted that mother's jealousy had prevented 'normal homosexual satisfaction ... a proper love-relation' between himself and father, and he recalled 'one interesting phase' in the analysis with Fairbairn in which he had wished for a stimulating rivalry in friendly activity with father, what he was most consistently aware of was 'a strong secret bond' which had grown with father and which had come out repeatedly in his dreams. It was, he believed, on the basis of this bond that he had been able to respond to his wife's love, and enter analysis. He did not consider that an ambivalent loving and hating relation to his father was a precondition for either.

However, the theme of unsupported revolt to independence of mother continued. when he dreamed that he fled from a woman – the phallic mother – chasing him with a snake, while in a further dream a woman was forcing a sexual relationship on a small male kitten, one of his 'stock symbols' for himself as a child. Winnicott pointed out that the dreams did not depict a little boy having spontaneous erections which were his own and which he could fantasy about, but forced, unrelated, split off excitements imposed by his mother's physical handling, which led nowhere and fragmented his ego. Guntrip had a further dream which, he felt, recalled the circumcision after his mother had excited him by cleaning his penis.

I had an operation on my thumb and later went to dig in the garden to see whether I could use it.

Again, as if in retaliation he dreamed of a woman whose fingers were raw and split down to the bone, but who was heroically carrying on. The latter dream, he interpreted himself as his mother working her fingers to the bone, but he also realised that anxiety masked the fact that, in fantasy, he had attacked and damaged her fingers, which she had used to penetrate his anus to make him defecate. Winnicott replied, 'The first time you've let your cruelty appear to me and its against her fingers with which she handled you.' As one might expect, Guntrip, whilst agreeing with the general point, could not accept 'cruelty' as a valid description of what he believed to be 'an inevitable reaction to what Fairbairn called the "Exciting and Rejecting Object", and hitting back at aggressive treatment' – the Nimrod theme. Here again, there was a serious issue at stake. The only way Guntrip knew of dealing with a non-understanding, a non-relationship, was to reinstate his 'schizoid intellectual defence' and his 'manically driven thinking process'. Winnicott's 'poor conceptualising', noted by Fairbairn, left him unreached and his 'negative transference' took the form of intellectual criticism as his only 'form of appeal'. His record does not make it clear, however, whether he spoke his criticism, or just 'thought it'. Winnicott, at any rate, persisted with the cruelty interpretation next day when Guntrip described having experienced a sharp anal spasm on witnessing an accident. He said, 'Your cruelty is this anal spasm. It is as if you are gripping mother's finger as she pushes the suppository in, and can't hurt her enough. When you saw the man's wounded leg in the accident, you felt you had done it.' Guntrip felt that this was the right interpretation but the wrong words: there was 'no cold-blooded intention to hurt'. However, what really mattered was whether the 'child' had felt reached by this interpretation – and on this occasion it would appear that he had for in the next dream Guntrip reported, 'I was a medical student and had just passed my exams, and my wife and I were engaged. I got my first job with Dr Danks and was delighted.' Danks was the Leeds doctor who referred his first patient to him, and he said, 'It feels a good dream, a new start.'

At the first session in December another interpretation in terms of 'aggression' forced Guntrip on to the defensive again. He had just received the news of what proved to be Fairbairn's last illness, and he expressed a fear that he may unconsciously have needed Fairbairn to die so that he could 'live and carry on' – a form of the 'one up and the other down' pattern which characterised the early stages of his analysis with Fairbairn. He added, 'I need a father who will help me to be active.'

Winnicott replied: 'You needed a father and brother to "compete" with, so as to have the full use of your aggression. It's against your make-up to have a nasty cruel side, but you need this possibility of potency.' Since he saw that Winnicott was equating 'energetic self-assertion in competition' with 'aggression' in an unthinking way, one might have expected Guntrip simply to accept the interpretation as it stood. However, the next day, he made a long and definitive statement of his standpoint: 'I've always felt repugnance and revulsion at aggression, cruelty, violence. My father was a peaceable man, didn't quarrel with mother, but once, when a man in the shop began to abuse her, father strode out angrily, and the man fled. Anger is justified, but violence, aggression isn't natural but motivated, and only becomes justified when it's necessary. The stable person is slow to anger, so Ernest Jones says. Habitually aggressive people are afraid that their world is hostile and feel they must get in the first blow. My childhood fantasies did get violent inside (the Nimrod picture) because I was at mother's mercy outside. If I hate anything, it is, ultimately mother's violence. I didn't fight at school, but just put up a creditable show boxing in the gym with boys of my own weight and enjoyed that, and developed plenty of aggression as a batsman and bowler at cricket, but that's not the same as violence or cruelty. I think Freud's term "aggression" is used too much indiscriminately, and isn't an instinct, but a reaction to menace. I had some bloody dreams in the Fairbairn period, some quite horrifying, but they were all clearly provoked by my fear of, and anger at mother.'

He then described the following dream:

I saw a whale swimming in the ocean. It had two lungs: one for leisurely breathing out in the ocean, and another for fast breathing in the loch it had swum into. A rope hung from it and some man somewhere pulled it, and it switched over from slow to fast breathing.

Winnicott at once said, 'Birth symbolism. Relaxed floating in the womb, then birth, the umbilical cord is pulled and you had to breathe fast: not automatic and unconscious breathing, but willed breathing. The whale is you being born. Probably you suffered some delay in being born which forced you to premature breathing effort. It may underlie your nasal catarrh which makes breathing hard, and a conscious effort. You feel you always had to keep yourself alive by your efforts. Your aggression has all been absorbed into the deliberate effort of keeping alive. You can't take your ongoing being for granted. You have to work hard to keep yourself in existence. Hence you can't retire. I hope we can alter that so that you can either retire or go on working for a different reason. You've had a hard-working life.' Guntrip concluded, 'I understood what Winnicott meant when he interpreted my early inhibitions, and his often astonishingly acute insight went to the heart of my problem.'

Notes

1   I noticed the painting by Cirano on the wall of Bertha's living-room on a recent visit. It retains its lambent quality: not all in 'the eye of the beholder'!

2   Home, H.J. (1966) 'The Concept of the Mind', *International Journal of Psycho-Analysis*, 47. Referred to by Guntrip in 'The Concept of Psychodynamic Science' (1967) in Hazell 1994, p. 251.

CHAPTER 17

1965

That winter the rigours of monthly travel to London were beginning to tell on Guntrip. On his way home before Christmas he
had been befogged on Doncaster station for an hour in dense fog
and the waiting rooms were so crowded that it was actually impossible to get in. Moreover, Fairbairn's death, which had occurred on
the last day of 1964, had saddened him deeply and he was unable
to go to London in January due to a combination of his own low
state and a fall in which Bertha fractured her knee. In the first
week of February, however, he was able to give the course of
lectures at the Davidson Clinic, referred to by Fairbairn in his final
letter, and he took the opportunity to have some long talks with
Marion Fairbairn, whom he sought to comfort in her bereavement.
When he returned to London he discussed the matter with Winnicott who issued a reminder of his own advancing age. He said,
'You've had to talk out with me Mrs Fairbairn's story of her
husband's death, and it's been very important to me personally. I
am not getting any younger.' But despite his feeling of reassurance
at Winnicott's 'fearless facing of facts about himself' Guntrip was
anxious that external events may have pushed the analysis aside,
and he said, 'I think I must be angry that the newly-born child-me
who was coming out so clearly here in December, has been pushed
out of the picture by external pressures.'

He recalled Fairbairn's death, feeling uncertain as to whether he
was mourning him or not. Winnicott said: 'You're not mourning for
him. You feel you haven't lost him in the part of you he helped. He
dealt with all of you that you brought him, but not with the part of
you that wasn't there. He didn't reach that.' Guntrip fell silent, and
Winnicott observed, 'Possibly you're feeling that you need not show
me your usual self, you needn't talk, but you feel I could still be
thinking about your other self that can't talk, that seems not to be
here.' On hearing this it would seem that Guntrip felt sufficiently
secure to lay aside his intellectual control. He said, 'I feel I can't
grasp what you are saying intellectually, but it doesn't matter. It's
gone in and reached my dissociated self that I can only safely let out

to you.' However, in their next session, a month later, he felt a strong need to discuss 'on an intellectual level' Winnicott's views on infantile ego-integration. The latter explained his view that the primitive feeling of wholeness given by womb-security was so quickly lost without maternal support, that in the first two weeks it could not last more than about three hours. Thus, consolidation of integration after birth was dependent on adequate mothering, although there could still be loss of spontaneity through too rigid and early cleanliness training. Although he had no direct evidence regarding his mother's handling of him in the first year, Guntrip had come to recognise her tendency to ascribe failings in herself to others – and in particular to Mrs Prentice, who had broken her children's spirits. Thus he had some 'well-founded suspicions' that this had been his own fate at his mother's hands. Regarding cleanliness-training, he was able to be more specific. His mother was an 'anal' character, with her love of money and obsessive interest in making it; her disconcerting tendency to leave the lavatory door open, and to object if Harry noticed and shut it; her use of suppositories on him, and so on. He recalled a dream in which he had felt that 'spontaneity was "forbidden shitting"', as if she had wanted to lock up all his spontaneity inside him, and then get out of him only what she had decided upon. He said, 'I strongly suspect that mother's cleanliness training began far too early and that she directed everything to preventing my being a nuisance to her, a live baby. If she ever had any maternalism, it was crushed out by having to be the overburdened "little mother" in her teens.' Winnicott replied 'You've mentioned that you often feel the need to defaecate at about six p.m., the time you usually come to a session with me; as if you feel free to bring out your faeces, or anything, spontaneously with me, and we could talk about them and find out what it means.' The fatherly tone in Winnicott's reply reminded Guntrip of the ease he occasionally felt with old friends, and with his father on his return from work in the evening, and he recalled a recent dream:

> I was visiting my old and valued friend Theo Holbrook. Then he seemed to be out and I felt someone was standing behind the curtain. I pulled it aside and there stood father looking at his best. I felt extremely glad to see him and he was glad to see me.

Winnicott began the next morning's session by saying 'That dream about your father was important', and Guntrip replied 'As you said that, your voice was very quiet, and gentle and sympathetic, and I knew you felt for and understood me. I sometimes wake feeling

I've been experiencing more real emotion in a dream than I can let myself feel when awake. I'm sure what you said last night enabled me to have this dream':

> I was in session with Fairbairn. The room was full of people as at his funeral, but he was there alive, and I lay on the couch. We had been talking but I was now lying quietly, nearly asleep, and feeling this was important and good and the first time I'd been able to do it. He accepted it. Then his first wife lay very ill, seemingly moribund, on a couch, as if she were finished. But when he went away she spoke to me and turned to me for help. Then Fairbairn and a son suggested we go for a walk and I agreed.

He continued, 'It's as if I've got to contact Fairbairn before I can let him die and mourn him. You said he dealt with all of me that I brought to him, but not the "me" I didn't bring to him. In fact I feel I tried to bring that deeper hidden "me" to him a number of times but he couldn't see that. I think I have expressed that in this dream of his wife. He didn't see she was alive, but I did and got a response . . . I've been bringing that "me" to you for some time now, and you've seen that and accepted it, and in doing that, it's as if you have drawn aside the curtain between father and myself in that earlier dream and our mutual love. I feel I couldn't bring my deep spontaneous self to father or Fairbairn because they couldn't let me see theirs. There was a curtain drawn across their love. You've enabled me to draw back that curtain, as I did in the dream, and discover a mutual love.' At this point, as if to express a longing for his mother also, Guntrip mentioned another dream 'about two women, a homely one and a business one, obviously Mary and mother. I loved the homely one and then wanted the business one to feel for me, but that didn't develop', and he concluded simply, 'I wanted mother's love but felt I never got it, clearly.' Winnicott believed that the two women could represent two aspects of mother herself. Perhaps he had in mind his opening statement of the previous session, regarding the preservation of a primitive feeling of wholeness given by womb-security, when he said, 'It's possible that childbirth aroused some maternalism in your mother for a short time. It does sometimes even in masculine women, but it didn't last. The curtain was drawn across not only mother but father; only Mary she wasn't jealous of. Mother could stimulate you, but only in a bad way. In curtaining herself and father off, she took away the spontaneous bit of you.' Guntrip

replied: 'In real life my wife comes in here. She has evoked whatever mother may have called out in me in the first few weeks, or
month or two, and what Mary called out as well.' Winnicott was
not to be deflected, however, from his postulation of an original
maternalism for Guntrip. He said, 'If your wife had only been
Mary to you, you would have been impotent. In fact you found in
her something good and exciting that even mother must have given
you at the beginning.'[1]

On his return in May, 'feeling physically very fit after a good
Easter holiday', Guntrip reported a sudden loss of potency 'after a
very happy union', which he felt inclined to connect with Winnicott's suggestion that his father and mother, in curtaining themselves off, had taken away his spontaneous self. He said, 'I feel I
became unable to react, to feel anything about them because, in a
way, they weren't there. This seems to have reactivated my early
"dead self", not active with either father or mother, that sank
devitalised on mother's lap and only revived away from her . . . I
never experienced any impotence until mother came to live with
us. Now I've moved forward from the "dead infancy" period and
am contacting mother and father again in my dreams, and suddenly go impotent.' He then reported 'two disturbing sex-dreams'.

In the first of these a group of people had a human monstrosity
in a bag, apparently without arms or legs, covered with brown
bristles, with a pointed shaped head. He said, 'It's the most bizarre
dream I can remember. It's certainly a penis-symbol, and I'm sure
expresses my mother's revulsion at sex. From what she said, father
had no such revulsion but she rejected him.' The second dream
seemed like a reaction to the first:

I saw a naked body of a man with no genitals, a sexless male.

Guntrip wondered if his potency had come to a premature end.
Winnicott replied, 'Only time can show. Loss of potency might
have evoked the fantasy, but the fantasy might have caused the
impotence. Perhaps the return of father involves you in impotence,
as living with mother did. You can't be potent in a competitive
relation with a father, because you didn't have one. You had no
Oedipal phase, no being in love with your mother, no competition
with father, nothing to help you discover and own your sexuality
early. You had to wait until you began to get away from them to
Madeleine and your wife, and could own your own adolescent sex.
Nothing in the earlier post-infancy period, no healthy possession of
mother, who never roused any real love in you. The human

monster is an unintegrated part-object, a part of yourself, and partly a penis or a breast, but not related to your adult self, which for the time being, loses potency when that bit of you comes up in a dream. You had no bodily stimulation, no healthy emotional sexuality from post-infancy to fifteen plus.'

At this time Guntrip was working at a deep level with his own patients, three of whom were recovering well after 'letting out their deep repressed child-self, akin to my ill child-self over Percy'. In the June session, he told Winnicott that the latter's interpretation of the Percy illness as a reliving of an earlier breakdown was probably the most important ever and he went on to mention that on three previous mornings he had wakened with a peculiar feeling that he couldn't end the state he was in, 'a static, unchanging, lifeless state, feeling that I can't move. Then I begin to know I can get up and end it any minute, and suddenly I do so. Then the feeling rapidly fades out.' Winnicott said, 'If 100% of you felt like that, then you probably really couldn't move, and would have to wait for someone to wake you.' This was surely the deepest problem: the 'vital heart' of Guntrip's personality was simply unevoked, unrelated and dissociated, entirely dependent for life upon someone's recognition. But, although he was later to cite the above as one of Winnicott's most penetrating insights (1975, in Hazell 1994, p. 362), Guntrip, at this stage of his analysis, could only connect his static state with sexual impotence. In response to Winnicott's deeply perceptive observation, he merely replied: 'After last month's session normal potency returned.' He then moved the analysis on to a different level, on which his own needs were deferred in consideration of his mother's sufferings. He reported a dream:

> At a meeting of analysts a woman asked me if my mother had had any traumatic experience with heat, because I had felt hot.

After ennumerating his mother's ample reasons for 'feeling heated': her tyrannical father, a mother who denied her an education, and left her to do all the work, causing her to run away at twelve years old; an elder brother who robbed her of the business her father had left her, to enable her to support her mother and four siblings, he added: 'Underneath a strong sense of family duty, she was embittered.' Winnicott followed Guntrip's change of direction. He said, 'She probably was and worked it out on you. Her dammed up heat exploded in anger on your body. I think it included working out her sexual frustration on you and involving you in it.' Winnicott's wisdom in allowing Guntrip to drift away from the deepest area, into the sado-masochistic region, is clear from the use the latter was able to make of this interpretation. He realised that he had never really considered that his mother might well have been sexually responsive to father if she had enjoyed a better childhood, nor had he been able to realise how Percy's death must have stirred up her frightful experience of having seen four siblings die. He said, 'Since you made contact with the deepest repressed "dead bit" of me, I feel you've put me in a position to experience my emotional involvements with my parents in the post infancy period in a new way. Better to feel involved in bloody battles and tortures than fade out into nothingness, deadness. But now we've unearthed my dead self, I'm beginning to be able to come to life and grow, and feel my involvement in the real family situations of my later childhood.' The turbulent emotion symbolised in the Nimrod story, and in his repeated insistence that his mother read it to him was now coming out in dreams about father and mother, in person or only thinly disguised. He had had three such dreams which revealed the extent to which he, and children generally, are deeply, if unconsciously affected by the hidden, inner, emotionally disturbed relationship of their parents – to a far greater extent than they, or parents, or people in general know about. The first dream, he felt, showed the extent to which he became involved in trying to manage his father's unexpressed rage with mother:

> I went to the lavatory twice and both times father had been and left the pan piled high with dirty paper. I got my fingers soiled in trying to clear it up.

In the second dream he was 'sending mother away. She wasn't behaving well', whilst in the third dream he was minister of a church and seemed quite unable to do anything in a service: 'I just sat and did nothing while it went on by itself. Then I suddenly remembered a terrible thing. I'd murdered a woman and couldn't remember anything about it, but was shocked and horrified.' In what seemed to Guntrip a 'daring but deeply penetrating interpretation', Winnicott said, 'I suggest that you were deeply and absolutely unconsciously involved in a fantasy of your father's that sex is murder of a woman. It made him impotent and interferes with your potency intermittently. Your sexuality is in two parts: one is your own, which is all right, but it's interfered with by the other, which is identified with father's rage – inhibited impotence and horror of sex as murder.' As Guntrip pondered on this, he realised that his emotional involvement with his parents' struggles went far beyond their sexual conflicts, so that he had somehow absorbed 'their unnatural, unhealthy, unconsciously motivated atmosphere', as a defence enabling him to survive Percy's death by 'living inwardly' in an internal bad-object world, and outwardly by getting away from home. A further facet of the 'home atmosphere' was revealed in a short dream that 'two brothers (actual men I knew) were cursing and swearing at each other'. Winnicott said, 'That's your first dream of competition between brothers. Percy didn't live long enough for any sustained competition between you. But we want to know how, after he died and you collapsed bewildered, you managed to salvage enough of yourself to go on living with, very energetically, and put the rest in a cocoon, repressed in your unconscious.[2] You daren't go to sleep for fear mother and father act out their fantasy murder.'

The following month, in his seventy-fifth session, Guntrip reported having woken with an erection 'and a fading dream of having got in touch with a bit of mother which was good, where she excited me and made me want her'. Winnicott pointed out that 'the erection didn't carry a fantasy of penetration genitally. It was aroused in connection with oral excitement, as a baby boy may have an erection while at the breast.' However, whilst this was the 'first real evidence' of mother having been a good object for him at the very beginning, Guntrip would seem to have winced away from its implications, for his next dream seemed to him to place the deteriorating relationship 'well inside the first year'. He again awoke with an erection, 'dreaming of our cat chasing a bird and couldn't get it. Both seemed lacking in energy. The cat would make a half-hearted pounce and the bird would flutter a few feet off. The bird would make a half-hearted peck at the cat.' Winnicott, however, continued to focus attention upon the earliest need. He said, 'This is an oral infant's desire for the breast in slow motion, inhibited to cancel out its ruthlessness. That's your trouble. Your oral desire for mother is ruthless, a shock for you, you might destroy her, eat her up without intending her destruction, so you have to damp everything down.' Despite the implication of 'basic oral ruthlessness' in Winnicott's interpretation, Guntrip was able to accept it in terms of his reaction to finding his mother gradually turning from being an 'initial good breast' into an 'impatient, physically off-putting automatic feeding-machine . . . after a few months at most.' The oral dream was followed, on the same night, by two further dreams which together show the extent to which Winnicott's deep insights had already begun to take root in Guntrip's dreaming unconscious. In the first he dreamed of telling a patient how a baby loses or doesn't grow a secure ego if failed by his mother. The patient was listening, walking as if in a dream, and as if disturbed by what was being said. The next dream was a momentous one:

> I met Freud at a conference. He was old but very much alive, pleasant looking, smiling with a wise, wrinkled face. We talked and seemed to understand each other excellently. He seemed very pleased I was doing psychotherapy. Then a younger woman, friendly, capable and stable was there, and I realised she was his wife. Then with Freud again [sic] and we talked. He had come to say 'Goodbye', and the atmosphere was straight-forwardly appreciative and supportive. There seemed a natural understanding between us, and he shook hands and left quickly, so as not to embarrass either of us by trying to put into words what was too deep for words.

Guntrip had awoken from the dream feeling better, stronger, and stabler, and feeling that he had breathed in the atmosphere of a healthy relationship. He felt that the Freuds stood for Winnicott and his wife Clare, and that Freud himself was not only Winnicott but also Fairbairn, Bertram Smith, and ultimately his father. He said, 'All that was best in all my father-figures has come to be summed up in you, because only you have seen and understood the bit of me that died in infancy, yet lived to put up whatever fight I could and use whatever help I could find, to grow a real self.' He felt that he had collected all his paternal good-objects to help him transcend the angry fight for life, forced upon him by his mother, whilst the stable female figure in the dream symbolised a combination of the good-breast mother of the first month or two and the kindly Mary who took over after that. At the end of the session, he recalled a part of the dream which he had forgotten to mention: 'Freud was retired.'

Next morning, Guntrip recalled 'a vague dream' in which Germany was making a savage attack on Russia, transporting all the food from the 'rich black soil' area and emptying Russia. He immediately provided his own interpretation in terms of his innate, energetic, 'will to live' out of which dangerously strong aggression had been generated by his mother's denial of him. He said, 'I must have been afraid that I would destroy her outright by my demands on her.' However, despite his belief that Winnicott and his wife (as depicted in the dream by the Freuds) had created an atmosphere in which he had 'come alive', thus enabling him to discover how ruthless his mother had driven him into being towards her, he questioned whether it would be safe to re-experience this in the transference with Winnicott. Moreover, the reference in the dream to Freud's retirement and farewell had raised the question of whether he ought now to end his analysis, and he told Winnicott, 'I've got at the heart of my problem with you, and have got from you the crucial insight and therapeutic relationship I needed, and now I feel I ought not to burden you any longer. You're nearly seventy.' Winnicott replied: 'That's realistic. I'm sixty nine and one day will die. You'll feel you've helped to kill me if this isn't worked through. You came to me because you felt it with Fairbairn. His work, his theory, has stood up to your demands on it and has survived, but he died as a person. Now you have to make use of me: in the way you talk, you are reaching out to touch me, mentally "feeling me all over" to get to know me, as you needed to and couldn't with mother and father as a child. You need me to stand up to it. That's why I rarely interrupt you. But it's safer, now that we can talk openly about it. You can "use me up" many times in fantasy and I'm still here in reality.' Guntrip later declared that this was 'a perfect example of genuine psychotherapeutic insight, based not on theory, but on sheer individual intuitive insight of a "seer"'. Whether he saw the significance of Winnicott's remark, 'Now it's safer' – namely that Guntrip's ruthless demandingness had been more dangerous for being unconscious – is not clear. He replied, 'I feel safe in making demands on you because when you are tired you say so, and when you know you must stop you will say so, and I feel I shall solve my problem before then. I must be a long way on that road now.'

From all the foregoing, Guntrip, having reached a sense of an original maternalism in his mother, saw clearly how his family circumstances had robbed him of that initial good experience, giving rise first to an experience of dying and then to 'real rage and ruthless hunger for the breast that had turned bad' on him. In his record of the analysis he wrote: 'That would explain the series of drawings I produced early in my analysis with Fairbairn, beginning with the "head staring in empty space", and then developing into a series of sadomasochistic representations of rape and castration, changing gradually into the depicting of a hungry baby biting the breast, alternating with the breast biting the baby.' He added, 'I do not know whether I mentioned these drawings to Winnicott. If I did not, it shows that I had a very powerful repression on all that destructive ruthless fantasy, of the well-fed baby, enraged by sudden deprivation of any genuine maternal handling and feeding.' It is hardly characteristic of Guntrip to be unsure about what he had told Winnicott. He had certainly felt extremely uncomfortable about this aspect of his experience hitherto. Now that the sado-masochistic phenomena had an explanatory context, however, the powerful repression could begin to lift. In the July session he said, 'I've been waking tired, feeling I was repressing some definite deep down tension.' He mentioned 'a dream of inhibition' in which he was back at Salem as minister after many years, but did not know what to do or how to go on. Guntrip was by now so aware of his anger at being forced into a self-sacrificing rôle that he interpreted the dream in terms of repressed resentment at being obliged to minister to others at home and at Salem whilst feeling unable to vent his anger and express his own growing self, so that, caught between these two extremes, he became paralysed. Sensing a sexual component, Winnicott said, 'Sexual excitement in sleep is really oral. The erect penis is a biting tooth. You let the surgeons rob you of your teeth too easily, and couldn't tolerate dentures, could-n't let yourself have teeth back.' Guntrip concurred, seeing his refusal to eat from three and a half to five years in terms of inhibited oral sadism, and recalling that his later fussiness over food had disappeared completely only when he left home. He was amazed at his unconscious compulsion to protect his mother from his angry need of her, so that, as he put it, 'the more angrily I wanted to bite, the more frightened I was to eat anything, and so the more hungry and angry I got'. He felt more than ever con-vinced that his real problem was a first-year breakdown or 'dying' that he had re-experienced when Percy died, and he saw that he had always felt a frustrated intensity, a drive, 'straining at the leash', while fearing to trust himself to let go, despite having managed on a conscious level to turn it into a constructive deter-mination to solve his basic problem.

Winnicott reminded him, 'Your oral transference involves your needing to make use of me and I must be able to stand it' – a timely redirecting of Guntrip's 'determination' into the transference which led him to recall a dream in which he had stopped going to Winnicott and had tried another London analyst, only to feel that he wasn't much good. Winnicott replied: 'If it's psychoanalysis you want or just maternal care, you can get that from another analyst, or Aunt Mary or Aunt Dolly. But what you want is Winnicott, or mother herself, and you can't get that anywhere else. You are afraid of compulsively wearing me out and wearing mother out. You've got to separate out the "wearing out" from the "oral sadism" that belongs to loving. It's frightening to bring up primitive destructiveness, but its when the patient can't get at his "oral sadism", can't find, admit and accept it, that he goes on and on, having analysis compulsively, and can't stop, and wears the analyst out. I'd like you to be able to end, because if the analyst can't let the patient go, the patient can't really end the analysis and get free. You weren't able to end properly with Fairbairn. You could only stop going and leave it unanalysed You can't end analysis until oral sadism is faced. You want to eat me and protect me!'

Next morning Guntrip acknowledged that he did indeed feel a powerful urge to devour the mother whose maternalism had failed him early on. Probably in the first year, with the business failing and Henry's job at risk, she had suddenly weaned him, with the consequence that he was aware of a devouring attitude to anyone he wanted or needed. He recognised how he could feel that he wanted to devour a good book, and after a time would suddenly lose interest in it, and that he felt that way about Winnicott's books and about Winnicott himself. But despite his realisation of how deeply this devouring attitude entered into his relationship with Winnicott, he declared, 'To me the deepest thing is not wanting to devour mother sadistically, but to have her for the security of maternal relationship so that I could feel "real", and I need you as a person to feel real with, not something called psychoanalysis.' Winnicott replied, 'There's a lot of things I must say now. First, about your mother. You felt she could provide enough food, but you were losing her as a person. She left you open to having to think about what you needed that she did not give. She didn't enable you not to need to think it out; and you've been having to think it out now with me, as if you don't know that I could know your need and meet it. You feel you've had to think it out and tell me what you want.'

Winnicott's second point was less welcome. He said, 'There's something else stirring in you at the level of the cruel Spaniard in the tomb-dream and a recent short dream of an Alsatian dog being put to sleep.[3] It involves anger, revenge against mother. The Alsatian dog is more primitive, just natural ruthlessness, the baby kicking out and finding he's hurt mother and didn't mean to.' He continued: 'Third, you didn't know how to want a person who knew what you wanted. Mother failed you there. So with Percy you had to build up a life of "not wanting" but of "giving" to someone who did not know your needs. You felt this was a reparation for your fantasy of destroying mother, but it turned out not to be; he died. You've had to perpetuate it therefore, as if you were saying:

"If I give my whole life to the service of others, I can at least get to and atone for the guilt over the damage I've done to mother in fantasy", and get at and let your primitive impulses come alive. If I could get you to your primitive impulses, you could then make reparation in a real, natural, non-compulsive way, write a book, have sexual intercourse. You can only get to your primitive ruthlessness, now you are an adult and not a child, if you've got a pattern of "reparation" and a vice versa of "concern". Now you're not an infant, you can only get to your oral sadism, if you know how to make reparation by being creative. Fourth, the Alsatian dog has two alternatives, death or reliving. Don't despise the first alternative. I'm wanting to help the dog to come alive, but I know the agony of living with the illness for a lifetime. It means at times that you would welcome dying, and if I were kind, I'd touch the spot and let you die. Not everyone wants to live the suffering and know it, to get better.'

Although it was apparent to Guntrip that, in his third point, Winnicott was emphasising his need for a 'truly personal relationship of mutuality', of which he had had no experience, and 'did not know how to want', he was certain that his 'giving' to Percy, although inevitably rather 'a one-sided affair', had evoked some return, since 'babies can react and show pleasure'. Moreover, he had no doubt that the eighteen-month-old Percy had 'done something fundamental in "habituating" [him] to a vocation of caring for others – which had acquired its own validity – since nothing in human life is so simple as to be 100% of any one element'. With regard to Winnicott's fourth point, although he realised that the alternative of welcoming death and giving up a hopeless struggle had been his experience when Percy and other 'brother-figures' died, he believed that 'the major forces' in his personality were against it and particularly his determination to resolve his problem. Finally he felt that both his own summing up of the total complex problem and Winnicott's emphatic response, had so clarified his position that, in spite of their one difference, which he now felt to be 'theoretical and marginal', no-one had ever understood his fundamental problem with so much insight as Winnicott, who thereby had given him the 'therapeutic relation' he had needed all his life. Using Winnicott's concept of 'Basic Ego-Relatedness', he had been able to see, to the benefit of his patients as well as himself, that the deepest part of him had always been 'ego-unrelated' with his mother so that he had always had to work hard to keep himself alive in a vacuum. When they reconvened in the autumn, Guntrip, with a profound sense of gratitude, recounted to Winnicott the latter's particular words and phrases which had meant so much to him:

'Mother couldn't be trusted to know your need, so you had to think it all out yourself and work hard to keep yourself alive . . . You talk in session like reaching out to touch me mentally, to get to me and to get to know me. Mother didn't let you do that. You need me to stand up to it.' For Guntrip at this time these words and phrases of Winnicott's were crucial for he felt that their sessions were his one chance to experience 'basic ego-relatedness' in a hitherto inaccessible part of himself. He later regarded the period from this point in October 1965 to December 1966 as the most intensive of the analysis.

Winnicott recapitulated: 'Mother gave you food but you were losing her as a person. You didn't know that I could know your need and meet it, without your explaining it.' With a deep feeling of relief Guntrip replied: 'Now I can relax in my analysis and begin to experience psychotherapy as a healing relation, not as a desperate effort to get in touch and get understood. Now I can be quiet and not feel lost in a gap of silence, because you give me a relationship of understanding to feel real in.' Winnicott replied 'You've left out one thing, play. I don't say you never played on the floor with tin soldiers and father there one Christmas, scalping Red Indians with Teddy Broadbent in the garden, cricket and football, climbing in Scotland, but there's been hard work in a lot of that play, proving yourself. You could play by going to Lords just to enjoy watching, but you read books to master them rather than enjoy them, as one might enjoy poetry.'

Guntrip replied, 'Our talking now is more like unrehearsed play. If I could take time off from working hard to keep going, I expect I'd sleep better.' It is significant that Guntrip had begun this important session by remarking that he had no dreams to report. He told Winnicott that up to this point his dreaming had mainly served a defensive function of 'working hard at night creating an inner world of sado-masochistic fantasy to keep some kind of deep down ego alive in', but that Winnicott's paper 'The Capacity to be Alone' (in Winnicott 1965) had brought his insight to a head, so that the feeling of their mutual interaction in session had come to feel 'more important than dreaming'.

Next day, in session eighty-two on 6 October, he said, 'Your words about play let me go away with a lighter mood. You are letting me out of the struggle to keep myself alive. I know that's got to grow deeper down yet.' Winnicott replied, 'Your problem is that the illness of collapse was never resolved, and you had both to keep yourself alive in spite of it, and also wanted mother to do it, and tried to coerce her by illnesses for eighteen months. But you had to take over your own mothering. Mother was the mother who let babies die. When Percy died, you took his place on her lap, to give her a chance to prove she could keep you alive and she failed. Aunt Dolly did something, but thereafter, while unconsciously wanting mother to do it, you had consciously to do it yourself. And it's left you afraid of gaps. You're afraid to stop acting, talking, or keeping awake. You feel you might die in a gap, like Percy, because if you stop acting mother can't do anything. You were bound to fear I can't keep you alive, so you link monthly sessions up for me, no gaps. You can't feel that to me you are a going concern. You know about being active, but not about "growing", just "breathing" and your heart just "beating" while you sleep, without your having to do anything about it to make them work.'

This vital interpretation went to the heart of Guntrip's problem (see Guntrip 1975, in Hazell 1994, p. 362): the threat of annihilation through the sheer failure of relationship. The next two sessions, in November, were crucial. They were to be followed by a major tragedy in Guntrip's professional career, and one cannot but think it fortuitous that the profound insights of these sessions were achieved before that tragedy occurred. In session eighty-three on 1 November, Guntrip reported a dream in which he was sitting with Winnicott who was reading a paper to him while he listened very intently, feeling very secure. He marvelled at how he was able to be silent, free from compulsion to talk hard to explain himself or to work hard to get Winnicott to understand. He said, 'I was secure enough to listen to you and not have to worry about keeping myself in being.' In the security he was able to recall how, in the 'fatal gap' after the death of Percy, his tent-bed illnesses had not really created a secure relationship, so that he had had to work hard to become self-sufficient, wandering alone in a park throughout one day trying to demonstrate it, until finally at eight years he had taken control his life and run his own interests. He reflected upon how he must have repressed the isolated child inside, and he told Winnicott, 'Now you've got in touch with me there, I can relax effort to do it all myself.' So saying he did relax in silence for a considerable time, until starting to grow rather anxious, he was relieved to hear Winnicott move. With 'uncanny intuition', Winnicott said, 'You began to feel afraid I had abandoned you. You feel silence as abandonment, which makes sleep a risk.'

In the eighty-fourth session the next morning, Guntrip said, 'In that dream I was able to be silent because you were talking, reading to me. In the session last night I began to feel somewhat anxious when I felt both of us were silent, a gap. When I returned from Aunt Dolly, I must have felt there had been a gap for I couldn't remember what happened.' Winnicott replied: 'The gap was not you forgetting mother, but feeling that mother had forgotten you.[4] You've relived that now with me. You feared mother couldn't keep you alive in her thought, so you had to take over keeping yourself alive in your own thought. You felt mother had abandoned you. I think in fact that the Percy trauma repeated an earlier trauma, which you might never recover without the help of the Percy trauma making you feel mother had abandoned you. You're trying to remember mother abandoning you, by transference on to me. You feel sleep risks falling into that gap.' He added, 'Children need to know for sure that mother has them in mind, and will make noises to let her know that they are about the house.'

The vital insights of these sessions in November 1965 are reflected in Chapters 8 and 9 of Guntrip's book, *Schizoid Phenomena, Object Relations and the Self* (1968), much of which Guntrip was sending to Winnicott in manuscript as he went along. These chapters in particular carry the unmistakable quality of hope emerging from the paralysing blankness of the unrelated state. Winnicott's written response to Guntrip's manuscript is worth reproducing at length:

> I am very glad you are writing this . . . the place where you discuss my concepts with healthy doubt concerns (I think) three things: (1) where you are in your personal analysis with me; (2) where I am right – or adequate; or wrong – or balmy; (3) where I am myself exploring in a paper . . . I hope to read to the Society in February.[5]
>
> In a book like yours you have to cash in on where you (and the rest of us) are at the time of writing. By the time it is published, you must inevitably wish to put certain paragraphs differently – for instance, a year from now, or more. A person like you goes a long way in a year.
>
> I like what you have written and also your expressions of doubt in specific places – Okay, Hooray.
>
> But perhaps I will take up one detail – at risk.
>
> This incommunicado position is the place where (non-derivative) creativity comes from. Only I am trying to describe this activity when it is at rest. It is the state of being alive, with infinite potential for experiencing living . . . But I discuss the alternatives BE and DO in this paper I am at.
>
> Every good wish – and I can't wait for your book to be on every shelf, green-bound and ever green in its freshness of presentation. (Personal communication, 14 November 1965.)

Guntrip's sense of 'quiet steady progress' at this time was cut short later that month by what he later described as the worst tragedy in his career as a therapist. In 1948 he had accepted a referral of a depressed and obsessional male patient on his discharge from hospital, and, due to the paucity of psychotherapists in Leeds, he also felt obliged to take on the patient's wife who was schizoid with some mild schizophrenic symptoms. Their joint treatment progressed steadily for eleven years, by which time they had stabilised their lives, made a home and produced a child. Guntrip heard nothing of them for two further years, except for a telephone call from the husband telling him of the birth of a second child. Then, late in 1961, the man rang in obvious distress and sessions had to be resumed. A combination of heavy extra work pressures, and serious troubles in the wider families of both husband and wife had broken him down, so that he returned to one session 'quite regressed, curled up on the couch like a baby in the womb', whilst Guntrip sat with him, holding his hand and saying nothing, till at last the man stirred, and was able to tell him what had happened. After a period of hospitalisation, during which the therapy continued, the man was able to resume work, but a deeper problem had emerged: he had a complete amnesia for the period immediately after his mother's death which had occurred when he was fourteen. He was left completely without help, and, overwhelmed by the loss, and responsibility for his younger sister, he collapsed. The boy and his sister were taken into care and educated by the Local Authority, until in due course they found partners and the man began an outstandingly successful professional career. From 1961 to the spring of 1965 Guntrip saw the man for once-weekly therapy, which was all that was possible since he lived fifty miles from Leeds. However, the sessions were supplemented by phone calls and the patient's amnesia began to recede, though 'to the accompaniment of intense anxiety at every step'. By the summer of 1965, he began to consider ending analysis. Then, just before Guntrip's August holiday, the patient expressed extreme concern for his safety; and when, on his safe return from holiday, the patient said he had feared Guntrip would die, the latter realised that by considering ending treatment the patient had unconsciously exposed himself to the possibility of reliving his mother's death. Slowly, he remembered his feelings of appalling weakness and isolation during his mother's last illness and afterwards, until one weekend 'he suddenly became totally regressed again, got himself to Leeds, and told me he was suicidal'. Guntrip put it to him that that was what he had felt when his mother died, and that his desire to end treatment had stirred up again an actual suicidal impulse at the age of fourteen. It was agreed between them that the patient should re-enter hospital while they sought to work through this dangerous traumatic memory, and the patient was much relieved when arrangements were made for his re-admission after the weekend. There had been 'a tense moment' in the session, when the patient had told Guntrip that before he could commit suicide, he would have to kill him, because he could not bear the thought that Guntrip would be alive to know that he had let him down. However, when Guntrip put it to him that he could be re-experiencing a suicidal despair that he had felt before his mother died, but which he could not bear for her to know, the patient seemed relieved.

But the patient did not enter hospital on the Monday as arranged. Instead his wife phoned Guntrip to say that they had had the happiest weekend she could remember, and that, in any case, she had told her husband that she could not cope with the children in his absence and could not stand his going into hospital again. Accordingly, he had gone into work that morning. But by midday his wife phoned again to say her husband had come home quite broken down. Guntrip spoke to him by phone, and told him, 'I'm not free to come over and see you, or you know I would come. But I'll write to you now. You must go to hospital.' Once again, arrangements were made for his re-admission, probably on the Wednesday of the same week. Meanwhile the wife was to visit Guntrip on the Friday, on her way to see her husband.

There was no further contact until the Thursday evening, when the police phoned: alerted by neighbours who had reported milk bottles not taken in for three days, the police had broken in, to find his wife and two children murdered in their beds, and the father lying dead on the sofa downstairs. It was established that he had had the scientific knowledge to enable him to kill them instantly and painlessly in their sleep. Guntrip realised, too late, that there was one bit of that traumatic memory of wanting to commit suicide, which he had not foreseen. The patient's original suicide wish at fourteen years was a product of his feeling of total isolation and despair at the loss of his mother, and of overwhelming responsibility for himself and his sister. But to accede to his wish would have meant leaving his sister alone in life, and he felt he should kill her first. He had collapsed unconscious at the horror of his predicament and was taken to hospital, where the memory of that traumatic situation was repressed – until the thought of ending analysis, losing Guntrip as a parent figure, revived it, hence the patient's fear that Guntrip might die on holiday. The one thing Guntrip did not foresee was the effect of his patient's wife's sudden realisation that she could not bear another loss of her husband to hospital. For the patient, the similarity to the original circumstances had really proved overwhelming: unable to 'escape' to the Local Authority/hospital, his conscious judgement was overwhelmed by the return of the repressed urge towards suicide, and once again, he felt the hopelessness of his position: to carry on felt impossible; to succumb would mean deserting his sister/wife and family. To him the only way out appeared to be to yield to his original impulse, to kill those dependent on him and then end his own life. Guntrip believed that his patient must have felt it was a 'mercy-killing', for the police photographs clearly showed his expression as he lay dead on the sofa to be one of peaceful relief. The Coroner and jury listened respectfully to Guntrip's account, and thanked him. But this was 'little consolation' for his feeling that, had he been just one step ahead in realising the full implications of his patient's reactions to his mother's death, he could have prevented the whole tragedy. When he finished his account of these horrifying events, Winnicott said, 'I think you were as near to a perfect "cure" in this case as you will ever be.'

At the last session of the year, next day, Guntrip wondered at the similarity of his own position to that of his patient. Had he, too, collapsed out of an unbearable situation – unable to support his brother's life with no real experience of support from his mother? The reverberations of the catastrophe in his own unconscious must surely have been extreme, and he reported that he and his wife both felt 'a gap, an emptiness, now that these two patients are no longer there to come for sessions or to ring up'. 'Life', he added, 'has lost some meaning, become trivialised.'6

This disaster occurred at the end of my second year of analysis with Guntrip. The latter revealed nothing of these events. But he was very rigid, stressing the need for psychotherapists to ensure medical cover, as the Coroner's court could be a very daunting experience.

Notes

1   Years later, Guntrip wrote in correspondence 'If one can conceive a *total* lack of ego or self, I think the baby would have died, lost even the capacity to feel as a "subject". The ego-potential at birth must be given something, however small, to begin to live by or it will die.' (Personal communication, 20 November 1971)

2   In 1975 (Hazell 1994, p. 362). Guntrip brought together Winnicott's two interpretations, 'If 100% of you . . .' and '. . . put the rest in a cocoon', as if they formed one sentence, probably the better to illustrate the origin of his 'lifeless state' and Winnicott's penetrating insight.

3   The dream was not recorded by Guntrip.

4   In his (1975) account of his experience of analysis, Guntrip merges Winnicott's interpretations in sessions eighty-three and eighty-four. Also the wording is slightly altered in the 1975 paper (Hazell 1994, p. 363): 'the gap is not you forgetting mother, but mother forgetting you'.

5   Winnicott's paper 'The Split-off Male and Female Elements to be found Clinically in Men and Women' was delivered to the British Psychoanalytic Society in February 1966. Guntrip's exposition is to be found in Chapter 9 of SPORS, p. 251ff.

6   Guntrip had written up the earlier stages of this case for a projected book on 'Borderline Cases' and he brought the account up to date for the Coroner's consideration. Winnicott had read the manuscript, and had congratulated Guntrip on it: 'For me it is absolutely first rate' (personal correspondence 5 January 1964). The book was never published.

CHAPTER 18

1966

The matter was foremost in Guntrip's mind when sessions were resumed in January. Winnicott pointed out to him that he could have survived the possibility of being murdered in that last session with his patient, and he added, 'You are frightened of the power of the dissociated Mr Hyde side of our Dr Jekylls, afraid of its power to take over. It could be in all of us. I might be a doctor of children to compensate for fantasies of killing children, as I used to kill insects as a boy. But you've been able to survive being destroyed as a therapist.'

Next morning Guntrip reported that he had woken in the night thinking of Winnicott's remark that he was frightened of what is dissociated. He felt that his patient's murder and suicide had stirred this up and for the first time he could feel that he hated Percy, not as a rival but for more subtle reasons, not least for having been unable to use his help to stay alive. He continued, 'His dying must have destroyed my faith in myself for the time being and I began to die . . . I began to fall ill and die because I came to feel my hate was destroying everyone and myself . . . My illness after his death was a kind of suicide, a hate of myself for failing, of mother for failing, of Percy for dying, and of life itself. That patient's suicide stirred up all that.' Winnicott reminded him that in adulthood one can only become aware of destructive impulses by having an established pattern of reparation.

Guntrip recalled how he had fallen ill when his Salem colleague left, and had dreamed of the Spaniard who hated the English Queen being buried alive in the tomb-room. Remembering his fear when the tomb-man threatened to emerge, he now felt inclined to believe that the latter also represented his repressed destructive self, which his patient had re-aroused by not letting Guntrip keep him alive. He remembered, too, his fantasy of destroying the painting of the Madonna and Child in the National Gallery, which he now felt had come to represent not mother and Percy but mother and himself, so that he had wanted to destroy the whole situation which could develop into such tragedies in later life. But he added: 'It also represented the one thing valuable which was denied me from the start.' Winnicott commented: 'You feel you can only possess the precious thing by destroying it. That's the dissociated bit. You can't know it. You can know and compensate for the repressed but not for the dissociated. I can know it's there for you. You could feel the only way to end analysis would be to possess me by killing me. The patient probably felt that about you. You need to accept killing me in fantasy while I stay alive.'

Although Guntrip could accept the idea of something 'dissociated' as distinct from 'repressed' as 'quite real', predictably the idea of 'possessing by killing' did not ring true. He did, however, determine to keep a sharp eye open to see if it became real in later sessions. For the present, Guntrip preferred to think of the destructive element as expressive of his need to 'blot out the whole terrible scene of Percy's death', by 'dissociating' it through amnesia. He recalled that the painting he fantasised destroying was da Vinci's 'Madonna of the Rocks' depicting the Mother and Child, and John the Baptist. It now seemed to him that the Madonna represented his mother, and Jesus Percy dead on her lap, with John the Baptist as himself looking on. He felt that the painting had threatened to bring the whole scene to consciousness so that he wanted both to blot it out, keep it dissociated, but also, by dissociation, secretly to possess, so that no-one could open it up and end it. He added, 'That patient no doubt felt that and felt my analysis was a threat to his secret possession of his mother and sister.' Guntrip observed that he had, within a few minutes, used the painting to express two different traumata: first the loss of the originally good mother, who so soon became tantalising through loss, and secondly the trauma of discovering Percy dead on his mother's lap. His reaction had been a dissociative amnesia of both the traumata. He believed that apart from one or two of what Fairbairn had called 'low-grade memories', which were a kind of sudden dark half-hallucination or picture of the baby dead on mother's lap, this was the nearest he had come to recovering an actual memory of the traumatic event.

Prompted by the recollection of his time with Fairbairn he dreamed, 'I called at Fairbairn's house. There was a large meeting of all his supporters. I knew nothing of it and felt I might have been invited. But they seemed to be Edinburgh people. Sutherland wasn't there. Fairbairn appeared not to see me. I greeted him and someone said, "Here's Dr Guntrip." He said, "Oh. Yes", and moved on. I felt out of it as if I didn't belong where I thought I did. When we all went, I found I'd left my coat at his house.'

Realising that the forgotten coat was probably an excuse to return and see if he was accepted after all, Guntrip confided to Winnicott, 'I may fear you may now lose faith in me: analysts may say: "He can't analyse aggression".' Winnicott replied: 'You feel that in the end, Fairbairn couldn't deal with what was coming up in you, the dissociated bit of you stirred up by this patient. You can't know your dissociated bit but you need to know if I can.'

Guntrip dreamed that his deceased patient came to him for a session, afraid of how he would be received after the murders he had done. But he looked much changed and was probably relieved when Guntrip took his hand in the dream and welcomed him. He asked Winnicott, 'Is this dream a response to your saying you could know the dissociated bit of me for me, so that I've brought him to consciousness in a dream to get him accepted by his analyst, and by myself?' Winnicott replied 'The dangerous bit of you died with Percy. You projected that bit of you into Percy. But it's only a myth that your sinister bit is in Percy, dead. It can't be final. You want to remember that part of you that you projected into Percy, though his death was your life for the rest of youself that could go on living afterwards, a life of reparation. The patient is Percy, but he is also that bit of you in Percy that you want to bring back but fear he'll pop up in the night if you let go.' Guntrip said, 'I'm feeling the burden and pressure of patients and can't stand it much longer.' Winnicott replied, 'Percy was your first patient. He died and you lived. You feel you must be rid of them to survive.'

In the session the following day, Guntrip simply reacted by saying: 'I'm having feelings of wanting to give up work and not do anything.' He had dreamed, twice, that someone got up to recite but forgot his piece and could not do anything, and he offered the opinion that the person represented himself afraid to do anything in case he should be destructive. His situation was indeed an unhappy one, and he felt nervous about going on with his work, in case other patients should have tragedies, and everyone would think he dealt with patients wrongly – a mood which found expression in another dream:

> I was wanting to get out of psychotherapy, and into the ministry, and then out of the ministry into some job with machine parts, impersonal, nothing to do with people.

Winnicott observed that the patient's tragedy had stirred up in Guntrip an unconscious need for each of his patients to die, because his work had become a struggle to prevent them dying. He said, 'They must get well or die, otherwise you're stuck with them in agony. It's the Percy situation.'

In the intervening month, Guntrip read Winnicott's paper 'The Split-off Male and Female Elements to be found Clinically in Men and Women', which the latter had read to the Society in early February. Guntrip discussed the paper extensively in the draft of Chapter 9 of *Schizoid Phenomena, Object Relations and the Self*, a copy of which Winnicott read and approved. Guntrip saw that the healthy female element of 'being' and the healthy male element of 'doing', which together form a complementary whole in both men and women, had pseudo-forms as 'passivity' and 'forced activity', which were reflected respectively in his father's being pushed into the background and in his mother's dominating behaviour. The relevance of the paper to Guntrip's own situation would appear to have re-established the vital sense of 'ego-relatedness', after the recent severe disruptions, for he dreamed:

> I saw a girl, quiet, pleasant, attractive, affectionate, just as it were 'being there'. I took her in my arms and she was pleased. We were just there together.

The dream reminded him of how Bertha had appeared to him when he first saw and loved her. He said: 'In this dream I'm finding the possibility of discovering my female element of "being" and so integrating, and allowing my "doing" to flow naturally, unforced.' Guntrip then proceeded clearly and firmly to equate 'sadism' with 'pseudo-male' activity. He told Winnicott, 'All your interpretations fall broadly into two groups, "sadism" and "being". You know I can't accept sadism as natural and innate. For me it can't be explained in its own terms. It is what develops in the pseudo-male compulsively active struggle to "be", to keep alive in the absence of a true sense of "being" in relation to a mother who isn't "being" for me. Your views about "being" have set things moving in me again, where I lost mother early in the first year and had to struggle to keep myself alive.' He was reminded of another recent dream:

> I was in bed with my wife and something made me get up, and I found she had been up and opened the bedroom door and front door and come back to bed. I felt disturbed and didn't like lying in bed with the doors open, but I didn't close them and went back to bed.

Winnicott said, 'You are using my theory of the female element, recognising your true female element, or capacity to lie at rest and not to be afraid to be open, though not doing anything.' Guntrip replied, 'I feel the situation is changing from one in which I did a heck of a lot of analysis, using you as someone to keep myself alive with, and becoming one in which I can growingly [sic] feel real without either of us doing anything but simply "being together". I'm real for you and so you are real for me and I'm growing more real for myself.'

During the intervening month, Guntrip was able to consolidate this experience of 'being' and 'being-with'. He said to Winnicott: 'I feel a decisive change is growing. I am feeling more energetic, sleeping better, but one night I woke and lay thinking of you as I see you in session, evidently manufacturing a relationship by thinking: my lifelong method. I'm not yet at the point where I possess it as an unconscious permanent experience, but I feel I'm on the way, and change has come to a decisive point.' He recalled the occasion in March 1963 when Winnicott loaned him his paper on 'Moral Education' and how he had felt that Winnicott had lost touch with the child in him, whereas the paper on 'Bisexuality' had had the opposite effect as if it were drawing together the long process of mutative interpretations that had been going on. He said, 'You are the first person to see the true meaning of my compulsive activity, working, talking, thinking, to manufacture something to keep in the gap of the non-existent sense of basic being. You have enabled me to get at an experience of being by giving me the kind of perceptive relationship mother could not give. Clearly, no-one had given it to her. Perhaps the critical turning point was in January 1963 when you said mother conceived me not as a live child, but as a dead one, a lump of clay, to be moulded into her shape, and my needing you to see me as having a life of my own.'

Guntrip's growing sense of 'being' was expressed in a simple dream in which Winnicott was helping him with his writing, reading what he had written. He reported this, and relaxed for the remainder of the session. After a time Winnicott came in with, 'I needn't say anything really, but I want to say that you have been able to work on your records of sessions, and do for both of us what possibly I should have done, and could only have done if I had kept records. You've shown how I have been slowly making a kind of container or shawl or pram of interpretations, inside which you could grow. You have done something for me in this. I've never had a patient who could do it before.' Guntrip found this a 'fascinating' comment – but shawls and prams did not quite do justice to what he felt, and he 'went one deeper', so to speak, by saying, 'Your understanding has made me a mental womb in which my deep down dead self could grow. I feel every main interpretation has been like food, something to take in and grow with. It's all the better because it wasn't a thought-out thing, not planned but a spontaneous umbilical flow of consistent understanding which I have taken into my unconscious as a basis for "being".' He added that their theoretical differences on the origin of aggression had really made no difference to the real heart of Winnicott's therapeutic analysis. In my view, Guntrip experienced Winnicott's views of 'innate sadism' primarily as a 'gap' in the so-needed sense of relationship, and retreated into intellectual argument as a defence to maintain some sense of personal viability. He needed to get the 'real' Winnicott back. In this session, with the sense of relatedness growing within, he could say, 'You haven't given me "interpretations", you have given me of your spontaneous understanding, which I don't hesitate to say goes deeper than anything I have ever met before.'

Next morning, Guntrip made reference to a Michelangelo painting and the three carvings to which he was later to refer in *Schizoid Phenomena, Object Relations and the Self* (p. 264) as illustrative of the way that spontaneous 'doing' arises from secure experience of 'being-in-relation'. That he himself now felt able to relax his competitive self-driving was demonstrated when he dreamed:

> Someone asked me to see a very ill child. He looked thin, drawn, strained. I was asked to take him on for treatment, but said I couldn't, and said he must be referred to someone for help, and wondered if he would be.

This highly important dream, in which Guntrip, with evident relief, arrived at the realisation that alone he was unable to treat either his own ill self, or that of his brother, marked the beginning of a steady regrowth, as he allowed his breakdown illness after Percy's death to emerge with Winnicott.

In April he reported having felt vaguely ill all month, like the ill boy in the dream that he could not treat, and he mentioned another dream of having a mental breakdown, and becoming confused and disorientated, until after he had rested, his wife came with a taxi, and he set off with her to return home. The dream had seemed almost like a vague memory of his illness after Percy died, and of being brought home to take up life again. Winnicott said, 'You have built up a big trust in my ability to see your illness and help you, but you need me to know the ill "you" who felt there was no-one who understands to turn to.' In a further dream a young man who was a patient brought another young man 'looking weak and ill', whom Guntrip saw for one session, though he was unable to take him on. He felt certain that the dream meant he was letting his ill self have his session with Winnicott, and he said, 'I'm needing to make the transition from "being ill" with you, to relaxing without being ill. I need to move from "compulsive doing" back to "being ill" and then to "being well with you", and on to "non-compulsive healthy doing".' He recalled Winnicott having said, early in the analysis, that a patient regresses with the analyst in order to find security to face the illness, and that he needed to know that Winnicott could help him find it. Winnicott replied, 'If I didn't see and find your dead or ill bit, no-one ever would.'

Next day, in the ninety-sixth session, Guntrip became gripped by an urgent need to reach and restore the 'basic dissociated female element, the capacity for "simple healthy being"' which so eluded him, convinced that he 'would not sleep' until he reached it. Fortunately, his unconscious took over, for he dreamed:

> I was addressing a Psychology Conference, and said, 'Gentlemen and Ladies. I start that way because men need more help in these things than women. Women know about people intuitively. Men only think they know.'

It is perhaps less the manifest content of the dream that indicates a change in Guntrip at this point, for as Winnicott had pointed out, the 'female element' of feeling and 'being' is basic for both men and women, but rather the humour of the dreamer in debunking his own 'pseudo-male element'. In one sense his next comment reveals a reversion to the old split between the two elements. He said, 'Since I gave up my church activities and became a psychotherapist who just sits and listens, I've felt an increased urge to urinate, a kind of protest against inactivity.' He also mentioned having gazed again at the Michelangelo Madonnas. Winnicott made a striking comment:

> Your talking had both manner and content: *1. Manner*[1] Talking is like urinating, a long stream that pours out till it stops because you have no more. That's the moment of rest, no

control, incontinence in the best sense. You don't have to drop control because there's nothing to control. You can just 'be' at rest, till more comes spontaneously. You can rest and just 'be' with me, and then become active spontaneously with me when you have something to say. 2. *Content*. You need me to talk about Michelangelo. Your mother was depressed. The Madonna wasn't depressed, and mother and child could just restfully 'be' together, and wait for spontaneous activity to arise of its own accord. Your mother was depressed and couldn't wait for you to become active in your own time. She had to stimulate you, make you active according to her ideas and what she wanted. When she wants you to pee and you have nothing to give, that's real impotence. Your only alternatives were her stimulating your forced activity, or illness, impotence. No 'rest' and 'being' leading to natural activity.

At this point Guntrip recalled a dream which he had forgotten to mention:

My aged neighbour began repairing his fence and putting up new posts.

Winnicott suggested that the neighbour could represent Guntrip's inactive father who gave him no living example to counteract mother's influence, but who in the dream came alive for him to identify with. He said, 'You need me to be both the mother who can "be" and enable you to "do", and also the father who can be active and 'doing' and enable you to "do".' Winnicott here seems to be transcending the influence of Guntrip's mother as an internalised bad object by manifesting a new quality in Guntrip's experience of which she was incapable. Moreover, he was ready to take on the function of 'role model', as a more active father-figure for him to identify with as a basis for his unilateral growth.

An example of the latter occurred at their next meeting in May, when the two men discussed frankly their professional experience. Guntrip had been told by a consultant that arthritic pains were due to 'wear and tear', but which he was inclined to associate with serious set-backs with two of his patients. He was greatly reassured by Winnicott's 'courageous realism' when the latter replied, 'I have a patient who has just begun to fall in love with her husband, and he is found to have cancer. I have to accept that I cannot get her well now. I have to go on doing child psychiatry because I need results to keep me going, and adult analyses tend to go on for ever.

You can't bank on results. Life may prevent them.' From here the content of the session moved easily into the reporting of a dream in which Guntrip 'saw a penis, just a stump with a soft top, formless, vaguely moving, as if there was just a bit of life in it'. He associated it with the 'broken pillar over a child's grave, a symbol of early promise cut short', and he said, 'It's both Percy and the bit of me that got cut-off short from further development when Percy died.' Winnicott replied, 'It may well represent Percy, and part of you identified with him, or else Percy identified with your penis, your keeping possession of him in yourself. Excitement could then be inside you and be prevented from getting into your penis.' Guntrip mentioned his circumcision at five years, and Winnicott said, 'It shouldn't have been done. You probably felt it inhibited you from feeling excited in the glans where you felt something was cut off, though you could feel it in your body.'

That night Guntrip could not sleep at all, but he dreamed, while dozing before rising,

> I was in a doctor's room and a man was showing how he could lie down and go straight to sleep.

He felt the dream to be expressing the fact that he could only relax through 'feeling a secure relation' to Winnicott, whereas with his mother, he 'fell into an emptiness'. The dream also led him to recall the occasion in the analysis when Winnicott himself had 'relaxed and slept' in his presence. However he may have felt at the time, Guntrip was now inclined to feel a sense of gratitude for such 'unguardedness' in Winnicott, who had 'proved the possibility of relaxing and sleeping in my presence by doing it; how to "be" without "doing"'. After pausing he spoke from the heart: 'I feel I must say that it is what you are that is most important to me. Fairbairn at his best was an acute intellect I respected, a courageous man who dared to think independently, and I found he had provided the psychoanalytical equivalent of my philosophical convictions, for which I was looking. I knew him at heart to be a kindly man, but as his health worsened, he began to disappear behind a wall of subtle defences. I felt I knew him best in his letters and somehow never really knew 'him'. You are not afraid to be known. I recently described you as the only man I know who seems to have no need of any ego-defences. You let me see your humanness, so that I don't have to hide my humanness with you now.' As he finished speaking he relaxed contentedly and just as he was beginning to feel a fear of isolation, Winnicott, sensing his need, said, 'I feel this silence is precious but now I'm feeling I ought to do something or speak, or you might feel I've forgotten you. But perhaps I ought not to have broken the silence. You could stand being silent and just "be" and enjoy it and feel safe, but mother couldn't.' Guntrip replied, 'Mother had to be "doing", fussing. That's probably one reason why I can't relax. You spoke just at the moment I began to need you to, but perhaps you also sensed that you had to re-enact mother's role, so I could see it and get over it, when you described it. Next time, I'll be better able to accept silence, relax and enjoy it.'

The intervening month was redolent of genuine ego-development for Guntrip. At their June session he observed that he was no longer working on the analysis between the sessions, but was aware of 'just growing', and of 'taking the strain of disturbed patients better'. But the new state felt precarious, and he told Winnicott how reassured he had felt when the latter had risked 'breaking the precious silence' in the previous session. In the security of this recollection, he relaxed in silence until the end of the session, without fear, either of abandonment or of impingement.

The next morning's session revealed the 'unevenness' that is so often characteristic of psychic growth. Guntrip mentioned a patient who had telephoned on Monday night in a panic because her GP had accused her of making up her mind beforehand not to take his pills which she felt paralysed her. Winnicott said, 'I think you may use this for a delusional transference. This began to worry you after your relaxation in last night's session. Unconsciously, you probably felt in one tiny bit of you a panic fear that I was your mother – like your patient's doctor – paralysing you, forcing you to relax for her sake because she couldn't stand your activity. You feel mother paralysed you to keep you quiet, or to prevent you developing a separate self apart from her, so that you had to get away in the end and be overactive.' Guntrip replied 'I did think you looked tired last night and I was glad that I didn't have to talk and demand your attention, but unconsciously I may well have felt it was mother making me keep quiet, though predominantly it was reassuring.' The accuracy of Winnicott's interpretation was confirmed by a vivid dream:

> I got away from home and wandered about and then needed to go back for some reason. Mother was near and I had to get in and away without her seeing me, to escape her. I did so helped by an aged woman.

Guntrip associated this aged female helper with Winnicott, in his maternal aspect, assisting his differentiation from his mother as an internalised bad object upon whom he could still feel unconsciously dependent. His fear that this dependence could never be outgrown was a real threat making him dread a worsening of his physical health and enforced retirement, which he unconsciously associated with his mother's paralysing influence. He felt doubtful as to whether his natural self, having at last secured recognition and relation at the deepest level, possessed the capacity to transcend the emptiness of his inner world. As the summer break drew near the power of the internal bad object seemed to be increasing, and Guntrip recounted a further dream in which he had heard a very different kind of 'aged woman' singing about 'Victory over devils', defiantly, energetically, whereupon he had laughed and said, 'Just how my mother would have sung it!' When he described this dream, Winnicott replied 'Mother's inner reality was full of dead, lifeless people and out of that you came; and she sought to keep everyone around her dead and lifeless so that only she was alive. Your sleep difficulty is to do with your falling back into her limbo, her dead world.' And, as on the occasion nine months previously when Guntrip had experienced a 'static lifeless state', Winnicott's response startled him into an identification with her in her difficult life: how in her teens she was a little mother, looking after her mother's children, four of whom had died and how she had then miscarried her first baby, and lost Percy. Winnicott, however, remained in touch with 'the child' who could not have made those objective judgements in mitigation. He said: 'Possibly she felt her destructiveness and sent you away, the one good thing she did do', and he added: 'Your wife can take over the original good-breast mother you had for the first two or three months, but it hides the other paralysing mother. You need me to stand for her so that you can get free': thus Winnicott sought to recognise and sponsor the growing personal life of his patient as he left for the summer break.

The Guntrips spent their summer holiday in Scotland 'doing the Corrieyarrack Pass', an impressive feat for two people in their mid-sixties. But the influence of the bad object was still powerful and when Guntrip returned to analysis in September, he was aware that he was carrying a deep-down sense of strain, which he associated with the fear of his mother's collapse, and the burden of having to support her weight. He dreamed of having to drag her large heavy wardrobe up a slope with his small car, with a fear that it would drag him back, and he recalled that his mother was always making sure everyone knew what a load she had to carry, and, behind his back, how useless father was. He mentioned one further dream of repairing an old overloaded car from the Salem days, and then, doubtless sensing that he was reverting to 'doing analysis' after a break, he said, 'I had some more dreams, but I feel I can leave them and lie back and relax.' His sense of relatedness had returned and Winnicott, who had remained quiet, said, after a longish silence, 'I don't think I need to say anything. You've had a long trek to reach a place of rest but you got there.'

The following morning Guntrip reported an intriguing dream in which he was dressing for a funeral service and found he had put on a coloured shirt and sports jacket. He was trying to change into a white shirt and black suit, and could not do it in time. Winnicott said, 'I think you want me to tell you about retirement. You feel you've been compelled to carry mother's burdens, herself, Percy, sinners, patients, and mustn't retire till you're worn out. A big conflict: you want to retire but feel you must go on. There's this "centre" or "core of self" or "creative tip of living" we discussed. But for mother, you might not have become a psychotherapist, but something you haven't discovered. You want time to discover it but feel you can't. But you feel now you can stop struggling and not fear being dragged down, and you don't take off your coloured clothes because mother has died.' Guntrip replied: 'I don't want to retire to useless senility as mother did, and I want mental freedom to arrange it without being worn out: to do psychotherapy as long as I realistically can because I enjoy it and get satisfying results. I don't know anything else that could give me real satisfaction, except being able to help a few patients as long as is sensible and be able to go on writing. My relation to you, in which I feel free to be myself is freeing me from mother.' Perhaps Guntrip sensed an ambiguity in Winnicott's interpretation: whose retirement was he referring to? Ostensibly Guntrip's – but his opening sentence, 'I think you want me to tell you about retirement', could well have startled Guntrip. However that may have been, the latter's response was unequivocal: he needed to remain and for Winnicott to remain. Moreover, at sixty-five, he was not inclined to change the course of his career, in which he was aware of experiencing a much greater sense of freedom and realism regarding the outcome of the therapeutic work.

In October, a month later, he demonstrated this realism by reference to a patient who had at last come to accept constructive therapeutic regression with him, only to find that her family could no longer tolerate her. He said, 'I may have to accept failure. I don't expect myself to do everything. I dreamed that I was asked to speak at a meeting and I said "No, I can't take on any more just now." Winnicott said, 'There are patients who can only get better when they've made you fail. They can't owe their cure to you. Melanie Klein failed completely with one patient and explained it by saying "You must have an extra lot of constitutional aggression." It was the wrong explanation, but some patients have to end and attribute their improvement to anything but their analyst. One of my patients left much better, and then a chiropodist cured some foot trouble and she went around attributing all her improvement to that.'

Such practical realism from a fellow psychotherapist, relating to him as a professional and emotional equal, had always had a marked effect on Guntrip. Next morning he said, 'I feel we are coming to the final stages of my analysis. The resolution of the hard core problem is emerging in the nature of the relationship between you and me, and in your seeing what I couldn't, that I had to keep myself alive and in being from moment to moment by ceaseless energy and activity, and that I had to do it all myself because there was no-one else who could or would. It led to a fear of dependence because I felt no-one was dependable, but also a sense of humiliation at needing help, at analysis being necessary at all.' He realised that whereas Fairbairn had critically analysed his fear of dependence as 'resistance', as his wanting to be 'his own psychologist', Winnicott had recognised and accepted his need to gain his own insights 'almost up to the last point', thereby enabling him to feel that his lonely struggle had validity. Nonetheless, Winnicott's perception of that dissociated part was still vital to him because he could not manage it alone. Thus he told Winnicott that he did not wish to end analysis on the basis of a feeling that he could do without him, which would be too similar to the way he had gained independence of his mother on a conscious level, but only when he could feel certain that the therapeutic relationship had so grown into him and become a part of him that ending the analysis would not be experienced as a parting. As he was speaking Guntrip recalled 'a peculiar dream'.

We had our neighbours to tea. Then they began to give us their clothes to dress in, and we had to give them ours.

The dream expressed a fear that involvement might become absorption, as it had with his mother, and he wondered aloud whether he could be fearing that this might happen with Winnicott. Winnicott replied: 'You need me to see something you can't see, because you never experienced it. Something about separation.

There's nothing for you in between "absorption in" and "cut-off from". You know what it is intellectually, but you haven't felt it as an experience.' Guntrip felt that the simple clarity of this interpretation brought his whole analysis to a decisive point.

November brought a further consolidation of Guntrip's developing 'capacity for being'. Winnicott's perception of the stark alternatives of absorption and separation had had a marked effect. He said, 'This morning I thought, "Time's running out. I can't go on indefinitely." Must I stop and admit that my basic problem of dying on mother's lap after Percy died there, is too disturbing to let out, and put up with insomnia as my defence against being absorbed into it?' As he mused on this, suddenly a new insight dawned on him, and he exclaimed, 'Ah! Yes. My insomnia is "fear of absorption", of going unconscious on mother's lap, absorption into mother, and dying as a separate person.' By contrast, he saw that staying awake 'was the opposite: feeling "cut off from", a conscious self-contained intellectual, a thinking individual' – and he concluded, 'I must have felt that dying on mother's lap was "becoming absorbed".' Winnicott said: 'What you experienced was not proper separation but dissociation from her.' Guntrip was later to describe dissociation as 'a more primitive phenomenon' than repression or withdrawal: 'some constitutional potentiality that has been left out at the beginning of the process of growth, something apart, unevoked, blocked off from the start, never integrated or given a chance to develop' (1968, p. 253). He refers to Winnicott's view of 'the dissociated' as 'something in the patient's make-up that he himself cannot know; it is outside the range of his ego-experience, conscious or unconscious. It is something the analyst must discern for the patient.' Guntrip concludes, 'This applies radically to the unevoked and undeveloped potential in the psyche' (ibid.). At this time in 1966, the new perception impressed upon Guntrip his need to experience 'proper separation' on the basis of a secure union with Winnicott. He said, 'Now I feel I must experience the "capacity to be alone in your presence", to be silent, forget you're there consciously while I know you're there unconsciously: a relationship that can't be broken inside.' Although Guntrip recalled having had some such experience with his father, the latter's passivity had prevented him demonstrating to his son how to be naturally 'active', and he now said to Winnicott, 'Only when my "basic ego-relatedness with you" includes my capacity to be active and unforced, because that's how you are, will I be able to sleep without anxiety and end analysis.' He added, 'I can't manufacture this but I feel it's in process of happening, and it will be a proper end of treatment and the birth of me as a person in relationship.'

Next morning he said, 'Last night's session cleared the ground. I don't want to talk but to let something go on between you and me. It's to do with not yet properly experiencing deep down the real relationship, which could be silent, and in between "being absorbed" and "cut off".' Acknowledging the relative value of his relationship with his father in that it had supported his being able to 'cut off' from his mother and 'grow away' from her, he said, 'He gave me some experience of "being", but not of "doing" to complete it.' Winnicott said, 'You had something good to give, and no one to give it to, a very sad thing.' The poignancy of his situation struck Guntrip. He said, 'I gave it to Percy and lost him, and must have despaired, as I lay dying on mother's lap.' Winnicott made a vital interpretation: 'You didn't sleep on mother's lap. You could only become ill and lost yourself.' Guntrip concurred, 'The "me" of the traumatic experience was cut-off, dissociated. I've never remembered it since. Ever since, I've been giving the good I had to substitutes for Percy, but that lost bit of me was cut off . . .   Now you've found that bit of me and hope is reborn.'

In the silence that followed, an image occurred to Guntrip reminiscent of his dream early in 1963. He saw 'a river flowing steadily with no real banks', which suggested to him his twin fears of absorption on the one hand and being cut-off on the other. He observed that the banks were fading, allowing him to become 'conscious of what's real in between, a natural flowing energy, flowing of its own accord', which he felt was his own real deep-down life beginning to flow naturally in 'silent relationship' with Winnicott. He recalled once again how, in his analysis with Fairbairn, he had dreamed of taking his beautiful bowl of golden urine to a woman who ignored him, and he said, 'The valuable thing I had wasn't wanted.' Winnicott suddenly said, 'I want to go and pee now', which he did. On his return, Guntrip said to him, 'In that way you've said to me, "You're afraid to give out. I must do it for you, to show it's all right."' It seemed to him that Winnicott was showing the way and making it safe in a way his father had been unable to do, and he felt that Winnicott had thus provided safe 'banks', 'a setting to flow in', and he added, 'Your presence, your room, me lying on this couch, like a river bed: my natural life flowing without effort.' Winnicott replied: 'Urinary symbolism goes right back to infancy. Sleep is related to it. At first the baby just pees when it wants, natural, and mother just accepts it, but later makes it bad, incontinence, which has to be stopped. Sexuality is like natural incontinence, unchecked flow of feeling, and has to be stopped, no free relationship, no flowing together allowed. Your bowl of golden urine symbolised your precious emotion and you were not allowed to pour it out spontaneously. So you fear to sleep and let your feelings flow. You have to wake and pee and get rid of it.'

When Guntrip returned in December, he reported that he had had a disturbed month. Winnicott's interpretation in their previous session had had the effect of exposing him during a sleepless night to the realisation that it was not enough that he should stop talking in sessions, but that he needed also to stop thinking as well and simply let his feeling flow. However, he saw also that his non-stop thinking was his defence against re-experiencing a return of that feeling of dying on mother's lap. Moreover he realised that with 'Percy gone as a buffer', he could not stand 'total exposure' to his mother's aggressive destructive personality. And yet, despite these upheavals and a return of the lifeless inert feeling, he had felt a deep sense of being 'in close touch' with Winnicott, as in the two previous sessions, and that morning, 6 December, he had dreamed of having a 'simple friendly chat' with Winnicott. He could not, however, rid himself of a sense of his mother's frightening face, 'cold, supercilious, thunderous', instilling in him a paranoid fear and suspicion 'of the whole modern world'. He mentioned that he had also experienced a strong reluctance for his wife to visit her mother in Scotland, and he recalled that although he had always known unconsciously what his mother was like, he had not allowed himself consciously to suspect how destructive she was until he had seen her turn against his wife. Winnicott replied, 'Your mother managed to put on enough dutiful mothering to give you something to believe in, but you sense her real inner destructiveness. She could have thought when Percy died, "Why doesn't God take the other one too?" She did not want children. When your sympathetic wife came on the scene she felt relieved of the need to put on the "good mother" act, and her real self was all that was left, hard and hostile. You kept thinking to stop the image and feeling of her coming through. You could fear finding her in me or even in your wife. Delusional transference. Here, you have always a very good, positive relation to me. In the long gap between, I could become the bad mother.'

Next morning, in session 110, the last before Christmas, Guntrip reported a dream, in which he felt that the negative delusional transference was again evident:

On holiday in Scotland, I wandered off and came to a village hall, and was accepted by a friendly group of people. Cakes were handed round and I was given some. Then a woman came and said my wife had rung up to see if I was there. She had been worried about me and was coming to fetch me, which she did.

In view of Winnicott's previous interpretation, Guntrip felt his wife in the dream represented his mother coming to collect him from Aunt Dolly's after Percy's death. He was disturbed by this negative transference on to his loving wife, and he added, 'It seems I have to use the reality of her and you to blot out the damage of seeing the bad mother, which makes me afraid to go to sleep.' Winnicott replied: 'Mother's death mask showed what she was really like. Your feeling that a paranoid bit of you is locked up with her gives you the delusion that you are a paranoid person. You feel paranoid because you feel tied to the paranoid deathly mother who dwells apart inside her world of decay and death inside you. You may feel she's me in your delusional transference, when you're not with me.'

Note

1   It is hard to know how to express the emphatic way Winnicott appears to have said this. At any rate – this is how Guntrip reported it.

CHAPTER 19

1967

On his return in January Guntrip realised with surprise that he had 'suppressed the whole problem of "the sinister woman behind the loving woman"', and had only been reminded of her when reading through his notes of the last session, five weeks earlier. He had, however, been aware of occasional body tensions at night, some of which had been so severe as to force him to get out of bed and exercise and work them off before he could get to sleep, 'rather like having to fight off mother first'. He recalled his dreams during the Fairbairn analysis, of fighting the fierce woman who stalked him behind rocks, and of his mother trying to get between him and his wife, on her first visit to them in their own home at Ipswich. He was again concerned at the possibility of a delusional transference on to his wife. Winnicott replied, 'There is something here about you needing a struggle with mother. You didn't experience satisfactory muscle eroticism with her. She didn't let you wrestle with her, only beat you. It makes it difficult for you to be muscularly active in your sexuality. Your wife could appreciate it.' Guntrip said, 'I suppose I unconsciously fear my hate of the sinister woman may hurt the woman I love. If I can dissociate vigorous energy from that hate of the violent-tempered mother, the wild woman, I may not get those occasional body-tensions. I used to get them in bed a lot in the Fairbairn period, but they faded out largely in that analysis. This Christmas they've come back suddenly after last session.' Winnicott said: 'I think you have diffused your need for struggle in going to Edinburgh and London, and in hard work, and earlier in cricket and football and climbing, and now you've lost most of those outlets. You struggle with ideas in your thinking and it's all to very good purpose, but it's not the same thing as muscle tension in bed. You've never been impotent, but there has been a recurring something, like an interfering brake on your activity; and sometimes it has got into your working life as well.'

Whatever Winnicott had meant by 'need for struggle' (there was no mention of 'hate') Guntrip had become 'defensive' – possibly because of his fear of a negative transference on to his wife. Thus he was somewhat taken unawares to find Winnicott on quite a different line, saying, 'I feel a big sadness in you over not being able to find a real relation to your father. You know he had been a fine, active, adventurous man before you were born, but you got no response from him. I feel your steady flow of talk is a kind of keeping the conversation going in the hope that, even yet, he may suddenly respond and discuss. You had no Oedipal relation because father didn't give you any friendly rivalry to stimulate you. He was for practical purposes a blank, but full of fine powers you could never get at. So instead of an Oedipal triangle you had an aggressive mother, a gentle Aunt Mary and you. You mustn't hurt the invalid Aunt, and you can only have a fight with your mother. It keeps some of your vitality out of your sex life, but not all of it.' Guntrip agreed: 'I do have a big sadness about father.' But the impact of the interpretation became lost when he was drawn once more into sympathetic identification with Henry, citing his courage in breaking away from his High Church and high Tory family to become a Nonconformist and a liberal in the 1890s, and attributing his passivity entirely to Harriet's inhibiting influence. However sadly true this state of affairs may have been, his father did 'choose' to marry his mother, and however expedient Henry may have felt it to prevent 'endless family rows' by remaining silent, there can be no doubt that he fell woefully short of giving Harry anything approaching a stimulating father–son relationship. Instead, he inappropriately engaged his sympathies at too early an age, engendering a kind of nostalgic longing for 'what might have been'. Accordingly, Winnicott persisted: 'Father handed over the whole problem of mother to you. You'd rather have a load of patients than mother living with you.' Guntrip, however, seized upon the reference to his mother to avoid further insight concerning his father and he replied emphatically, 'Yes. She split my image of woman and hate of her has always, I suppose, drawn off enough energy inside to make me have to over-drive in real life.'

In February Guntrip discussed the manuscript of Winnicott's fine paper, 'The Location of the Cultural Experience' (in Winnicott 1971), which the latter had given him to read. In answer to Winnicott's query he assured him that the paper had not disturbed him, but had helped him 'enormously'. In particular he had been struck by Winnicott's view 'that analysis must end in silence to leave room for the patient's own self to emerge'. He had also felt the force of the 'x+y+z formulation', where x+y minutes denotes the time a baby can stand mother's absence, and x+y+z minutes absence disintegrates the baby's nascent ego. In the same paper,

Winnicott had belatedly acknowledged that he was 'in the territory of Fairbairn's (1941) concept of "object-seeking"' as distinct from "satisfaction-seeking" – an acknowledgement which Guntrip felt was partly due to the effects of his own testing arguments in sessions with Winnicott, who had often said to him, 'There, that's what I feel, Harry. You go and think it out for me.'

Later in the session he described a dream in which he and his wife were refurbishing the dining room in the Lordship Lane house by sending all the furniture to be cleaned, restored and replaced. He said, 'My family were simply not there', adding 'Father could have been there and he wouldn't have been disturbing.' He then reaffirmed his belief in his father as a good object, saying 'mother couldn't destroy him in the end, and it was me he turned to in the end to say his smiling and triumphant 'Goodbye'. He told Winnicott: 'Now in silence with you I find my faith in the indestructibility of my internal good objects and can relax and feel safe.' Thus it would seem that, despite his shortcomings as an active personality after marriage, Henry had retained an original integrity, which for Guntrip was the quality that had facilitated his attachment to successive father-figures and made it possible for him to co-operate with male analysts. That night he dreamed that Winnicott, as part of the analysis, had sent him to Fairbairn. He associated the Fairbairn of his dream with his father, because he knew the former's health had been undermined by 'some bad women patients', so that he felt he had, in a sense, lost his father twice over. Winnicott said, 'You came to me to get over the breakdown of Fairbairn. You want me to get you back to the good father you've kept inside.' Guntrip affirmed: 'Yes, I've always dreamed a lot about supportive good father figures. You've become the good father whom mother can't destroy in my inner world. In silence with you, I just then remembered that at mother's death, though I saw her cynical face, I felt that her breast looked beautiful.'

Guntrip then felt that Winnicott had enabled him to recover an early experience, not only of a good father, but also of the original good mother: the good breast he had had for a brief time at the beginning, and that had remained buried beneath all the later bad experience. Winnicott said 'Mother probably had a good female body which she could have used to love, and she didn't want it, at least not after the earliest period of her marriage. But there was at first a mother your father could love and who loved him. You can get back to realising that they fell in love at first, whatever happened later.' Guntrip suddenly saw that this underlying 'basic good', which Winnicott had helped him to rediscover and re-experience, had been the true source of his capacity to care for Percy, and to become a psycho-therapist. It had become the basis of a secret belief in 'an indestruct-ible basic good', that Winnicott had enabled him to get in touch with. It is surely significant that Guntrip wrote a number of papers on religious themes at this time (for example 1967b and 1967c, see Hazell 1994, pp. 23–4) which bring out strongly the influence of his experience with Winnicott. In March a minor operation resulted in loss of sleep, and Guntrip's ambivalence over taking sleeping pills stirred the ambivalence over his mother's breast. This was expressed in two dreams: in the first of which he 'heroically' opposed and expelled a heckler at Salem who was chanting something about being against the use of pills. In the second dream he found 'two heaps of dead white slugs, set solid', which he buried with a spade, feeling unable to touch them. He spontaneously associated both the slugs and the Mogadon tablets with 'dead breasts', which one aspect of himself was driven to need, whilst in another part of himself he was determined to do without them. In order to resolve his ambivalence he realised that he needed to regain the secure possession of his original good objects. Bringing to mind Winnicott's remark about the original good in both his mother and his father, and their falling in love, he had a fantasy of 'mother's greatest hour', in which he pic-tured her, in the moment when she realised that his father had fallen in love with her. He felt that after her troubled, overburdened and embittering childhood, it must have seemed an escape to paradise when father had proposed marriage, and in his fantasy he saw her standing looking up into Henry's face with a radiant smile as he smiled back at her. He realised that their love could only have lasted a year or two before the tensions began to rise, and Harriet's inner destructive self from early life took control. Nevertheless, he said to Winnicott, 'I feel there was a good time for them at the beginning, the first time I've ever seen that possibility. She was very likely a good breast for the first two months or so.' Winnicott replied 'It was hidden by the deadly mother, but now you seem about to bury her.' Guntrip realised that he had been unable to let his mother go, even after she had died, because he had been unable to recover contact with his original good objects: 'the earliest good mother and father', and he told Winnicott, 'Now I feel you have become the focus and representative to me of my primary good parents and of their viability as good internalised objects in me. Now I feel I could bury the dead mother, and remember her only by what was good, and rest peacefully without pills, as symbolic objects, good or bad, because I have become sure of my real good objects, good parents in you.' In making this rather deliberate summary Guntrip felt that he was 'recapitulating his gains in order to possess them more securely', rather than 'conducting his own analysis'. Certainly it appears that a decisive stage of the analysis had been reached, in which he felt genuinely and deeply healed. His fantasy of Harriet's greatest hour seems quite plausible. She had indeed loved and admired Henry, ascribing all the Christian qualities to him ('the Christian for her') and was content to work hard by his side. Only when reality in the form of an actively needy baby confronted her with her own inner unmet childhood need, had she become destructive, doubtless in an attempt to ward off collapse.

Next morning, Guntrip observed how the purpose and meaning of the sessions had changed for him. At first he had collected material to talk out because it was on his mind. Then the talking had come to feel a necessity as the means both of keeping Winnicott's attention, and himself 'alive', until he had finally discovered 'the possibility of being silent, and still "being in touch". Now, he felt he had moved beyond even that, to a need to absorb a relationship in silence' and he said, 'I feel as real a relationship to you now, when I'm not here as when I am, and when I'm not talking as when I do talk. You've come into the gap mother left.' Thus he felt convinced that Winnicott had at last neutralised his mother's destructive influence in his internal world. At the April meeting Guntrip mentioned that he was feeling a deeper relaxation when lying with his wife, and described a remarkable and 'important' dream:

> An elderly woman analyst, very stable and motherly, was seeing me. I told her where I was in my analysis with Winnicott. She said, 'Yes. Your mother is now out of the way. She won't be able to come in now, will she?' I said 'No' and felt safe from her intervention. The analyst said, 'Now I want to kiss your breast' and quite straightforwardly did so. My breast seemed full. We were still, like that Madonna and Child.

He woke from the dream feeling reassured by a good stable mother, showing affection and finding good in him. Winnicott made a striking observation: 'You had a good breast, something good to give. You've always been able to give more than take. The analyst is good for you, but you are good for your analyst.[1] Doing your analysis is about the most reassuring thing that happens to me. The chap before you makes me feel I'm no good at all. You don't have to be good for me. I don't need it and can cope without it; but in fact you are good for me.' Guntrip responded warmly, 'You enable me to be good for you, without my having to try to do it You have enabled me to be good for you by just enabling me to be me. With mother I had to be what she wanted me to be, and tried her utmost to make me be.'

Ever since 1964, the year of Fairbairn's death, Guntrip had been working on the manuscript of a paper on 'The Concept of Psychodynamic Science' (1967, in Hazell 1994, p. 251). Both Fairbairn and Winnicott had wondered whether he would have been a physical scientist had his psychopathology not drawn him into the psychoanalytical area. The paper, which was published in the *International Journal*, amply attests to both sides of Guntrip's complex personality, but the final section particularly reveals the influence of the above session in which Winnicott affirmed the reciprocal benefit of their relationship. Guntrip wrote:

> Psychodynamics is the study of that type of experience in which there is *reciprocity* between subject and object, and of the experience of ego-emptying and ego-loss when relationship and reciprocity fail . . .   Object relations theory has not come sufficiently to grips with conceptualising . . .   the complex fact of . . .   two persons being ego and object to one another at the same time, and in such a way that their reality as persons becomes, as it develops in the relationship, what neither of them would have become apart from the relationship. This is what . . .   psychotherapy seeks to make possible for the patient who cannot achieve it in normal living. (In Hazell 1994, pp. 268–9)

Next morning there was further integration of bad experience on the basis of the security of the therapeutic relationship – perhaps the beginning of real healing, a process which was to last longer than Guntrip's positive conscious affirmations might suggest. He mentioned a vague memory of a dream of being ill at Salem, and returning there to find it all changed, and feeling unable to bear the burden any longer. He said, 'It feels like a vague memory of coming back home after Percy's death and my stay at Aunt Dolly's, and feeling the whole home set-up was different, and somehow I broke off.' It was the nearest he had come to recovering memory of that estranged period, which he now felt able to re-experience in the security of his relatedness to Winnicott. His night-time tension had also eased, but it had crossed his mind that a fire might break out in his hotel. Winnicott replied, 'You no longer feel a distinct threat of the bad mother inside you, getting between you and your good objects, but you feel she is somewhere. Something in you wants to remember the worst: the worst that you experienced at the pre-verbal level or at Percy's death; to re-experience it, relive it; but you also want to make it never come back. Somewhere there's a destructive Winnicott, masking a destructive mother, hidden, not intruding, but not buried. You need to remember the few moments on mother's lap when you felt destructive forces that weren't just mother – because she sent you away from whatever was destructive, not just herself. They could destroy you, no help for it. You have to re-experience it to be rid of the fear of it. You remember everything after it but not that.' Guntrip took Winnicott to mean that when he saw Percy dead, he must have felt suddenly that the entire world ('my little world') had become destructive. He makes no reference in his record to the postulated destructive forces within himself.

During the intervening month Guntrip became troubled by a feeling that Winnicott, now over seventy, considered him a nuisance and was really seeing him out of obligation. Winnicott said, 'When I said last time that you were good for me, I knew it was the end of an era, and you'd have to have a different disturbed relation to me. You felt mother didn't really love you after the very beginning. She didn't want you and looked after you as a duty. You feel I may be like mother now, going on with you as a duty, and no real love relation to support your ego. It's painful to get back to experiencing her changing from the earliest loving which you had made contact with, to her only doing her duty. If you'd had a real ego-relatedness to mother you wouldn't have needed to go outside to live. You'd have turned to father, and gone back and forth between them in real relations to both. But mother shut you off from father.'

In July the possibility occurred to Guntrip that he may have used a second minor operation as the 'threat of illness' in order to keep the very early part of him buried in the unconscious. Whereas he had previously associated the burial in the tomb only with repression of hate for his mother, from three and a half to five years, he now considered that the buried alive part of him may be his very early self from birth to three and a half years, the only part of him that he now believed to have had some feeling of being in a home. He realised that he must have found some way of protesting between six months and two years, when his mother became absorbed in her business, and before he had Percy 'to feel real with' – surely it had been his 'protest' that had caused Mrs Prentice to exclaim 'I've had one of your children. I'm not putting up with another!'

Next morning, the feeling of going over all the old material, but with a new meaning, was still powerfully there. He said to Winnicott, 'Because you got in touch with the deepest bit of me, new feeling comes at the higher levels also.' In particular he noted how, after Percy's death when he could find no life with mother, Aunt Dolly demonstrated how a life was possible away from mother, thus enabling him to enter actively into the life of a succession of schools. In fact his memory of his teachers, Miss Turner and Mrs East, in the setting of their homes was clearer than that of his mother in his own home, with the one exception of the biggest beating. He concluded: 'I was well for six years at College and only unwell at home on Vacations.' Winnicott made an elaborate interpretation:

> You remember your centrifugal life going out from home, but not your centripetal life seeking in to mother. Now you want to find your centripetal life, back to the centre. But it's hidden by that period of stifled anger between the early good breast and having Percy. She made you the passive recipient of what she did. She put a phallic breast into your mouth and put you in the cot to sleep till she was ready for you again, smothered your active personality. You became unable to accept that. It was like death in life. When Percy died and left you alone with mother, you went like that, lost your active self, appeared to be dying. So she made sleep seem dangerous, like losing all your active self to mother. Mother gave you food but not a relationship. You went to Fairbairn because he stood for 'object-relations'. Mother satisfied your hunger but threatened to kill your soul. Instinctive oral satisfaction is not enough.

Guntrip later recorded his satisfaction at this unequivocal 'personal relations' statement from Winnicott, adding only that he would prefer to substitute 'appetitive' for 'instinctive'.

During the summer break Guntrip was busily occupied with August conferences and preparation for a lecture tour in January in New York and Washington at the invitation of Carl Witenberg of the Alanson White Institute of Psychiatry, Psychoanalysis and Psychology. Nevertheless, he contrived to wrench his shoulder skimming a stone, while on holiday in the Lake District, and set up osteo-arthritic pains in his left arm, for which an orthopaedic surgeon ordered traction in hospital. It was typical of Guntrip's clinical dedication that he had explained to the surgeon that he was determined not to fail his patients during the autumn before his visit to the States. Arriving for a session one day, I was amazed

to see a large metal hook in the lintel of the consulting room
doorway. He explained that he gave himself traction each morning
using a harness from the hospital, so that he could continue to see
his patients. But, despite it all, as September approached his 'unconscious' revealed its secret activity, and when he resumed his
sessions with Winnicott he described a dream of carrying on some
activity with his father there, looking on, a very pleasant, comforting, reassuring person, friendly and interested, not interfering, but
encouraging and supportive in a quiet way. He told Winnicott, 'He
was like father without his withdrawnness, like Fairbairn without
his touch of austerity, and like you in natural friendliness.' Winnicott said, 'I feel you are wanting to get at the possibility of your
silently "playing" freely in father's presence and mine.' Guntrip,
however, did not feel capable of such relaxed 'playing' at that stage,
fearing that it might cause him to relive the Percy period and the
early experiences 'with live emotion'.

Nevertheless, he described a dream which 'went back before
Percy':

> I was living with two women I know, married to the gentle one.
> The other one went out to work and I locked the door to keep
> her out. Yet we all seemed to have rooms in the same house.

He felt this to be a reference to his wanting to lock mother out in
her shop and stay safely with Mary, though he was aware in the
dream of the strain of 'having to adapt first to one and then to the
other'. At that point he became aware of another part of the dream
he had forgotten: The situation was about to be upset. It had
changed to the College and new students were about to arrive. He
was re-experiencing the atmosphere in the immediate offing of Percy's birth.

Next morning, Guntrip reported a further dream which seemed
to emphasise his fear of 'centripetal life':

> A Salvation Army Officer was criticising me for not doing
> psychoanalysis properly. I argued back, but felt rejected.

He commented, 'I can't be orthodox, tied to anybody's system. I
must preserve my freedom to think for myself. I'm not a compulsive disagreer, but I must be free to use my own judgement. Outside the Salvation Army, outside the Church, outside the Psychoanalytical Society. But I would feel outside a family altogether
without a good father-Fairbairn-Winnicott, who leaves me free to

play mentally, to grow, create and find and be myself.' Winnicott succinctly observed, 'I give you that situation. You can't quite fully take it and use it.'

In October Guntrip recounted a dream which had about it the quality of 'playing' in a secure setting which he so badly needed:

> We arranged a birthday party for father in the back upstairs dining room at Lordship Lane. My wife and daughter, mother and father and myself, and Aunt Mary, and also baby Percy were all there. Father was very pleased and I was very keen to make it a really good birthday party for him, and to get the full value out of it.

He said to Winnicott, 'I've here created an astonishing family, united, to belong to, and I've got Percy into a dream, though I can't see a dream picture of him.' He felt that he had arrived at a state of feeling in which it had become possible to bring together all his 'good objects', on the foundation of his father's underlying integrity, and had even included 'the earliest good mother' among them. He felt that he had retained a basic faith in the viability of good objects in the end. Winnicott replied 'You have a good family dream repressed in which mother didn't overshadow father, and all seems happy and helpful, and in it the females are helping you to be active. Just a shade of the old mother butting in but you aren't disturbed by it. You could not let yourself remember this good dream because it would have got mixed up with the bad dream of last time (the dream of the two women) but now you can let it come, having got that bad dream out last time.' Guntrip remarked that in his dream the females were 'letting the males have their proper place, as mother didn't do', as a consequence of which he was able to 'let the females have their proper place', as in a further recent dream in which Bertha was mini-skirted in a wedding dress and went off looking in shop windows. He commented: 'My wife is rejuvenated, and having her own independent interest. I'm not seeing her merely as Aunt Mary. According to my early experiences, there were only two types of women, the bossy one and the passive one. Now I bring in a third possibility, the lively young girl with interests of her own, a very attractive person.' Winnicott replied, 'You're giving your wife a bit of adolescent girlishness. In that "good family" dream you have almost altered the past, but possibly also have recovered a real bit of mother's earliest maternalism.'

Guntrip later recorded his feeling that Winnicott had helped him grow out of a sense of pessimism and deadlock that was the legacy of his childhood. He asserted once more his conviction that such growth was possible only because there was some very important positive good in his father, which his mother was never able to extinguish, and upon which Winnicott was able to build, together with something good in the gentle invalid Mary. He believed that Winnicott, by building on that foundation, had enabled him ultimately to reach back to the almost totally obscured maternalism in his mother, most of which 'had been exhausted in caring for younger brothers and sisters, including the harrowing experience of four babies dying'. It was, nonetheless, he felt, Winnicott's enabling him to get back into touch with the 'earliest and therefore indestructible good mother', and to build a whole good family around that as a secure basis for living, that had enabled him to re-experience the deep significance of his nearly dying after Percy's death.

Next day, he reported a relevant dream:

> I had to go with two parents to a Coroner's Inquest on the suicide of their child.

The mother in the dream had reminded him of a former patient 'who was very masculine'. Winnicott said, 'The child dies of despair of a non-maternal mother. You had a maternal mother at first but she changed; she ceased to be a maternal lap and was controlled by her delusional penis. You ceased to have a maternal lap and Percy had no maternal lap at all. While mother was the male who worked, you had to mother Percy. You mother patients in psychotherapy. All our patients need us to be a mother in the end. The mother–child relation is the model of psychotherapy. You and Percy merely lay across her knees. Her delusional penis ended her maternalism and she killed Percy and nearly killed you, and feared she might, and saved you by sending you away from her. Your illness expressed a kind of passive suicidal despair, like the child in the dream.' It occurred to Guntrip that his mother's saving action in sending him away to Aunt Dolly must have represented her own deep-down surviving bit of maternalism, evoked by the doctor's blunt statement. 'He's dying of grief. If your mother-wit can't save him, I can't.'

The strain imposed upon Winnicott by Guntrip's need for him to 'be a mother in the end' was revealed in November when Guntrip reintroduced the theme of suicidal despair by referring to a suicidal young patient of his. Winnicott suddenly jumped up and went out to have a pee, and then walked up and down the room, saying, 'What have I got to do with this kid away in Yorkshire!' He then explained: 'You must have felt despair of being understood. It was your own despair of mother that I felt the pressure of, the despair you nearly died of.' Of course, the 'kid away in Yorkshire' was Guntrip, and Winnicott was feeling the weight of a 'suicidal kid' in a man of sixty-six years. Moreover, this was the penultimate session before an extended break in the analysis, since Guntrip needed intensive daily treatment for cervical arthritis before his American tour. Guntrip seems to have been strangely unaware of the gravity of this impending separation at such a crucial point in the analysis. Perhaps the memory of the suicide of his own patient, two years earlier, with whom he had to a considerable extent been identified, was still too poignant to recall. Winnicott however, aware that the 'child' in his patient should not be expected to adapt to his 'mother-therapist', interpreted once more, 'The mother who is not a mother made you feel suicidal despair. You saw that she wasn't a mother to Percy so you took over the role, and when he died, you were lost. You could keep alive by being a mother, but you could only die of suicidal despair with the woman who couldn't be a mother to you. You have that buried in you and you had to get away from mother, and keep alive by being a mother to others. And you couldn't risk sleep which meant slipping down to where the deadly non-mother was, and feeling suicidal despair; and you feared you'd die if you relaxed and slept.' At this the 'child' in Guntrip felt reached. He answered: 'It has always felt to me, when those one or two odd illnesses overtook me, that I collapsed deep inside. Life just felt to be oozing away and I became exhausted. No need to do anything to commit suicide in the presence of my deadly mother. I could only lie helpless and die. The end of analysis will come by facing and getting past the deadly mother and finding in you the mother with whom I can just "be" quietly and effortlessly alive. Then I'll be able to sleep.'

The final session of 1967, an evening appointment, was no less arduous, though much less was said. Winnicott realised that Guntrip was registering in his body the strain of the imminent separation, when the latter said, 'I need to be quiet. My arms ached last night with the arthritis after carrying my travelling bag. I can let my left arm rest here.' Winnicott, bearing in mind the deeper need, replied, 'I've got to discount X-rays, and shrunken muscles and cervical arthritis now, and point out that you have tension in your arms and fingers all the time. You can hold but you feel you have no hope of being held since mother failed you. You need here to have the experience of being held and then you could sleep. It's most important that you should feel supported by me here.'

The manifest experience of the American lectures was, by Guntrip's account, 'a most stimulating two weeks at the White Institute, and a weekend at the Washington School, including visiting
to lecture at the National Institute of Mental Health and the
Stockbridge Hospital'. The response was generally enthusiastic, and
is reflected in a foreword to Guntrip's book, *Psychoanalytic Theory,
Therapy and the Self* (1971) in which his seminars are recorded.
Dr Earl G. Witenberg expresses deep appreciation of the 'zest,
warmth and sparkling humour' which Guntrip brought to his
material, and continues, 'His intense interest, his patience, and his
serious caring enlivened and stimulated a whole group of people to
think more clearly about their ideas and their way of practising
. . . First and foremost, he feels the experience with the patient,
and from the experience, he conceptualises so that theory is very
close to experience. Though Guntrip is most clearly associated with
Fairbairn and Winnicott, he is not identified with any school.' It is
perhaps salutary to have this 'independent view' of Guntrip, the
professional, as a counterbalance to the serious intensity conveyed
by this account of the analysis. As his analysis with Winnicott
became mutative he did indeed develop a warmth to augment his
general vigour, and his public speaking was always lively and compelling. Nevertheless, Dr Witenberg's enthusiasm was by no means
universal, and for Guntrip, the stimulating quality of the visit was
somewhat soured by the fixity of the doctrinal schisms he found in
America. In particular, he was shocked by some news that the
New York Psychoanalytic Society had attempted to expel Dr Clara
Thompson and two other analysts from membership because of
their acceptance of some 'heretical views' of Dr Karen Horney.
According to the report, the three analysts went to court, complain-
ing of monopolistic practices and the New York Society had to
reinstate them, but Guntrip's reaction was extreme. On his return,
he told Winnicott, 'I feel a sense of horror at finding in psychoanalysis the same "closed shop", dogmatic, authoritarian schools as
I came up against in Theology and the Church. I feel this is death
to progress.' Perhaps Guntrip had been over-optimistic in hoping
for a more liberal attitude in the USA than in Britain. Certainly
Winnicott himself encountered much criticism the following
autumn when he gave his controversial paper on 'The Use of the
Object' (in Winnicott 1971) to the New York Psychoanalytic Society, and Guntrip was to encounter further reverberations on his
visit to Los Angeles the following spring. Overall, however, he
greatly enjoyed and profited from his visit, and, on his return to
Britain found himself 'defending Freud' and psychoanalytic therapy

in the pages of the *Listener* (in Hazell 1994, p. 405) against Dr Max Hammerton of Cambridge who had broadcast a talk on the Third Programme of the BBC entitled 'Freud, The Status of an Illusion'. Hammerton claimed that psychoanalysis was not a science and that Freud's work had only entertainment value, providing the amusement of trying to psychoanalyse famous men. Guntrip's opening reply was characteristically terse: 'Opponents of Freud often attack him with ridicule. He is a disturbing thinker to take seriously.' The debate continued for months, involving among others Sir Henry Miller, then recently installed as Dean of Medicine at Newcastle University, who, according to the *Guardian* (7 December 1968) 'spent many column inches of the *Listener* in scorning Freud and everything derived from him'. The following week Lord Platt, no less, responded in a letter to that Journal: 'I was not', he said, 'very interested in what Henry Miller thinks of Freud. I would be much more interested in what Freud would have thought of Henry Miller!' Guntrip, of course, was most concerned to convince these opponents of psychoanalysis that 'feelings', emotional experience, had the status of 'facts' which can only be 'known' in the security of an analytically enlightened and caring personal relationship. He wrote 'A psychotherapist is not a doctor carrying out an impersonal scientific treatment, but an experienced person offering a disturbed human being a certain kind of human relationship . . . No advances in purely physical medical science can solve the problems of the "person" as distinct from the "organism". But we owe it above all to Freud that this most important of all healing arts, the healing of "the personal self", has become a field of systematic research, yielding results capable of being applied in practice by those who are sufficiently motivated to tackle human problems on this basic level.' In August 1969 Guntrip wrote to Sutherland: 'I may be prejudiced but I feel I've had the best of both rounds.'!

Note

1   Guntrip changed the wording in his 1975 paper (in Hazell 1994, pp. 363–4). (D.W.W. 'You are good for me.') He also gives the impression that Winnicott added this statement regarding 'object use' a year later.

CHAPTER 20

1968

The first session of the New Year took place in March after Winnicott had recovered from an illness in February. Guntrip had enjoyed his American tour and announced that throughout he had 'retained a clear picture' of Winnicott – of his 'calm pleasant face'. In fact, he had felt so inwardly secure that he had experienced 'the first undisguised negative transference', which he associated with their last session having been at 8.15 p.m. He had had a strong feeling, both that it was too late for Winnicott to be working, and also that he himself was being given 'the fag end of the day' after all the important business had been concluded. He did not mention Winnicott's recent illness, which must surely have been relevant, but he was not slow to associate this feeling with those stirred up by his mother putting her business before him and only giving him the 'fag end of the day' after she had done with the shop. Guntrip made clear his view that he could use the negative transference constructively because of the certainty of his inner relationship to Winnicott 'as a good parent, both mother and father'. He recalled the 'monopolistic practices' of which he had become aware in the New York Psychoanalytic Society and he said, 'I feel this is death to progress. I feel that Fairbairn and Winnicott must never become schools.' Winnicott at once replied, 'That's the most important thing you've said. I feel you're feeling your way to "playing in my presence". Schools, dogma, etc. are the end of that spontaneous creativity, and that's what you want to reach.'

Did Guntrip feel a fear of the freedom of this 'new world'? It would seem likely, for he reported a dream,

> I was looking down our lawn and garden. It was all lit up and people were wandering about there, as if it was a fete, and as if they were intruders who had got in over the fence. Then I saw my study lit up and found two men there, and said, 'What are you doing here?' They answered in a friendly way but I was not sure if they could be trusted. They could only have got in

through the window uninvited, but it wasn't broken. I was
rather anxious and uncertain how to act. Should I drive them
out? It seems I did.

Guntrip was still not altogether at ease in social situations outside
psychotherapy. Perhaps the dream reflects his fear of the more
sociable aspects of his American trip. He observed that whereas,
usually he felt it was 'dark outside and burglars breaking in' – the
scene in his dream represented the opposite: 'It's light and live and
friendly people come in.' He exclaimed: 'This must be my "live
self" emerging, not that "dead self" I had to find before. But I am
somewhat anxious in case my ego-defences are not working.' Winnicott interpreted: 'The dark outside would be psychotic forces
erupting into consciousness. When I was ill you may have felt I
was an internalised bad object masking the internalised bad
mother, not there for you. But you have me as a real good object
to be alive with, and you see me as such consciously as someone
who is creative and enables you to findand release a similar part of
yourself. You can only be alive because of a real relationship. The
introjected world is psychotic.'
  In the intervening month Guntrip dreamed intensely around the
theme of the possible emergence of his 'live self', and of the
dilemma over whether he should stay with his familiar driven
'working self', or risk simply 'being' and 'playing'. He dreamed:

> Winnicott was staying with us. We went out in the evening for a
> walk and came to a small hall where there was a social function
> in aid of something. We went in. I would have passed but he said,
> 'Let's go in and see what it is.' Quite a little crowd of people. He
> bought an apple and had a method of whipping it into an appetis-
> ing frothy pulp. I was however anxious to get home to check on
> my consulting rooms being decorated. I put them straight and was
> very pleased to have Winnicott visiting us.

There were two more dreams on the same theme: one in which a
waiter landed him and Bertha on holiday with a mentally ill
patient, whom they managed to get moved; another where he 'accidentally' failed to disembark from a steamer bound for 'beyond the
north of Scotland' after seeing someone aboard. He commented
that his USA trip had resulted in increased pressure of work, which
had crowded out his leisure-time with Bertha. Winnicott said,
'You've left no time to "play" in my presence. Your patients
resented you leaving them for the USA, and you feel their

increased pressure now, and want to get away from them. And you could have unconsciously resented my leaving you to go to the USA without me. Consciously you had me with you, but unconsciously you may have felt you'd lost me.' This is surely correct, despite Guntrip's insistence that he had not felt cut off in the USA. He was, after all, apt to 'insist' on emotional gains once his rapid intelligence had grasped and confirmed their positive significance. Moreover, the two sessions immediately before his departure had been highly disturbing.

Next day he was ready to allow that the separation had made him feel he had lost Winnicott, and he then acknowledged the further impact of Winnicott's illness after his return. He said, 'Since that four months break,[1] my dreams have been full of danger', though, as he also pointed out, the 'good father' was never far away. Thus, in one dream in which he was assailed by 'a queer paranoid man', Dr Dicks appeared and introduced them, trying to pacify and humour the man. Guntrip associated the 'madness' of this dream with his having not sufficiently secured possession of 'the earliest good mother', so that when separated from Winnicott he had fallen back into the power of the paranoid mother who made him paranoid in turn.

In other disturbing dreams he was back in the Salvation Army or the Church, and in danger from huge bombs which reminded him of his mother's explosive tempers. In two of the dreams father or his representative was present, and in one the mother- and father-figures both died, but the father-figure was restored to life. He realised, however, that the only way he could 'go past' the 'dead mother' in his deep unconscious to the 'earliest good mother' was by means of a deep and secure relatedness to Winnicott – a truth which he felt was expressed in another dream in which he met again the patient who murdered his wife and committed suicide:

> He looked wasted and thin and he said, 'Do you believe in God?' Guntrip replied in the dream, 'I'm not going to answer that in words, theories. But I'll say this: that if you meet your wife again, you'll find she still loves you.'

Guntrip associated the dream with his fear of losing the earliest good mother, and his need to know that she could not be destroyed by his hungry need of her. He said to Winnicott, 'I must have feared you would die when you were ill, and that I would feel the loss of you, and the final loss of the good mother.' Winnicott replied, 'That's because mother could not accept your vigorous love. She feared you would destroy her, and she exploded angrily on you, and became a bad destructive mother. You had to split off the original good breast and keep her as an ideal mother, repressed, but lost as a real person. Mother became, or was, the destructive paranoid self that she feared you would be to her. She must have had the same experience with her mother and it made her paranoid, full of hate, and she made part of you like that. So you feel you can't make use of the ideal mother, you fear you'll destroy her. You feared you'd done that to me when I was ill. Now through me, however, you recover the good mother, and have to risk using me, and find I can survive it and you're not destroying me. I have to be used in your destructive fantasies, and you find I survive in reality.'

It is worth noting that Winnicott at this stage referred not to 'innate sadism' but to a 'vigorous love' that intensified destructively under the influence of fear, when its needs were not met. Moreover, although no reference was made to Guntrip's fantasy of destroying the Madonna and Child, the same issues are at stake. At that time, two years earlier and just after the patient's tragedy, Winnicott had said, 'You feel you can only possess the precious thing by destroying it. That's the dissociated bit you can't know.' As things stood then, Guntrip could not use the interpretation, but now the 'risk of using' Winnicott by 'vigorous loving' and finding he could survive it had new and vital relevance for him.

Shortly afterwards, Bertha had an illness, and Guntrip was alarmed by his reaction to it. As he saw it, if his 'good-mother' was unwell he must have caused it, because his real mother had been unable to stand his needs. He saw that it reminded him of Winnicott's illness and, ultimately, of the basic problem of his mother, not only of her paranoid destructive aspect, but even more seriously of her non-relating, non-responsive aspect. He felt stuck and said, 'I don't know where to go from here.' It seems that he may have felt that the analysis had in some sense failed. Certainly, he realised that the recovery of his 'earliest good mother' experience had not evacuated his bad experiences, as he may have hoped. He wondered whether he might have been quite unable to care for Bertha and himself during her illness if he had had no analysis, and supposed that he would have had the same experience, but not made the connections, and most importantly, that he would have 'remained static in the deeper experience'. He recalled his first session with Fairbairn, and that he had said, 'I've a lot that I must talk about and then I'll get a block.' Winnicott replied, 'The first session is important. Your block was your feeling of hopeless despair, because you had a mother deep down from whom you could never get a real emotional response, a barren rocky field. You have a delusional transference of that on to me. You mentioned an article of Bion's on "treatment" and you thought it a schizoid concept of treatment; somewhere you feel I'm the schizoid Bion, giving no personal relation, though consciously you see me as very personal. Let's get this cleared before I get too old.' Guntrip perversely argued, 'Your view that the core of the person is a permanent isolate that must not be contacted makes me feel that there's no way of relating to you.' Winnicott replied, 'Your not seeing me for four months stirred up that fear, the delusional transference: the mad schizoid bit that sees people as quite different from what they are. Your mother had her "depressed child-beating father" in her, but also her mother who could not love.' Guntrip assented: 'Yes, her mother would go out and leave her to manage and she ran away at twelve, and four babies died.' It seems that Guntrip despaired of Winnicott and analysis in this session, and it took all Winnicott's directness in telling him he was 'mad' and 'deluded' to break the power of the delusional transference. Winnicott also felt it necessary to cut through Guntrip's view of him as 'very personal' in order to get at the delusional transference 'before he got too old!' – a realistic but risky way of breaking through, in view of Guntrip's reaction to his illness. The effectiveness of Winnicott's approach was demonstrated by Guntrip's reply to the effect that anyone who could describe the core of the self as an isolate could not be related to – old or not! Was there, perhaps, in this sharp interchange, a greater confidence beginning to grow, leading in the direction of 'using the object, and finding it survives'?

When he returned in June, Guntrip was feeling exhausted by a combination of work and family pressures. He was at this time proof-reading and indexing *Schizoid Phenomena, Object Relations and the Self*, and had extra lectures at the University. He reported that although he was getting off to sleep more easily, he had again been beset by 'separation anxiety' when his wife was absent: 'one afternoon I felt tired and sat in a deck chair on the lawn in the sun. My wife had to go out, and I began a fierce mental argument with mother . . . it was quite compulsive.' Strangely, at this time in 1968, Guntrip was quite perplexed by this, and went again into the old sado-masochistic interpretations of the Fairbairn analysis, though in his sessional record in the 1970s he inserted 'I had forgotten momentarily that bad objects are better then none.' But why had he forgotten? Surely because his four months' absence, crowded though it was with stimulating activity, had combined with Winnicott's illness and ageing to produce a deep insecurity. Thus, his preoccupation with the old sado-masochistic experiences led back again to the realisation of his mother's lack of maternal feeling for him. He said, 'There was something about mother's atmosphere that wasn't good for a baby, not truly maternal, managing not mothering, directing not supporting, moulding not loving, doing good work, but with inner paranoid hates and fears, always quarrelling with someone.'

Next morning he described having awoken all month in a 'kind of timeless state', unable to remember the date or time. He associated this state with his need to escape from the devitalising effect of his mother's atmosphere after Percy died, so that when asleep or nearly so he would fall into the schizoid devitalised infantile state, neither dead, nor living. He went on to describe the contradictions of his mother's personality, as if curious about her. Despite her good works and good intentions, she had lacked the qualities of character father had, and deep within herself, she was violently disturbed. He needed to experience her 're-emergence inside', and he lay quiet, hoping that his introjection of Winnicott's quiet, safe presence might make this possible. For a moment he felt safe to sit up, with the warm June sunshine suffusing the room. But then, as he resolved to go away with this experience and let it work, he was assailed by remembering his difficulty in tolerating his dentures, how he had wanted to vomit them out, as if they represented the bad mother who had 'got inside' him. In fact his mother had had a habit of always playing with her own dentures. Winnicott observed: 'If you cast them out, project mother when someone's there, you feel you'll project them into that person and must fight or be devitalised. So you can't have negative transference. You can only keep it all repressed and discharge tension in constant activity, work, restless bodily movements. If you project mother in negative transference, you'd have to part, as mother sent you away to survive.'

The effect of the interpretation was registered the following month when they met for their 139th session. Guntrip reported having had 'three dreams of violence', but added that he was reassured that three women patients in therapy with him had improved greatly and were ending treatment. In the first of the dreams a twelve-year-old boy stabbed another of the same age, which Guntrip took to represent his self-attack because he could not hit back at mother, for he had, in fact, recently mis-written his present address as Lordship Lane as if he still lived there. In the second dream he saw a man bash a woman's face, with blood flowing, while he felt horrified, but was unable to get there to stop

it. The third dream, that very morning, had been of burglars breaking in and taking things by force. Winnicott said, 'It's a wonder
you could rescue your sexual potency for your wife. You were
helped to feel safe with good objects by father and Mary. But now
this is between you and me. One of us is stabbing the other and
you need to know if I can survive your aggression and destructive
impulse. You were talking of patients ending treatment, and you
are thinking now of your being able to end treatment, and me
surviving intact. Fairbairn died.' Guntrip pointed out that Fairbairn
died after he had 'ended treatment', and added that although he
was aware of sometimes having strained Winnicott by hard talking.
he felt safe in the knowledge that Winnicott could protect himself
'by sleeping'. But he added: 'I do feel anxious for you when you
have to give me a late session.'

Next morning, Guntrip reported a remarkable dream, of the
previous night: 'I was with you for a session. I sat on the end of the
couch and you sat on it and put your feet up naturally, relaxed and
very at ease. You gave me a kiss, as a father would kiss a son with
straightforward affection, and I returned it. This seemed an entirely
natural relationship and I felt very well.' Guntrip attributed this
harmonious dream to the previous day's session. He told Winnicott:
'I think you are bringing up my fears of my effect on you and I need
to know I'm not harmful to you. Last evening reassured me.'

On 12 August Guntrip gave the Mary Hemingway Rees
Memorial Lecture at the Seventh International Congress of Mental Health. His paper, entitled 'Religion in Relation to Personal
Integration' (Guntrip 1969, in Hazell 1994, p. 271), was published in the *British Journal of Medical Psychology* the following
year. The paper is redolent of the therapeutic relationship with
Winnicott, drawing attention to the need for the patient to discover with the therapist 'a different kind of knowing like the
mother's non-intellectual, emotional understanding of the baby
through personal relating' (p. 279). However, when he returned
in September Guntrip was restless, as if the gap of the summer
holiday had stirred his deep feeling of isolation. He told Winnicott that he had been acutely aware with his own patients of
'the isolated infant' which lay behind all that could be analysed,
with its absolute need to be found and related to, and he added
that he had had repeated dreams of feeling somehow attached to
some situation, only to find he didn't really belong, but had to
part from it, and resettle in a different situation, only to find no
permanent belonging in any situation. This dream, he felt,
expressed his feeling on his return home after Percy's death, and

of his having been in and out of situations ever since, Alleyns, the Salvation Army, University, Ipswich, Salem, and the Department of Psychiatry. It was only psychotherapy, 'the search for a real solution', that he did not want to move out of. As if to confirm the truth of his last remark, he described a further dream which was extraordinary in that it seemed less like a dream than a fully conscious reflection, as if his conscious understanding had joined forces with his dream-level feeling, as a result of his developing integration. He dreamed simply, 'The bottom fell out of my little world as a baby', and he said, 'Mother didn't have the art of communicating with a baby, even before Percy died, even before the shop. The shop and Percy's death emptied my world and I had to start again and live a lonely self-sufficient life, keeping myself going.' Winnicott replied, 'Mother could communicate to but not with, do things but not be en rapport. We are dealing now, not with the bad mother inside, but with the bad you, that you feel she made you. You fear I can't stand its emergence.'

Guntrip's only recollection of the following morning's session was that he met Mrs Winnicott as he left. But when he returned a month later, in October, he mentioned a dream of having visited Bertrand Russell's house and later met him at a gathering at another house. He was quiet and happily married. The dream seemed to be associated with an actual gathering of analysts that Guntrip had attended the previous month at the home of Masud Khan, and at which Winnicott had been present. That the dream also masked anxiety about Winnicott's health, and a need for him to be well cared-for, emerged more clearly when Guntrip dreamed again of having been delayed and unable to find a taxi to get to a session, only to find that Winnicott had been taken ill, and was unavailable anyway.

Winnicott was indeed not in robust health. He was now over seventy and as Guntrip recalled how frail he had looked at the gathering of analysts, he realised how this situation was stirring latent anxieties over seeing Fairbairn's health deteriorate. Guntrip realised that the Bertrand Russell dream revealed a subtle process of substitution, of symbolic replacement of one person by another to disguise his anxiety that he might lose Winnicott. Thus, in another dream his actual mother was masked by the figure of his wife. He dreamed:

My wife and I were living in the house at Lordship Lane. It was all very dilapidated, altered, no proper fencing at the back. My wife went off up Lordship Lane and didn't come back. I had no meal and went to look for her. I'd had a lonely meal and then found her in some café with friends, eating and wasn't coming home. I said, 'What will I do for meals?' She made no reply. I went back to the house alone, and suddenly was faced with an enormous black Alsatian dog which blocked my way, and got hold of me in its mouth. It was sitting, and was twice as tall as I was and had a long pointed face. [2]

He commented: 'My rage, which is that fierce dog, came out in childhood as heat-spots. I turned it against myself by repressing it inside.' Winnicott said, 'The dog had a savage mouth and a pointed face, both a mouth and a penis, areas of the body where angry excited need could be concentrated and irritate you, because as a child, that did at least make mother do something to soothe you, to remove irritation.' Next morning Guntrip reported a dream of the previous night, in which he had again substituted a harmonious family atmosphere, in which all was well:

My wife and I were on holiday in Scotland staying with her mother and aunt. We took my wife's father in the person of Dr Danks. We sang them part songs which they all liked.

Guntrip saw that he was trying to cancel out all the old depressing home atmosphere by an imagined 'Winnicott atmosphere', based partly perhaps on his having seen Winnicott's younger wife. At the same time he was also aware of an undercurrent of anxiety about Winnicott, for Fairbairn's younger wife had been unable to save him. He said, 'I feel I ought not to burden you now' – undoubtedly expressing a fear of overwhelming Winnicott, which emerged clearly in his next two dreams. In the first of these some patients turned hostile to him and he said, 'If you feel like that you'd better finish', but then calmed down and continued treatment. A doctor asked him, why he did not just get rid of them, but he replied, 'You can't just dismiss them and let them down. You'd have suicides.' The dream was fraught with tension and anxiety, for he was clearly fearing that Winnicott may secretly want to be rid of him, and only keep him out of fear of the consequences. Nonetheless, he was able to see that Winnicott had made it possible for such frankness in a way that Fairbairn had been unable to do. The second dream was about Czechoslovakia, where he felt communism was being attacked by its own aggression, in a way which made him feel 'endangered' as if 'anything might happen to anybody'. Winnicott replied, 'Yes, I felt sick when I heard of Kosygin going to Finland, where I have friends.' Guntrip concluded, 'I'm needing to prove I can be greedy and make demands on you and you can survive them. Then I can accept my nature as good, and end analysis. I couldn't get that reassurance with mother and so was never able to get free of her inside, but only outside in adult life. Last night after the session I slept peacefully for six hours' – presumably having felt sure enough of Winnicott for that period. Winnicott remarked 'If you lived in London, you'd want to come every day, live with me. You bring me into your home in dreams, but you can't let yourself into mine. You stay alone with that fierce Alsatian turning against yourself while your mother neglects you. Your sense of not belonging in your early home is very important. The Alsatian is like the lion in the Nimrod story. Is the lion you or your mother and who will kill whom?'

In October (session 145) the endangered feeling still prevailed. Guntrip had an odd feeling of being a nervous boy of eight to eleven years, in the school of toughs at Denmark Hill, Camberwell, and he dreamed:

Our garden was invaded by young hooligans and it took me a long time to get them to go.

As he said, the dream showed that he was finding it hard to suppress his 'Alsatian dog bit'. His next dream strongly suggested that his relation to Winnicott had indeed matured to the point of enabling him to integrate the destructive aggression aroused by his mother, for it had, most vitally, evoked in Guntrip 'Good potentialities' that he had not known he possessed. He dreamed

Winnicott came, in a group of people, to our house, for a gathering. He wandered down our lawn and I went down later and found some beautiful flowers I did not know we had. I showed them to him and he knew all their names.[3]

Winnicott commented realistically: 'You are needing this sense of belonging, in a hostile world, afraid of persecutors, mother with the cane. You couldn't analyse paranoid fears in Czechoslovakia or Denmark Hill because they would be all too real. But you can analyse them now.' And he added, as if to emphasise that the 'good potentialities' needed to grow in vigorous contradistinction to himself – to 'individuate' – 'You fear to come alive and make vital demands on me.'

The session the following morning was a decisive one. Guntrip embarked upon an enthusiastic review of his dreams about his back garden and lawn, noting how there had been a gradual progression out of the original paranoid fears of robbers in the dark breaking in, through a mixed dream of the lit garden-fête and two ostensibly friendly men in his study, of whom he could not feel sure, to the present dream in which Winnicott, in the midst of a relaxed gathering, had enabled him to find a hitherto undiscovered floral richness. He said, 'You've helped me find a dissociated good part of myself, some potentiality mother never evoked, your "female element" of creative Being.' Winnicott replied: 'It's like giving birth to a beautiful baby with my help. I help you to know what it is. You gave me half an hour of concentrated talk, rich in content. I felt strained in listening and holding the situation for you. You were bringing a baby to birth. You had to know that I could stand your violence, your talking hard at me and my not being destroyed, and find you are not destructive but creative. I had to stand it while you were in labour, and produced something live, finding your creative, not masochistic or sadistic self. Psychiatric drugs "hold" violence but in an impersonal way, and it does no good.' Guntrip replied, 'You've held my violent talking, the only way I could permit myself to express it, and you felt the strain but you stood it. Now you have helped me not to be afraid of myself and feeling [sic] I can be creative and soon can stop analysis.' This experience constituted arrival at a 'real result' for Guntrip, the culmination of the gradual improvement of the previous two years. In a real sense it was just in time, before another four-month break in sessions during which Winnicott lectured to the New York Psychoanalytic Society, and at the Alanson White Institute. While there he fell seriously ill with a chest infection which affected his vulnerable heart and he nearly died. He was in the process of falling ill while giving his paper on 'The Use of an Object'.[4] in New York on 12 November, and had to cancel his second lecture at the White Institute the following day. It is worth noting that Guntrip, in his account of his analyses, associates Winnicott's mutative interpretation in their previous session with his recent concept of 'object-use'. Indeed, in that paper, Guntrip quotes Winnicott somewhat differently from the account cited here. Not only does he omit to mention Winnicott's references to his 'violence' and 'sadistic' or 'masochistic' selves, but he reports Winnicott as saying, 'You are talking about "object-relating", "using the object" and finding you don't destroy it. I couldn't have made that interpretation five years ago' (Guntrip 1975, in Hazell 1994, p. 363). The essence of the interpretation is, of course, maintained, and it is necessary to remember that it is only because of Guntrip's remarkable memory that either record is available to us, as he intended them to be. In fact the addition was transposed from a later session (150) – no doubt because Guntrip in his profound gratitude to Winnicott felt eager to stress that part of an interpretation to which he owed so much, and perhaps more especially because he had heard that Winnicott had been strongly criticised by some of the members when he gave his paper in New York, and had only just managed to get home by Christmas. Guntrip records his 'suspicion' that the criticism Winnicott's paper evoked was a measure of the anxiety it evoked in orthodox analysts, for he had little doubt that much 'psychoanalytic technique' was the analyst's defence against his patient. Recalling how Fairbairn, as his health declined, had fallen back on orthodox technique to defend himself against the deepest problems, Guntrip wrote 'I think there is reason to believe that the majority of analysts stop short at this point. My analysis with Winnicott was of such enormous importance because he had not only the insight but the personal courage to go beyond that "defensive technique" and take on himself the strain of the patient's disturbance.'

Notes

1   8 November 1967 to 5 March 1968 – a month longer than anticipated due to Winnicott's illness.
2   Guntrip recorded a slightly altered version of this dream, which he attributed to 'a male patient' on p. 187 of *Psychoanalytic Theory, Therapy and the Self* (1971), in which his New York lectures are documented. Presumably he added the dream when writing up the material for publication, since, while the book was not published until 1971, the lectures themselves ante-dated the dream. His account of the history of the 'male patient' leaves little room for doubt that he was describing his own situation, though with reference to his mother, not his wife (p. 188), and he makes the point that behind the 'oral sadism' represented by the Alsatian dog, lay the empty house and the absent mother.
3   Guntrip noted that 'Fairbairn knew the Latin names of flowers, trees etc.'
4   The paper was read in the New York Psychoanalytic Society on 12 November 1968, and was published in the *International Journal of Psycho-Analysis*, Vol. 50 (1969). A revised version appears in Chapter 6 of Winnicott's book *Playing and Reality* (1971).

CHAPTER 21

1969

By February, Winnicott was sufficiently recovered to resume work and he wrote to say he could see Guntrip, who attended six scattered sessions with him. At their first meeting they chatted about his illness and about Guntrip's projected visit in the spring to address the Los Angeles Psychoanalytical Society. Guntrip was delighted with his gains. He had maintained his sleep improvement in spite of an extra-heavy work programme: preparing the Los Angeles lectures, writing up the New York lectures in book form,[1] seeing *Schizoid Phenomena, Object Relations and the Self* in publication just in time to precede the Los Angeles tour, preparing lectures for a Psychiatric Social Workers' course in the department and seeing difficult but decisive developments in three important cases. The new three-term course on the 'The Development of Personality' was a breakthrough in the Department of Psychiatry, and was directly attributable to Guntrip's influence. It ranked equally in his mind with the American lectures, in terms of significance. He concluded, 'I've been tired but enjoyed it all.' He then reported an 'extremely relevant dream' which he believed may have anticipated Winnicott's paper on 'The Use of an Object'.

> I was lecturing in the presence of a senior psychotherapist and Fairbairn, on patients' oral needs that must be met and understood. They both got hot and critical and said, 'What are you going to do if a couple of patients get manic and make persecutory demands on you?' I stuck to my point, saying, 'That's just the very point where you can but musn't let the patients down or fail them.' They couldn't accept it and I felt it was because they were afraid of the problem.

He believed that in the dream he was recognising how Winnicott had accepted the strain of his energetic need to express himself orally by talking and had stood it and survived. He said, 'Your understanding of my fear of my violent starved oral need, and accepting it and surviving has enabled me to understand it, and frees me of that fear.'

He recalled how, after their October session, he had had to work off
bodily tension several nights before sleeping, so that Bertha, with
great insight, had asked 'Does that tomb-man dream bear on it?' He
had realised at once that it did, and that the tomb-man represented
not merely his repressed aggression against a hostile mother, but his
essential vitality, his basic vital self breaking through, only to be
pushed and crushed, first by his mother and then by himself, in the
form of his exhaustion-illnesses. It had all been expressed in that
early dream, his terror of his own basic vital self: in his own terms,
his regressed libidinal ego, exhausted, withdrawn and repressed, and
yet retaining its libidinal quality, for, as he then told Winnicott: 'He
remained alive and you have let him out!'

Next day, after such celebratory boldness, Guntrip experienced
his familiar misgiving that he had imposed a strain on Winnicott.
During a restless night he had dreamed of walking down from the
Lordship Lane house to the Goose Green shop, when he pointed to
a window and told someone, 'I used to live there and looked out of
that window for father.' With the open honesty so typical of him,
Winnicott said: 'You were looking for a good father to help you in
your problem with Mother and Mary. I may not be quite a father-
figure. I'm a good mother-figure, but you're not sure of my maleness. Mother wouldn't accept you as a male, wouldn't be a target
for your male eagerness and activity. So you'd no-one to develop
your maleness to, though it's there. And Father didn't give you a
vigorous male example, though you found he'd been male and
active earlier. He had it in him. But you are male beneath the
female that mother tried to force on you. You show an active male
self in your writing and lecturing, and you get hold of ideas and
organise them and write books in a way that I can't, but I see it.'

Guntrip saw that Winnicott, like a 'good mother' was sponsoring
his 'male' vitality. He said, 'You help me to develop my male "doing"
side by seeing and appreciating it in a way mother didn't, and you
accepted having to be a target for my eager, urgent, active self-expression. Now I feel I need not assert my active self here. You've cleared
away mother's opposition and I can be male and active in the rest of
life elsewhere', and most significantly, he added, 'If occasionally I see
you I can be quiet and grow.' He then reported a dream of 13 December, at the time of Winnicott's illness, which seemed to him to
confirm his confidence that all was well: 'I went back to University to
take another degree, but the class was unimpressive and the teaching
poor. Outside I met Fairbairn looking fit and vigorous and he said,
"What do you want to be taking another degree for? You don't need
it!" I felt he believed I could now stand on my experience and what I

had achieved.' There was certainly a big change in Guntrip's reaction
to this most recent illness of Winnicott as compared with his reaction to his illness a year earlier. He himself felt that the dream was
a 'reaction of hopefulness' both regarding Winnicott's illness and his
own intention of ending analysis. He said, 'I never doubted you
would recover from your illness, and here Fairbairn is revitalised, and
I can end analysis.' Winnicott interpreted, 'Mother turned your
potency into aggression and frustrated your active development. I
accept your eagerness and let your aggression turn back into creative-
ness. You felt my impressive summing up in October was a male act
and you used and kept it.'

At this point there was a three-month break in sessions, from
February to May, during Guntrip's lecturing visit to Los Angeles. The
tour was a demanding one, involving 'two weeks of case study seminars, personal and private discussions with individuals, lectures at a
number of hospitals to their staffs, and a lecture to a joint meeting of
the Los Angeles and South Californian Psychoanalytic Societies'.
Although conscious of the fact that he was overworked, Guntrip
revelled in the experience. On his return he told Winnicott, 'They
gave me a magnificently generous and appreciative reception, and
eager, stimulating discussion, so much so that I just did not realise
how tired I was physically until we stopped off in New York, to give
one lecture at the White Institute on the way home.' The physical
strains were telling, and, more than a year later, he was conscious of
having worked against over-fatigue 'ever since Los Angeles'. Moreover, there were the usual rumblings among the orthodox members
of the Los Angeles Society, to such an extent that when one pointed
out some schizoid aspects of a case of fetishism he was treated to a
denunciatory harangue, ending with 'this is Guntrip!'. The member
was refused acceptance as a training analyst, and it was said that one
of the appointing committee had exclaimed of Guntrip: 'Do you
know what this man stands for? He'll destroy psychoanalysis.' Guntrip was clearly downcast at this reaction, though less surprised than
before. However, the longer-term effect of his visit was more positive.
There was a wave of indignation among the members and the decision was reversed. Overall the tour had been a success, and Guntrip
told Winnicott that he was aware of being 'on top form' in a way that
he attributed to Winnicott's acceptance of his 'talking hard' whilst
seeing him as creative: 'as able to give birth to something, while you
were not destroyed'. He continued, 'You have released my capacity
for active living in a spontaneous way, not "having to work hard to
keep myself alive". You've cancelled out mother's basic inhibitory
influence on me [and] enabled me to resurrect my buried alive self

out of that tomb. I'm sure I'm of more use and help to people now than when I had to force my activity over and above what spontaneity I had.'[2]

Next day in the 150th session Winnicott said, 'I feel you are talking about object-relating and also about using the object and finding you don't destroy it. So you and the object can be together and separate and then together again, and you can both be both together and both apart. It's like the foot and the shoe, both can go along together and part and join again. It's like my two hands, one on top of the other and then apart side by side and then together again. I couldn't have said that ten years, or even five years ago.' As Winnicott spoke, Guntrip realised that his whole analysis had fallen within that ten-year period. With a profound sense of gratitude and privilege, he lay back on the couch and relaxed. And, as if in confirmation of that 'separateness which is a form of union', Winnicott for the first time moved his small chair forward alongside so that Guntrip could see him.[3] Guntrip lay peacefully, musing, 'We can be together and apart and together again, mentally related and yet separate persons.'

The final two sessions took place in July. Guntrip felt able to leave because of the freeing of his 'basic vital self'; not a wholesale evacuation of bad experience, but rather, a basic 'ego-relatedness', and consequent 'ego-strength' capable of re-experiencing and integrating that experience. Thus against a background of 'all round improvement, too general to be itemised or defined' and 'good family dreams', Guntrip recalled 'one element of the sinister from childhood' that had not been cleared up. Although he knew of the event he had never actually broken through his amnesia to re-experience directly Percy's death and his relation to his mother at that time. Unaware of how portentous his words would prove to be he added, 'But I'm sure it will come in its own time.'

Meanwhile he described a harmonious family dream redolent of the best in his early family life,

My mother and father came to visit us, a pleasant visit. Then later I went to visit them. Mother was away to the left in the house when I went in. Father opened the door and was clearly pleased to see me, and called to mother that it was me. Both were pleased, a pleasant visit.

Not surprisingly this was followed by a disturbing dream, for Guntrip, on the point of ending his analysis with Winnicott, was clearly experiencing some anxiety, despite his manifest gains.

Doubtless seeking to link his good experience with whatever of himself was still tied to the past, he had dreamed

> Winnicott and I were going to a conference and arrived at a large empty house, where we were to stay. We looked over it, and found some proper letters that had been delivered and fallen into a pile of rubbish. We decided to sort them out. While we were in a back room I heard a voice and said, 'There's someone here in the hall.' I went through quickly and saw a slightly built boy of ten to twelve in a long white nightgown [such as Guntrip himself had worn as a child] dart across the hall and up the stairs. I was afraid and struggled to call out.

He had woken making choked noises, causing Bertha to ask what was the matter. He told Winnicott, 'That boy was clearly me. It must be the old family home emptied of the old bad mother and insufficiently active father, but not all the rubbish cleared yet, and some good messages to be opened. I met the ghost of my child self. He darted across just like the little black, bad, boy of a half-waking dream years ago but this one is white. If he's the inoffensive child mother wanted me to be, I'd rather be the black boy, but this white boy is also trying to escape.' Winnicott merely replied, 'You're meeting a lost part of yourself', no doubt feeling that the major part of their work had now been done, and that 'lost parts of the self' would continue to be reintegrated in the course of time. Thus steadied, Guntrip recalled another good family dream, the last he brought to Winnicott:

> My wife and I were travelling in a car on holiday with our daughter and her husband, and we called on my wife's mother and aunt. They welcomed us and it was all very pleasant.

In his review of this session Guntrip wrote, 'So I had finished my last session but one, with dreams of surrounding myself with "good objects", and of having Winnicott with me to help me face something still capable of flitting disturbingly from my past over my dream scene.' It is also noticeable that Bertha had come more into prominence in the sessional material as the analysis moved towards its conclusion.

In their 152nd session on 16 July 1969, it would seem that Guntrip was 'mentally stocking up' against whatever remained to be faced. He reported a sleepless night in which he had been 'kept awake by a fear of that boy in white', and by thinking obsessionally of the parable of the seven devils.[4] The parable describes how 'when the unclean spirit has gone out of the man, he passes through waterless places seeking rest', and how, when unable to find it, he conscripts 'seven other spirits more evil than himself' to reinhabit the 'swept and garnished' empty house from which he came. In both biblical accounts the conclusion is that 'the last state of that man is worse than the first'. Clearly, Guntrip was apprehensive of experiencing a vacuum after finishing his analysis, in which, as so often before, he would feel himself assailed by his bad objects, which for so long had been the only alternative to the void. Indeed this would appear to have already occurred in a minor way when, in his interpretation of his penultimate dream, he had introduced a conflictual situation between the boy in white and a 'bad' black boy, who had not appeared in the actual dream at all. Nor did it occur to him to associate the agile boy in white with his newly realised vitality or even with his rediscovered 'female element'. However, the ending of an analysis is often marked by a flare-up of 'separation-anxiety' in which access is sought to previously vacated 'bad-object situations', for, as Fairbairn pointed out (and as Guntrip often quoted), 'emotion can be drained out of the old patterns by new experience, but water can always flow again in the old dried up water courses'. And as Guntrip finally pointed out to Winnicott, 'In the dream I had you there to stand by me!' In his deepest conviction he was no longer alone.

Notes

1 *Psychoanalytic Theory, Therapy and the Self* (1971).
2 I have described my own experience of the change in Guntrip *as an analyst* as he himself began to work towards a solution with Winnicott. Hazell, J. (1991) 'Reflections on my Experience of Psychoanalysis with Guntrip', *Contemporary Psychoanalysis* Vol. 27 (1), pp. 148–66. An earlier form of the paper was written in 1975 as a tribute to Guntrip after his death.
3 Winnicott would appear to have been more 'orthodox' than Fairbairn in this respect, for Fairbairn (1958) stated that he had come to prefer the use of chairs to the couch. Guntrip used chairs and/or couch and certainly by 1969 he was accustomed to sitting alongside when a patient used the couch.
4 Matthew 12: 43–45, Luke 11: 24–26. Revised Standard Version 1946. Guntrip had referred to this parable in his early paper, 'The Therapeutic Factor in Psychotherapy' (1953, in Hazell 1994, p. 63), as one 'which psychotherapists would do well to ponder', since 'If we could succeed in ridding patients of their symptoms without giving them a constructive relationship with ourselves to build on, we would do them more harm than good in the end' (p. 79)

Resolution

CHAPTER 22

1969–75

The reason why Guntrip concluded the Winnicott analysis when he did is not made explicit, and although Winnicott had made quite frequent references to his mortality during the sessions, he continued in practice for at least a further year before his death early in 1971. One is reminded of Guntrip's fear of staying in analysis with Fairbairn until the latter died. Had Winnicott similarly become a brother to Guntrip in the transference thus presenting him with a similar dilemma of 'having to end his analysis to get a chance to finish it', only to find he had no-one to help him with the resultant trauma? Another reason might well have been Guntrip's own deteriorating health. For, although he later dated 'a process of compelling regression' from February 1970 when he was warned medically that he was seriously overworked, and that if he did not retire, 'Nature would make him', it would appear from his letters to Sutherland that the process of regression had begun during his tour of Los Angeles, shortly before he finished with Winnicott. Moreover, although he felt that Winnicott had released his 'capacity for active living in a spontaneous way', he nevertheless had to spend 'ten days flat on [his] back' with a disc lesion in August 1969 after finishing with Winnicott in July, and he was unable to respond to an invitation from Sutherland to speak at a conference in Edinburgh that September. By January 1970, he had been forced to decide on 'virtual clinical retirement', and, by October he himself had come to feel that a further medical insistence that he retire was the culmination and not the start of a regressive progress. He wrote to Sutherland that a marked decline in his physical resources since Los Angeles had 'simply pulled the trigger on a loaded situation' (personal communication, 10 September 1970). An awareness of ageing, and the sense of a newly acquired capacity for spontaneous living had combined with unprecedented opportunities in America, London and Leeds, to deny him a gradual and steady integration of his new-found energies. The result was a particularly unwelcome series of minor breakdowns as his physical powers declined faster than he realised, while his work increased, bringing about something like his former 'manic defence', and while his physical state was indicating a need for 'therapeutic regression'.

Thus, while he was wise enough to cancel the Edinburgh conference on account of his disc lesion, he nevertheless responded that August to an urgent request from the editor of *New Society* that he should write a reply of 2000 words at two days' notice, to an article by Eysenck on 'Behaviour Therapy versus Psychotherapy' (personal communication, 8 August 1969). In addition he accepted an invitation to give a 'staff lecture' that October in the Department of Psychiatry at Leeds on his Los Angeles tour. It was the first invitation of this kind in twenty years in that department, neither had he been invited in all that time to present a case at the regular case-conferences, despite offering to do so (personal communication, 16 December 1970). He believed the reason for his exclusion to be that the two professors, first Hargreaves, and then Hamilton, found 'the way I presented cases, the kind of problems I "exposed to view" in patients they would only prescribe pills for . . . too disturbing for them' (personal communication, to J.D. Sutherland, 16 December 1970). Indeed, Hargreaves, while initially more supportive, had refused to write a foreword for *Healing the Sick Mind*, saying he'd lost faith in psychotherapy, while Hamilton, professing to do psychotherapy, was reported by a visiting colleague to have rapped out questions, demanding a short answer 'Yes' or 'No' , and then to have said, 'It's curious, the diagnosis of most patients I see is "agitated depression"' (personal communication, 16 December 1970). In such a context it is clear why Guntrip felt he must respond to the invitation to give a staff lecture, whatever the cost. He wrote, 'The staff-room was packed and it was clear that quite a number of people from the staffs of our four hospitals had come. I fancy the "winds of change" are beginning to blow rather strongly around our Professor, for when I told him I was resigning my clinical work in the Department (NHS) he begged me not to resign as a lecturer. After having been kept in the background for so many years I find the situation intriguing, and I feel it's a pity I'm not ten years younger' (personal communication, to J.D. Sutherland, 7 October 1969). Indeed, such was the impact upon him of the new recognition that over and above his existing lecturing commitments, Guntrip responded to an 'eleventh hour' request by the professor of Psychology, Dr Gwynne Jones, to undertake a three-term course of lectures on psychoanalysis and psychotherapy to second-year postgraduate Clinical Psychology trainees, and this in addition to his lectures to Social Workers: 'two lectures every Monday a.m. have been added: no-one else to do it' (J.D.S., 10 September 1970). The lectures attracted much interest from qualified Clinical Psychologists working in nearby mental hospitals who asked if they could attend, and who requested that Guntrip should run a weekly clinical session where they could discuss their cases. It is not surprising that Guntrip's enthusiasm for these simultaneous developments was counterbalanced by ill health. The energy and zest with which he pursued his tasks was formidable, and one wonders whether he may have recalled Winnicott's prediction that although he was 'at the centre of the growing point of psychoanalysis . . . and may well go on and do better work than Fairbairn' or himself, he may yet be hampered by anxiety that in doing so he might injure his 'analyst-fathers' if he went on 'being alive and achieving things and enjoying it in old age'. At any rate, he could not or did not stop! – contributing a chapter to a festschrift for Erich Fromm's seventieth birthday, revising his book *You and Your Nerves* for re-publication under a new title *Your Mind and Your Health* with two extra chapters, considering a companion to Paul Halmos' *Faith of the Counsellors* entitled *Psychodynamics for Counsellors* and finalising his book *Psychoanalytic Theory, Therapy and the Self* for publication in the USA. By December 1969 he was obliged to rest in bed for two weeks with a flare-up of the disc lesion, following an attack of vertigo and a fall in September. By January he had arrived at his decision on 'virtual clinical retirement' at the end of the year, reserving himself for 'a bit more writing and lecturing, and one or two who will be finishing off training analysis' (personal communication, 21 January 1970). Between February and March 1970 he experienced such 'sudden severe vertigo' that a consultant warned him that his cervical arthritis could impede the blood supply to the head, and advised him against sudden head movement. The consultant also made the comment to which Guntrip later attributed his 'compulsion to go back to the past' to find out all that had happened to him: 'You are seriously overworked. If you don't cut down nature will make you' (J.D.S., 10 September 1970).

But Guntrip did not 'cut down': 'I must have felt unconsciously that that was a threat that "Mother Nature" would at last crush my active self', (1975, in Hazell 1994, p. 364). Not only did he begin some 'detective work' on his personal history and two analyses, upon which much of this book has been based, but early in May he agreed to be interviewed by Derek Hart for the BBC television programme *Viewpoint*. He wrote 'I thought the TV thing went well, but paid a high price. Three hours of being glared [sic] by three powerful arc lights at close range in my room meant that pains in the eyes and head kept me off work for 2 weeks and started up vertigo' (personal communication, 17 July 1970). All sessions had to be cancelled. It was a state remarkably similar to his 'photophobia' and exhaustion as a student: 'My wife cancelled everyone and everything for a week, and then a second week. I just had to spend most of the time in bed, with curtains drawn and dark glasses on' (personal communication, 1 June 1970). The state recurred during the summer holiday when he 'foolishly watched the TV World Cup final . . . the glittering screen brought back eye-strain and vertigo. It took me another two weeks to get over it and it spoiled the holiday. If only I had worn sun-glasses' (personal communication, 17 July 1970). It must however be emphasised that it was certainly more than 'fear that Mother Nature would crush his active self' that motivated Guntrip in the aftermath of his analysis. His letters were full of a genuine love of life and interest in his friends and ex-patients, such as myself. Nor was it simply the 'determination' inherited from his mother. Those who knew him, including myself, attest to the fact that he was no longer 'an evangelist without a gospel', but a warm and vigorous old man, with very little vestige of his former aloofness. At the time of receiving these letters, I was sorry, but not worried for him. Indeed, he was still an inspiration. Thus, it came as no surprise when, on 18 September 1970, he travelled to Aberdeen to lecture on 'The Ego Psychology of Freud and Adler, re-examined in 1970s' (Guntrip 1971, in Hazell 1994, p. 287). The lecture, which marked the centenary of Adler's birth, was to inaugurate the Psychotherapy and Social Psychiatry Section of the Royal Medical-Psychological Association. It was a great occasion and Guntrip, in a letter to Sutherland, defended his decision to see it through: 'I would not like to have missed Aberdeen (though I hadn't bargained for that long reception afterwards), nor the necessity it gave me for formulating the Adler–Freud Ego Theory Situation: which is more interesting than I had previously realised' (16 December 1970). He went on to attribute his subsequent collapse not to the Aberdeen lecture, but to 'the Department's call after not making much use of me for over 20 years to do some really serious lecturing' (J.D.S., 16 December 1970). In fact the collapse must largely have been due to his inability not to respond to any and every opportunity to promote his message. He promptly accepted an invitation to speak on a radio programme *Pause for Thought*, and set to work on a revision of his book *Psychology for Ministers and Social Workers*.

It was in October 1970 that Guntrip, sensing that he had

finally outstripped his resources, wrote to Sutherland with a new urgency: 'I appreciate very much your giving me a couple of hours of your time on a Sunday, especially when you have visitors coming. I would not make such a request except for a very important reason. I have arrived at what I believe to be a very important conclusion in some post-analytical detective-work on myself.' The letter continues, 'I have always known that my analyses with Fairbairn and Winnicott did not reach a definitive conclusion, but did prepare the way for it; and that somehow, sometime I would have to find my own way to the clearing up of a serious emotional trauma at the age of 3½ when my brother aged 2 died, and I was thought to be dying for no apparent reason other than the "grief" the doctor suggested.' He went on to describe how deaths and 'endings' had provoked exhaustion attacks all through his life, and how his retirement warning in February had led to the 'detective work' which he felt convinced would reveal the trauma. He then made an emotional appeal to Sutherland: 'It so happens that, for reasons you will recognise, you are the one person who can help me to relatively finalise [sic] the result I am reaching. Neither Fairbairn nor Winnicott could do it, for reasons I can show.' Guntrip then described in detail his deteriorating physical health, making the important point that at no stage in his enforced bed-rests had he been able to relax his mind. He continued, 'Clearly, lowering of physical resistance has let a cat out of the bag, and I have had no choice but to keep going over the emotional implications of the various instances of "exhaustion-attacks". I have seen them clearly as screen-memories, repeating, but hiding, the trauma of Percy's death and my relation to my mother; and to my father and Aunt, who both went passive under her dominance. I believe I have got somewhere with the re-arousal of all that by the threat of retirement, and for reasons I will explain you are the one person with whom I can finalise this and free myself. You have meant more to me than you knew' (J.D.S., 10 September 1970). The reasons for Guntrip's faith in Sutherland are not difficult to assess. Sutherland was one of the two analysts whom Guntrip had contemplated approaching when he had considered finishing with Fairbairn. He had also been instrumental in the publication of Guntrip's first psychoanalytic paper in 1952. He had himself been in analysis with Fairbairn, and he knew Winnicott and Balint, and was sympathetic to 'object-relations' therapy. Moreover, although Guntrip later denied it, the personal tone of his appeal suggests that he saw in Sutherland a brother-figure in rude good health who had the experience and capacity both to facilitate and survive his attempt to clear up the legacy of Percy's death. With Sutherland, he at least had an answer to the dilemma of how to end analysis – involving, he felt sure, a full-scale eruption of the trauma of his brother's death – and have someone to help him with it: above all, Sutherland was there! As repression and his physical powers continued to weaken, he needed someone of Sutherland's stature to relate to.

A week after his appeal to Sutherland Guntrip collapsed with pneumonia, and spent the ensuing five weeks in hospital and three more laid up at home. He wrote to me, 'I came out of hospital three stones lighter than I went in, weak, unsteady and dizzy . . . I get up for meals for an hour, write a letter (like this), and return to bed for 2 to 3 hours. I have to return to hospital for an X-ray and final check up in January, and was told I must accept a long slow convalescence. In mid-Winter nothing else is possible anyway and I think it will take the Summer to put me right' (personal communication, 29 November 1970). I should add that the tone of this letter was as warm and engaging as ever, and full of interest in my own news.

Apart from the friendly letter in December in which Guntrip blames his illness on the strains of extra departmental pressure, there is no record of further correspondence with Sutherland until March. The tone of that letter is in fact distinctly cavalier, in stark contrast to that of the October letter. After grumbling about his treatment by the professors, Guntrip ends: 'Hey Ho! It's a very human world. You can't blame folk, it's their parents: and you can't blame parents, it's the grandparents – back to Adam and Eve, and that wretched snake who was probably Freud's oldest ancestor' (J.D.S., 16 December 1970). Perhaps Guntrip, having, so to speak, satisfied himself that Sutherland was 'there for him', felt able to relax. Moreover, it seems probable that the two men were in contact by telephone, and that the ground was prepared as well as it could be, for Guntrip to 'finalise' his detective work and free himself. At any rate, it was in these circumstances, in a state of enforced convalescence punctuated by hospital attendances, that the ultimate 'trigger' of Winnicott's death, in January 1971, set off in Guntrip an 'autonomously regressing dream sequence' in which the death of Percy, for so long the focus of analytic investigation, was itself revealed as a 'screen memory' for a profoundly depersonalised experience with their emotionally exhausted mother. Guntrip's own words (Guntrip 1975, in Hazell 1994, pp. 364–5), convey the immediacy of his experience. On the very night that Winnicott died, he had a 'startling dream. I *saw my mother*, black, immobile, staring fixedly into space, *totally ignoring me* as I stood at one side staring at her and feeling myself frozen into immobility: the first time I had ever seen her in a dream like that. Before she had always been attacking me. My first thought was: "I've lost Winnicott and am left alone with mother, sunk in depression, ignoring me. That's how I felt when Percy died." His immediate feeling was that he had 'taken the loss of Winnicott as a repetition of the Percy trauma': the very fear he had had about Fairbairn when, after his serious illness, the latter assumed the significance of a brother in the transference. But on this occasion there were vital differences: 'That dream started a compelling dream-sequence, which went on night after night, taking me back in chronological order through every house I had lived in, in Leeds, Ipswich, College, the second Dulwich shop, and finally to the first shop and house of the first bad seven years. Family figures, my wife, daughter, Aunt Mary, father and mother kept recurring: father always supportive, mother always hostile, but no sign of Percy. I was trying to stay in the post-Percy period of battles with mother. Then, after some two months two dreams at last broke that amnesia for Percy's life and death. I was astonished to see myself in a dream, clearly aged about three, recognisably me, holding a pram in which was my brother, aged about a year old. I was strained, looking anxiously over to the left at mother, to see if she would take any notice of us. But she was staring fixedly into the distance, ignoring us, as in the first dream of that series.' The following night Guntrip had what he described as 'the most dramatic dream ever' which 'must be regarded as proof that Winnicott had enabled me to find the truth about this trauma'. He dreamed:

> I was standing with another man, the double of myself, both reaching out to get hold of a dead object. Suddenly, the other man collapsed in a heap. Immediately the dream changed to a lighted room where I saw Percy again. I knew it was him, sitting on the lap of a woman who had no face, arms, or breasts. She was merely a lap to sit on, not a person. He looked deeply depressed, with the corners of his mouth turned down, and I was trying to make him smile.

Guntrip realised that in this dream he had broken the amnesia for Percy's death. His feeling was that he dreamed of the collapse first because that had been his initial reaction 'of terrified hopelessness' at the shock of finding Percy dead on his mother's lap. He then dreamed of 'trying to make him smile' in an attempt to 'stay alive by finding others to live for' – ultimately his patients. But, more than this, he had 'actually gone back in both dreams to the earlier time before he died, to see the "faceless", depersonalised mother, and the black depressed mother, who totally failed to relate to both of us' (Guntrip 1975, in Hazell 1994, p. 365).

It will be noticed that the dream of the faceless, depersonalised mother with the depressed Percy on her lap is strikingly similar to what Fairbairn had described as 'vague visions' or 'low-grade memories' in November 1949. Harry was approaching the first major break in analysis at that time, and was desperately needing an identificatory union with Fairbairn, which the latter interpreted as 'a great source of resistance'. Similarly, Fairbairn interpreted Harry's shut-in lifeless state as a reaction to feeling 'deserted' by his analyst. Fairbairn, at that time could not see, and neither could Harry articulate, the need of the unrelated infant, which underlay the kaleidoscopic changes of the 'one-up-and-one-down' relationships, and the catastrophic trauma of Percy's death.

Now Guntrip realised that although Winnicott's death had reminded him of Percy's, his experience was 'entirely different' to that debilitating feeling of illness which had attended the deaths of Percy and Tizard, and the loss of his ministerial colleague of the Salem days. With great joy he began to realise that what had given him strength in his 'deep unconscious to face again that basic trauma of Percy's death' and their mother's 'total failure to relate' to them, had been the eternal quality of his relation to Winnicott, who 'was not, and could not be, dead' for him, 'and certainly for many others'. He wrote, 'Winnicott had come into living relation with precisely that earlier lost part of me that fell ill because mother failed me. *He has taken her place and made it possible and safe to remember her in an actual dream-reliving of her paralysing schizoid aloofness.* Slowly that became a firm conviction growing in me, and I recovered from the volcanic upheaval of that autonomously regressing compelling dream-series, feeling that I had at last reaped the gains I had sought in analysis over some twenty years' (1975, in Hazell 1994, p. 366).

Guntrip was clear that analysis cannnot give anyone a different life history, and that *'we have to accept that when analysis reaches down to the deeper level, as I believe mine did with Winnicott, that does not constitute an immediate full "cure". There is no such thing. What does happen is that one is put in a stronger position internally* to experience, with fuller understanding the ways in which the old ingrown bad-relation patterns are aroused and disturbed by present day affairs . . . *If the past is*

never totally outgrown, neither is the whole personal self static
. . . while a genuine therapeutic relationship is being experienced'
(sessional record of Winnicott analysis). Thus, while Guntrip felt
that Fairbairn had resolved the negative transference, and that
Winnicott had 'entered the emptiness' left by his non-relating
mother, he still felt 'a mood of sadness for my mother who was so
damaged in childhood that she could neither be, nor enable me to
be, our true selves' (1975, in Hazell 1994, p. 366), and while his
dreaming 'slowly faded out' it was replaced by 'feeling consciously
in the grip of a state of mind I began to realise I had been in
unconsciously deep down ever since: a dull mechanical lifeless
mood, no interest in anything, silent, shut in to myself, going
through routine motions with a sense of loss of all meaning in
existence. I experienced this for a number of consecutive mornings
till I began to find that it was fading out into a normal interest in
life: which after all seems to be what one would expect' (1975, in
Hazell 1994, p. 367).

Guntrip believed that the dream-sequence confirmed his long-
held belief that his dreams were a symbolic record of originally
external bad experience which had to be internalised because it
could not be accepted and used for ego-development. It marked the
culmination of his faithfully maintained record of his dreams,
which he took as evidence that his unconscious had 'known its
own business best' and had 'gone its own way', uninfluenced by
those psychoanalytic theories which did not match it. He wrote
(1975, in Hazell 1994, p. 367), 'so far as psychopathological
experience is concerned, dreaming expresses our endopsychic structure. It is a' way of experiencing on the fringes of consciousness,
our internalised conflicts, our memories and fantasies of conflicts
that have become our inner reality, to keep "object relations" alive,
even if only "bad object relations", because we need them to retain
possession of our "ego".'

It is surely significant that Guntrip was in this extremely
regressed state when he relived in his dream sequence that ultimate trauma. One cannot help but think that, 'outside analysis',
his body represented his psychic needs, and 'got him into care' at
just the right moment. He was nursed by Bertha through that
crucial stage, with doctors in attendance due to his convalescent
state, and Sutherland fully apprised of the likely turn of events.
Such environmental care would hardly have been compatible with
his journeys to Edinburgh or London. Bertha maintained a sound
and loving presence, as she had throughout their life together. In
his account of his gratitude to Fairbairn and Winnicott (1975, in

Hazell 1994, p. 155), Guntrip adds that without Bertha's understanding and support he 'could not have had those analyses or
achieved this result'. In his private record he was more expansive:

> It is impossible for me to do justice to my wife's forbearance
> and patience over the nine years my mother finally lived with
> us. My debt to her is enormous, more especially as the only
> way for me to get a training analysis with Dr Fairbairn (or
> indeed with anyone else, for there were no analysts in York-
> shire) was to travel to Edinburgh from Tuesday a.m. to Thurs-
> day midday, and doing my work in Leeds from Thursday p.m.
> to Monday night every week. For 7 years my wife accepted the
> necessity of that programme, and for the first 3½ years under-
> took the strain of my mother alone for two days each week.

For her part, Bertha experienced all the strains and ambivalence
attendant upon supporting a partner in analysis. In 1983, eight
years after Harry's death, she wrote,

> I myself felt deeply disappointed that Harry's problems with his
> mother cut him off from allowing our own relationship to heal
> his hurt self. However, I loved him truly, backing him at all
> times in his long search. He worked with all his might and
> strength to solve his own problems, and I am glad that his
> work . . . lives on in his writings, aiding others. (Personal cor-
> respondence, 23 March 1983)

It was indeed propitious for Guntrip, that, at a time when he was
unaided by psychoanalytic insight, he should have been able to
respond to such a supportive and loving person, so utterly different
from his mother. There were clear signs from time to time that he
himself was identified with his mother's dominant personality (as
Crichton-Miller quickly spotted), and it is probable that the analysis and the marriage partnership were mutually protective and supportive, for Bertha would surely have been even more severely tried
by projections on to her of Harry's internalised bad mother, had
Fairbairn not so assiduously 'detoxified' them.

After the momentous events of New Year 1971 – perhaps as a
consequence – the letters to Sutherland in April and May returned
to their former pleasant, business-like style, about such matters as
the revision of the Aberdeen lecture for publication, and preparation of a new double-length chapter on 'British Psychoanalytic
Object Relations Theory: the Fairbairn–Guntrip approach', for in-

clusion in the revised *American Handbook of Psychiatry*. The chapter, an outstanding example of the clear and energetic writing of the seventy-year-old Guntrip, is perhaps the clearest, concise account of the work of the 'British School', and includes references to the contributions of Winnicott and Balint. The instructions issued by the chief editor, Dr Arieti, presented quite a challenge:

> One should visualise the *Handbook* as an authoritative reference work, not only for your colleagues but for residents in psychiatry and psychology and interested students in the other behavioural sciences. This requires each contribution to be more detailed and comprehensive than a text book but not so detached as the typical monograph.

The *Handbook* was eventually published by Basic Books Inc. in 1974.[1]

No reference was made in the correspondence to the 'detective work' or its outcome. The letters to myself at this time are suggestive of an easing of Guntrip's inner burden, though he and Bertha both showed signs of strain. They were able to enjoy a visit to Marjorie Brierley's house at Rowling End at Whitsun and managed a holiday in June; but Bertha was discovered to have fairly advanced osteoarthritis of the left knee, which meant very limited walking and then only with two sticks, while Harry's cervical arthritis obliged him to wear a surgical collar. Their physical condition had been exacerbated by the growing responsibility of looking after Bertha's mother, now ninety and crippled, and her aunt, eighty-five, and nearly blind, whom the Guntrips had housed some years earlier in Aberford, a village some ten miles from Leeds. Now that the health of all concerned dictated that the physical burden should be kept to a minimum, Harry and Bertha were fortunate to find a detached bungalow for themselves next door to the old people.

Harry had begun to re-engage in clinical work in February, just a month after his dream-sequence, seeing a small number of patients (two monthly and two fortnightly), and it was important that the new house was in reach of Leeds, both for the patients and also for Harry's visits to the University. Moreover, Aberford itself had a certain symbolic significance for Harry, for the Swan Inn was the ancient staging-post on the Great North Road, exactly midway between Edinburgh and London! The bungalow, into which the Guntrips moved in late August 1971, and where Bertha still lives, became the 'centre of operations', both clinical and literary, until the end of Harry's life. He and Bertha managed a short holiday after the strain of the move, and by November there were unmistakable signs of returning vigour at the professional level. The tone of the letters that month is buoyant, with no sign of the appallingly low physical state of twelve months earlier, or indeed of the urgent need of support expressed to Sutherland the previous October. Instead, Guntrip briskly discussed his plans to visit London later in the month to give the inaugural lecture to the newly established specialist Psychotherapists' section of the Royal College of Psychiatrists, where he had been 'particularly requested to repeat the Aberdeen lecture'. He wrote to Sutherland: 'I have improved a good deal in the last couple of months and feel equal to this London venture.' Indeed the lecture was very well received. Mrs Winnicott, in particular, was very enthusiastic and commented, 'Nothing like this can be got anywhere in London, and not in the Psychoanalytical Society.' The lecture became the basis for a paper published in the *British Journal of Medical Psychology* (vol. 44, pp. 305–18) in that same year.

Harry had also resumed his lectures at the rate of one a week to the trainee Clinical Psychologists. He wrote: 'I find this important as it . . . gives me human contacts. I really get my class asking questions and engaging in animated discussion as I go along, which I find stimulating' (personal communication, 9 November 1971). It was these questions and discussions that prompted Guntrip to write his paper 'Orthodoxy and Revolution in Psychology' (1972, in Hazell 1994, p. 305). Life in the village was not, of course, devoid of 'human contacts', but the weight of need of the older people next door must surely have provoked a corresponding need for external stimulus in Harry, despite his evident concern for them. A welcome further stimulus for Harry at this time in 1972 was provided by a number of visits by other psychotherapists and psychiatrists from London and New York who 'thought it worth making the journey' to discuss their work with him. One of the latter, the New York psychoanalyst Bernard Landis, subsequently recorded his impression of Harry as 'exceptionally considerate and generous'. He described how, after meeting him at the station Harry 'moved swiftly and with agility as [they] strode towards his car, a tan Morris Minor that had seen better days'. He amusingly recalls that Harry was not a natural driver: 'his rapid driving, fast turns and constant side glances as he spoke did not inspire confidence. Nonetheless, he was attentive in pointing out the sights, and courteous and warm in his manner.' When Landis discussed a patient he found Harry 'alert, his attention locked-in, his comments informed and straight-forward. He was opposed to sentimentality which stood in the way of unequivocal emotional commitment to the therapeutic endeavour.' In particular, Landis noted, Guntrip believed that 'the analyst must be able to find something of substantial value in the patient that he can reliably confirm, something pertaining to the patient's own capacity to nurture and create' (ibid., p. 117). Bertha's needs for 'human contacts' were partly served by her continued active membership of the church in Leeds, while in Aberford she was quickly becoming what her daughter later described as 'a natural counsellor who listens to her neighbours problems in such a therapeutic way that she is in great demand' (personal communication, 4 June 1991).

It would be misleading to suggest that Harry was solely interested in himself and his own activities. On the contrary, he was positively supportive of Sutherland in a way that suggests he had not forgotten the latter's readiness to listen when he had been crucially in need. Accordingly, when a wealthy former patient of his, Mr Geoffrey Ellis, became keen to support the promotion of psychotherapy, Guntrip acquainted him with Sutherland's plans to form a Scottish Institute of Human Relations in Edinburgh, and put the two men in touch with each other. Ellis subsequently made a considerable financial contribution to the new institute. Again I personally recall Guntrip's enthusiastic support of a paper of mine, expressing 'very great interest' in my work, and other ex-patients of his have remarked on his active and encouraging involvement in their undertakings at this time.

There is more in the tone of Harry's letters than simple recovery from illness. They suggest a 'renaissance', a regrowing of his basic personality after a therapeutic regression. Harry had always emphasised the value of 'post-analytic improvement', which he believed to be especially likely if the patient had good family support. It is therefore quite consistent with his view that his own regression should have been attended by Bertha, the 'natural counsellor', after the professionals had prepared the way. There is hardly any reference in the correspondence to Winnicott's death, doubtless because of Guntrip's conviction that Winnicott was, as he felt his own father to be, 'in a deep way alive' in him. However, in January 1972 Guntrip was again in London, 'by invitation', at the memorial meeting for Winnicott at the Psychoanalytic Institute, where he was greatly encouraged by Martin James who said that he was 'constantly being asked to lecture on Fairbairn, Winnicott – and Guntrip!' (personal communication, 19 January 1972). Perhaps the foregoing is sufficient reflection of Harry's rejuvenated capacity for living at this time, a year after his compelling dream-sequence. I myself, and 'certainly many others', were staggered by it. It was quite irrepressible, and much more than one asked for, or expected, which was already considerable! On re-reading the letters I am amazed afresh. However incomplete a result psychoanalytical therapy may have achieved within the limitations of its treatment, it had succeeded in establishing him at last in a state of mind to respond to and profit immeasurably from the love of his family, and to relate to his own patients, past and present, as valued friends. Thus, although he could still find himself, in dreams, exposed to 'the dread of aloneness' (see Landis 1981, p. 115), it seems fitting also that in January 1973 Harry had a vivid dream which seemed to him to confirm the strong sense of fatherly support expressed by his very first recorded dream in 1936. The dream was triggered by his study of his sessions with Fairbairn in 1949, and was as follows:

> Story of a great siege. I seemed to be besieged and father the immediate one conducting it. Yet we were together in the same place. I was saying firmly that whatever happened I would never give in. He realised that was true, and at length went to the final authority and said this. It was accepted and the siege was called off.[2]

He concluded: 'It was as if father was telling mother it was useless to think I would surrender to her, and she had to accept this; which she did' (sessional record of Fairbairn analysis 1949). The dream led Harry to feel that when his mother had occasionally called on his father to get him to submit to her in his early teens, Henry had retained some independence of her, and, as in the dream, had co-operated 'only so far as his own judgement went and then told her clearly that she must accept my growing away into independence of her'. Guntrip was much cheered by this dream as he pondered it, feeling 'a distinct mental relief, a settled state of mind that is hard to describe', and concluding 'so a problem created in childhood is never too late to mend, and if we know how to let our unconscious speak to us, a lifelong tension can be relieved even in the seventies. Age does not necessarily bring loss of capacity for emotional change and relief of longstanding tension' (ibid.).

In the spring of 1973 a new mission emerged when a group of psychiatrists to whom Harry was lecturing on psychotherapy in preparation for the Royal College examination complained of being unable to obtain Fairbairn's book *Psychoanalytic Studies of the*

Personality. Guntrip had lectured to more than seventy psychiatrists in the previous twelve months on psychoanalysis and psychotherapy and wished fervently to influence the Royal College training in an 'Object Relations' direction for which Fairbairn's later clinical material was an essential basis. Instead he saw an ominous tendency towards orthodoxy. In his view, 'The psychotherapy section of the Royal College of Psychiatrists must ultimately stimulate research . . . independently of the official society whose journal articles are often repetitive and dull' (personal communication, to J.D.S., 20 May 1973). The psychiatrists had been told by the publishers Kegan Paul that the book was out of print and not to be reprinted. Much discussion followed between Guntrip, Sutherland and Masud Khan, editor of the International Psychoanalytic Library. An additional problem was that Fairbairn's most progressive papers, on Hysteria and Therapy (Fairbairn 1954; 1958) which contained the phenomenological evidence for his recasting of the theory of endo-psychic structure, had been written after the book, and Kegan Paul would not agree to a revision to include them; neither would they release the copyright to another publisher. Guntrip, who did not think the book worth reprinting in its existing form, went to enormous lengths contacting Fairbairn's family, and drawing up a completely revised scheme for a comprehensive Fairbairn book which he submitted to other publishers; and to which he proposed to write an introduction: 'It would give me a chance to deal with the new anti-positivist "Realist Philosophy" which psychoanalysis needs, and which would have rejoiced Ronald.' By March 1973 he was writing to Sutherland that he was considering approaching Science House, New York, about an independent 'Fairbairn volume' of unpublished papers, and he invited Sutherland to contribute 'an introductory biography' of Fairbairn (personal communication, 20 July 1973). In the event Kegan Paul, probably aware of a rising tide of interest in 'object-relations theory', reprinted Fairbairn's book in its original form, and only recently in 1994 has Jason Aronson of New Jersey, USA, published two volumes of Fairbairn's collected papers, jointly edited by his daughter, Ellinor Fairbairn Birtles and Dr David E. Scharff.[3] However, although his project failed in 1973, Guntrip was fired with a still more ambitious mission: to use his own sessional notes of both his analyses in an innovative way, not least in order to show the significance of his own development of Fairbairn's theory. It was a mammoth project which was to remain the major preoccupation of Guntrip's remaining years. In March 1973 he wrote to Sutherland that his review of his session notes had prompted him to 'question: what is analysis?', adding, 'I share your view that if it is not therapeutic (Oedipal analysis misses the real problem too much to be more than superficially therapeutic), it is merely "analysis" an intellectual exercise' (personal communication, 20 March 1973). A month later Guntrip had warmed to his new theme. Making no reference to his trenchant letter of 10 October 1970, he wrote again to Sutherland:

> I have had it in mind for some time to write you [sic] about an unusual piece of research . . . which could be a study of a unique kind . . . You may remember my telling you of my amnesia for my brother's death when I was 3½ and of my reaction to it. That was never uncovered by either Fairbairn or Winnicott but to my surprise erupted spontaneously in a long compelling dream-sequence after my pneumonia illness.

He then unfolded the idea of 'an autobiographical psychoanalytic study of the continuous dreaming process' which would provide

> 'factual data' about the psychodynamic processes, of a kind that critics of psychoanalysis have no access to. It could be a study of dreams parallel to Marion Milner's study of drawings in *The Hands of the Living God*. (Personal communication, (24 April 1973).

Guntrip's phrase 'You may remember . . .', must have struck Sutherland as a trifle 'cool', in view of the urgent and deeply confiding tone of his letter two-and-a-half years earlier. Guntrip continued,

> I always felt I had an Oedipal and not an Object Relations analysis with Ronald and now I am beginning to see why I felt that.

From the vantage point of 1973, Guntrip began, with considerable excitement, to see in truer perspective the long journey he had been engaged on in his search for understanding. He saw, for example, how Fairbairn after his wife's death, and in failing health, began too late to conceptualise an 'object-relations therapy' to match his theory. He realised that, although Fairbairn accepted his suggestion of 'a final Ego-split, a Regressed Ego, as completing his theory, he could only see Regression as "Hysteric dependence on and exploitation of the analyst", not as "the patient needing his analyst to Recognise (Balint) that he needs the analyst to see his inability to relate to a non-relating to mother". He realised that Fairbairn had never really appreciated what 'schizoid' had come to mean to him – not 'repressed split-egos relating to split objects – Klein's inner world', but the 'sense of unreality, depersonalisation, a living death, withdrawal into a vacuum, the experience of having a mother *who doesn't relate* – all that Winnicott made so clinically plain a decade later, though he too failed to interpret that properly with his oddly inconsistent classic 'Id-theory' (personal communication, 24 March 1973). All this Guntrip made clear to Sutherland in this letter, so redolent of the extraordinary sense of enthusiasm and urgency that characterised him at this time. At the age of almost seventy-two, after twenty years of analysis, he felt fully alive in a way he never had before, despite his ailing physical health. His reputation continued to grow, increasingly in London, where his new self-revelatory style had attracted further interest, both at the Institute of Psychoanalysis, and at the Tavistock Clinic where he addressed the staff on 'Psychotherapy and Psychoanalysis', using 'a brief view of my own analysis to illustrate my argument as to "what is analysis". . . if it is not therapeutic, it is useless'. Also during the course of 1973 he published two papers, 'Sigmund Freud and Bertrand Russell' (1973a, in Hazell 1994, p. 315) and 'Science, Psychodynamic Reality and Autistic Thinking' (1973b, in Hazell 1994, p. 331), and when Jason Aronson wished to publish his collected papers, Guntrip was enthusiastic about this possibility, wishing especially 'to preserve the Aberdeen paper and the American papers', but was thwarted by shortage of time and the pressure of his new project. It gave me great pleasure to co-operate with Jason Aronson twenty years later in the production of a volume of Guntrip's papers.[4]

Guntrip's direct exposure of the limitations of Fairbairn's theory and analysis can hardly have been welcome from Sutherland's point of view, since Fairbairn had been his own analyst, and he queried the point that 'Fairbairn's theoretical advance did not get fully reflected in his psychotherapy.' Maybe he felt somewhat under pressure from Guntrip's determination, which the letters certainly convey – that he should co-operate in his new venture, and indeed in other lesser ventures, for there were many more requests that he should read through and comment upon Guntrip's lectures and papers. Maybe he also wondered whether he, like Fairbairn, had become Percy in transference, and subject to the dominance of a bossy elder brother, for he tentatively suggested that he and Harry might be 'siblings'. The response was unequivocal:

As to our being siblings, when I was an infant in psychoanalysis, you were, from my point of view, one of its venerable fathers, and you were literary godfather to my first papers and two most important books. I did not at first know you had had an analysis with Ronald. What our relationship has grown into is an intriguing question, but I know I can always get from you the most balanced judgement on any psychoanalytical matter. (Personal communication, 7 July 1973)

In fact, notwithstanding his late start as a psychotherapist, Guntrip was some four years Sutherland's senior in years, and it must indeed have seemed alarming to the latter to become the object of projections of venerable fatherhood. He therefore offered the further suggestion that there might be colleagues in Leeds with whom Guntrip could collaborate. Again, Guntrip's reaction was immediate and emphatic: 'You are all the more valuable because of my isolation here', and he went on to describe again the dearth of colleagues in the Department of Psychiatry, concluding,

The only people I could really discuss with are people like Padel, Milner, Martin James, Gosling, but even if I were in the Society, which I feel no desire to be, Leeds is so far away. If ever I need to discuss anything, you are the one person with whom I feel I have a genuine understanding. (Personal communication, 7 July 1973)

Sutherland seems to have accepted the responsibility willingly enough, and the Sunday evening phone conversations became something of a fixture. Clearly, underlying doubts remained over Guntrip's criticism of Fairbairn, despite a very clear – and fair – explanation from the former:

What in my experience (Fairbairn) assumed was that the IBO [Internalised Bad Object] relations being interpreted would enable the patient to give them up because he had a relationship with the analyst. He did not grasp that it is not a question of taking the place of the IBOs, but of the analyst seeing that the alternative to IBOs is originally having no objects at all: that that situation disintegrates the infant ego who cannot relate to the analyst unless he specifically sees and interprets that. He must be not just a GO [Good Object] but a 'GO who finds the patient in his empty world' where a non-maternal mother simply did not relate. What Winnicott did interpret with great clarity was what I had begun to know I was needing, that if IBOs are given up one is left with nothing and cannot do anything, cannot relate to the analyst as a good object, but can only wait for the analyst to do the relating; just as the infant has to wait for the mother to do the mothering. (Personal communication, 7 July 1973)

For the next year Sutherland received regularly copies of whole sections of a projected book on 'Fairbairn in Historical Perspective' with repeated requests that he should write 'the biographical introduction' and many reminders of the same. There was a strongly supportive quality in Sutherland's personality – stronger at times than his personal ambition. Thus, after Harry's death, he wrote to Gwen Greenald:

I have never indulged in much writing myself. I always seem to get involved in midwifery, i.e. getting other people's work born! – but I have been a great fan of your father's work because he was such a good expounder. Students certainly find his work most useful.

Guntrip had certainly chosen his 'literary godfather' well! Thus, although, from their correspondence, one gets the feeling that Sutherland was somewhat 'peppered', there is no hint of any great resistance, apart from a hint in one letter from Guntrip in October 1973, that he sensed some reluctance on the part of Sutherland to locate a fairly easily accessible Fairbairn reference and to supply the name and orientation of Fairbairn's analyst. Guntrip's letter ends, unsigned and with none of the customary good wishes, with a denunciation of Fairbairn's tripartite ego-splitting theory:

Incidentally, Ronald's Ego-splitting theory adhered too strictly to Freud's Tripartite scheme. Anti-LE–RO only accounts for aggression as *identification* with the RO against the LE, but not for *direct aggression*, anger, against the RO. Hence his CE is left to be simply Winnicott's 'False Self' on a conformity basis, which is a very incomplete analysis. (Personal communication, 4 December 1973)

There followed a post-script: 'I hope you will do an Introductory Biography.' Despite its acerbic tone, the criticism was cogent. In fact Guntrip became increasingly dissatisfied with theory, which according to Landis (1981) he came to regard as 'just a schizoid defence'. Landis later believed that, had he lived longer, Guntrip would have gone on to a major revision of object-relations theory where the internalised world would include all significant figures, not the mother alone. The tone of this letter is not at all characteristic, and it is probable that he felt threatened by three possibilities: first, that Sutherland might not wish to participate in his project; second, that he himself might run out of time before it was complete; and third, that his own development of Fairbairn's theory, although acknowledged by the latter, would remain unrecognised, and that he would be regarded as Fairbairn's pupil, having no distinct contribution of his own. This third concern became more powerful as time went on, and the first was clearly evident in his next letter to Sutherland, a month later, in which Guntrip announced his intention of sending Sutherland Chapters 2 to 5 of the Fairbairn book, amounting to about ninety pages. The letter ends,

> I should be very glad if, before I go further with this, and embark on the purely theory part of the book, chapters 6–8, you would let me have any criticisms, comments, emendations, etc. on chapters 2–5 . . . I also feel that you will want to know the kind of book I am writing, in order to know what kind of 'Biography' by you would best introduce it.

His awareness of the passage of time was clear when he stated that, despite 'not getting any younger', he intended a similar appraisal of Winnicott's work, including his own 1954 'letters of disagreement' to Winnicott, and 'also based on my sessional knowledge of how he went to work, in a very different way from Ronald – the kind of more personal, less abstract theoretical *presentation* that I feel psychoanalysis needs to make it "come alive"' (personal communication, 2 November 1973). An additional reason for 'getting a move on' he told Sutherland was mounting pressure from Spanish and Danish publishers who intended to include Fairbairn's papers on Hysteria and Art in their own productions. The third fear, mentioned above, of being, so to speak, associated too closely with Fairbairn, was expressed in a letter to Gwen and Denis Greenald. Referring to Chapters 2–5, Guntrip wrote: 'This is a necessary undertaking as my views cannot now be identified with Fairbairn's in some important respects, but my name is being linked with his.' Citing a recent (1972) paper, by Stephen Morse who referred to the 'Fairbairn–Guntrip metaphor', he continued, 'This kind of reference identifies me more exactly with Fairbairn than is now true, and I must clarify the issue' (personal communication, 10 December 1973). It is still not unusual to hear Guntrip described as a 'disciple', 'follower' or even 'pupil' of Fairbairn. But this view is now gradually changing, as for example in Josephine Klein's helpful book, *Our Need for Others and its Roots in Infancy* (1987) where she describes Guntrip as 'a considerable scholar of the old school. Deeply respecting the thoughts of others he characteristically wrote as if he were only clarifying what others had said: he is only gradually coming to be recognised as a thinker with a unique perspective of his own . . . the dating of his writing is relevant as being either post-Fairbairnian, or as after both Fairbairn and Winnicott' (p. 305). In fact Guntrip was generally enthusiastic about Morse's paper which put forward the view that the Fairbairn–Guntrip metaphor 'descriptively explained the data presented by Winnicott and Balint'. But he also claimed that he had 'anticipated Morse by some 20 years in his "letters of disagreement" with Winnicott in 1954.

After the contretemps of October 1973 the rate of correspondence increased markedly, with enquiries as to Sutherland's health and with the hope expressed that he kept 'fit and well'! Sutherland was due to go away on a trip to India in the New Year of 1974, which caused Guntrip to dispatch the carbon copies of Chapters 2–5 to him less than a week after he had first mentioned them. At the end of November Guntrip wrote, 'By the time you get back from India I hope to be well ahead with the "re-study of theory" chapters and I would like to have the book completed by soon after Easter or early summer; as I want to follow it up with one on Winnicott before I get much older . . . All good wishes for your India trip and I shall look forward to hearing from you, I suppose sometime in February 1974.' Guntrip himself mentions the strains imposed by looking after the old people, but reports, 'Fortunately my health holds good, except that I tire more quickly than I used to do' (personal communication, 27 November 1973). In the event, Sutherland's trip had to be cancelled, but, as may be anticipated from the foregoing, Guntrip did not spend much time on elaborate expression of sympathy. On 19 December, he wrote, 'Sorry your trip had to be cancelled. Meanwhile, I have decided, owing to the amount of material I had, to divide chapter 5 into two chapters': One to 'illustrate Fairbairn from his correspondence and discussions after sessions' and the other to 'illustrate Fairbairn in his interpretations in sessions, where they have theoretical bearings. Both, taken together, will show on the basis of my own analysis how my own psychopathology became the basis of my own theoretical development beyond Fairbairn and how he accepted that', and there was a post-script; 'I am enclosing the first twelve pages of chapter 7.' By late January he was planning 'a radical alteration' of the chapter order, so as to begin with the development of Fairbairn's theoretical views in a way which would emphasise how he had anticipated the new philosophy of science propounded by Karl Popper, which 'literally demolished' the nineteenth-century philosophy of science 'espoused by Freud', namely Positivist Empiricism (personal communication, 22 January 1974). He would then trace the development of Fairbairn's views through his Freudian, Kleinian, and Fairbairnian periods, 1923–35; 1935–39; 1940–54, thus emerging into the period of his own analysis with Fairbairn, by reference to which he would show 'signs of gradual change that led him to accept my extension of his theory', which would in turn lead on to the Winnicott formulations. Meanwhile there was still the question of Sutherland's 'Biographical first chapter'. India must have seemed very attractive! But despite the pressure and a certain importunate tone at times (for example, he needed Sutherland's opinion on whether an autobiographical section of his paper to the Independent Group 'would prove acceptable'), the spirit of the letters is one of bustling good will – invigorating on a good day and never impersonal.

The tone of the letters to the family at this period, towards the end of 1973, is warm and affectionate:

> Dear Gwen and Den, Mum says the riding lessons are £1.10 and you said weekly for six months, plus 3 for yourself. I said we'd go fifty-fifty, so I reckon 26 plus 3 at £1.10 is £31.90. Here's a cheque for £16. We shan't be in the Work House yet. For the first time in history the Income Tax people have sent me a cheque.

The royalties for one of his major books had accidentally been entered twice. £100 of the refund went immediately into 'Mum's Abbey National'.

> I feel she must have a sizeable sum she could draw on at need in case of any emergency to me: so we are saving while I am still able to earn with five patients and lectures. (Personal communication, 18 September 1973)

At this time, the 'tiring' he had mentioned to Sutherland was bringing attendant fears over financial insecurity. He had no pension, and it is characteristic that in such matters, he thought first of Bertha. He was now giving eight patient sessions a week for his five patients, and one regular lecture every week for two terms in the Department (twenty weeks) plus extras at the Tavistock, where the staff had welcomed the autobiographical section of his previous talk, and the Institute of Psychoanalysis, where Bowlby and Gosling had invited him to give a paper. At seventy-two, he was feeling the strain, and he was beginning to realise that he could not expect to do that amount of work 'for more than another two years'. However, he did not at that time extend his prognosis to written work. He wrote:

> When patients and lectures come to an end, I have enough publishing work on the stocks to last several years, possibly from books, Fairbairn's Collected Papers, my own Collected Papers, which New York have invited me to send them, and two new studies of Fairbairn and Winnicott based on some fascinating material I've found in my records of my own analyses. (ibid.)

He pointed out that this 'summary view of his plans for the immediate future' was conditional upon,

> what happens next door. I do all I can to help Mum, but there's so much a man can't do for two old ladies, that mostly I have to do what I can take off her hands here – to free her for next door. (ibid.)

Harry's involvement in the care of the old ladies, one of whom, Bertha's aunt, was becoming increasingly disturbed and difficult, was deeply sincere. Bertha's mother (now ninety-two) had been a tremendous support throughout their marriage, especially during the trials caused by Harry's own mother. This letter of September 1973 is a good example of the development of Harry's relationship with Gwen and her family. He had learned from the encounter nearly twenty years earlier, and the remainder of the letter includes references to his recent paper on Freud and Russell, a reprint of which he enclosed, enquiries after his grandchildren ('How about the boys? If there's anything cropping up for them comparable to Alison's riding, let us know'), interest in Alison's progress at a new school, and a poignant reference to the sudden demise of the wife of Earl Witenberg who had hosted Harry and Bertha's first trip to America:

> She was a splendid person, in children's work, and had just received the printer's proofs of her first book *The Emerging Child*. (1973)

The letter ends, 'With our love to everyone, Mum and Dad.' I have chosen to quote at length from the letter because it is a true

example of how Guntrip's whole personality expanded after his
analysis with Winnicott. He was in no sense cut-off from his
family. On the contrary, *he related personally at every level* and in
every area of his experience, whether he was discussing 'family
matters' or the new philosophy of science. Professional colleagues
felt 'conversed with' by a friend: never 'lectured to'. Life had
acquired the feeling of an adventure for him and he wanted to take
others along with him! He felt the journey was not worth making
if it excluded anyone else. At the same time no-one was left in
doubt as to his views. His response to a cutting about American
Humanistic Psychology sent by Gwen was typical:

> It was right about Behaviourism being mechanistic, failed to
> appreciate that psychoanalysis as 'deterministic' only applies to
> classic orthodox Freud, and as for 'Humanistic Psychology', this
> is only seriously represented by post-Freudian 'personal relation
> theory' – certainly not by American crazes for a new group
> psychology, the destructive results of their 'Encounter Groups'
> and the final advice given in the cutting, that in groups people
> should introduce themselves to each other by 'feeling each other
> all over and talking of their sex life'. Could anything be more
> contrived, stagey and artificial? (Personal communication, 12
> October 1973).

The letters to the family are so packed with so wide a variety of
views and opinions that they seem at times more like those of a
young man in his twenties. At this stage, too, in the winter of
1973 his physical powers were holding good, despite the weariness
and some slight memory impairment. He and Bertha were able to
get someone to help with the old ladies,

> giving Mum and me a chance to get out walking for 3 days and
> do some shopping in Wetherby. One day we did a four hour
> walk, all through fields.

Although regular visits to Salem Church in Leeds were not now
possible, Harry preached a sermon at the 189th Anniversary of the
Church. He had lost none of his reforming zeal:

> The Kingdom of God, of love, is a far larger concept than of the
> Church. It exists and grows wherever basic human rights and
> needs are honoured . . .   The Kingdom of God is the slow decay
> of fear, and it's main by-product, cruelty, and the growth of

co-operation and love ... The Church is the fellowship of those who consciously seek to help each other to serve the growth of the Kingdom in this world, a world which is always groaning with the labour pains of yet larger and more significant growth towards unity and mutual responsibility.

This was typical of the optimism he felt about human nature. He really believed in the intrinsic value of man – and that his 'social nature', 'from the religious point of view his God-given nature', was the most profound product of the evolutionary process. It was the task of religions and psychotherapeutic endeavours alike to work towards the full realisation of the social nature of man in personal relations. He was a great orator, with an international reputation, and copies of his sermon were produced and sold, and the proceeds sent to 'Christian Aid'. He was still giving public lectures at this time: the Hargreaves Memorial lecture in Leeds, and the Kincardine lecture at Bristol University – 'Facts and Values in Psychoanalytic Psychotherapy' – in addition to the lectures in his own department to MSc psychologists, and also to psychiatrists sitting the Royal College Examinations. Guntrip felt especially concerned for those psychiatrists who had qualified before the Royal College was established and who were now required to sit an examination for membership. He was lecturing on a 'crash course' for them.

Guntrip's religious and psychological preoccupations did not blind him to the importance of politics. In a letter to the family in March 1974, when the miner's strike forced the country to prepare for an early election, he was characteristically definite in his views. The *Guardian* newspaper had favoured a coalition of the Labour and Liberal parties. Guntrip disagreed:

Any coalition would, it seems to me, risk sabotaging the remarkable upsurge of Liberal opinion, and I'm for the Liberals holding on to their integrity as a distinct political force which could make a very big stride forward when the next election comes. When it does we shall vote for them.

He hoped for an end to 'two-party warfare' 'by a middle-of-the-road alternative', in which the problems of the time (the miner's strike and cost-of-living inflation) could be confronted with 'moderation and good sense'. He felt that, whereas proportional representation would only fragment the electorate, nonetheless

when the third party can poll 50% of the votes obtained by each of
the other two respectively, such a big chunk of national opinion
has a right to a bigger say in the process of government.

The provocation for this political statement was a remark of his
daughter's that she 'suspected that he and Bertha voted Conservative', which brought the old battle between them to modified life.
He replied,

It sounded as if you thought we were becoming ageing old fogies
playing for safety . . .   whatever you thought, you were out of
touch with our thinking. I have always been basically anti-Tory
as my father was. I dislike the mentality of the general run-
of-the-mill landed aristocracy (who are being taxed out steadily
by death duties) and the 'ugly face of capitalism' and financial
speculators! – though we are all better off under them than we
would be in any brand of 'totalitarianism'.

Guntrip's reservations about the Labour Government were partly on
account of his distrust of Harold Wilson, but also to do with its stand
against the European Common Market. He wrote prophetically:

I won't vote Labour while they are so anti-Common market. I
don't think we shall gain materially by being in, but it's a far
bigger issue than that. In 20 to 50 years time, between USA
and Soviet Russia, a fast-growing China and a developing third
world, a disunited Europe will be at the mercy of world events
with no effective voice or power. Ultimately I believe a United
Europe is as necessary as a United Nations, even if it is hard to
get. Labour's antagonism is based on short term mercenary
motives, 'prices' rather than 'principles'. (Personal communication, 3 March 1974)

The seriousness of this letter is softened by a humorous cutting
from *The Frog Book*, sadly anonymous, as follows:

What a wonderful bird the frog are –
When he stands, he sit almost
When he hop he fly almost.
He ain't got no sense hardly;
He ain't got no tail hardly either
When he sit, he sit on what he ain't
got almost.

Guntrip had underlined the last line in ink, and commented, 'Heath or Wilson!'

At the end of March Harry and Bertha managed a 'full five days' in the Yorkshire Dales, following a particularly taxing week with the old ladies. Bertha had been driven to highly untypical anger, and Harry had succumbed to eye strain, headaches and fatigue. He had become afraid that he would not finish his writing:

> If I had to leave my final research project unfinished, especially now that I've done at least half of it in the first draft, I would feel depressed. A week away, a proper holiday this time, around our beloved Pen-y-Ghent, will do us a lot of good. (Personal communication, 29 March 1974)

On their return Harry and Bertha had to accept that the old ladies' condition had deteriorated to a point beyond their capacity to look after them at home. The doctor was consulted and a nursing home selected, and paid for by the old people's savings, wisely invested. Despite a routine of twice-weekly visits of twenty-two miles each way, Harry and Bertha's freedom of movement, severely restricted over the last year, was now restored. Guntrip wrote to Gwen and Denis, 'It should be possible now for us, when we get settled to our "new life", to pop over (to Chester) to see you for a day or two now and again.' Moreover, the old ladies' house was still available for use and arrangements were made for Gwen, Denis and their three children ('the trio') to come to stay there between Christmas and the New Year 'and have a chance to see one or two of our lovely walks here if the weather is good. Make it a few days if you can' (23 August 1974). Regrettably, however, the accumulated strain of nursing the old folk marred the 'new life' considerably and, as the Guntrips prepared for another holiday that September – 'the first holiday for 15 months which we can enjoy in a really carefree state of mind' – Bertha developed a skin irritation all over her back and Harry was 'getting a tight head and eye strain whenever I read or type'. He added,

> I have felt very disturbed recently, feeling that age is catching up on both of us, and I may not be able to complete my research plans which will take another two years at least; but I begin to feel again that I'll manage it. I've completed about half of the final 'Fairbairn book'. (23 August 1974)

It seems likely that his use of 'final' meant that he could not

confidently contemplate a 'Winnicott' book as he had hoped, or
even a book of his own collected papers. In a spirit of compromise,
he decided to offer a condensed 'psychoanalytic autobiographical
study' of his experience of analysis with Fairbairn and Winnicott to
the International Review of Psychoanalysis, 'who are considering it
but probably find it too disturbing for the orthodox'. He felt the
material had aroused so much interest that 'it must be published
somewhere' (ibid., 23 August 1974). In the same remarkable letter
to his daughter and son-in-law, which ranged over so many issues,
both professional and personal, Guntrip wrote,

> Our experience with the old ladies has made us feel we must
> never risk landing you with such a problem, and whenever our
> final move has to be made we would hope that it would at first
> be to a small place of our own near to you, and give us a
> chance to have a look around at whatever 'Residential Homes
> for Elderly People' there may be, and select one and keep
> enough capital to pay for that and leave some for you. Our
> expenses are small, and in the meantime, we shall save hard
> and still enjoy ourselves. (ibid., 23 August 1974)

The letter concluded: 'Mum and I are now going to wash up, and
go out for a care-free stroll.' Guntrip's lecturing was still generating
a small income, but he only had four patients continuing from the
ten he had kept when they moved from Leeds three years before.
The rest of his income came from the royalties on his books which
were selling world-wide, and from public engagements, a notable
example of which was the arrival in Aberford, in the last week of
August, of

> two professors from Tennessee, who came and stayed at the Swan
> Hotel and videotaped four sessions of 1½ hours each discussion,
> plying me with questions on 'British Object-Relations Theory',
> which is growing markedly in America'. (ibid., 23 August 1974)

They were Harold J. Fine, PhD, Professor of Psychology and Director of the Clinical Training programme at the University of Tennessee, and Dr Jack Barlow, Clinical Psychologist at the Helen
Ross McNab Centre, 'a non-profit corporation for the diagnosis,
treatment and prevention of emotional illness'. On the basis of
their visit, Fine and Barlow established the Harry J.S. Guntrip
Postgraduate Training Institute in Knoxville, Tennessee. In the
prospectus, Barlow described Guntrip as

a spry, talkative man who seemed to take great pleasure in thinking and teaching. He was one of the kindest men I ever met, yet he showed a sense of assurance and independence which made it clear that no-one was to take advantage of this aspect of him – lest one sense it as a weakness rather than a strength . . . He outlines his practice as a personal venture which must, by the very nature of persons, be devoid of manipulation, trickery or techniques. Because of this . . . 'relatedness' is the central efficacious aspect of any analytic endeavour.

One of the stated aims of the Institute was 'to allow the time that is necessary for substantial development of the individual to take place' despite a 'managerial miasma of "quick care"'. When Barlow consulted Guntrip on how this might be achieved, the latter's 'off-the-cuff' response was characteristic,

It is a matter of how you can do the best possible under the necessity of conforming to the irrational demands of an uncomprehending environment (pause, laughter) I personally would fight it. I know you may not be able to; and probably I'd be kicked out.

On return from holiday Guntrip was again in touch with Sutherland. He had by then received a first draft of Sutherland's 'Biographical chapter' but was concerned that '"the real man" was lost in the final pages. . .; just where I am sure "hard evidence" is needed that he did not just peter out into senility'. Guntrip supplied the evidence in the form of a number of 'treasured letters' which showed how Fairbairn had declined badly between 1958 and 1961, when he was very ill; but how he rallied from 1962 onwards, and

clearly read quite a bit of psychoanalytic stuff and saw some patients . . . [and] gave me clear evidence that he understood and appreciated what I was doing, and so to speak, specifically took me into partnership in the development of his theory. (Personal communication, 24 September 1974)

Guntrip wished Sutherland to grasp the fact, not only that Fairbairn had accepted and valued his own development of theory, but that he had been mentally alert when he did so! He also made it clear that he intended to use the letters in the final chapter of his book ('The Creative Years') so that it would be very appropriate if you could make use of them to give a condensed closing page or two of your chapter, to leave the impression of a Fairbairn, not senile and out of touch, but still reading and thinking psychoanalytically, and actively supporting me in the further development of his basic views. (ibid. 24 September 1974)

He added that Marion Fairbairn, Fairbairn's widow, had written that he and Bertha, by their visits, had 'helped to keep the real Ronald, the thinking analyst, alive in him almost to the end'.

As the new University term began that October, Guntrip was greatly encouraged by

the tremendous news, though it's come too late for my liking, our department (mainly because of the outlook and drive of our fine clinical psychologist, Alan Dobbs, a Tavistock man), is creating a two-term course for a 'Diploma in Psychotherapy', which will be open, not only to psychiatrists (like the Aberdeen diploma), but to Educational Psychologists, Child Care Workers, etc., i.e. non-medicals who have a University degree or diploma in psychology of a broad kind. Certainly the standing I have acquired on behalf of psychotherapy over the years has played a big part in preparing the ground for Leeds to be the first British University to create a 'Psychotherapy' qualification. I am asked to take a 50% rôle in the course. (Personal communication, to Gwen and Denis, 12 November 1974)

The lectures which were to take place on Tuesday evenings from six o'clock were a considerable addition to Guntrip's workload. He was still lecturing to post-graduate clinical psychologists and psychiatrists, and he confided to Gwen and Denis, 'I feel doubtful if I can cope, but will be bitterly disappointed if I can't.'

Guntrip's doubt over his ability to cope was due to what he believed to be a 'stomach-strain' caused by lifting Bertha's mother after an accident at the nursing home. The strain was later misdiagnosed as a hiatal hernia, for which Harry was advised that surgery was rarely successful. Harry's eating difficulties and Bertha's skin irritation had robbed their September holiday of the restorative effect that they had hoped for, and they were feeling 'very cut off from personal contacts' as winter approached. Harry was, however, delighted by Sutherland's introductory chapter, and still aiming to finish Volume 1 of the Fairbairn book by Easter. A further encouragement that autumn came in the form of a most pressing invitation to go to the Menninger Psycho-therapy Clinic, Topeka, Kansas early next year as chief guest speaker at their 50th Anniversary Celebration. It is a famous and progressive American foundation and has always favoured Fairbairn's views. I had a letter from the founder, Dr Karl Men-ninger, a good many years ago. How I'd love to be able to accept, but I can't. Even if I were physically fit enough, I could-n't go away for ten days to America and leave Mum to see to everything. (Personal communication, to Gwen and Denis, 15 October 1974)

Guntrip's earlier letter from Karl Menninger had been to inform him that he was pleased to have a copy of *Personality Structure and Human Interaction* for the Menninger library. The letter from the present 'Head of the Menninger' was indeed inviting:

I am sending this invitation to you to deliver the lecture on our program on behalf of many of my colleagues who have urged me to convey their gratitude for your pace-setting work in clini-cal theory and therapeutic practice. They have so often wished to meet you. (ibid., 15 October 1974)

Guntrip had to decline, but promised to write a paper for the occasion – which, however, he was unable to produce.

Guntrip was now obliged to accept the limitation imposed by his own deteriorating physical health, but he could still sometimes think in terms of two further books when the Fairbairn one was finished. He wrote to Gwen and Denis:

I think what makes me more tense than I want to be is the knowledge that recent events have put me a good six months behind with my research writing. If I am to complete what I regard as my 'life-work', and I have much encouragement to feel it is worth doing, I shall need to keep fit enough for hard concentrated study for at least another two if not three years. As yet I find I lecture as well as ever, but I'm so much more tired afterwards that I realise I am up against physical limits I have not experienced before. I think it is this sense of 'pressure of time' when other things prevent me getting on with the Fairbairn book, which would be the first of the three. I have done about two thirds of it, but much of that will need final revision yet. (ibid., 15 October 1974)

Ever the pragmatist, Guntrip added that a further incentive to press
on with his writing was the knowledge that the book would sell
well in America. 'As income from lecture fees and patients fades
out, it will be a help to have an income from American dollars.'
(The rate of exchange at the time was £1.00 = $2.40.)

By mid-November, Guntrip had 'practically finished Fairbairn
parts 1 and 2' (to the end of the Kleinian period) and 'hoped to
start on the "creative period", 1940–54 before Christmas'. 'If I can
do that', he wrote to Sutherland, 'the whole should be completed
by the middle of next year. We are both hoping that a good holiday
will give us more energy than we feel we have at present. All good
wishes to you both for your holiday. Yours Harry' (personal communication, 12 November 1974). He wrote again a fortnight later
that he was 'fairly satisfied' on re-reading Parts 1 and 2 (Chapters
2–5) and that he was embarking on the 'Creative Years' (Chapter
6). This would conclude Volume 1; and Volume 2 would

> have to comprise the period of my later analysis with [Fair-
> bairn], his acceptance of my extension of his theory, and a
> study of its limitations of the kind that necessitates Winnicott's
> work as the real post-Fairbairnian development of 'Personal
> Object-Relations Theory' on the lines of my paper to the Insti-
> tute, (now accepted by Sandler for the new International Re-
> view), and using my own sessional material, much as I did in
> that paper. (Personal communication, 26 November 74)

There is no record of further communication with Sutherland by
letter, though they may have been in touch by telephone. It seems
that the bulk of the material for the Fairbairn book remained with
the Guntrip family until, in accordance with Harry's wishes, they
entrusted it to Sutherland.

Harry's correspondence with the family continued as before
through January, with that unique combination of vigour and
intimacy. He and Bertha had managed to sell 'No. 3' – the bungalow
previously occupied by the old ladies, and with their consent, had
made over some furnishings to Gwen and Denis. But the extra strain
of the house sale had made them realise 'how perilously near exhaustion we have been pushed. It's curious how one can rise to an occasion when you have to and only find out afterwards how much you
have been pushing yourself' (personal communication, 24 January
1975). The situation was indeed serious. Although Harry did not
know it, the condition diagnosed as a hiatal hernia was really cancer
of the oesophagus. The letters of that period in January 1975, had a

retrospective tone, as Harry compared the physical energy of his daughter and son-in-law to his own and that of Bertha.

> We rather envy you your physical fitness, but as we look back we feel we were fortunate. We had my mother living with us for 9 years altogether, 1942–43, and then 1944–52, and pretty awful it was very often. But, when after she died, we began our 'climbing careers' in the Lakes and then Glencoe and the Cairngorms, we were in our fifties, older than you are now. We were lucky, we feel, to have been able to collect so many happy memories after so late a start.

He had even become more reconciled to Harold Wilson and the Labour Party, and was impressed by Len Murray, the TUC Secretary – 'even though a Communist, he shows judgement and sound sense'. By contrast he felt that the Tory Party was fading into impotence with no clear leader: 'Heaven help them if they choose Margaret Thatcher'! However, his love of his family and his lively interest in the world could not conceal the reality of his physical deterioration and he wrote:

> All through December up to Wednesday 15 January when the house was sold, the strain mounted and the fact that that coincided with the period of maximum lecture pressure for me was real bad luck. On Tuesday evening, 14 January, I think for the first time ever, I felt tired and having to push myself while actually giving the lecture. Now that the immediate pressure is off, we feel the 'will' to push ourselves anymore has gone for the time being ... The last few days I have had to give up serious work and just lie on the bed like a log for 1½ hours two or three times a day. Unfortunately Mum can't do that, it only makes her more restless. However, we are laying off all we can and letting things slide till we regain our energy ... mum is worried because I have gone so thin, lost over a stone [in] weight in the last three months. I'm sure the hernia has a lot to do with it ... We feel that the last 1½ years have pushed us two or three years too soon into old age, and I feel distinct anxiety about whether I can now complete enough of my final research project to publish. We must wait and see, and meanwhile we support each other as best we can.

Harry was still seeing four patients that January, one of whom had broken down under severe external pressures into a suicidal state.

Another was near to death following a road accident. It is clear
from the the letter that Harry responded to these demands as a
matter of urgent priority. This letter written at the end of January
was his last to the whole family. It ended:

> However, we shall perk up in time, but for now we can do
> nothing to force the pace: only be patient. I hope to be able to
> write more cheerfully in due course.
>   Our love to you all – Mum and Dad.

Harry's last letter was written from hospital on the night before his
operation (12 February 1974), after a visit by Gwen and Bertha.
The letter was to his son-in-law, Denis, to whom he wished to
express his appreciation for his 'most generous and affectionate
support in making it possible for Gwen to come here and be such
a support to Mum'. He had by then spoken with the surgeon who
had been 'kindly frank' in explaining that the cancer might be too
widespread and malignant to eradicate. Harry's main concern was
not for himself: 'I can and will face whatever has to be.' He wished
Denis to know that he had three main concerns: firstly Bertha: 'If I
have to go first I shall feel secure in Gwen and yourself standing
by her'; secondly

> I dearly wanted to complete my life work in research. The Fair-
> bairn–Winnicott final stage of it is 50% completed and now, it
> may be I can't finish it. That would be a bitter disappointment.

thirdly:

> The deep affection and interest in which both Mum and I
> follow all the busy, fascinating activities and interests of your
> doings with Gwen and the trio. I don't want to be robbed of
> that. But I shall face whatever comes, and I want you to know
> that you, yourself, and Gwen, and the trio are a very great
> solace and support to me. By tomorrow night I may know the
> worst and/or best. Mum would join me in sending our very
> warm affection to you all.
>   Yours, Dad.

As usual there was a postcript: 'Please thank the boys for their
letters. I'll write to Ali (not Muhammed) as soon as I am able after
the operation. Her letters delight the staff here.'
    Harry died six days later, on 18 February 1975. There can be no
finer tribute to his memory than the Obituary written by his son-

in-law, Denis, and published in the *Bulletin of the British Psychological Society* in September 1975.

H.J.S. GUNTRIP (1901–75)

Harry Guntrip was my father-in-law – I married his only daughter Gwen in 1950 and knew him well for 25 years. Our relationship was a particularly happy one – I found in him the capacity to discuss a wide range of political and philosophical issues without the element of confrontation which marred similar discussions with my own father; he found in me, I like to think, the son he never had. He was the most open and honest man I have ever known – and this trait was central not only to his undogmatic approach to psychology and religion but also to his family relationships. To us as a young couple he was a model of non-directive support – never repressive or demanding, generous with his time and interest yet expressing a quiet confidence in our ability to manage our own affairs.

The practice and theory of psychotherapy dominated his life and in the time I knew him he became the doyen of British psychotherapists with a reputation that was world-wide. He carried introspection and the probing of his own psyche to a depth which few have dared. Hundreds of hours of analytic sessions with Allen, Maberley, Fairbairn and Winnicott, together with every dream were all carefully recorded along with his attempts to extract meaning from them. His aim was to discover with the help of others the truth about himself not by answering standardised questionnaires, but in the laboratory of his own mind. This, he argued cogently, had every claim to scientific validity, and those who sought to exclude such matters from 'science' were merely imposing a semantic restriction to meet their own criteria. Although he recognised the value of drug treatment and behavioural techniques he was too conscious of the ethical problems inherent in any attempt to manipulate and predict human behaviour, to accept them unreservedly. He saw his patients with potential for psychological growth but inhibited by psychic conflicts from functioning effectively: his job was that of a catalyst who would provide the facilitating environment which had been denied them in infancy. The almost obsessive search for this in himself might have resulted in egocentricity – instead it was used with prodigious energy and a rare creative flair to help his patients and to carry forward the development of theoretical psychoanalysis. Theory and practice were for him inseparable – theory as an end in itself, which did not inform practice was sterile; practise must illuminate and modify theory. Nearly all his theoretical writings are enlivened and humanized by an apt quotation from an actual psychothera-peutic session. People and their relationships with each other were his central concern and he felt that some aspects of clini-cal psychology and orthodox psychiatry tended to ignore this. This tendency reached perhaps a high point in the sixties and one of the more heartening developments to him in recent years was the growing number of articles in this Bulletin which emphasized the interaction of human beings as the proper concern of psychology.

Although 73, his death could genuinely be said to be untimely – four or five more years were all he asked for. He discussed this, many times – 'there are just three more books I'd like to write'. There was no flagging of his intellectual vigour and questing spirit: we, his family and his professional colleagues, will miss him greatly.

Later that year, Bertha received a letter from Sir Martin Roth, then President of the Royal College of Psychiatrists, saying that the Court of Electors had decided in January to confer on Harry an Honorary Fellowship, with a citation paying tribute to his work – the highest honour the college could offer. The ceremony was to have been in August – too late; but such a rare honour for a 'non-medical'.

Dr J.D. Sutherland took over the responsibility for editing Gun-trip's outstanding work. After much considered discussion with the family it was mutually agreed that Sutherland should offer Guntrip's writing on science and psychoanalysis to the *British Journal of Medi-cal Psychology*, where it duly appeared under the title 'Psychoanalysis and some Scientific and Philosophical Critics' (1978, in Hazell 1994, p. 371). In a footnote Sutherland stated that the paper, which was prepared by Guntrip himself just before he died, was a 'shortened version of the first part of a fresh systematic appraisal of Object Relations theory', and added 'The quality and independence of Dr Guntrip's thinking in clarifying issues that have bedevilled the status of psychodynamic thought add greatly to our regret that his larger work had not progressed enough for publication.' The 'larger work', consisting of the chapters on the development of Fairbairn's thought, and the psychoanalytic and autobiographical material were judged by Sutherland to be too disorganised and repetitious to form a book. Bertha herself had felt 'uncomfortable about the repetitions in Harry's work, which I realise mark Harry's beliefs and intense urge to spread the gospel'. She felt that 'Harry was far more ill than he realised over a long period, and sad as it is, and devastatingly disappointing to him, prevented his progress' (personal communication, 21 September 1976). Gwen wrote to Sutherland, 'We feel that the "book" as such, should definitely, in view of your comment, be abandoned. To attempt to finish it would be too demanding for anyone else. I feel quite happy in making this decision, as I am sure my father would have agreed . . . Had the book been virtually finished, and needed only trimming, editing, etc., it would have been a very different matter' (personal communication, to J.D.S., 7 October 1976).

The family finally agreed with Sutherland's suggestion that he should 'ask the Psychoanalytic Society in the first place about the autobiography . . . on the grounds that it would be more fitting for the manuscript to stay in the UK. On the other hand, if there is little likelihood of them doing anything with it, e.g. making it known as available for study to senior students, then we'd better go to the USA' (letter from J.D.S. to G.G., 15 October 1976). The autobiography and the account of the analyses were subsequently stored at the Menninger library, where they are preserved for the attention of 'senior students'. It seems likely that Sutherland was able to use some of the material on the development of Fairbairn's thought in his book, *Fairbairn's Journey into the Interior*, for he wrote to Gwen: 'If you are agreeable, I'll hold on to the manuscript I have of the Fairbairn book as I might be able to make some use of it for another article – probably by substantial quotations. It was, of course disappointing that the Fairbairn book hadn't more to it' (letter from J.D.S. to G.G., 15 October 1976).

In 1984, he wrote to Bertha Guntrip, 'Harry's work is immensely important, and more and more people in the USA are recognising it. I felt somewhat embarrassed at being described as Harry's literary executor, as it was a rather grand title I never claimed. I am glad, however, that his autobiography is at the Menninger, as they will look after it, as well as making it available to bona fide students. I am sure that one day, perhaps not too far off, someone will manage to make a shorter account that can be published widely. There is no doubt that he became one of the psychoanalytic immortals' (letter to B.G. from J.D.S., 1 October 1984).

Notes

1   Silvano Arieti (ed.), 1974, *American Handbook of Psychiatry*, 2nd edn, Volume 1: *The Foundations of Psychiatry*, Chapter 39 B. Psychoanalytic Object Relations Theory: The Fairbairn–Guntrip Approach.

2   This dream bears a close resemblance to that quoted by Guntrip in
     his published account of his analyses (Guntrip 1975, in Hazell 1994,
     p. 356). They are probably one and the same.
3   *From Instinct to Self: Selected Papers of W.R.D. Fairbairn*, Vol. I:
     Clinical and Theoretical Contributions; Vol. II: *Applications and Early
     Contributions.* Jason Aronson 1994.
4   *Personal Relations Therapy: The Collected Papers of H.J.S. Guntrip.*
     Hazell (1994).

Bibliography

Bacal, H. and Newman, K. (1990) *Theories of Object Relations: Bridges to Self Psychology*. New York: Columbia University Press.

Balint, M. (1968) *The Basic Fault: Therapeutic Aspects of Regression*. London: Tavistock.

Dicks, H.V. (1939) *Clinical Studies in Psychopathology*. London: Arnold.

Fairbairn, W.R.D. (1952) *Psychoanalytic Studies of the Personality*. London: Tavistock.

— (1954) 'Observations on the Nature of Hysterical States'. *British Journal of Medical Psychology* 27:105–25.

— (1958) 'On the Nature and Aims of Psychoanalytical Treatment'. *International Journal of Psychoanalysis* 39:374–85.

Flugel, J.C. (1933) *A Hundred Years of Psychology*. London: Duckworth.

Greenald, D. (1975) 'H.J.S. Guntrip (1901–1975)'. *Bulletin of the British Psychological Society*.

Guntrip, H.J.S. **Books**

— (1944) *Smith and Wrigley: The Story of a Great Pastorate*. London: Independent Press.

— (1949) *Psychology for Ministers and Social Workers*. London: Independent Press.

— (1951) *You and Your Nerves* (reprinted 1970 with additional chapters and retitled *Your Mind and Your Health*). London: Allen and Unwin.

— (1956) *Mental Pain and the Cure of Souls*. London: Independent Press.

— (1961) *Personality Structure and Human Interaction*. London: Hogarth.

— (1964) *Healing the Sick Mind*. London: Allen and Unwin.

— (1968) *Schizoid Phenomena, Object Relations and the Self*. London: Hogarth and the Institute of Psychoanalysis.

— (1971) *Psychoanalytic Theory, Therapy and the Self*. New York: Basic Books.

— (1974) 'Psychoanalytic Object Relations Theory: The Fairbairn-Guntrip Approach', in *American Handbook of Psychiatry*. Second Edition. Silvano Arieti, ed.; Volume I. Ch. 39: 'The Foundations of Psychiatry'. New York: Basic Books.

Guntrip, H.J.S. **Papers** in Hazell, J. (ed.) (1994) *Personal Relations Therapy: The Collected Papers of H.J.S. Guntrip*. New Jersey: Aronson.

Hazell, J. (1991) 'Reflections on My Experience of Psychoanalysis with Guntrip', *Contemporary Psychoanalysis* 27(1): 148–66.

Holbrook, D. (1972) *The Masks of Hate*. London: Pergamon.

Home, H.J. (1966) 'The Concept of Mind'. *International Journal of Psychoanalysis* 47.

Klein, J. (1987) *Our Need for Others and its Roots in Infancy*. London: Tavistock.

Landis, B. (1981) 'Discussions with Harry Guntrip'. *Contemporary Psychoanalysis* 17(1): 112–17.

MacMurray, J. (1933) *Interpreting the Universe*. London: Faber.

— (1935) *Reason and Emotion*. London: Faber.

— (1939) *The Boundaries of Science*. London: Faber.

McDougal, W. (1912) *Psychology, the Study of Behaviour*. Home University Library.

Milner, M. (1950) *On Not Being Able to Paint*. New York: International Universities Press Inc.

— (1969) *The Hands of the Living God*. New York: International Universities Press Inc.

Morse, S. (1972) 'Structure and Reconstruction: a critical comparison of Michael Balint and D.W. Winnicott', *International Journal of Psychoanalysis* 53:487–500.

Popper, Sir K. (1959) *The Logic of Scientific Discovery*. London: Hutchinson.

Scharff, D.E. and Fairbairn-Birtles, E. (1994) *From Instinct to Self: Selected Papers of W.R.D. Fairbairn*. New Jersey: Aronson.

Segal, H. (1964) *Introduction to the Work of Melanie Klein*. London: Heinemann.

Sutherland, J.D. (1989) *Fairbairn's Journey into the Interior*. London: Free Association Books.

Tizard, L. and Guntrip, H. (1959) *Facing Life and Death*. London: Allen and Unwin.

— (1959) *Middle Age*. London: Allen and Unwin.

Winnicott, D.W. and Kahn, M. (1953) 'Review of Psychoanalytic Studies of the Personality by W.R.D. Fairbairn', in *International Journal of Psychoanalysis* Vol. 34, part 4: 329–33.

Winnicott, D.W. (1954) 'Metapsychological and Clinical Aspects of

Regression within the Psychoanalytical Set-up', in Winnicott 1958.

— (1955) 'Clinical Varieties of Transference' in Winnicott 1958.
— (1958) *Through Paediatrics to Psychoanalysis*. London: Hogarth.
— (1960) 'Ego Distortion in Terms of True and False Self' in Winnicott 1965.
— (1963) 'On Communicating and Not Communicating, Leading to a Study of Certain Opposites' in Winnicott 1965.
— (1965) *The Maturational Processes and the Facility Environment*. London: Hogarth.
— (1967) 'The Location of the Cultural Experience' in Winnicott 1971.
— (1968) 'The Use of the Object and Relating through Identification' (unpublished paper) in Winnicott 1971.
— (1971) *Playing and Reality*. London: Hogarth.
Witenberg, M.J. and Brusiloff, P. (1973) *The Emerging Child*. New York: Jason Aronson.

Index

absorption, discussed in Winnicott
analysis 267–8, 269
academic career
Leeds University Psychiatry
Department 50, 61–2, 67,
298, 308–9, 318, 331, 336
see also lectures and public
speaking
academic study
HG's Ph.D. 116
see also education
'acting out' in analysis 142, 145,
147
ageing, HG's dreams of 216, 217
aggression
HG's attitudes to 228, 234–5
symbolism in HG's dreams 87–8
see also anger; destructiveness
Allen, Dr Clifford 26, 28, 32, 39, 76
American Handbook of Psychiatry
200, 316–17
amnesia of Percy's death 6, 86, 256
breaking through 79, 277, 301,
313–14
analysis see psychoanalysis
anger
HG's repression of 35, 37, 43–4,
224
HG's towards Harriet 58–9, 68

Barlow, Jack 334–5
Beard, Norman 61
Blows, Alfie 8, 12
brother-figures
Alfie Blows 8, 12
Henry Dicks 65
W.R.D. Fairbairn 187

brother-figures cont.
J.D. Sutherland 311, 323–4
Leslie Tizard 21, 181
Mr Turner 36

career see professional career
castration anxiety 101, 140, 148
circumcision 8, 43, 77, 82, 86, 101,
111, 263
Civil Service, HG's career in 12, 13
communication in analysis 217–18
'Concept of Psychodynamic Science,
The' 277
Crichton-Miller, Dr
HG's analysis with 26–7, 28, 31–2,
33, 34, 37, 38, 41
as supervisor of HG's psychotherapy work 45
Crucifixion Neurosis 125–6

Danks, Dr 45
death
HG's fear of own 37, 211–12
HG's identification with 38
of part of HG's personality 220,
230, 231, 241
Percy's see Percy Guntrip
destructiveness
discussed in Winnicott analysis
210, 215–16, 228, 242, 246–7,
255–6
Harriet's 270
diaries 49, 65
Devotional Diary 13, 14–15, 133
Dicks, Henry V. 43, 61, 63, 64, 65
differentiation 125, 127
dissociation 191, 255, 256–7, 268

drapers business 3, 4, 7, 11–12, 13, 158

drawings 106–11, 115, 244–5

dreams
of 'good family' 281, 301, 302
HG's autobiographical study of 322
HG's record of 27, 46
HG's views of 27–8, 102, 248, 315
invalid dream 8, 56–7, 83
oral-sadistic dreams 96–7
of Percy after Winnicott's death 312–14, 315
procession dream 28, 76
tomb-man dream 36–8, 86, 159, 255, 299
violence in HG's 291–2
worm and wild woman dreams 123–4, 128, 134

education 8, 11, 12, 279
University 18, 20–2

ego
ego-weakness and Fairbairn analysis 119, 186–7, 198–9
ego-weakness in HG's patients 63
in Fairbairn analysis 119, 122, 124, 140, 179, 185
HG keeping possession of 192
HG's writings on regressed ego 190, 195
Winnicott's concept of ego-relatedness 247–8, 258
Winnicott's views on ego-integration 237

'Ego Weakness, the Core of the Problem of Psychotherapy' 190–1

emotion
HG's difficulty in expressing 48, 92, 141, 209, 238
intellect as means of repressing 65, 76–7, 80, 116, 131
see also intellectualising

endo-psychic structure xi, 124, 166, 188, 190

Facing Life and Death 181

Fairbairn analysis
breaks in
due to Fairbairn's illness 97–8, 181, 183–4, 186
HG's dreams during 79, 98, 138–9
HG's financial reasons for 81–2
HG's schizoid experience during 89, 90
HG's separation anxiety over 78, 93, 104–5, 117
ending of 118, 119, 157, 185, 193–4
fears, resistance and anxiety in 74–8, 80, 82, 86, 95, 100, 107, 187
fees and financing of 74, 81–2, 177
HG's choice of and faith in Fairbairn 73, 123, 126, 162, 167–8
issues in
concentration on guilt 95–6, 99, 100
Crucifixion Neurosis 125–6
Fairbairn's objections to regression 172–3, 174–5, 189, 191–2
HG's need for love 105–6, 118
HG's obsessionism 168, 173
interpretations of drawings 106–11, 115, 244
primal scene phenomena 91, 115, 118, 175–6
orientation of
change to ego-weakness 186–7, 198–9
oedipal interpretations 75, 76, 117–18, 174
physical context 78, 119–20, 146
progress and achievements in 106, 120, 130, 133–5, 154–6, 157, 178
HG's frustration at lack of 138, 160, 161–2, 173–4
professional benefits 95, 155
reaching the main problem 79, 87, 114–15

Fairbairn analysis *cont.*
  relationship in 158–9
    'on–the–level' professional
      relationship 90, 126, 127,
      141, 178
    therapeutic relationship 88–9,
      120, 141–2, 144, 150, 154,
      165, 178–9, 180
  transference
    Fairbairn as brother 187
    Fairbairn as father-figure 85,
      88, 106, 113, 114, 129,
      152, 153, 183
    Fairbairn as mother 75, 77,
      79, 80, 97, 141, 142, 144,
      146, 155
    Fairbairn as mother and
      father 76, 85, 112
Fairbairn, Dr W.R.D.
  BJMP honouring of work of
    199–200
  choice as HG's analyst 67–8, 73
  death and mourning of 187, 201,
    236, 238
  deteriorating health of 149–50,
    181, 183, 185, 187, 189, 193,
    195
  financial situation 177
  Glover's review of work of 142,
    143
  HG's book on 325, 326, 327–8,
    335–6, 338, 343
  HG's fear of being seen as
    follower of 166, 326–7
  HG's intellectual discussions
    with 103, 141
  HG's need to talk about 210–11
  HG's representations of ideas of
    132–3, 135–7, 321
  limitations of theory and analysis
    of 322–3, 324–5
  'Observations of the Nature of
    Hysterical States' 166
  professional support of HG
    135–6, 141, 143, 178, 184,
    195–7, 202
  relationship with Winnicott
    166–7, 184–5

Fairbairn, Dr W.R.D. *cont.*
  theoretical move toward ego-
    weakness 186–7, 198–9
  theory of endo-psychic structure
    xi, 124, 166, 188, 190
  upbringing 155
family
  care of Bertha's 317, 329, 333
  emotional inadequacy in HG's
    early years 3, 90
  family life in later years 328,
    329–30, 333, 334
  HG growing away from 11, 133,
    232
family drapers business 3, 4, 7
  HG declines to join mother in 13,
    158
  move to Lordship Lane 11–12
father-figures 39
  Bertram Smith 47
  Henry Dicks 64, 65
  W.R.D. Fairbairn 85, 88, 106,
    113, 114, 129, 152, 153, 183
  D.W. Winnicott 243, 274
feelings *see* emotion
Fine, Harold J. 334
Freud, S.
  Centenary Celebrations 175
  HG's defence of 284–5
  HG's dream about 243
Freudian theory
  HG's views of 32, 117–18, 175
  see also oedipal interpretations
friendships
  Alfie Blows 8, 12
  Theo Holbrook 14
  Jack Hunt 15
  Leslie Tizard 20–1, 181, 182

Glover, Edward 142, 143
Greenald, Denis 57–8, 171, 340–1
Greenald, Gwen (*née* Guntrip)
  (daughter)
  birth of 24
  adolescence 57–8
  HG's dream about 30, 170
  HG's relationship and correspond-
    ence with 168–71, 172, 332

Greenald, Gwen *cont.*
  marriage to Denis 98, 113
guilt 95–6, 99, 100
Guntrip, Bertha (*née* Kind) (wife)
  background 18–19
  care of mother and aunt 317,
    329, 333
  delusional transference onto
    270–1, 272
  HG's dependence on 58, 66
  HG's reaction to illness of 289
  meeting with and marriage to
    HG 18–20, 23
  as 'natural counsellor' 48, 319
  relationship with Harriet 18, 19,
    42, 58, 64, 270
  role in HG's life 48, 239
  support during and after HG's
    analysis 74, 169–70, 171,
    315–16, 319
Guntrip, Harriet (*née* Jessop)
  (mother)
  background of 1–2, 240–1, 265
  as 'bad-object' 60, 75–6, 93, 153,
    265
  beatings of HG 9, 95–6, 124,
    128
  becoming disturbed in old age
    32, 46
  care for HG during childhood
    illnesses 7–8
  character of 68, 122, 133–4, 237,
    265, 270, 291
  as 'good object' 274–5, 282
  HG growing away from 11, 125,
    133, 232
  HG's anger toward 24, 58–9, 68
  HG's dreams of 64–5
  HG's identification with 84, 99,
    103–4, 125, 127, 133, 134
  illness and death of 147–9,
    150–1
  jealousy of HG's family relation-
    ships 19, 59–60
  lack of close relationship with
    HG 132
  marriage to and relationship with
    Henry 2, 3, 7, 241–2, 274–5

Guntrip, Harriet *cont.*
  maternalism 238, 275, 282
  lack of 3, 5, 6–7, 111, 156–7, 237,
    270, 291
  reaction to death of Mary 2, 24
  relationship with Bertha 18, 19,
    23, 42, 58, 64, 270
    visits to and residence with HG
      and Bertha 24, 42, 46, 55–6,
      58–60, 68
Guntrip, Harry
  autobiographical study ix, 321–2,
    333–4, 337–8, 343
  birth of 3
  career
    in Civil Service 12, 13
    lecturing *see* lecturing and pub-
      lic speaking
    pastoral work *see* pastoral work
    psychotherapy *see* psycho-
      therapy career
    in Salvation Army 13, 14–17
    see also professional career
  character
    compulsive activity 57, 67,
      192, 249, 259, 261, 264
    obsessionism 11, 168, 170,
      172–3
    vitality in later years 319–20,
      323, 330
  education 8, 11, 12, 18, 20–2, 279
  hobbies and leisure interests 12,
    20, 181, 230, 265
  illnesses *see* illness
  meeting and marriage to Bertha
    18–20, 23
  obituary and death of 340–2
  published works
    books 117, 181–2, 201, 309,
      316–17
    papers 190, 195–6, 200, 201,
      277, 292, 318, 323, 334
    *Personality Structure and
      Human Interaction* 116, 184,
      186, 189, 196–7, 200
    *Schizoid Phenomena, Object
      Relations and the Self* 96,
      190, 250–1, 258, 290

Guntrip, Henry (father)
    background of 1
    capacity for 'passive resistance' 3
    death of and HG's grief for 22–3,
        31, 37, 153
    as 'good object' 153, 274, 275
    HG's dreams about 28, 31, 36–7,
        47, 88, 320
    HG's identification with 22–3,
        106, 112, 122, 127, 133
    HG's relationship with 12, 37,
        60, 83–4, 217, 232–3, 273,
        274
    HG's resentment of inactivity of
        126
    marriage to and relationship with
        Harriet 2, 3, 7, 241–2, 274,
        275
    repression of emotion and anger
        37, 84, 88, 209
    Salvation Army speech 14
Guntrip, Percy (brother)
    death of 5
    effect on HG of death of 188,
        208, 213, 222, 229, 255, 257
    Harriet's accounts of death of 6
    HG sent to Aunt Dolly after
        death of 6, 229, 279, 282
    HG's amnesia of death of 6, 86,
        256
        breaking through 79, 277,
            301, 313–14
    HG's devotion to 4, 5, 188,
        246–7, 282, 283
    in HG's dreams 39–40, 312–14,
        315
    HG's illness after death of 5–6,
        188, 208, 255, 260–1
    sibling rivalry 29–30, 222, 242
    unconscious references in HG's
        diary to 14

hallucinations 32
Hammerton, Max 285
hobbies and leisure interests 12, 20,
    181, 230, 265
Holbrook, David 197, 202

Holbrook, Theo 14
house-moves 11, 138, 139, 317
Hunt, Jack 15

illness
    after Percy's death 5–6, 260–1
        interpretations of 188, 208,
            213, 255
    in Fairbairn analysis 187
    HG's childhood illnesses 7–8, 43,
        89–90, 124, 220–1, 233
    HG's deteriorating health and
        death 307–8, 309–11, 312,
        336, 337, 338–40
    HG's insomnia 26, 38, 42, 66–7,
        268
    HG's recurring 'exhaustion illness-
        es' 19, 21–2, 26, 36, 38, 65,
        220, 311
    HG's sinus problems 54, 100–1,
        115, 117
    HG's turn to religion 15–16
instinct theory 45–6
intellectual interests, growth of HG's
    13–14, 15
intellectualising
    as means of repressing emotional
        trauma 65, 76–7, 80, 83, 86,
        116, 131, 183–4
    as means of uncovering emotional
        trauma 139
Ipswich pastorate 22, 23–4

Jessop, Harriet see Harriet Guntrip
Jessop, Mary (aunt) 2, 3
    death of 24, 57
    in HG's dreams 8, 57, 128, 188,
        238
    HG's identification with 92

Klein, Josephine 327

Landis, Bernard 318–19, 325
lectures and public speaking 230–1,
    292, 310, 318, 331
    invitations to USA 279, 284, 298,
        300, 337

lectures and public speaking *cont.*
   lectures at Leeds University
   Psychiatry Department 50,
   61, 298, 308–9, 318, 331,
   336
   for Royal College of Psychiatrists
   318, 320–1, 331
Leeds, pastoral work in *see* pastoral
   work
Leeds University *see* academic
   career
libidinal ego 104, 121, 124, 190–1,
   193
libido, Fairbairn's definition of 103
'Location of the Cultural Experience,
   The' 273–4

Maberley, Alan 50–1, 52, 53, 54, 61,
   76
McAdam, William 50
MacCalman, D.R. 67
male (doing) and female (being)
   elements in Winnicott analysis
   258–9, 261–2, 264, 268, 299
'Manic Depressive Problem in the
   Light of the Schizoid Process,
   The' 181, 195–6
Middle Age 181
Morse, Stephen 326, 327

'Nature and Aims of Psychoanalytic
   Treatment, The' 180
Nimrod theme 9–10, 85, 104, 148,
   232
object-relations theory xii
   HG's move toward and need for
   48, 68
   HG's wish to influence training
   in direction of 321
'Observations of the Nature of Hysterical States' 166
obsessionism, HG's 11, 168, 170,
   172–3
oedipal interpretations
   in Allen and Crichton–Miller
   analyses 27, 28, 31–2, 33
   in Fairbairn analysis 75, 76, 174

oral sadism 96–7, 244, 245–6, 247
'Orthodoxy and Revolution in Psychology' 318

pastoral work
   St John's Church, Ipswich 22,
   23–4
   Salem Church, Leeds 24–5, 26,
   28–9, 38
   arrival of Sproxton 50, 57
   combined with HG's psychotherapy work 45, 47, 50, 55
   effect of Harriet on 59
   HG's anniversary sermon
   330–1
   HG's dreams and anxiety concerning 29–35, 77
   thoughts of leaving 51, 60–1
   Turner's departure 36
   wartime work 41–2
*Personality Structure and Human
   Interaction* 116, 184, 186, 189,
   196–7, 200
politics, HG's views of 331–3, 339
Prentice, Mrs, (domestic help) 4
primal scene phenomena 91, 109,
   110, 115, 118, 175–6
professional career
   contact with other professionals
   230–1, 318–19, 334
   see also Fairbairn; Sutherland;
   Winnicott
   and finances in later years 328–9,
   334
   HG's status and confidence in own
   work 95, 130, 202, 216–17,
   309, 323, 326–7
   lecturing *see* lecturing and public
   speaking
   overwork 171–2, 186, 192, 307–11
   see also illness
   in psychotherapy *see* psychotherapy career
psychoanalysis
   with Allen 26, 28, 32, 39, 76
   with Crichton-Miller 26–7, 28,
   31–2, 33, 34, 37, 38, 41

psychoanalysis *cont.*
    effect on HG's domestic life and
        Bertha's support of 74,
        169–70, 171–2, 315–16, 319
    with Fairbairn *see* Fairbairn
        analysis
    HG's move from Fairbairn to
        Winnicott 199
    HG's records of own ix, 74
    HG's self–analysis 27, 29–32,
        33–6, 42–4, 68, 119
    HG's views on nature and ben-
        efits of 314–15, 321–2
    with Maberley 50–4, 61, 76
    need for nurturant holding in
        165, 166
    with Winnicott *see* Winnicott
        analysis
Psychoanalytic Studies of the Person-
    ality 136–7, 320–1
psychoanalytic theory
    HG's defence of Freud 284–5
    HG's development of Fairbairn's
        132–3, 135–7, 188, 190–1,
        321
    HG's writing on 316–17
    orthodox views in USA 284, 300
Psychoanalytic theory, Therapy and
    the Self 309
Psychodynamics for Counsellors 309
psychotherapeutic relationship
    HG's views and writings on 141,
        165
    see also Fairbairn analysis; Win-
        nicott analysis
psychotherapy
    analyst as mother figure in 282
    HG's view of essence of xii, 69
    HG's views on therapist's capac-
        ity to love 183
    HG's wish to influence training
        in 321
psychotherapy career
    beginning of HG's 23–4, 45
    burden of HG's patients 215,
        223, 227, 228
    clinical work in later years 317,
        334, 339–40

psychotherapy career *cont.*
    combination with pastoral work
        45, 47, 50, 55, 60–1
    at Department of Psychiatry clinic
        63, 194, 308
    HG's realism regarding therapeutic
        outcomes 266–7
    HG's retirement from clinical
        work 266, 307, 308, 309
    regressing patients 165, 194–5,
        209, 215, 221
    tragedy of patient's murders and
        suicide 251–3, 255, 257–8
regression
    Fairbairn's objections to 172–3,
        174–5, 179, 189, 191–2
    HG's dealings with regressing
        patients 165, 194–5, 209, 215,
        221
    in HG's writings 190
    Winnicott's views of 165–6, 261
relaxation, in Winnicott analysis
    209–10, 264
religion
    Henry's involvement in 1
    HG's Devotional Diary 13, 14–15
    HG's involvement in Salvation
        Army 11, 13, 14–17
    see also pastoral work
'Religion in Relation to Personal Inte-
    gration' 292
retirement from clinical work 266,
    307, 308, 309

sadism
    HG's views of 258
    oral sadism 96–7, 244, 245–6, 247
sado-masochistic phenomena 100,
    157
    in drawings 109–11, 244–5
Salem pastorate *see* pastoral work
Salvation Army, HG's involvement in
    11, 13, 14–17
schizoid element of HG's personality
    14, 48, 188, 190, 322–3
    schizoid experiences 89, 90, 96,
        105, 230

schizoid patients 105, 120–1
*Schizoid Phenomena, Object Rela-
tions and the Self* 96, 190,
250–1, 258, 290
*Schizoid Problem and Psycho-
therapy, The* 201
'Schizoid Problem, Regression and
the Struggle to Preserve an Ego'
195
schizoid withdrawal 190, 191
school *see* education
separation
from mother 125, 198, 268
see also Fairbairn analysis; Winnicott analysis
separation anxiety 125, 157, 198,
199, 290, 303
sexual symbolism in dreams 87–8
sexuality, development of HG's 91,
92, 93, 239
shop *see* family drapers business
sibling rivalry 29, 222, 242
Smith, Bertram 24, 25, 47
'Split-off Male and Female Elements
to be found Clinically in Men
and Women, The' 258
Sproxton, Vernon 50, 55, 57, 61
Sutherland, J.D.
as brother-figure 311, 323–4
HG's appeal to 311–12
as HG's 'literary godfather' x,
324, 325, 342–3
HG's relationship and correspondence with 316, 321–2,
323–6, 327–8, 335–6, 338
HG's support for 319
Szasz, Thomas 180

theory
HG's use in self–analysis of 42–4
see also intellectualising; Object
Relations Theory; psychoanalytic theory
'Therapeutic Factor in Psychotherapy, The' 132–3, 141
therapy *see* psychotherapy
Tizard, Leslie 20–1, 181, 182

tomb-man dream 36–8, 86, 159, 255,
299
training
Harry J.S. Guntrip Postgraduate
Training Institute (Knoxville)
334–5
HG's training sessions with
Maberley 50–4
HG's wish to influence psycho-
therapy training 321
transference *see* Fairbairn analysis;
Winnicott analysis
Treasury, HG's work in 13
Turner, Mr 25, 26, 28–9, 36

violence
Harriet's beatings of HG 9, 95–6,
124, 128
in Harriet's childhood 2
HG's attitudes to 234–5
HG's childhood preoccupation
with theme of 9–10
in HG's drawings 109
in HG's dreams 291–2
Webber, Madeleine 12–13
Winnicott analysis
beginning 198, 207–8
ending 244, 267, 301–3, 307
issues in
communication 217–18
effect of patient's murders and
suicide 255, 257–8
HG's male (doing) and female
(being) elements 258–9,
261–2, 264, 268, 299
HG's need to talk about Fairbairn 211
oral sadism 245–6
timid and brave child selves
212, 213
progress and achievements 208,
213–14, 229, 264, 276, 296–7
relationship in
mutual benefits of 276–7
professional relationship 266–7
therapeutic relationship 163–4,
224, 244, 247–8, 259–60,
292, 294, 295

Winnicott analysis *cont.*
    separation and breaks in 230–1,
        283, 288, 296, 300
    transference 286, 290
        Winnicott as father-figure
            243, 274
        Winnicott as mother 225–6,
            245, 270
        Winnicott as mother and
            father 262
Winnicott, D.W.
    effect on HG of death of 312–14
    'ego-distortion in Terms of True
        and False Self' 190
    HG's introduction to 155, 165
    HG's reactions to illness of 293,
        296, 300
    HG's relationship with 263–4,
        266–7
    HG's theoretical differences with
        167, 210, 234–5, 260

Winnicott, D.W. *cont.*
    HG's wish to write book on 326,
        334
    relationship with Fairbairn 166–7,
        184–5
    response to *Schizoid Phenomena,
        Object Relations and the Self*
        250–1
    'The Location of the Cultural
        Experience' 273–4
    views on regression 165, 166
    withdrawal 114–15, 140, 190, 191
    work *see* professional career

You and Your Nerves (republished as
    Your Mind and Your Health) 117,
    309

Index by Judith Lavender